Pogue's War

Pogue's War

Diaries of a WWII Combat Historian

Forrest C. Pogue

THE UNIVERSITY PRESS OF KENTUCKY

Publication of this volume was made possible in part by a grant from the
National Endowment for the Humanities.

Published by The University Press of Kentucky
Scholarly publisher for the Commonwealth,
serving Bellarmine University, Berea College, Centre College of Kentucky,
Eastern Kentucky University, The Filson Historical Society, Georgetown College,
Kentucky Historical Society, Kentucky State University,
Morehead State University, Murray State University, Northern Kentucky
University, Transylvania University, University of Kentucky, University of
Louisville, and Western Kentucky University.
All rights reserved.

Editorial and Sales Offices: The University Press of Kentucky
663 South Limestone Street, Lexington, Kentucky 40508-4008
www.kentuckypress.com

10 09 08 07 06   5 4 3 2 1

Frontispiece: Sergeant Forrest Pogue in Normandy, June 1944.

The Library of Congress has cataloged the hardcover edition as follows:

Pogue, Forrest C.
    Diaries of a WWII combat historian / Forrest C. Pogue.
        p.   cm.
    Includes bibliographical references and index.
    ISBN 0-8131-2216-3 (cloth : alk. paper)
    1. Pogue, Forrest C.—Diaries. 2. Military historians—United States—Diaries.
3. World War, 1939–1945—Campaigns—Western Front. 4. World War, 1939–
1945—Personal narratives, American. I. Title: Diaries of a World War Two
combat historian. II. Title: Diaries of a World War 2 combat historian. III. Title.
D811.P566 A3 2001
940.54′8173—dc21   2001003411

Paper ISBN-10 0-8131-9160-2
Paper ISBN-13 978-0-8131-9160-7

 Member of the Association of
American University Presses

To Jeannine, with love
23 December 1933–18 March 2001

Contents

Foreword

Forrest Pogue may well have been one of the best-educated ser-geants in the U.S. Army in World War II. At age eighteen he had earned a bachelor's degree at Murray State Teachers College in Murray, Kentucky; at nineteen he had a master's degree in Euro-pean history from the University of Kentucky; and at twenty-four he had a Ph.D. in European history from Clark University in Worcester, Massachusetts. In 1937–38 he studied at the Univer-sity of Paris and became fluent in the French language. (So fluent that after the war he could interview Charles de Gaulle without an interpreter.)

Wherever he went during the war, whether in England or France or Belgium or Luxembourg or Germany, he knew the castles, the monuments, the local heroes, the ups and downs in the various wars of the region, the commerce, the literary and philosophical outpourings, and, of course, the history.

Pogue was certainly one of the smartest sergeants in the U.S. Army, indeed one of the smartest individuals. It was inevitable that Pogue would be chosen when Army Chief of Staff George C. Marshall decided to organize a unit of combat historians to write the history of the war as it occurred for the benefit of the training staffs and later for the edification of the general public. Their task was to interview GIs and their officers immediately after combat and gather eyewitness accounts for the narratives.

He was the first historian of D-Day. His work was based on interviews that began on 7 June 1944 and continued through most of the remainder of the year. The product was widely disseminated and used. It remains authoritative. He also learned and wrote about the hedgerow battles in Normandy, the dash across France, the awful battle at the Huertgen Forest, the Battle of the Bulge, the crossing of the Rhine, and the final phases of the war in Europe. Along with his associates, they produced the finest history ever written about a war, exactly as General Marshall had wanted.

For all those who followed in studying and writing about the war in Europe, Pogue and his fellows are an inspiration. After the war, Pogue did the penultimate volume of the Army's official history, *The Supreme Command*. He later wrote a four-volume biography of General Marshall and many other books. Together, they occupy a prominent place in every World War II historian's library. They are of such quality that when one of us looks at them on our shelves, we smile, nod, and thank God. They are always consulted, never given away. They mean more to us than any other possession.

Knowing Forrest was best of all. He was extraordinarily generous with his knowledge, time, and friendliness. He learned the importance of so being from his society, his grandfather, and his father. Above all, his gracefulness was taught to him by his mother, whose death in December 1945 when he was still overseas brought from him a tribute to her that in a few pages is the finest biography that great American biographer ever wrote.

Here is his wartime diary. It is priceless. He was in a unique position and wrote in his own way. Throughout, one can hear him speaking. Everywhere one learns how to research and write history, but so much more as well. I know of no other account of the war that even approaches it as a view of the U.S. Army in Europe from 6 June 1944 to 7 May 1945. This was due to Pogue's methods. He was on the front lines and in the rear areas, at company, battalion, regimental, division, and corps headquarters. He knew the plans well before D-Day (one shudders to think of what might have happened had the Germans captured him in May and gotten him over to France for interrogation), well before the big offensive at Saint-Lô and later across France and on the edge of Germany. Mostly, he did his job, interviewing the junior officers, the noncommissioned officers, and the privates—often at or near the front lines. He was shelled, he ducked machine-gun and rifle fire, and he was bombed. He seldom got a chance to change clothes, had only cold water sponge baths, ate C rations, carried his weapons along with his briefcase and writing instruments, slept on the ground, and suffered from the cold and the almost constant rain.

He saw and talked to and wrote about the Americans in Europe. He was often at or near the action. There are heroes and all-but-unbelievable actions and brilliant maneuvers. There also are skunks—cowards, thieves, officers who are relieved of command, and quartermasters who appropriate and then sell on the black market gasoline, cigarettes, food, clothes, and more. There are famous entertainers and there are frauds. We meet men and women from across America, each of them caught up in the great drama and reacting in their own way. We meet many of the intellectuals in Paris, including his prewar professors, along with Picasso, Gertrude Stein, and others. He takes us to wartime London, Salisbury, Bristol, and other English places; to the small villages of Normandy and the liberation of Paris; to the destruction of Liege, Cologne, and elsewhere.

Pogue was at Torgau for the linkup of the Red Army and the U.S. Army, and he was in Pilzen, Czechoslovakia, with General George Patton's Third Army when the war ended. We see it all through his eyes, hear through his ears, and make our assessments through his brain.

Some glances at Pogue's experiences include: 14 June 1944, in Normandy, at the 115th Regiment's headquarters, when he was studying the advance into the hedgerow country on the maps and learning about the casualties: "The score was kept each day . . . as the first sergeants and the sergeant majors totted their lists and said: 3 KIA, 12 WIA, and 4 MIA. How like a drugstore when getting the latest ball scores or an election headquarters when returns are coming in."

22 June 1944: "How to win [a] war . . . 'Keep your sense of humor and the infantry in front of you.'"

25 June 1944: "Landscape looked like a Corot painting last night."

1 December 1944: "When the First U.S. Army moved into the Huertgen Forest in November 1944, it was much like the other wooded areas of Germany—carefully preserved by forest masters who saw that the undergrowth was cleared away and who superintended the cutting of any trees in the area. There was nothing sinister about it, and there were few, if any, legends connected with it. Within four weeks after the Americans had entered the forest, their initial force had been badly battered and the forest itself was smashed. Once-proud trees were in ruin; blackened stumps remained where great wooded giants had stood. There

were no birds, no sighing winds, no carpeted paths. There was desolation such as one associated with the Battle of the Wilderness. An American general who had fought through one of the battles of the forest offered $5 for every tree his men could find unmarked by shelling and got no takers."

17 December: The German counteroffensive in what came to be known as the Battle of the Bulge had started the previous day. That evening, at First Army headquarters in Spa: "It apparently was generally felt that no real crisis existed, because we managed to hold one of our usual parties with toasts being drunk to the safe arrival of the captains, to my promotion [to master sergeant], and everything else we could think of. . . . As the party grew louder, I could not forbear quoting the lines about the eve of Waterloo— 'there were sounds of revelry by night.'" (The most famous party ever held, in Brussels, the eve before Waterloo).

8 April 1945. French slave-workers were liberated in a German camp. "These people did not seem bitter, but they were thoughtful. None were the pale, anemic type of Paris. I felt helped by their spirit. It is wonderful to see how they look when they are going home. It is one of the finest things we have done. They won't forget us. . . . Saw PWs in afternoon. Some were very young. Fathers, mothers, wives had been bringing them in. As the guard said—'Once they leave here they've got it made.' He said they were told to treat SS soldiers as rough as they could under the Geneva Convention. He said after they had beaten one SS officer severely, he said 'You are too soft; we would kill somebody.'"

1 May 1945. "Hitler's death announced. Admiral [Karl] Doenitz takes over. Deaths of [Heinrich] Himmler, [Joseph] Goebbels also reported. . . . Mussolini shot in Milan. Got pie-eyed."

Throughout the campaign, Pogue lived with men who swore constantly. And so on. But there is not one swear word of his in the diary, and in decades of knowing him, I never once heard Forrest swear. He learned from his mother: "Without studying psychology she knew child care. Seldom using punishment, she taught by example, teaching me to correct bad speech when she wanted to cure me of childhood swear words."

Pogue's interview with Lieutenant John Spaulding, who led

the first platoon up the bluff at Omaha Beach, is the single best interview I've ever read. The book as a whole is so superior that I can't think of words of praise that could express how good it is.

Stephen E. Ambrose

Preface

Forrest and Fannie Pogue reared their family of six children during the early years of the twentieth century, through World War I and the Great Depression. During those years they experienced the good but harsh life of rural people living in and around the small towns of Dycusburg and Frances, located in Crittenden County, Kentucky.

Forrest's parents, Marion Forrest and Betty Matthews Pogue, owned property in Frances and a farm that enabled them to scratch out a living. Experiencing firsthand the world of hard work, the Pogue children learned how to provide for themselves and others.

Their oldest son, Forrest Carlisle Pogue Jr., was born 17 September 1912. He exhibited at a very young age the academic promise that was to be his calling. Because of his intellect and the early attention and tutoring he received from his mother and grandfather, he moved quickly on to advanced classes, which enabled him to graduate from high school at the tender age of fourteen.

Money was scarce, so he was unable to attend college his first year out of high school. However, he managed to enroll at Murray State Teachers College in Murray, Kentucky, the next year, and graduated from Murray State at eighteen. He then enrolled at the University of Kentucky and received his master's degree at age nineteen.

Forrest completed his doctorate at Clark University in Worcester, Massachusetts, in 1936. He then went to France to study at the University of Paris in 1937–38, where he observed firsthand the rise of Nazism in Germany and was able to feel the effect those events had on the people of France and of Europe. He also learned to speak and understand the French language fluently, which proved valuable to the American troops with whom he served. He left France and returned to the United States in 1939, just as Hitler and his Wehrmacht invaded Poland. He joined the faculty

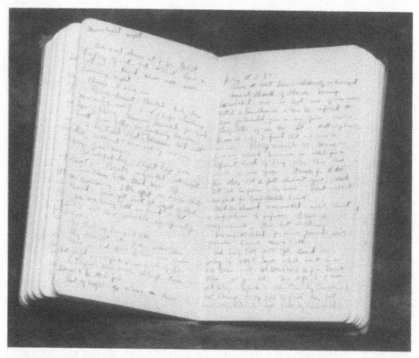

Sergeant Pogue's diary.

at Western Kentucky College in Bowling Green and a year later became a teacher at Murray State Teachers College.

With the declaration of war against Japan and Germany, thousands of young American men and women volunteered for or were drafted into the armed forces. Forrest and Fannie had four sons, all of whom served in the army. Roswell and Marion Carter served in the Pacific, and Tommy and Forrest Jr. in the European theater of operations. Tommy served as a crewman on a tank destroyer and took part in many of the battles in Europe. Each of these sons returned home virtually unscratched, although each had been in harm's way many times.

Forrest was selected to be a combat historian and served with V Corps. He began his interviews on 7 June 1944, aboard an LST, which had become a hospital ship for those who were wounded on Omaha Beach on D-Day, the sixth of June. He went ashore at

Omaha Beach on 8 June and continued to interview troops until
the end of the war in Europe.

He lived in the field at or near the front from D-Day until after
the breakout at Saint-Lô, and entered Paris very soon after the
Allies recaptured that famous city. He returned to the field in September in time to record the Huertgen Forest battle and then experienced the famous Battle of the Bulge. He was present at
Torgau, Germany, when the U.S. Army met the Russian army. He
was one of the first witnesses to the holocaust that had taken place
at Buchenwald. After the Germans surrendered in May 1945, he
was ordered back to Paris to start writing the history that had
been collected by the combat historians.

While my wife and I were visiting with the Pogues one day,
Forrest suddenly got up and went to another room. He soon returned with an armload of little gray books that were old and
weather beaten. As a combat historian, Forrest had carried these
pocket diaries with him in the field so events could be recorded
as they happened or soon thereafter. He said that he had intended
to write a book based on the diaries, but was unable to finish it
after he had lost most of his sight. He said he had tried to find
someone to complete the work for him, but all who had tried were
unable to read his writing. Those who have corresponded with
Forrest know firsthand the physician-like script that he uses in
his correspondence. (He told me once that he developed his short-
hand style when he was a young lad). I looked at those books in
astonishment and awe and realized that they were valuable documents that needed to be transcribed and, if possible, published. I
told him that my wife, Jeannine, who had corresponded with him
for years, was the one person the other family members would
ask to read his letters to them, and that with her help we would
attempt to finish his book.

Because of the illegibility of Forrest's handwriting and the
condition of some of the old, worn pages, I have found it necessary to indicate gaps using ellipses, unintelligible words with
————, and [?] where a word is partially decipherable. For clar-
ity, I have also spelled out ranks and other basic abbreviations
that are used in the diary.

Christine Brown Pogue, Forrest's wife of forty-five years, has
provided me with access to her library, as well as encouragement

and direction. She was my official proofreader and has held me to a high standard, for which I am most appreciative.

Stephen E. Ambrose, noted historian and author of many fine books and a colleague and friend of Forrest's, has helped us immensely by providing direction and support.

Edward M. Coffman, a fellow historian and author and colleague of Forrest's, read the manuscript and made many helpful suggestions.

Jacqueline Murray, whose native language is French, provided expert translation of the French phrases.

I purchased a computer and, with the help of my granddaughter, Ashley Nicole Tinsley, who showed me how to operate the machine, finished Forrest's book.

Franklin D. Anderson

Chapter 1

London in the
Spring of 1944

England in the spring of 1944 was weighed down by the masses of guns and equipment which the British and Americans had brought together for an early return to the continent. Wags said that but for the barrage balloons, which could be seen straining at their cables throughout the country, the island would sink beneath the waves. The Western world had gathered its might for an unprecedented amphibious attack against Hitler's Festung Europa.

Among the hundreds of thousands of Americans helping to swell the population of the United Kingdom was a small group of combat historians, of whom the author was one, flown by the War Department to London in the early days of April 1944 to prepare for the task of recording the history of the American armies in the field.

To many old-timers who already feared that the army had been corrupted by USO shows and Coca-Cola, this business of furnishing assistants to History to record the asides of conflict was the last straw. Some efforts had been made in this direction in World War I, but the U.S. forces considered such "wandering troubadours" useless. Proposals in the 1930s to outline such a program for the future in case troops were sent abroad again had been dismissed as nonsense.

With the coming of World War II to the United States, the army established historical sections with the various armies and major commands, and units in the field were required to render periodic after action reports. The Ground Forces Headquarters, in order to learn battle lessons and to build infantry morale, sent a

few experts to several battlefronts. Combat history got its opportunity when General George C. Marshall, desiring to give
wounded men a chance to read about the actions in which they
were hit, ordered the Historical Branch, War Department G-2, to
prepare a series of pamphlets for this purpose. The first chief of
the branch was a young West Pointer, Colonel John Kemper, who
came from several generations of army officers. He had taught
history at the Academy and was energetic, persuasive, and charming. The fact our group had been brought into existence was largely
due to his efforts.

To gather material for the pamphlets, the Historical Branch
brought together by the spring of 1944 some twenty combat historians, ranging in rank from private to lieutenant colonel and
including former historians, lawyers, and newspapermen. By the
time I reached Washington, historians had already been sent to
the Pacific and Italian theaters. After several weeks of indoctrina-
tion in military history of past wars and in World War II after-
action reports and official records, some nine or ten of us were
sent in the first half of April to the European theater of operations
for assignment to the First and Third Armies.

With us went the executive officer of the Historical Branch,
Lieutenant Colonel Charles H. Taylor, professor of medieval history at Harvard, who combined the meticulousness of the student of the Middle Ages with an active interest in the present. He
often said that while modern war was better documented than
conflicts of the past, the task of piecing together the truth was just
as difficult.

Chosen to head one of the historical teams in the field was
Major Hugh M. Cole, professor of military history at the University of Chicago, who had written his dissertation at the University of Minnesota on the early development of the Prussian army.
He had a voluminous knowledge of warfare and armies and knew
when a particular army adopted leggings or when basic changes
were made in certain weapons. With it all went a thorough ac-
quaintanceship with the modern army and a flair for collecting
information. Impatient of authority, certain of his own knowledge,
and aggressive to the nth degree, he was one of the most effective
historians in the field and a capable administrator when we came
back to Paris at the war's end. For those who worked with him at

Third Army, he was a delightful companion. With his thirst for detailed information on military matters went varied interests which included the development of early jazz, Chicago honky-tonks, and burlesque routines. A fine sprinkling of Runyonesque argot characterized his speech. Nearly everyone below the rank of general was called "Doc," and he often added "you old bastard" as a term of affection for his closer friends.

Others in our group were Captain Frank Ferriss, a Yale graduate who had practiced law in St. Louis. Inclined to carry a biting courtroom tone into his interviews, he scared accurate answers out of many of his subjects who must have felt that they were being cross-examined on a murder charge. The careful work of his early interviews was often held up to us as a model. Much milder in manner, but just as persistent, was Lieutenant Roland G. Ruppenthal, who had a Wisconsin Ph.D. in European history. Coming from a German family, he displayed the industry and intensity of purpose often attributed to people of Teutonic origin.

Among the other officers was Lieutenant Kenneth Hechler, a former instructor in political science who had used classroom interviews of outstanding political leaders to gain the interest of his students. He had served as a historian in the Ground Forces. One of the younger officers was Lieutenant Blair Clark, a graduate of Harvard. Blair's private school background had been tempered with newspaper experience so that he could combine great urbanity with a capacity for scrounging equipment for his historical unit.

Three enlisted men made up the remainder of the team that went over in early April. One was Staff Sergeant David Garth, author of *Bermuda Calling*, which had appeared a short time before, and of several other novels that had been turned into movies. He had traveled over much of the world and his talk helped enliven many evenings. One of his hobbies was the study of Civil War history. This helped him not only in his combat history work but proved externally useful on one occasion at Fort Myer, Virginia, when we were trying to get from the supply sergeant some items not normally issued to enlisted men. They were on our orders, but the situation was unusual and the sergeant was standing by the good old army rule of suspecting anything new. He was adamant about the matter until Garth got him into a discussion of the Civil War. The sergeant, a Brooklynite who had apparently made a career of studying the battle of Franklin, was a sucker for a question about that encounter. Garth not only got most of the items on our orders, but also toilet paper and GI soap, reported to be in short supply in the ETO and definitely not listed in our travel papers.

Sergeant Gordon Harrison, graduate of Harvard and Oxford and a former instructor at Harvard, had served for a time as a medic and as an MP before coming to the Historical Section. Looking more like a prizefighter than a scholar, he was well versed in literature, music, and history, and was one of the best interviewers and writers we had. He had an eye for terrain, a knack for getting at the heart of the matter, and a facility for finding the right word which all of us envied. Like me, he had been recommended for a direct commission in military government, and was near his lieutenant's bars when such commissions were stopped by the Secretary of War.

As for myself, I had taken a doctorate in European history and diplomacy at Clark University, had studied diplomatic history on an exchange fellowship at the University of Paris in 1937–38, and had taught history at Murray State College in western Kentucky from 1933–36 and 1939–42. Drafted in 1942, I spent a year as a clerk at the Reception Center, Fort Harrison, Indiana. There my duties consisted initially of typing locator cards in forwarding mail and in searching recruits for whiskey, pornographic literature, and concealed weapons. My only literary efforts consisted of writing down the names of individuals found by the doctors to have some form of VD. When it was learned that I had been a professor, I was sometimes given the task of giving orientation lectures on world affairs. At the end of seven months I had made sergeant and was given additional duties of calling the roll of recruits when there was an unusual number of foreign names, of explaining the means of taking a certain hygienic examination, and of persuading new men to join the paratroopers.

Despite the nature of the work, I learned a great deal of military history. Since I was on night duty for twelve to fourteen hours daily, and since our major shipments of recruits came at two- and three-hour intervals, I often drew on the post library for books to fill up the time. The collection ran heavily to military subjects, and I managed before the year was out to learn something more about Jomini and Clausewitz and the standard books on maneuver and strategy than I had picked up from my textbooks several years before.

In February 1943, I was shipped to the basic training center at Fort McClellan, Alabama. Since I had never been given proper basic training, I had been discouraged from applying for officer's candidate school. I, therefore, asked for a demotion from sergeant to private and the transfer to McClellan on the theory that I was on the road to OCS.

Near the end of my training at the IRTC, where I learned enough about squad, platoon, and company action to understand the men I later interviewed, I was ordered to Headquarters, Second Army, Memphis, to help the historian, Lieutenant Bell I. Wiley, who had been history department head at the University of Mississippi, write a history of Second Army. In the course of a year, working with Wiley and his successor, Lieutenant Thomas P. Govan, who had taught history at the University of the South, I had learned a great deal about the forty-odd divisions trained by Second Army.

At the recommendation of Wiley, who had gone to Washington with the Army Ground Forces historical section in 1943 to work with Lieutenant Colonel Kent R. Greenfield, I was transferred from Second Army to the War Department G-2 on 15 March 1944. Shots, training, and the drawing of equipment began at once, and within less than a month I was on the way with Ferriss, Clark, and Garth by C-54 to London. With our rank, we had feared that we would never get on a plane, but our priorities were finally upped sufficiently that we not only went by air, but we traveled with Major General Charles P. Gross, the chief of army transportation, and three or four members of his office. We were much impressed by the company and by the secret orders under which we traveled. They were so classified that Garth and I, being enlisted men, were not allowed to carry them but had to hand them over to Lieutenant Clark whenever we got around other officers.

The flight to London, my first plane ride of any consequence, proved uneventful except for fog over Stevensville that forced us to spend the evening at Presque Isle, Maine. Garth and I remembered that base mainly for the mud, the overheated and noisy barracks, and the first sergeant who tried to put us on latrine orderly duty the next morning. I successfully pulled rank (General Gross's that is) on him and we got away before he could recover. General Gross proved to be very friendly on the way across and won our gratitude when, at suppertime, after saying that the lowest ranking man aboard had to serve the sandwiches, pointed to the lieutenant as the man to do the job.

We landed in Prestwick on the morning of 12 April and were told we would have to go down by train. However, the General invited us to go along in the bomber that was sent up from London.

Our bus from Hendon Airport took us to the billeting office on North Audley Street where we were met by Harrison and others who had preceded us to London. We checked in briefly at the Historical Section's offices at Headquarters, European Theater of Operations, located on Grosvenor Square. Not far away was the American Embassy and on every side were American-occupied buildings. The prevalence of American uniforms had already gained for the square the name of Eisenhowerplatz.

Harrison had been in London long enough to know the ropes. Therefore, instead of our going to the barracks on Green Street, where we would have to drill and stand inspections, he wangled permission for us to stay with him at the transient enlisted men's billets on Cadogan Square. (For those who went to reveille—we arranged amongst ourselves that every room would have one or two representatives every morning—there was usually two minutes of exercise, consisting of double-timing in place. Theoretically there were inspections, but we always had to be at headquarters when these were announced.)

There were some penalties, however, since our nice apartment houses were not heated and the water was never warm. We slept on straw mattresses, which years before had been hardened into the uncomfortable shapes we found to be unchangeable.

Tired as we were the first evening, we were pleased by the sight of the beds. But the Germans and friendly ack-ack and our charge of quarters did what they could to keep us awake. We had just fallen off to sleep when the young corporal, who was held responsible for our safety and attendance at formations, rushed into the room. Fully dressed, even to helmet and gas mask, he urged us to go to the cellar. Meanwhile, the air-raid sirens were sounding and the ack-ack guns located in the park outside our window were making a terrible fuss. Since we were told that day that Germans were really not dangerous any more and that only reconnaissance planes came over, we were not inclined to leave our beds. We peered out at the searchlights for a few minutes and went back under the blankets. The corporal, who whined at intervals, "C'mon fellows, do you want to get killed," finally gave up. He never bothered us thereafter. However, there were a few minutes that night—especially when we heard what we thought was the drone of many planes and the sound of bomb explosions—when we wondered if we had made a mistake.

Harrison, Garth, and I managed to act like junior executives while in London. Carrying our shiny briefcases, with which the War Department had generously provided us, we would stride out each morning, hail a bus or taxi, and head for one of the hotels near Grosvenor Square for breakfast. On our first morning at the Cumberland Hotel, many of whose rooms were reserved for officers, we found ourselves surrounded by majors and colonels. However, the headwaiter greeted us impassively and we felt at home when one of the colonels who had been on the plane with us stopped and said hello. The breakfast at the Cumberland and the other hotels was never very exciting, since the eggs were powdered, the meat contained cereal that tasted like sawdust, and the milk for the cereal was heavily diluted with water. Still, the waiters were correct in their dress and manners, and we tended to prefer the good service and bad food to the slightly better food— and earlier hours—at the enlisted men's mess.

The breakfasts were also made interesting by the people we met there—often pilots of planes who were taking a forty-eight-hour pass after flying missions over the Pas de Calais, the Normandy coast, or sometimes into Germany itself.

In those days we searched eagerly for any information that would give us "the big picture," something we had expected when we reached London and which, we found, the people there did not have. They were able to fill us in on details of preparations and the names of units slated for the invasion, but as yet they did not have the exact plan or time of landing. So far a small group of historians had been sent on some of the landing exercises, and the chief of the Historical Section, Colonel William A. Ganoe, had received from General Omar N. Bradley an agreement to let historians operate in his area. The agreement had been oral, but Colonel Ganoe ultimately outlined the nature of the conversation in a letter and General Bradley initialed it. This constituted our credentials in the field.

Our briefings at ETOUSA consisted mainly of lectures somewhat like those we had heard previously in Washington, in which tables of organization and equipment of various types of units were discussed and we were given manuals on infantry and armored tactics to study. Occasionally, we had a talk by some outsider on phases of the battle we might see. I remember only one, Lieutenant Ware of the navy, who, in discussing amphibious landings, said that we could write the story of the early hours in a phrase: "Confusion reigned on the beaches."

Theater Historian Ganoe, under whose general direction we were to work, was an interesting old gentleman who had come out of retirement to head the ETOUSA historical program. A one-time instructor in history at West Point, where he had taught Eisenhower and Bradley, and author of a standard history on the American army, he seemed a logical choice for the job. His appearance reminded one of mousy Hollywood actor Donald Meek. The colonel interviewed each of us separately as we arrived, going through a routine that included a discussion of opera (he had once been something of a singer), the French short story, and the writing of history. In my case, the conversation included the Baltic and the Zola, something of the Italian opera, and reference to his book, which I managed to get into the discussion. It so happened that he talked to Garth and me the same morning, and Garth's impressive lists of short stories impressed him. For months afterwards, he confused the two of us, and every time I saw him he would ask if I had written anything lately.

The colonel, in contrast to the officers of the War Department, held that it was impossible to get a connected account of operations. He preferred instead the collection of colorful details that could be used to enliven the dull pages of battle history. This view led him to send out several freelance historians who wandered at will through the field units, picking up choice bits of gossip and color that they sent back in handwritten letters to the colonel. It was characteristic of army custom that because the colonel was very senior in rank and had been appointed by the theater commander, he could use the War Department historians sent over to follow Washington directives in a manner almost directly contrary to their original instructions. Of course, being practical-minded members of the War Department contingent, they tended to follow the line they had been initially taught.

Despite the differences between the War Department and the theater regarding combat history, and the natural feeling that the newcomers were going to interfere with a going program, Colonel Ganoe, so far as we were individually concerned, did not show any difference in treatment between his own historians and those brought from Washington. He handled his enlisted men with great kindness, praising us on many occasions and sometimes shocking his officers by saying that many of them have been commissioned by accident while many of the unlisted men had escaped being commissioned in the same way. He, like his successor, Colonel S.L.A. Marshall, while requiring proper discipline from us, always demanded that in the field the enlisted historians and artists be given every possible consideration by his officers. At Christmastime in 1944 he won our gratitude by personally writing our families to say that he appreciated the work we were doing.

Until the spring of 1944, Colonel Ganoe's chief interest had been in the program of writing the history of the services of supply. His historians included Major Wood Gray, head of the history department at George Washington University, and Captain Robert C. Healey, a graduate in literature from Georgetown University, who had come to London in 1942. In addition, the colonel took special pride in the battlefield art program. Outstanding among the men in this group was Technical Sergeant Olin Dows of Rhinebeck, New York, a neighbor and friend of Franklin Roosevelt and formerly deputy head of the federal art program. Olin had done the murals at the Hyde Park post office at the request of the president.

Our mornings, as I had said, were spent studying organization and tactics of the army. Our afternoons were pretty much free and we spent considerable time in an activity called "looking for a Bailey Bridge." Colonel Ganoe, either for lack of anything for us to do or perhaps to give us a chance to get out of the office, urged us to inspect a Bailey Bridge. To this task we dedicated many hours but used very little sense of direction. The search frequently took us to Selfridge's for tea and scones and got us back only in time for tea at the office. Often our guide was Russ Jones, a onetime Minnesota newpaperman, who had come to the United Kingdom with the 34th Division and then had gone to North Africa. He worked on the original *Stars and Stripes* there and later came to London, but a disagreement with his colonel led him to choose the Historical Section. He knew London well and showed us many places to look for a Bailey Bridge pleasantly without any chance of finding it.

But it is not for these army experiences that I shall remember London that spring of 1944. One of the high spots was a trip to Parliament. Arranged by a charming North Carolina–born, British-wed woman, whose husband and son were in the army, and sponsored by the English Speaking Union, the visit included a tour led by Lord Fermoy through the bombed-out House of Commons, then to the Lobby to see the procession of the Lord Speaker as he went to the new place of meeting, and finally to the gallery to see the House in action. We sat in the Dominions Gallery because our tickets bore the names of two Canadian colonels. An ancient but courteous guide showed us to our seats and, in loud stage whispers, pointed out various celebrities on the floor. We arrived just at the opening of the question period—something we do not have under our system of government—and saw nearly every member of the Cabinet perform. Of those we wanted to see, only Churchill was absent—and it was not until November 1944, when he and de Gaulle marched in the Armistice Day Parade in Paris, that we were to see that great Englishman. But in the course of an hour, we saw and heard the dapper Eden, the ponderous Bevin, the biting Bevan, the blunt Morrison, the modest Attlee, and the stolid Sir John Anderson. There were a number of pointed questions—one on the terrible quality of cigarettes furnished the troops—which pleased the soldiers in the galleries.

On other occasions we turned plain tourist and gawked. We were pleased to see that clean-up activities were under way and to find that improvement societies were handing out tracts describing the London of 1950.

Near Fleet Street, on one of the trips, we visited the ruins of a church whose chapel went back to the time of the Templars. A German bomb had done in seconds what time had not accomplished in centuries. Not far away was a museum dedicated to Samuel Johnson. The custodian welcomed us, saying that many American scholars had visited there before the war. She told us the story, which undoubtedly had been told before to other professors, of the American teacher who had come to London to find the answer to some obscure point about Samuel Johnson. After he had searched for some time, he found someone who said that the authority on that phase of Johnson's life was an American professor. The name, of course, that was mentioned was that of the man who had come seeking knowledge.

Around St. Paul's could still be seen the effects of some of the worst bombing which London had suffered. The church itself had suffered and its historic crypt had had to be closed, but it still stood proudly amidst the damage. I could remember the wonderful photograph made during the height of the bombings with St. Paul's silhouetted against the burning buildings of the city. It had represented then, as it still did, the courage and lasting quality of London.

Westminster Abbey, with all its relics of the past, drew us like a touchstone. The strength and power of the ages stood guard there and met firmly the challenge from across the Channel. On the first Christmas after victory, I was to come again to the Abbey and hear its vaults resound with paeans of peace.

From the Abbey we went to Whitehall and saw the old room from which Charles I had gone out to his execution. And we reflected on the manner in which a tyrant met his fate, gaining in that time of trouble some consolation from that outcome, but were sobered somewhat by the knowledge that his conqueror became a greater dictator than he.

At times we journeyed singly to the other sights, such as London Tower or Tower Bridge. The Tower was open then only to Allied troops and their guests. However, the Beefeaters, gorgeous no longer since they had shed their medieval costumes for modern battle dress, always assumed that the child who joined you at the gate was your own. I took a little girl in with me and she was impressed by the tales the guide told us no less than by the sight of the famous birds of the Tower.

However, my chief recollection of this visit was a meeting with a little lad near Tower Bridge. He informed me that he was from Deptford, pronouncing it as if the first syllable had choked him, and asked if I had anything to give him. First he wanted candy, and then, in order, gum, shoulder patches, uniform buttons, or anything else of value to a boy. When I convinced him that I had given all these things away to other children, he slapped me on the back and said, "That's all right, chum, I like you anyway." Having eliminated remunerative considerations, he turned to history and Anglo-American relations. He showed his knowledge of American history by asking if I were a Rebel or Yankee, and said that another soldier had told him the difference. (He also wanted to hear of the history of the Tower, which he had never visited, although he often played beside it). When I told him that I had heard the name of Drake connected with his town of Deptford, he seemed pleased to find that a Yank knew something of that fellow-countryman of his. Our conversation was brought to an abrupt halt when a girl of about twenty approached, bade him be on his way, and asked for a cigarette for herself. She was not interested in history.

Another day, I visited the Inns and the ruined Guildhall and wondered if these ruins were similar to those at the time of the Great Fire. Suddenly a mob of urchins yelling "Any gum, chum?" engulfed me. I soon came to dread these floods of children because my weekly ration was soon exhausted and the unfortunate ones seemed sad and resentful because of their ill luck. One day, when I had been fallen upon by such a group near London Bridge, an old man ordered them away and asked my pardon for the "begging" of the children. He said he was ashamed because it wasn't like the English children to be like that, and it was all a symptom of the war. Although he himself was ragged and poor, he had his pride for London and for England.

Later, as I walked across the bridge, I stopped to talk to a Welsh miner who told me of the woes of coal mining and waxed fiercely Socialistic. A veteran of World War I, wearing his medals of that conflict, a little man from up Yorkshire way also told me of the terrible things which the Tories had done to England, and he recited tales of the terrible days of the real Blitz and the proud deeds of the Londoners as they withstood it. A Jewish lad, standing far-

ther along the great span, told me tales of terror in Germany before he had escaped, first to Paris and then to London. He, too,
had frightful tales to tell of the London raids, for of the few members of his family who had escaped from the Nazis, two died during a raid on a winter night, victims of the long arm of German
airpower. So it went on every walk—or at a pub—or at a restaurant—one could meet people from every sort of background. From
them all there came the recounting of the fright and sorrow of the
dreadful days when Germany threatened to be master of earth
and sky. And then there was the quiet pride of a people who had
won the big fight and who now waited only for the chance to end
the conflict, of whose outcome they had no doubt.

The story of the days of terror could still be read in the faces
of those who still came, not in thousands as of old but in the hundreds at least, to sleep in the various subway stations. Although
the great raids by planes had come to an end, a few aircraft still
came each evening to keep alive the threat of death, and some
frightened souls still sought the refuge of the friendly Tube. Beds
were still set up—in tiers along the platforms—and individuals
were allowed to register for the same place each night. There, as
we went home at night from shows or the Red Cross clubs, we
could see them huddled together, spreading their beds. Children
were weeping, and some were ill natured because of a lack of
sleep since the lights would not go off nor the cars stop until late
at night. My vision of the Blitz at its worst is not found in the
photographs of falling bombs, of flaming ruins, nor of battered
rows of buildings, but in the blank face of the white-haired old
lady who restlessly smoothed her bed and in the pinched faces of
nervous children who had never known a night of peace.

Ah, those nights in London. From their blackness, we could
still get an idea of the darkness of war. We had seen brownouts
and practiced blackouts in the United States, and I had my boy-
hood recollections of an ink-black countryside on a moonless night.
Back home, since 1942, we had had block wardens, and there were
occasional attempts at camouflage and jests about those houses
whose blackout curtains let through the light. But here it was no
joke. Plays and movies opened in late afternoon so that the streets
might be well emptied by the time darkness fell. The entrance to
each building was darkened with heavy curtains, although it is

doubtful if much light could have shown through the great piles of sandbags that still stood in front of many of the structures. If one knew his way about, the blackout was not as difficult as a London fog, but we did not soon forget our first encounter with the pitch-black streets and unfamiliar ways. Only here and there was there a light in a traffic island—which gave only the thinnest cat-eye of illumination, and one had to grope his way around street corners and try to develop a blind man's sixth sense of feeling a landmark without actually knowing it was there. But the dark was good; the people were still unhappy when there was a moon. While they were sure that the RAF had conquered, there was always the chance that the Boche would return for one night or two of terror before the invasion. And indeed, it had not been long since strikes had been made at the city and at Bristol. And while it was not the old Blitz, people still died.

Without its lights, London could still be alive at night. There were numerous plays to entertain a crowd and, even as in New York, the accent was on escapism. The success of the sugary musicals of Ivor Novello showed what was wanted at the moment. GIs tended to gather at the Rainbow Corner, at the Washington Club, Hans Crescent, or some of the city's soldier clubs. Rainbow Corner was the best known because of its Piccadilly location. Occasionally entertainment was given at the clubs, but mainly they served as places to get food, to get a shower, a kind word, to meet a friend, or write a letter. The food was not exciting because we were following a British diet in the clubs, and the sandwiches, made of austerity bread, ran to cress, herring, and odds and ends of onions and pickled fish. The soda pop was weak stuff, indeed, bearing the same relation to American colas that wartime "arf and arf" and "mild and bitter" bore to prewar British beer and ale. With all that, the clubs provided a welcome spot—a little more like home than a crowded pub around the corner.

And if the clubs were not exciting, there was always Piccadilly. No longer brightly lighted, and with the statue of Eros away for the duration (his counterfeit spirit was still around, however), there was little at first sight to remind one that here was the Times Square of the British Empire. However, in the faint light of the dying day, one could see enough to know why Piccadilly had found its way in the songs of Britishers of the First World War.

In a short walk, one could see soldiers and sailors from all parts of the earth. Although at the moment, the Yank threatened to submerge the representatives of the Empire and the troops of the Governments-in-Exile, the different accents of the British soldiers and shoulder patches of the foreign forces, most of whom wore British battle dress, made clear the cosmopolitan nature of this corner of London.

Where roving men of the world gather there also may be found the painted ladies of the street. Piccadilly, I take it, always had its quota of streetwalkers, but the prices offered as the troops came up to London for that last furlough before they shoved off for the Continent brought girls from all the haunts of the United Kingdom. Looking the more glamorous with a fur coat bought from the proceeds of one month's activities, the former four-shilling girls of the London slums, who once had been badgered by the Bobbies, suddenly found themselves squired by sergeants and sometimes colonels. No longer need they lead furtive existences, for these Yanks with flying pay, or overseas pay, or cash that they might never live to spend if they saved it, went out on the town with their Piccadilly Commandos. Fastidious nightspots, opened to American officers as a courtesy, often found that their hospitality was extended to women "the likes of which they hadn't seen before."

But evenings out weren't always that sordid. Many a Yank in Normandy solaced himself with the memory of a young teacher, a young stenographer, an ATS girl, or a Land Army lass on leave. Quite a number of our men met girls they married before D-Day or shortly after the war. For others, these girls represented merely a passing date that quite often ended in Hyde Park. It was a standing joke in London music halls that one had to watch where he stepped in Hyde Park because there might be a Yank in the grass. And there were doorways, air-raid shelters, and alleys—all of which were preached against by ETOUSA headquarters as it appealed to American soldiers to behave better while away from home. Major General John C.H. Lee, the services of supply commander, sought to keep order and maintain discipline by putting his MPs in white helmets and giving them white gloves, so that they were known as Snowballs, and sent them about telling the good word to the heathen. He was strict on saluting—even in corridors—and troops marched to breakfast and for a time, until bombs fell near one formation, to work. But they didn't stop the "fraternizing" and the promiscuity. The English girls, for their part, taught the American lads all the naughty words to "Bell-Bottom Trousers," and "Roll Me Over in the Clover" threatened to become a sort of international theme song.

The pub has been too often described to require much discussion here, but it was part of the life of the Yank in England and must be remembered by the scriptwriter who does the European war movie. Always crowded, the air foul, with barmaids who looked as if they were hired more for their ability as bouncers than as dispensers of brew, the public houses came perilously close to losing their ancient reputations as places where the folk of the neighborhood could gather for a social glass. The good burghers had to shove their way through crowds of assorted soldiers to buy their one glass of "mild and bitter." It seemed always doubtful if even the watered stock would last for a second round. The dart players had to take their chance on hitting some of the players or, worse still, to submit to the disgrace of being beaten by some Yank who had picked up the habit over a number of glasses of beer in one of the southern counties. The people of the smaller pubs taught the Yanks not only the game of darts but also the rules of "Shove Ha'penny" and the words of a dozen songs. It is hard to know what folklore they gathered in return, but the shilling a mug for beer helped to balance the international trade balance, as the Exchequer gratefully pointed out.

For a time it also appeared that the Yanks' gift to the British birthrate might equalize the decline suffered by the continued absence of thousands of soldiers. Tommy Trinder wore thin this joke: "In the next war you will only have to send the uniforms." The *Economist* indicated that the birthrate went up most rapidly near camps occupied by Canadian troops, but the Yanks indignantly declared that this was merely another case of Imperial Preference.

In the midst of the drinking and the lovemaking and the furloughs there were many signs that the invasion was near at hand. Nearly every day the regular traffic would be stopped to let pass the great convoys of men and equipment moving eastward and to the south. The British were headed toward the old ports of

Dover and Rye, while the Americans went toward Devon and Cornwall. At other times one talked to a pilot or a gunner. Tired, weary, but avid for a different excitement from what they had been experiencing, they would describe the work being done over the Pas de Calais. Six missions in a row over Flak Corner on the "Milk Run" was the story of one gunner, who spelled out tales of recklessness, heroism, fear, and fatigue. He was sure that things were about to pop because the intensity of the attack could not continue. As yet unbriefed as to the real area of the invasion, we tried to figure it from the pattern of air attacks and troop movements, only to make the same mistake the Germans made. Our planners were clever. They wrote the script so that long-range bombings would fool the enemy as to the direction of the attack while destroying his lines of communications.

With all this movement there was still time to see what remained in the art galleries, to visit bookstalls, and to talk politics. There was also time to eat out, but the strict rationing made even the biggest restaurants uninteresting places to dine. Gordon took us one evening to a place in Soho that he had known while a student in Oxford. We ended by paying a pound for tough hare, the inevitable Brussels sprouts, and a thin bit of trifle.

One of the unexpected treats of the stay in London, and one which could happen only in an army which drew on men from all walks of life, came one night at the Hans Crescent club in Knightsbridge. Garth, Gordon, and I had stopped in for our usual nightcap of pop, when we heard from the music room a master sergeant playing a minuet of Mozart as it was seldom done in those precincts of jazz. The music also drew the attention of two checkers playing lads, who, observing that they had a "classical" pianist in their midst, asked for "The Blue Danube." When the sergeant shrugged away their request with the reply that he didn't have the music, we asked if he would play for us. I asked him for something of Scarlatti's, which I had heard in Washington shortly before I left for London. Then Gordon, who had once played piano a great deal, asked for Chopin. For two hours the sergeant played request after request, and then for a time the two played together, one starting a number somewhere in the middle and the other taking it up again at a given point. We learned that the performer had been a professional—Mueller, Russian-born—who had joined the American army in order to do something for his native country. He looked sadly at his fingers and said that he would never be able to play again some of the more difficult numbers, since he was unable to practice regularly. But he still had magic there, and I heard him in the Paris Rainbow Corner some months later, holding a GI audience enthralled.

During my last week in London I had talks with a number of friends from the United States who came up from nearby stations for their last visit to the city before the invasion. A former schoolmate, Captain Hal Houston, came by to say he would go in with the first hospital unit. I was to see his unit in Normandy and to visit him much later during the Bulge. Lieutenant Daniel Boone, a former student who complained of the kidding he got because of his name, came by to say hello. On the streets one day, I ran into Jim Allison, also a former student from Murray, who I had last seen in the Pentagon. And there was "Woody" Spencer, in whose home I had often visited in Worcester while a student at Clark. We had a sandwich and a Coke at Rainbow Corner and talked of his family, of his brother "Red" in Italy, and of the tough job he would face as an infantryman in the 4th Division. Several weeks later, in Normandy, he was severely wounded and sent back to the States. One former student canceled his trip to London, being ordered back to his ship near Plymouth just before he was to leave. Just before D-Day he wrote me a pleasant note, one of the last he ever penned, because he was reported missing on 6 June and his body was never found.

All of this happened between the twelfth and twenty-eighth of April as we saw London, got briefed on preparations, held our ear to the keyhole of history, and got our gear together. The decision was made in late April that Cole, Hechler, and Harrison would go with Third Army, while Garth, Ferriss, Ruppenthal, and I would go with members of the ETOUSA historical staff to First Army. The chief of the First Army team was to be Major Jeremiah O'Sullivan, who had been "dean" of our morning conferences at ETOUSA. "Jerry," a professor of history at Fordham, had studied at Trinity in Ireland, at the Sorbonne, and at the University of Pennsylvania. His studies in medieval history had taken him throughout the Continent and he had a great knowledge of its history. He was a typical Irishman with a big heart and a twinkle, a bit of a brogue, a way of disregarding rank, and a fine voice for "I've Got Sixpence," and "Beer, Beer, Beer, Said the Private." He had written history for a time for the air force and then, not long before we came to London, had joined Colonel Ganoe's group. With him to First Army went two other ETOUSA officers. One was John Howe, a Rutgers graduate and teacher of history in a New Jersey school, who was our executive officer. The other was Lieutenant William J. Fox, a UP man from Brooklyn. As Irish as Jerry, he lacked the brogue and some of the air. Still, he was inclined to be belligerent on occasion and he liked to philosophize over a drink of cognac. "Bill" had taken ROTC in college and came into the army as a reservist. He arrived in England in 1942 with the 29th Division as a platoon leader and learned his soldiering the hard way. Fellow officers later told me how his feet, unused to such punishment, had bled on the first long march, and how he hobbled on and finished with the company. With all the cockiness common to men small of stature, he was always ready for an argument, but he found it difficult to hold a grudge. Like Cole, he disposed of the opposition with a withering "those bastards" and went on to other matters. It turned out that he was to spend more days in the field than any of the other historians.

With the selection of teams our London phase was over. A few of our group were to get back again before 6 June, but Garth and I were not to make it until the summer of 1945.

Chapter 2

We Learn Top Secrets or We Are BIGOTED

With our fellow members of the First Army historical team, Garth and I in late April journeyed down to Bristol, where First Army was located in the grounds and buildings of Clifton College. For the first time since I had left Memphis I became conscious of the difference of rank at the railway station in London. Tickets for Garth, a staff sergeant, and for the officers were first class. I was only a buck sergeant and had to ride in second class with a corporal who also came along. As a gesture of solidarity, the others joined us, and the officers helped push the cart with our baggage at the station. We never encouraged them to act differently and they seldom did. Once a newcomer asked me to carry his bag, and I said I would be glad to help him with his if he would help me with mine. The matter ended there.

The stay in Bristol was quite brief. The first night in transient quarters was enough to drive us away, since sleeping in a clammy and frigid basement with very little cover was not calculated to endear one to the accommodations. For the rest of our stay, Garth and I sought refuge in a private home where we found the first decent beds since we had arrived in England.

Sunday and Monday, 29–30 April

Captain Ferriss, Lieutenants Fox and Rafferty, and Sergeants Ruffenberg and Garth came to Bristol. Talked things over with Major O'Sullivan and Lieutenant Howe. On Sunday to V Corps. Met Colonel R.B. Patterson and Major Teague, Adjutant General.

In Bristol, the historians were separated into corps teams. After a meeting with Colonel Truman C. Thorson, the First Army G-3, who asked our names and qualifications, shook our hands, and promised us the First Army's backing, we were assigned to corps. Fox and I were to go with V Corps, Ferriss and Garth to XIX, Ruppenthal and Lange to VII. O'Sullivan, Howe, and Hall were to stay with First Army and assist any corps that needed help.

Before leaving Bristol, I managed to see something of the city from which John Cabot had sailed on his voyage to America. I was especially interested in Clifton College, the site of First Army headquarters, whose beautiful halls and lawns seemed ill at ease in the presence of so many soldiers. Cricket had been replaced on the playing fields by baseball, but the spirit of a great college was still there, although the clatter of mess gear in the cloistered dining rooms seemed strange.

Other memories include the interesting restaurant Mauretania, whose furnishings had came from the famous ship of that name; the Centre, Bristol's Broadway and Times Square; the damaged cathedral; and the recently bombed buildings, whose uncleared debris made the city seem more deeply wounded than London. Perhaps the most impressive sight in the city was the Cabot Monument, which one reached only after a long climb up Cabot Hill. The great shaft, looking out toward America, proclaimed the part England had played in our settlement and growth and bore testimony to our kinship. However, the first English representative I saw here, a rather rugged spinster type, proved impervious to any international goodwill, glowering at my first hello and hastening away at my first question about the monument. Fortunately, two older ladies decided that I wouldn't compromise them, and became quite friendly. We discussed politics, and they proved to be rather socialistic, predicting changes at the next election. Of course, they pointed out, "we are not from the south of England." It developed that they had come down from the north some thirty years before. They spoke severely of Edward VIII and his wicked marriage. "We could have accepted an American wife," they reassured me, "but not a divorced one."

I suggested that the ladies probably had received bad impressions of American soldiers, but they insisted on blaming the British girls who were taking advantage of "the poor lads." Some were even trying to get them to marry them before the invasion, so they would have an allowance from the army, and "they don't care if they don't come back." They then added that no matter what the grown-ups might think, the British children would never forget the generosity of the Yanks. They told me, almost in tears, of the first Christmas when the Americans had come, and the way in which they had saved their rations of fruit and candy and given great parties. "And even now they give gladly. No, the children will never forget."

Fox and I moved at the end of April to V Corps, to which we were assigned for the rest of the war. In a jeep heavily loaded with our gear, including my precious briefcase, which I was never to have the nerve to take with me on a single interview, we wound across the pleasant hills and through the valleys east of Bristol, enjoying the beauties of an English spring. As we passed along the narrow lanes, we were reminded that war was there because the hedges along the way had suffered badly from vehicles too outsized for such a tiny countryside. And in the little towns, we noted how the huge tanks, not built for maneuvering in such cramped space, had knocked out pieces of corner buildings as they attempted to make sharp turns on a little street that had never been expected to cope with anything worse than a coach and four.

At Norton Manor near Taunton, the location of Major General L.T. Gerow's V Corps, we began to get for the first time the real feel of war. Here we changed from blouses to field jackets, and began to check our field gear for use. Instead of quarters in pleasant Georgian style apartments, we were back in open barracks. The beds were in double-tiered wooden bunks and chicken wire served as springs. There were supposed to be hard pads for mattresses, but the supply had given out, so I slept on the springs with a total of three blankets, one a thin British one which did not suffice to keep out the cold. Sometimes the chill of April made it necessary to sleep in my fatigues and to bundle up as best I could in an improvised blanket roll. After a time, my next bunk neighbor, Sergeant Nelson, got me some extra blankets and my life became pleasanter. However, nothing made life comfortable in the morning. Reveille was at 6 A.M.—late by basic training standards—but the frost that met us each day was a little hard to take. We were spared calisthenics and inspections, however, and we would race, nearly freezing, from the morning roll call to the steamy mess huts for our breakfasts of soggy French toast and porridge, with cups of scalding coffee. Here, as elsewhere, the barber mug type coffee cups had no handles and we burned our hands and mouths in the process of drinking.

Since field headquarters worked on Sundays as well as other days, V Corps was operating the afternoon we arrived and we were taken at once to the adjutant general, Colonel R.B. Patterson, a delightful regular army officer, bald of pate and heavy of midriff, who had shown a great interest in our work. The colonel had been adjutant general of Second Army until the spring of 1944 but had asked for a combat assignment and had been given one at V Corps. Since he had helped to compile the army's order of battle of the First World War while on duty with the small historical section of the army, and since he had written the memorandum for Second Army's history (on which I had worked), he was friendly to our cause. Although for the moment we were attached to the G-3 section, we were destined for much of the war to be under Colonel Patterson's watchful eye. He could be stern and tough, but mainly he was a delightful gentleman who did his job well. After the war I met him once at Bad Homburg where he was attending an all Beethoven symphony concert, but I remembered him best musically for the way in which he would stride through the building singing the popular tune "She Danced All Night with a Hole in Her Stocking." He held to the theory that everyone should know what the war was about, and he was in the habit of calling in officers and men for a briefing on coming campaigns.

That evening, after Colonel Patterson told us he would issue instructions to the divisions to cooperate with us, we felt that we were at last started. Bill was anxious to get on the way. About twenty-five, he was still an idealist, although disillusionment on several scores made him swear bitterly, and at times he would try to be cynical. But it never quite came off because his natural buoyancy would always come through. We chatted until late, trying to imagine what the attack would be like. We agreed that we did not fear death, but feared more the mark that the coming battles would leave on our thinking, our lives, and our world. We were somewhat unhappy because of the conflict between Washington's and ETOUSA's ideas of combat history, and we were not sure exactly what to look for. This conflict was not settled until near the end of the war, when the Washington view was finally established. In the meantime, we were more or less on our own.

The corps to which we had come was the first U.S. corps headquarters to reach the United Kingdom. Located at first in Ireland in 1942, it had then moved to Bristol, and finally in 1943, after General Gerow became its commander, to Norton Manor. Some of its members had been overseas as long as I had been in the army. General Gerow, who was chief of the War Plans Division of the War Department in 1941, had turned it over early in 1942 to General Eisenhower and had come to Europe as commander of the 29th Division. He proved to be a capable officer without fuss or pretense. His chief fault, so far as the men were concerned, was a tendency in combat to move his headquarters too close to the front. This proclivity sometimes put his forward command post on the line, and I can recall in Normandy actually going back a little way from corps to reach a division CP. He was also noted for his desire to be up where the action was. Once, when we were trying to reach a 29th Division forward position and our jeep was held up in a traffic jam, a major behind us began to swear and to tell us to get moving. Suddenly we saw General Gerow coming up from behind and saying bitingly to the major, "What's the matter, can't you walk?"

We got well settled during our first week at corps. Colonel Hill, the G-3, assigned us a place with the liaison group attached to his section, and Colonel (later Brigadier General) Matchett, the chief of staff, promised us transportation. At Colonel Patterson's request, Fox and I began to draft a memorandum that he would send to all the divisions indicating the material to be preserved for historical use.

On my first weekend at Norton Manor, I got a pass to visit my brother Tommy, who had been overseas several months with the 703rd Tank Destroyer Battalion of the 3rd Armored Division. He was located in the town of Mere in Wiltshire. Wartime situations were such that although he was only a few miles away, it took two changes of trains, nearly a mile walk, and two efforts at hitchhiking before I got there. Fortunately at Wincanton, the first chap I asked for a ride was a mail orderly from Tommy's battalion, and he delivered me to the front door.

Tommy invited me to spend the night, and I made the mistake of accepting. If Norton Manor's accommodations were Spartan, those at Mere were primitive. Living quarters were Nissen huts, toilet facilities were open-air, and there was little heat. I had already experienced piercing, bone-chilling cold in England, but this was something extra. Everyone contributed blankets to keep me warm, but although I was almost crushed beneath their weight, my teeth continued chattering for some time after I went to bed.

Any regret I had for staying over in such a cold hut was dispelled next day by the delightful visit I had with the Grays of Mere. Tommy and many other soldiers had found the home of this Welsh shoemaker and his family the best equivalent of their own homes they had seen in England. Later, when I met American soldiers who were bitter at the English or who said they were aloof or rude, I was sorry that they had not met the Grays. Mere was an old town with Celtic, Roman, and Norman remains. There was little excitement, despite the efforts of ladies of the city to make the local soldiers' club a pleasant spot. But here at the Grays there was a spark of home. As we walked along the country lane on the way to the Grays, we were caught in a downpour that soon had us gasping for breath before we reached the house. Mr. Gray built up a roaring fire and hung our wet things in front of it while we warmed ourselves. Despite the severity of rationing, he and his wife soon set out cakes and tea, not only for us, but for the dozen chaps who came in during the four hours that we stayed there. They played symphonies for us on their phonograph and followed these with choral music, but seemed to get their greatest enjoyment out of a recording of "The Man Who Comes to Our House When Papa Goes Away." I was told that these gatherings took place every night. Our meeting was a little saddened by the fact that all signs pointed to an early departure. These people, not because we were Yanks to be welcomed, but because they were friendly folk, wrote our parents back home not to worry, and did for us the wonderfully thoughtful things that make up true hospitality.

Saturday, 6 May–Tuesday, 9 May

Outlined Standard Operating Procedure for reporting on activities. To Bristol with Lieutenant Fox in P.M.

On our second Saturday at corps, Fox and I journeyed back to Bristol for final instructions. Garth and Ferriss came up from Knutsford, and Colonel Ganoe and Captain Thurman later joined the discussion. It was clear that there was still no settled policy on the coverage of history, although the tendency now was to stress small-unit actions. Our big argument was that the colonel was permitting peripatetic representatives to roam through our areas without our being notified, so that we looked blank when we visited units and were asked, "Jesus Christ, how many of you people are going to come in here?" We were promised that this practice would be stopped, but we left with a feeling of uncertainty. The parting had a touch of finality because the colonel had brought word that Y day was the thirty-first of May and that the invasion would come any day thereafter. We also learned that the attack would be made in Normandy.

Before going to Bristol, I had made a number of friends among my barracks mates. In addition to Nelson my immediate next-bunk partner, a valiant soul who never once threatened me about my snoring—which had tried the patience of many older friends than he—I became friendly with Sergeant Reagan of G-1, Smitty, a clerk in AG who entertained us with testimony from some of the court-martials, and Sergeant Macauley of Ordnance. This group and others, who were veterans of several field exercises, correctly suspected I would never get anywhere without help and they found equipment for me and helped me scrounge articles of clothing I would need. Nelson got me a knife for my pistol belt that made me look properly martial in my photographs. "Mac" decided that I needed to know about the new army vehicles and insisted on showing me the finer workings of the new Weasel, the carrier that clambered about in mud and water with equal ease. Knowing that he had a greenhorn aboard, he sent the carrier up almost vertical heights and then later came splashing down in the water in a nearby proving hole until I was sure we would be capsized or drowned.

Wednesday, 10 May–Tuesday, 16 May

Two WD observers attached to G-3. So we to switch to G-1. Will stay in troop movement and liaison office here with Major Nurmburger, Captain

Sleyer, Captain O'Connor, Captain Shannon and Captain Digby. Saw informal order attaching us to G-1; was dated yesterday. ——— with Master Sergeant Sorenson, chief clerk of G-1 and Staff Sergeant Francis Ragen. They will be nice fellows to work with. Met Major Hamlin briefly.

Ten days after we arrived at corps, we were BIGOTED. I had never realized that I could achieve any special merit by having this term applied to me, but I asked that it be done. This term meant that in common with quite a lot of people, we now had the privilege of working with high-level documents dealing with NEPTUNE. The general code name for the invasion plan was OVERLORD. However, since this name had been used for some months, the decision was made to call the initial assault phase of the invasion NEPTUNE and to give all plans and papers concerning this phase the special BIGOT classification. This drastically limited the number of people with access to this information. After very little ceremony, G-2 was satisfied as to our trustworthiness and we were told that we could examine the plans. We assumed that such secrets would be under heavy locks and carefully guarded, but we discovered that the planning building in which copies of the plan were kept had no special sentry and that the room in which a stack of the papers could be found was secured only by a Yale lock. After introducing ourselves to Lieutenant Degnan, Sergeant Shain, and Corporal Kelly, we were shown to a room that seemed to be filled with paint buckets and brushes used to stencil boxes. In one corner was a large wooden cabinet, with no lock, and in it on the floor were the various sections of V Corps's plans for the landings. For several days this room was to be the center of our activity as we memorized sections of the basic plan so that we could talk intelligently to officers and men about it when we were ashore.

For once the complacency was knocked out of us. In London, we had been around rumormongers with the "hot dope" long enough that we tended to assume an air that "there isn't much you can tell us." But here was chapter and verse. Beginning with the original directive, issued in February, the plans outlined the activities of V Corps on Omaha Beach on D-Day and the first ten days thereafter. Since this was the set of plans issued by corps with the amendments written in, we were able to follow the course of planning, especially since Colonel B.B. Talley, the chief corps planner, put at our disposal his personal correspondence file regarding the planning.

In a few days, we became aware of the immensity of the D-Day plan. While the plan we were studying was only that of V Corps, it included the broad outline of the First Army plan with a sketch of the action to be followed by the British—and a copy of the full navy plan. Three weeks before we had felt "in the know" because we knew the order of battle for D-Day. Now we had in detail the main phases of the attack with maps and charts showing the exact spots of landings.

Feverishly we digested the material. We soon knew that General Collins's VII Corps was to attack on Utah Beach, on the Cherbourg Peninsula; that General Gerow was to attack on Omaha Beach in the center; and that British XXX Corps was to attack on the left. The planners had chosen the landing beaches for a variety of reasons. They were distant from German airfields and near our own, they were believed to be lightly held, and they could not be easily reinforced. These were some of the points that had led to their selection. It was hoped that the building of artificial ports with materials floated over for that purpose would compensate for the lack of ports in the area.

The area chosen was, however, unpromising looking on a map. From the minute, yard-by-yard descriptions and silhouette photographs of the coast, the beaches were unlovely things on which to land. The beaches, backed by cliffs, were rimmed by ledges from which antitank guns and automatic weapons could bring murderous fire on the invader. Reports from the French underground, from aerial photos, and from special landing parties that had been set ashore to conduct reconnaissance virtually pinpointed the defenses, the paths, the winding roads, the stone walls, the length of beach, the height of shingle. More important, they knew almost how many machine guns were there, where they were pointed, the rifle pits, the strands of wire, the communications trenches between pillboxes, the tank ditch that cut off access to exits from the beach, and then the awful photographs of the underwater barricades. Gate-like "Element C," standing ten feet high with slanting steel supports topped by teller mines; hedgehogs, ugly affairs made of crisscrossed steel beams from five to six feet in height; and log ramps and posts with ragged edges and mines to rip and explode landing craft all protected the beaches. Thus a devilish collection of pitfalls waited for the troops coming in for a landing. The presence of these obstructions required the planners to arrange their assault at low tide, so that the first waves of troops could go in when the barriers were exposed, thus avoiding the underwater terror and carrying demolitions teams to clear away these barriers before the later waves of men would come in.

The soldier faced the risk of explosion to his ship, fire from the guns situated out of sight behind the cliffs, the obstructions at the beach, antitank ditches, minefields, wire, and fire from pillboxes. In addition, it was possible that he would have to wade in water up to his neck and run across wet sand while heavily loaded with weapons and equipment.

The planners had tried to think of everything. The intelligence people had drawn from old road maps, hotel guides, tourist information, postcards, recollections of visitors, French Resistance information, and the like in order to depict for the soldier the area he was to invade. V Corps was to go into Calvados, which like the rest of Normandy was an ancient part of France, conservative by nature, pluralistic, and made up of "tight-fisted, hard-headed, shrewd folk." There were few Gaullists among the group, but it seemed likely that they could be depended on once we got ashore.

The V Corps invasion area was sparsely settled, with Saint-Lô and Isigny the largest towns. The rest were largely fishing or tourist villages, such as Saint-Laurent-sur-Mer, Colleville-sur-Mer, and Vierville-sur-Mer, on which the main V Corps attack was to be directed.

Omaha Beach was said to be defended by approximately eight hundred troops, thirty-five pillboxes, some twenty antitank guns, and from eight to twelve howitzers. There was some fear of effective counterattacks by troops inland at the end of the second or third day, but there seemed to be a feeling that the opposition on the beaches from troops, who were believed to be largely Polish or Russian, would not be heavy. On reading this, I noted in my diary for 11 May: "Optimism about probable opposition on beaches likely to change."

In an effort to knock out or spike six guns that were believed to be in place at the western flank of V Corps's attack, the planners had arranged a Ranger attack on Pointe du Hoe. Because of the rugged cliffs in that area, an elaborate plan had been worked out for the use of scaling ladders, scaling ropes, and the like. To our minds, this operation seemed the crucial one on Omaha Beach.

Second in interest to the Rangers were the DD tanks, newfangled weapons made by encasing tanks in canvas coverings so they could be floated in under their own power from five miles out. Corps correspondence indicated that some officers were worried about the possibility that the tanks might sink, that they would become landlocked once they reached the beach, or that they would behave as poorly as they had done in previous trials. However, the need for tank support for infantry in the opening minutes of the attack tipped the scales in favor of these monsters. Rocket ships were also added to give additional power.

The chief support on the beaches, of course, was supposed to be provided by the ships and planes. Ships were expected not only to drench the beaches with shells before the attack, but also to give close-in support during the first hours and days of the landings. The bombers, which had been at work for weeks against factories, railroads, and bridges, were to concentrate in the hours just before the landings on the bridges of the Seine, the highways leading to the beaches, and the beach defenses.

Naturally, invasion planning did not stop with these activities. Many appendices of the master plan included such matters as civil government, supply, medical questions, and the like. One plan listed the amounts of cocoa, wheat, meat and vegetables to be distributed in towns where food shortages were acute. The quartermaster was given estimates of uniforms, bandages, Purple Hearts, and even Bronze Stars he would be expected to provide. The Medical Section reassured us that there were no poisonous serpents in the area, while omitting the information that in a local apple brandy called calvados, the region had a potent antidote against snake bite. We were even told where the Germans had their chief administrative headquarters, which local officials had been friendly to the enemy, and there were sometimes lists of prostitutes who might be able to supply information concerning the Germans.

The task of learning the plan was staggering. We asked each other, if we can't even read the plan in a month, how can we expect in that length of time to get a story of what happened? We realized, of course, that we must depend heavily on the company, battalion, and regimental clerks, the sergeants major, the officers and men who kept the journals and the message files, the clerks who kept the war room map, the officer who made the situation reports and the overlays. All these recorded the battle as it was seen at headquarters. The journal contained all written messages, overlays, periodic reports, situation reports, weekly summaries, and the like. In some headquarters, a careful record was also kept of important telephone calls. Supplementing these were after-action reports to be issued once a month and unit histories that some organizations prepared if there was time and talent. Our task in the remaining days before the invasion was to sell part of the people in the invasion units on the value of preserving additional pieces of information that were not loaded down by army regulations. We realized that the heart of our postwar history lay in the integrity of the journal. Here was where they were likely to record the situation as it was known to a unit at a given moment. Since the keeper of the journal stuck in the pieces of history as they came in, the journal was likely to reflect the fears and hopes of the sender at a given moment in history. Unfortunately, the record was not always accurate, since it showed sometimes not the danger of defeat but the fear of defeat; not the size of the enemy force on a given front but the distortion of the size of the force as it existed in the mind of the originator of the message. Sometimes a commander, anxious to get for his men the glory of taking a town, reported its capture when he was only in sight of it—and then had to see other troops sent up to seize it a day or two later. But this record, however incomplete, was an unconscious listing of evidence and, therefore, worth preserving. Often, the journal was not complete when it reached the rear echelons, since material needed for operations was borrowed and a salient page replaced with a memo: "Major Blank has this." To the historian several years later, such annotation would be of little aid.

Wednesday, 17 May

The necessity of contacting the various units in order to sell our idea of combat history before the battle began gave us a chance to see southern England in the spring—one of those army junkets that enables one to enjoy the countryside while carrying on one's work. My first visit was made on 17 May to the 1st Division at Blandford. The headquarters was located in a former manor house that had been requisitioned by British forces and turned over to us.

But I had made the visit much too early, inasmuch as the division was preparing to move out for the marshalling area and officers and men were running in and out of offices with equipment. I found that there was little need to sell the idea of history to this division. The 1st Division, conscious of its past history and with a staff already trained for battle, was well prepared to tell its story. Lieutenant Colonel Charles Ware, the G-1, and the adjutant general, Lieutenant Colonel Leonidas Gavilas, who were charged with preparing a history, promised to prepare material for our later use. This task was delegated to Corporal J.J. Pirhalla, a graduate of New York University and Columbia and a former teacher, who was vitally interested in the project.

The division offered us quarters for the evening, but my driver, Private de Rosa, who had made this trip before, persuaded me to go instead to nearby Bournemouth for the night. Most of the great hotels overlooking the sea had been turned over to the American forces and it was possible to have a comfortable room and to sit in a lobby with photographs of American cities, maps of the United States, and the latest pinup girls. This contrasted strongly with the beach outside, which was armed against invaders. Since the beautiful beaches invited the enemy, the sands were covered with wire and mines, and the area overlooking the beaches with steel and concrete antitank barriers. One thought of the possible battle there in 1940 had the Germans made their Channel push, and also of the fact that in two weeks some of the men then enjoying a last weekend at the seashore would be clambering over beaches and obstructions like this.

Thursday, 18 May

We reluctantly left Bournemouth the next morning and went to Tidworth, where the 2d Armored Division, scheduled to land shortly after D-Day, was located. The unit was away on a field problem and it was nearly dark before a group of grimy and exhausted U.S. soldiers came back from a rough day. No one was in the mood to talk history, and I had to be content with discussing the problem with a public relations officer—a Captain Volk—who promised to talk to the right people about maintaining a unit history.

Salisbury was our stopping place the second night. We reached there near dusk and I was disappointed not to get in the cathedral grounds to get a look at the famous church. "Obvious reasons," an old Scotswoman told me when I asked about the closing, glowering all the while at a soldier who was passing along the street with a young British girl he had just met. The old lady made plain that she was not English, although she had been in Salisbury more than twenty years.

Friday, 19 May

I rose early the next morning and got into the cathedral as soon as it was opened. There was sunlight and brightness and the old building looked especially magnificent. Even de Rosa, who had been showing disdain for such places, seemed impressed.

As we drove back toward Taunton across the Plain of Salisbury, we picked up a British soldier who, finding us willing to listen without arguing, vented his grievances against the American soldier. He laid the success of the Yanks with British girls to the munificent pay received by American soldiers. He was good enough to admit, however, that in 1939 in France, British soldiers had pressed their advantage when they found they were paid more than the French.

De Rosa, knowing that I had a brother at Mere, managed to take a road that brought us by the 703rd Battalion, and I took a few minutes to say good-bye. There was a dread about our meeting that we did not mention. Like other parting conversations, the talk was not of the invasion, but of recent news from home, of his bedroll, and of a photograph of our young niece, Dianne Stevens Corts. We posed for a photograph, I saw one of the new tank destroyers and Tommy told me how it worked. We talked about some of his friends whom I had met on my former visit and he kidded me about wearing a tie. We wondered why no mail had come. (Unknown to us, mail both to and from the United

Kingdom was being impounded for security reasons until after the attack.) We walked to a beautiful hill overlooking Mere and gazed down on numerous little towns spread in ordered beauty at our feet. I mentioned the history of the area and we agreed that so old and great a land was worth defending. We went back silently to the hutted camp, where Tommy put into my briefcase a number of pamphlets and souvenirs which he would be unable to take to the Continent (even road maps had to be left in England lest they fall into the hands of the enemy and perhaps later serve their purposes). Still without mentioning possible danger to ourselves, we expressed sympathy for our brothers, Jim and Rip, who had the tough luck to be in New Guinea, and said good-bye. The fears we left unspoken never had reality, since we and our two brothers in the Pacific came through the war unscratched. But before my next meeting with Tommy in the cold and mud and snow of Germany, I was to relive often that moment of farewell.

Saturday, 20 May–Monday, 22 May

The last three days were spent in ridding ourselves of surplus clothing and equipment. Headquarters SOP had listed in detail the things we could and could not take. Men in assault groups were limited to a helmet, two shirts, two pairs of trousers, and two pairs of shoes (the extra pair of each item had to be heavily doused with gas impregnated preparation which meant they were heavy with lime and smelled to high heaven), several pairs of socks, their weapons, and field equipment. Headquarters personnel were permitted to carry a little more clothing and to wear impregnated coveralls. Since corps sections had many boxes for documents that they had not yet collected, nearly everyone fudged on regulations by putting some additional things in boxes marked "Secret Papers." Even then we got down to fundamentals—a musette bag and a half-filled duffel bag contained the gear we would need for several months. I sent a request back to London with Lieutenant Fox asking for my blouse, extra shirts, low-cut shoes, and some fifty books. The clothing was supposed to be brought to Paris by our ETOUSA friends when they came, but they declared to me in September 1944 that everything had been lost. After the war, a captain who had also left a Valpack and some clothing found that most of my things were in his bag. The books were never found.

In addition to impregnated clothing, we drew seasick pills, vomit bags (and they proved helpful before we landed), and anti-lice powder. The PX was closing out, so we bought a quantity of cigarettes. I bought my share, at the urging of friends, and exchanged the popular brands for the cartons of Fleetwoods that everyone had to take.

The final days were made interesting by NAAFI shows and a final party—with Land Army girls as guests and cider and cookies as refreshments—to end the social season.

Our nights were still enlivened by broadcasts of "Axis Annie," who interspersed good American music with BBC-type newscasts in which she told of crop failures in England accompanied by riots in London, of the wasteful high living in the United States, of the frightful toll the Germans were taking of Allied planes, and of the men who would be fished out of the Channel if an invasion were attempted. I could see no effect of these talks on the men who listened. Most of them had been overseas since the spring of 1942. They knew that the battle had to get started before they could go home. They would swear at times and say, "I hope this ain't just another maneuver." But they knew in their bones it wasn't, and no one took the chance of leaving behind some vital part of equipment as they had done on previous exercises.

That last mad night we reviewed our almost forgotten knowledge of tying up full field packs and got our gear in shape. Overcoats and other extra equipment was turned in. All but two blankets were left behind. Someone discarded a heavy olive-drab muffler that the Christian Science Church of Boston had sent him, so I took it. We drew new combat shoes and tried to work dubbing into the leather. Then we took a last shower. Of course, there was little sleep. Some did not sleep at all, as the lights for once were not put out.

Chapter 3

Waiting in Cornwall

Tuesday, 23 May

Cold.

For the stay in the marshaling area, and for the invasion, we had been shifted from the G-3 to the G-1 section, and lumped with a miscellaneous party of War Department observers and liaison officers. At 8:30 on the morning of 23 May we started with them from Norton Manor to Cornwall. The area back of G-3 headquarters was in an uproar from daybreak on as the vehicles were assembled and everyone tried to find his proper place. I had been assigned the back of a covered truck which contained—in addition to Colonel Talley's sleeping quarters, office equipment, and papers—some fifty or sixty boxes of K rations that filled the bed of the vehicle so full that I could not sit up straight. As luck would have it, the truck developed trouble and had to be sent to a maintenance station for repairs. Lieutenant Fox thought he should go back with the driver, so I took his place in a jeep with Major J.P. McKnight, an attorney from Auburn, Nebraska, who was attached to G-1 as a War Department observer.

Our destination was the 29th Division's marshaling area near Redruth. The morning was cold as we started, but slowly the chill was dispersed by the sun, and the day at last became one which made me willing for once to be in England now that spring was there. It is easy to remember the peaceful hills and valleys, and the occasional breathless moments when we sat on a hilltop and saw on a dozen roads of the valleys below us thousands of trucks, jammed with men and equipment, moving to the south.

Major McKnight, remembering something of his English history, asked me to refresh his memory. So, as we went along the road through Exeter toward Land's End, we talked of the Celts, the Roman invaders, and the Northmen. We could see about us ruined castles, peaceful homes, and happy scenes. Yet all about, if one looked closely, there was the grimness of war. There were half-concealed airfields, meadows that hid tanks and jeeps, and hedgerows harboring piles of shells. The little towns, still filled with century-old quaintness, looked out of place as troops streamed through in a floodtide toward the sea. Once, we stopped at a simple little house, from whose front door a scrawled sign proclaimed: "Tea for sale." The pleasant old lady showed us to her parlor, filled with the knickknacks of a past era. On the walls were photographs of her daughter, a WAAF in London, and a son, a lance corporal in India. She had no cookies, so we opened our K rations, the first that most of us had eaten, and got the sugars and crackers for our meal. She told us of her son and daughter and wished us well on our trip, although she didn't know for certain—and we didn't say—that this maneuver was for keeps. We saw cows in the pasture from the front room and, since we were nearly all farm boys, we talked of the cattle that had come from the British Isles. There was no jarring note, just a friendly cup of tea with a friend—no talk of war, although we were "accoutered in martial cloth and armed with deadly fire."

After stopping for half an hour, we proceeded on our way, but got lost and went past Penzance before we were put on the right road and came at last to our concentration area at 5:30 P.M. We were attached for rations and quarters to Company K, 175th Infantry, of the 29th Division. Our camp was in a series of small fields, along a country lane, placed between small hills which hid us from the sea, twelve miles away from Falmouth and a bit closer from the west. At this isolated camp, we felt for the first time the imminence of the invasion. Since we were to be briefed on the time and place of the attack, we were forbidden to leave the area without permission. At the entrance to each field were guards with orders to shoot anyone trying to leave. Other guards stood at regular intervals along the road, acting as airplane watchers and carrying specially prepared armbands that were treated so that they would indicate the presence of gas. We went to chow in small parties and were spaced at intervals so that an exploding bomb would kill only a few of us. Every man in the line hid his shining mess kit, which in peaceful times we had had to polish carefully for inspection, so that there would be no telltale reflection to attract the enemy.

To inculcate proper habits of discipline, the camp authorities required us to arrange our arms and helmets properly when we went out. At the moment, the chinstrap of the helmet had to be buckled. Later the rule was changed because of a report that the force of a blast near men with tightly buckled chinstraps had broken their necks. Later still, the tight chinstrap was ordered back because of reports that too many men were losing their helmets.

The field that was our home held about eight pyramidal tents, a latrine complete with honey bucket, a tub for washing clothes, a donkey cart, and a donkey that showed much wear. The two latter items were not army issue, but seemed to go with the field. Unfortunately, the men had little to do but to play with the donkey. In a few days, he was terribly bloated as the result of a diet of candy drops (paper not removed), chocolate, cigarettes, prophylactics, and chewing tobacco. At times when his goat-like diet proved too much for his stomach, he would give vent to horrible braying and run up and down the enclosure next to us, looking resentfully at everyone in GI clothing. His owner would then beg the gang to desist, but next morning, the donkey would be up to the fence, braying softly and begging for more handouts.

Wednesday, 24 May

Clear and beautiful day.

My first day in camp included a trip to Redruth for writing supplies. I recall the day mostly because this was the first town I had seen in England where I saw no soldiers. Also memorable was the fact that this was the last day until 2 August that I had a bath in proper bathing facilities. I would be taking sponge baths from a helmet and an occasional dip in an ice-cold pool in June and July, but this bath in a huge tub filled with hot water was to be an experience to be cherished in the early days in Normandy.

Thursday, 25 May

Cold and rainy. Very disagreeable. Stayed near cot most of the day.

Friday, 26 May

Regular men of group briefed. Our men will later. Examined map of this area. Discussed English history with Major McKnight. . . . Captain Johnson is from Mississippi. Still cool and misty. Played cards with Smith, Huff and Richards. Briefed by Major McKnight and paid partial payment.

Our days and nights were spent in sleep, card playing, reading, and occasional hikes. The hiking was stopped for the attached party after one four-mile march when several of our people got blisters. We had gone in the first place only because the Company K gang—who had declared that this was the quietest week they had had since 1942—took the ten-mile hikes daily just to keep in practice.

On Friday we were briefed. This was not a new experience for Fox and me, since we had read the plan and knew the actual day planned for the invasion—something the briefing officer did not know. Nonetheless, it was fascinating to watch the reaction of the various groups. In some cases, the briefing officers set up silhouette photographs of the coast, showing the beach as it looked at one-half mile, two miles, and five miles out. In other cases, the men gathered around sand tables or maps spread on the ground. They listened closely to the story of D-Day as it was outlined, still not clear as to the overall plan. They were told that under the full support of air and naval power they would go in on beaches that would be cleared of opposition. (This attempt to encourage them concerning the success of the landing led later to the accusation by the infantry that the air force had let them down. On 26 May, when they were briefed, the air planners did intend to neutralize shore defenses and perhaps make craters on the beach that the infantry could use. But, forty-eight hours before the invasion, the Air Corps notified General Eisenhower that bad weather would make it impossible to drop their bombs on the beaches without endangering the men. The project was abandoned as a result.)

As the plan was unfolded and as the platoon and squad leaders learned their specific mission on the beach, the men showed greater animation than I was to see at any other time during the invasion. With the growing grins that one sees on the faces of listeners who anticipate the denouncement of a risqué joke, the men showed their pleasure at the prospect of getting the attack started. "Jesus," one of them remarked, "now we can get started on the way home." They were tired of waiting, these men of the 29th Division. They had trained in Ireland for North African service and then had been left behind to aid in the defense of the United Kingdom. "The bulk of England's defense command," they liked to boast. For what seemed an endless time, they had marched up and down England, participated in exercises, and drilled in assault training centers, until it seemed that they would never do anything but practice war. They had feared that our 23 May move would be just another maneuver. But here at last their time had come. Just do this job and they could start back to Pennsylvania, Maryland, and Virginia, where many of them came from. So, without worry about the fact that the first day of battle might be their final day of life, they hailed the announcement of the invasion with great joy.

The invasion, as they had guessed, was to be in France. Uncertain, heretofore, as to the exact place of landing since they, like the Germans, had been fooled by our feints toward the Pas de Calais, they found at last that it was to be Normandy. They knew little of that part of France except that some had heard it connected with "apple blossom time." Cherbourg was known to some, but few had heard of fabled Bayeux or ancient Caen. Even had they heard of these spots, it is unlikely that their knowledge would have included Saint-Laurent-sur-Mere or Trevières or Isigny and, perhaps, not even of Saint-Lô, the little Norman town whose name will be always associated with that of the 29th.

Most of the briefers did little more than state the bald facts of the unit's job, and then indicate, "That's it." A few, more eloquent than the rest, desirous of saying a word for history, but self-conscious in the face of destiny, pictured to their men how all their months of drill and toil and preparation had been for this. The dress rehearsal had been held without their knowing that it was the final practice. The battle would soon tell how well they knew their lines.

Effective use of sound knowledge and some luck would determine if they survived. To assure them, some of the commanders repeated the familiar army cliché: "You have the best damn equipment and are in the best damn outfit from the best damn country in the world." There was little talk of Nazi monsters, although recent psychological warfare releases had suggested that "Hate the Hun" themes be emphasized, or a few statements about the lads battling bravely on a dozen fronts. They had been too tired of slogans, too wary of false sentiment, to use historic statements at the end.

Saturday, 27 May

Washed clothes.

Sunday, 28 May

Stayed in bed most of day. Beautiful weather. Read and slept. To church service at ten.

Monday, 29 May

Loafed most of the day reading detective stories and magazines. Weather prettier than ever; welcome contrast to cold and rainy weather of past two weeks. News of Anzio push. Bombings increase in intensity.

Tuesday, 30 May

Still killing time. We are beginning to get a few things ready every day: haircuts, waterproofing of gas masks, working clothes, etc.

Wednesday, 31 May

Got nice short haircut. Moved our truck and jeep to final marshalling area. Talked to several of the fellows who are getting ready to go. They show little excitement, since they have gone through numerous training exercises similar to this. They seem ready for a fight and well hardened. . . . The chief topic is concerned with the amount of French sufficient to make contact with French mademoiselles. Played cards at night.

Thursday, 1 June

Rained late yesterday afternoon. Cold this morning.
Got life belts, rations for one week, instruction on abandoning ship.
Will start move to boat tomorrow. Everything still quiet; unmarked by
excitement. Cards in the afternoon. Put impregnate (against gas) on
shoes at night. Will wear gas protection on coveralls, leggings and shoes
tomorrow. Weather cool and blustery.

With the briefing finished, it was a matter of waiting. Shoes
were to be impregnated and vehicles waterproofed so they could
run through heavy tides undamaged by the sea. The company barber, returning to recruit haircut styles, prepared the men against
possible attacks by vermin by taking off all the hair. Clothes were
washed; helmets were improvised into wash kettles and bathtubs.
Some time was taken in the making of partial payments. In order
that we might have at least a little French money when we reached
the far shore, four dollars in invasion money was issued to each
soldier and officer, and he was urged to convert the rest of his cash
into this currency. Poker players learned that it sounded bigger to bet
a hundred francs than ten shillings, although the value was the same.

One of the more interesting pastimes was that of learning
French words from the numerous phrase books that were passed
around. After several informal sessions of trying to learn the definite and indefinite articles, and of trying to solve the mystery of
the French "u," they reduced the matter to *"combien," "vin rouge,"*
and a few intimate phrases to be addressed to the first mademoiselles they chanced to meet. I must confess I never saw such avid
pupils, nor, judging by their later successes, have I ever seen effort repaid with such returns.

When card playing and detective stories proved dull, we
turned to conversation, usually of women. Fearful that we would
be long absent from feminine companionship, we sought to keep
the savor of the last romantic meetings by warming up the memories of the final trysts. A darkened doorway, a comfortable apartment, a dance at a club, a drink at a pub, each one had some final
recollection. Outrageous memories, pleasant thoughts, and tender reminiscences were ours to hold until some later meeting
dulled or obscured them.

There was little talk of Germans; I saw no sign of hatred there. We spoke of this strange attitude, but no one worried. They were sure that when the shooting started and friends were killed, they would hate the Germans enough. "After all," said one artillery-man, "we don't see the men we kill anyway." There was no great worry about the chance of getting hit. The *Stars and Stripes*, in an effort to keep down worry on this score, explained in a series of articles carefully distributed to the troops how shock kept the patient from feeling much pain, and that there were few cases where the hurt persisted long before unconsciousness or morphia gave relief. General Bradley, who proved to be an accurate prophet, had struck out against wild estimates of casualties which, based on Tarawa percentages, threatened us with the loss of fifty thousand men in the first few hours.

Despite thoughts of home, few men seemed greatly interested in writing at the end. Perhaps it seemed too dramatic, this epistolary leave-taking, or, perhaps the censor, who now threatened to blot out every line, destroyed the desire to write. But in the last days, the officers suggested that the men write now so that the families might have a letter shortly after D-Day and feel that their men were safe. Most of the fellows in my tent complied, all save the nineteen-year-old from Oklahoma. He temporized until, at last, at the lieutenant's suggestion, I asked if I could write a letter for him. He said no one cared where he was, but I wrote one anyway and asked if he would sign it. He chuckled at the idea that anyone would believe the sentiments I expressed, but signed nonetheless, and seemed pleased when he informed the lieutenant that he had performed the task.

Our final Sunday in camp was extremely beautiful. The day was much like any other, until someone interrupted the card game and said there would be services in the mess hall. I half persuaded another chap to go, but when one of the players said it was a fine thing to be going from cards to church, he said he would stay behind and not be a hypocrite. Some twenty of us met in the mess tent, sitting on the rude benches where we usually ate, while a young, red-haired chaplain from Virginia led us in a group of songs from which "Onward Christian Soldiers" and "The Son of God Goes Forth to War" were omitted. He preached simply on the text "Suffer little children to come unto me." There was no threat of death nor talk of hate nor smell of battle in that tent, although his helmet, set before him on a table, served as a pulpit, and we held our guns, even as had the Puritans, close at hand while we prayed.

Chapter 4

Crossing the Channel
One Day Late

Friday, 2 June–Thursday, 8 June (D+2)

The first day of June was our last day in the marshaling area. We had spent the last few days cut off from the outside—no papers and no mail, although occasionally a rumor came in. Word reached us that a push had at last started in the Anzio region. "Good," we said, "that will hold some of the Germans away from the north." We had a scare on the evening of 30 May when a German plane hit an oil dump near Falmouth. As the great flashes of flame appeared and a heavy curtain of smoke overhung the sky, the dread we had of a German air attack came strong upon us and we wondered if at last they had searched us out, because it seemed impossible for them to miss hitting something if they once came over. All next day, as clouds of smoke obscured the sun, we hoped that we could get away before more planes followed the first one.

Our last day was readiness day. Life belts were issued, inner tube types of things that we were supposed to half-fill with air when we put them on. In case of a sinking, we needed only press a valve that punctured a hole in a gas cartridge and released air to fill the tube immediately. All this was explained carefully, together with a warning that if we jumped overboard we should not allow the belt to get under our chins since the force might knock us out. There was no excitement among the men, merely the practiced boredom of a group that had been through this sort of drill at least twice before. For me there was something chilling about the whole business that put any idea of a holiday air about the expedition out of my mind.

Friday, 2 June

We were awakened at the usual time, 0700, on 2 June and told to don our gas impregnated clothing. At 1015, after breakfasting, we left E-14 area and went to E-11, where we joined a convoy. At noon we were fed at an improvised mess hall along the way. Two hours later we stopped and were fed again. We continued to repeat the joke about the condemned man eating a hearty breakfast. As we passed along the road toward the sea, we saw little evidence among the English people we met to indicate that they knew we were on our way across. They had seen several such maneuvers as this in the past few days, and they probably thought that was what we were doing again. At times someone would come to the door and look curiously at the quiet groups of helmeted men going down to the sea. Now and then a mother would hold up her child to see the passing troops, perhaps dimly realizing that her lad could tell when he was old, "I saw the Yanks as they set off for the shores of France."

Land's end for us was the edge of a small cove near Helston, such an inlet as pirates or smugglers might have used, or a spot where Phoenicians might have anchored when they came two thousand years ago to seek Cornish tin. The British had realized that it was such a place as enemy intruders might seek out for entry and they had built machine-gun nests and barricades on the hills around.

At Helston we discovered that we had been billeted with the wrong company, and that we were to go across the Channel with Company C, 175th Infantry. Three LSTs were in the cove, and we watched them being loaded. The troops went up rope ladders on the sides, while vehicles went into the gaping maws of the strange ships. I had seen photographs of these peculiar craft, but I was not prepared for the real things. The vessels were built much like a freighter that has had one end cut off squarely and a great ramp substituted in its place. This ramp was let down onto the concrete piers—"hards"—set at the edge of the sand. The vessel seemed to swallow up casually the vehicles as they were driven aboard. Since we in our party were in vehicles, we went in with them, backing up the ramp. As soon as possible we went topside to see the infantry come over the sides. We would have thought of likening them to sea marauders as they clambered aboard, but for the heavy packs that weighed them down. We sympathized with most of them, but we laughed at the fat major who had to be hauled on deck when it appeared that he might fall backward into the water.

By 8:30 in the evening LST 516 (army number 487) was loaded and we were ready to sail. Not until 9:15 did we leave the cove. As we sailed for Falmouth, we met some of the crew. It added nothing to our sense of security to find that the crewmembers, like the LST, were on their first voyage. Many of them had been drafted only six months before. A few had been in Italy, but most of them were still so new that the captain, after giving a nautical command, would translate it into layman's language.

In the first hour aboard, details had been assigned to the soldiers. A boat commander, in the person of the senior army man aboard, had been appointed, and he in turn named his officer of the day, his provost marshal, his sergeant of the guard, and assigned men to preserve order, observe blackout discipline, and do KP duty.

Loading vehicles into LSTs like the one in which Sergeant Pogue crossed the Channel.

The boat was jammed with troops and a decision had been made to give all bunks to the infantry. The rest of us were to sleep on the deck, in jeeps, or in trucks. Corporal Kelly and I chose the truck that was to be Colonel Talley's office and sleeping van. Kelly got the bed and I slept on the K rations. Billy Cooper, the driver, slept in the cab. I was not comfortable, but despite everything— including the cold that came through my blankets, coveralls, regular uniform, and underwear—I managed to sleep rather soundly.

Saturday, 3 June

Weather very beautiful; quite warm. Harbor is nice. . . . Talked to a medical lieutenant who says, there are 101 LST's with hospital facilities, and that they can handle 20,000 casualties if necessary.

No tension among troops; are very confident; intent on getting home. Very few seemed sorry to leave England after 12–20 months here. . . . Our friendliness to the English children . . . has endeared us to many parents and will undoubtedly keep our memory green in the minds of the children. . . .

There is an absolute lack of heroics about these soldiers. They have been told in briefing that the navy and air forces will make us equal to the best the Germans have and these fellows believe that as a basis of equality. They will win.

I have seen little feeling about politics or labor. Many of the boys say they want Roosevelt until the war is over and then Dewey afterwards. We ——— Roosevelt people are long-time Republicans. I have seldom heard labor discussed.

The Negro problem has attracted considerable attention and we hear possibly exaggerated accounts of trouble in Bristol and other places which led to restrictions of whites three nights a week.

There is no great hatred of the Germans, although most of the men I have talked to think that hatred will follow our first casualties.

The chief topics are: women, whiskey and home in that order. Only a few attended church Sunday (about 20 of us). . . . We are certainly well-equipped. We carry around our waist—pistol belt, lensatic compass, pistol, canteen, medical kit, knife (a heavy brushed object given me by Sergeant Nelson of Iowa). I carry gas mask and dispatch case plus musette bag. Add a life belt, steel helmet, impregnated coveralls (smelling to high heaven) over heavy underwear and you have a great combination.

The first day in Falmouth harbor was beautiful and warm, which made me regret my choice of heavy underwear, which I had found comfortable the night before. The harbor at this point had nine LSTs while just in sight outside the harbor was the reassuring sight of a cruiser and two smaller navel craft. Considerable signaling went on between ship and shore and we imagined that exciting messages were being conveyed.

Sunday, 4 June

On Sunday the weather was foul. Sometime during the day we heard that Eisenhower had postponed the invasion one day and there was some griping by the men who feared that they would have to go back. The plan had indicated that only three days in the first part of June were satisfactory for the invasion. If they could not be used, then the men had to be taken off the boats and back to the marshaling area to wait for two weeks more. No one wanted that.

In the afternoon we had our first battle stations drill. We were told the guns and boats we should stand by and we were introduced to the call for General Quarters. The affair was not taken seriously and proved to be as unceremonious as a drill on a peacetime passenger ship.

Monday, 5 June

At nine in the morning on 5 June, we started from Falmouth Harbor, picking our way slowly eastward. By 3 P.M. there were twenty-eight LSTs visible in three long lanes, while out beyond on the horizon could be seen three or four destroyers, shedding confidence on us as they circled and turned to stand between us and the perils of the deep. Above were plane escorts, and the two barrage balloons that floated above each LST gave a holiday touch to the occasion. Behind us we towed a curious raft known as a "Rhino ferry." Other vessels pulled along strange pieces of concrete and steel that were to be part of the artificial port.

Everything was quiet aboard ship. The sky was somewhat overcast, but the sea was relatively calm and the sun came through

Sailing eastward from Falmouth on 5 June 1944 with barrage balloons over each LST.

now and then. "Abandon ship" drill was perfunctory, despite the sobering statement of the captain that the next General Quarters would be the real thing.

At noon we received General Eisenhower's order of the day together with our cookies. Those who read it said little. The only comment I got down in my diary was that several said "Bull." Fox and I compared notes and we agreed that the men were somewhat cynical and uninspired about their task, but determined. They spent their time no longer at cards now that the money was in the hands of a few, but swapped yarns and exchanged items of clothing with the sailors. This pastime, which threatened to change the colors of the services, was eventually forbidden. The evening was cool and windy, and we made little speed. We went to bed early since we supposed we would be awakened by firing.

Tuesday, 6 June (D-Day)

> *Awakened at 10 to hear that it had been announced that after heavy bombing and bombardment U.S. and British troops had landed on the French coast. No great enthusiasm evinced by troop, although they were pleased.*
>
> *Started turning southward from English coast at 7 p.m. There are now 60–70 craft in sight (the radio says 4000 took part). Water relatively calm (although we rocked a bit at noon and I felt a little sick). Became*

cool near evening. At 7 as we turned towards France a message was read from General Eisenhower urging proper treatment of peoples of France. Another message—from General Montgomery—wished the men good hunting. Neither message got any response from the men. It has been difficult to get any atmosphere of ——— or preparation. The Captain found it necessary to urge watchfulness and care in the Navy personnel since they were imitating the Army's lack of care. In the midst of so many boats, the idea of despair seems to them remote and absurd. There is absolutely nothing to indicate that the men are stirred in the least.

We have been told that we will stand off the coast of France between 6–7 and that we will go off on Rhino ferries and LCI's. We were told to expect air attack.

The clouds lifted in afternoon and except for cool breeze the weather is fine. Planes were in evidence throughout the day.

Land barely in sight astern at 7:30. At 9:30 were told we were 54 miles from French coast. Bed at 11. Slept poorly because 5 of us were sleeping on top of 5 cases of K rations in truck.

During the next six weeks, it was to be the task of some five combat historians to collect as much as we could of the D-Day story from officers and men of the 1st and 29th Divisions, the Rangers, the 4th Division, and the 82d and 101st Airborne Divisions. My share was the interviewing of assault troops from the 116th and 115th Regimental Combat Teams and a few from the 16th Infantry Regiment. Lieutenant Fox and the division historians did the bulk of the work on the 1st Division. Colonel Taylor interviewed the Rangers, Colonel Marshall the two airborne divisions, and Ruppenthal the 4th Division. The material we collected was checked against the official records and went into the War Department pamphlets *Omaha Beach, Utah Beach to Cherbourg,* and *Small Unit Actions* (about the Ranger action at Pointe du Hoe), and the Army's official histories.

My own picture of D-Day was gleaned from dozens of interviews with officers and men who went in during the morning of 6 June. Some I talked to shortly after they were wounded, others I interviewed as they rested near the front lines, and some gave their stories weeks later. A short outline of that morning is given below.

The ships that took the assault elements to Normandy had

been loaded, much like ours, in many coves and inlets in Wales, southern England, and the eastern counties. On the evening of 5 June they had proceeded from the rendezvous area near the Isle of Wight southward toward France. Shortly after midnight, minesweepers of the Allied fleet began to clear channels through the minefields for the ships. British and American airborne units took off from English fields and flew overhead to drop over their objectives—the British east of the Orne and the Americans in the Cotentin Peninsula. The British reached their bridgehead early and secured it, while the American forces, scattered to a considerable degree, had a tough job of assembling for concerted action.

Toward daylight the planes and ships took up their task of softening up the enemy, the chief change in plan being that mentioned earlier in which the air force struck a few miles inland instead of at the beaches. On the western limit of Omaha Beach, the Rangers scrambled ashore to find that the six guns they were to knock out were pulled back out of their way.

By daylight, ship channels had been cleared to the beaches and the small landing craft had been filled with men from the LSTs and larger transports and were on their way in from rendezvous points some ten miles out. The floating tanks were started in, as were guns in small craft. Only five out of thirty-two DDs survived of those that attempted to float in under their own power, while most of those in the other tank battalion, sent in at the last minute by boat, got in safely. In one field artillery battalion all but one gun was lost when the craft carrying them capsized.

The accounts of the early landings tend to follow the same pattern. Heavy seas threatened to swamp the smaller craft and made many of the soldiers seasick. Enemy fire struck numerous craft or forced navy crews to unload in deep water. Poor visibility, obstacles, and inexperience led other navy crews to land on the wrong beaches. Many of the soldiers in the first waves had to wade ashore carrying heavy equipment, which they often disposed of in deep water. At the extreme ends of the beaches, the cliffs interfered to some extent with the enemy fire and gave our troops some protection. In front of Vierville, the men hid behind the seawall that ran along the beach, and near Saint-Laurent-sur-Mer they found mounds of shingles to use as cover. Accounts of the first hours on the beaches speak of efforts of officers and noncoms to organize their units and get them off the beaches, but often those who tried to direct the attack fell as soon as they exposed themselves to the enemy. In some cases, platoons stuck together, but in others sections landed some distance apart—and there were instances where dispersed elements attached themselves to entirely different regiments and divisions and did not return to their parent organization for two or three days.

The first real effort to give direction to the attack came after the regimental commanders landed. The command group of the 116th Regimental Combat Team, which included Brigadier General Norman D. Cota, the assistant division commander, and Colonel C.D.W. Canham, the regimental commander, came in at about 7:30 A.M. The S-4 of the regiment was killed near the water's edge and other members of the command group were hit. Colonel Canham was wounded as he tried to organize the attack, but after receiving first aid he returned to his task. One of the most active commanders was General Cota, who, according to the accounts of the soldiers, was apparently everywhere that morning. Some spoke of his handling the bangalore torpedo that breached the wire at one of the exits, and others had him handling a Browning automatic rifle. His activities in the first weeks ashore made him almost a legendary figure. Noncoms were also called on to give leadership, as heavy casualties were inflicted on the junior officers. In one case, a private who had worked until a short time before in the regimental Post Exchange rallied the men of his unit by calling them by name and persuading them to follow him over the seawall.

On the 16th Infantry's beaches, Colonel George Taylor, the RCT commander, gained lasting fame by saying to his officers and men: "The only people on the beach are the dead and those who are going to die—now let's get the hell out of here." In a short time he had the men in his sector moving. He and Colonel Canham were promoted to the rank of brigadier general for their work on D-Day.

The manner of the advance up the bluffs differed somewhat among the various units. Some stayed behind the seawall until units in the second and third waves came in through them and went up the cliffs. Others, after being reorganized, pressed forward and by noon were on top of the bluffs.

By midnight on 6 June all of the regiments in the 1st Division (the 16th, 18th, and 26th) and two from the 29th (the 116th and 115th) had been landed on Omaha Beach. The 2d and 5th Ranger Battalions were in position to their right. Heavy seas, landings on the wrong beaches, intense fire from well-entrenched positions, the foundering of DD tanks and artillery pieces, abnormally high casualties among officers, failure to open all the beach exits, beach congestion, the slowness of some of the assault waves to move forward from the seawall, the difficulty of using the full force of naval gunfire because of the fear of inflicting losses on the infantrymen, the lack of sufficient gaps in underwater obstacles and beach obstacles, and the failure, for various reasons, of air bombardment to take out beach fortifications all placed V Corps a considerable distance from its D-Day objectives, and, as a result of the presence of the German 352d Division in the area, in danger of a counterattack before the time estimated. In the face of this situation, the regiments were reorganized, defenses were set up for the night, and preparations made for a vigorous offensive to attain the D-Day objectives as quickly as possible.

We had missed any part in the day's action because the 175th Infantry to which we were attached was a follow-up unit. It was supposed to go in on the afternoon of D-Day, but the delay on Omaha Beach and the massing of troops in the constricted space held by V Corps led us to wait in English waters until the late afternoon of the sixth. As we finally moved out toward France, there were some sixty to seventy craft in sight, planes overhead, and destroyers on our flanks. Now there were five instead of the three parallel lines we had seen on the fourth. The ships were about half a mile apart, stretching as far as we could see. Halfway across the Channel we began to meet LSTs returning to England for more men and supplies.

As we turned toward Normandy, the captain read us the supreme commander's message urging proper treatment for the people of France and General Montgomery's order of the day wishing the men "good hunting." Much more interesting was the announcement that we would stand off the French coast between six and seven the next morning. The captain found it necessary to urge a sense of watchfulness by the crewmen, since they were imitating the army's casualness. In the midst of so many boats, the notion of possible danger from submarines or planes seemed absurd.

The night was unpleasant for sleeping because by now four soldiers had decided to share my ration-box bed in the truck. As we crammed ourselves into the narrow space, Trooper James caused an outburst of laughter by yelling, "If any of you fellows get any closer, you will have to marry me." The ration boxes had become upended as we scrambled in and out, and I felt that special ridges in my back and side would become permanent features of my anatomy. We still slept in all our clothes, except our shoes, and we wished that we had kept them on in the morning when five of us tried to divide the shoe gear.

Wednesday, 7 June (D+1)

The seventh was cold and the waves choppy. I got completely sick and filled my two vomit bags, but that was due in part to the 4 A.M. reveille and the greasy 4:30 breakfast. At 8:00 we had our first sight of Normandy, which had been hidden for some hours by mist and smoke. At 9:45 we could see ships shelling targets well inland, and about 10:15 we anchored two miles offshore.

> *Craft increased until there were some 90 in sight. . . . Numerous planes overhead. . . . One report has it that the night before the attack 31,000 airmen made 7100 sorties, dropping 10,000 tons of bombs. . . . I heard that 6 battleships are taking part.*

The captain made his official farewell to us at 9:15 A.M. when he read a special prayer for our success. For the first time the soldiers began to show signs of animation. A group near our truck began a song session which, I noted in my diary, included "Clementine," "Working on the Railroad," "Mademoiselle from Armentieres," "Over There," "I Got Shoes," "John Brown's Body," and several bawdy numbers.

Troops of C Company, 175th Infantry, went off in small boats between 12:30 and 1:00; part of the attached engineers went two hours later. We were to stay aboard until the next day. Although the men who had gone ashore knew they were to be committed to action almost as soon as they went beyond the range of the first hills, they exhibited no special qualms, no bravado, no "well boys, let's give it the old try" spirit. In the boats they may have been given a stirring message that took them ashore in a fighting mood, or they may have had visions of home, "Mom's blueberry pie," and "Old Rover" for whom they were fighting, but they certainly kept any such sentiments secret when they left. Perhaps great crises have their own drug for the emotions so that people under heavy stress act more nonchalantly than people going to work, but these men, as I had noted over a period of days, acted as if nothing unusual was amiss.

Gunfire seems in the distance, although it is in plain sight.

Naval craft off the beaches fired sporadically. Everyone seemed pleased that French ships were joining in the attack on shore positions. Destroyers lay near the shore and fired on shore positions several miles in. The Germans replied occasionally to the fire, but without effect, and as for German air, we saw only one enemy plane, a reconnaissance aircraft, during the day. British and American planes were over in force all day. In one fifteen-minute period we counted five flights of eighteen Marauders each.

After three o'clock the skies cleared except for a few clouds over the fighting area and it turned hot, to our great discomfort. We wanted to go ashore, but orders came out that only people with rifles, who were prepared to use them, were to go in. So we parasites, armed for the most part with pistols, stayed aboard as spectators of this second act. Standing on jeeps and trucks, we watched developments off Omaha Beach as if we were at a fair. Actually, we could make out very little on the shore. Signs of movement were obscured by smoke from the firing, fires that had been started by shells, and by the demolition of mines. I did not see how it was possible for troops to have recognized any landmarks, nor have I been able to understand how correspondents, who watched the D-Day attack from ten miles out, ever got such vivid pictures of the shore.

At seven in the evening we moved closer in and the beach became plainer. We were told that a delay had occurred ashore because Germans had moved back into some of the pillboxes. Vehicles had piled up at the exits and the beach masters didn't want more trucks and jeeps cluttering up the beaches. However, demolition people were needed, so our remaining engineers were taken off. Some of the last men over flaunted, as a sort of banner, gaily decorated field jackets—usually drawings of scantily clad girls in bust relief. One such girl was quoted as saying, "I have big things ahead of me."

We have an excellent vantage point for the bombardment, since we are on the inside column of the 7 or 8 columns of ships. There do not seem to be as many ships in evidence as there were earlier in the day. . . .

The sea is almost completely calm.

This part of the countryside is not as pretty as the English one, but the general appearance is somewhat similar.

Heavy fire and, perhaps, depth charges seem to be cooking up several types of marine life. At last we could see the building that had loomed large on our map—the one commanding the approach to Easy Red exit. It seemed to be only a shell, although something of the village overlooking the beach appeared to be standing. The town to the east was burning.

Seven o'clock also marked the climax of a thirty- to forty-minute heavy barrage laid down by five or six ships to the east and west of Easy Beach. Some of the shells seemed to be dropping over a road just behind the hill. Others were falling on it.

Our meal that evening consisted for the first time entirely of K rations. We had eaten them before as a supplement to other food, but now we were able to test just what they would do to an appetite when tried by themselves. I noted that the cheese was good, although "we didn't care for energy biscuits, lemonade extract and malt tablets," an opinion I never had reason to change in the field. According to Major McKnight, they fared better at the captain's table. Later, when we were in the mud in Normandy, he liked to tell of the rough way he saw D-Day, at the captain's table being waited on by a waiter in a white mess jacket. However, the navy, which had done well by all of us, was about out of food as a result of our extra day aboard ship. They were also inclined to become disinterested. We had cold water, in one pail only, in which to wash our mess kits (not having hot water for the mess kits is a cardinal sin in the army) and we were disgusted because we had to push greasy scum aside to wash out the scraps. When we protested, the navy suggested that we heat some water ourselves.

We rather expect an air attack tonight but no one seems worried.

Wounded begin to come aboard after 7, about 20 were brought to the boat. Of these two were Germans (one, shot through the lungs, died, the

other, a Pole, was glad to be captured). Two were English, and the others
were from the 1st and 29th Divisions. One man merely had a dislocated
shoulder. An army captain was shot through the hand.
    Fire from ships continued until 11:10. Apparently shooting fire to
the west.

My first interview was with a young corporal from Beaver
Falls, Pennsylvania, who had a dislocated shoulder. A member of
the 18th Infantry, he had gotten ashore all right and was halfway
up the hill "when we began to catch hell from the snipers." From
him I got the first word about the 29th. He said that the 116th had
failed to complete its mission and the 115th had to take over.

My second victim, a captain from the 110th Field Artillery
Battalion, attached to the 29th Division, who was shot through
both hands, greeted me eagerly and expressed his willingness to
talk if I would hold a milk bottle while he relieved himself. Someone had handed him the receptacle, forgetting that he was too
completely swathed in bandages to make use of it. Thus, feeling
not at all like Florence Nightingale, I started my interview.

The captain was quite angry at himself for getting hit. He said
that he would "bust any man of mine who did a damn fool thing
like I did," for he had climbed a tree to observe German fire and
had been shot through both hands as he lifted them to the branches
above his head.

The officer was also angry because his unit had been put ashore
on the wrong beach. He felt that the area had been unnecessarily
crowded with heavy trucks not needed for combat. He believed
that there should have been fewer vehicles with bedrolls and hot
coffee and more carrying ammunition. I remarked that Lieutenant General Ben Lear had said after the Tennessee maneuvers that
trucks carrying packs and Coca-Colas would not win the war.
The captain felt that the Germans were not well prepared, but
that they were doing good work with their 88mm guns. He felt
that the U.S. assault troops had been improperly briefed when
they were taught that the terrain near the beaches would be like
that in Cornwall. Instead, he said, a bit nostalgically, it was more
like South Carolina.

The night was moonlit, which displeased us, because at 1:30
the droning of a German plane overhead brought a call to battle

stations. Before I could get out of the truck, the ack-ack gun beside us had opened up with a terrific clatter. Recalling the jagged
pieces of metal that I had seen fall from the guns in London, I did
not want to remain in a truck covered only by canvas. In three
minutes the entire Baie de La Seine was alive with ack-ack firing
from the ships around us, the nearby flak boats, and the batteries
ashore. Tracers began to light the sky and we could spot the plane
high above our heads as it circled. We expected at any moment to
be rocked by a bomb from it, but it became apparent that it was
merely on reconnaissance. We thought for a moment that we had
him as a bullet found a mark and there was a burst, but to our
chagrin the thousands of rounds of ammunition from hundreds
of guns had succeeded only in bringing down a barrage balloon.

Despite other ack-ack bursts during the night, we ultimately
managed to get some sleep, only to be awakened in the early
morning when the ships began their morning firing. Two of the
sturdy vessels of the day before were back at work. Two Free
French ships, flying the largest flags I had ever seen, were getting
in their licks. Again and again the same little drama was played.
There would be a release of heavy black smoke and a flash, then
we would count "1–2–3–4" before we heard the boom. Our boat
would shake from the blast and waves would be started in the
water. We never tired of the sight, although our interest was diverted occasionally as the cruiser *Augusta* passed in and out among
the ships. By that time also, special guide boats came by to ask us
what we had aboard. When we itemized our passenger list they
quickly passed us by.

One of our patients died during the night, and everyone
pressed to the side of the ship to see his body taken off. No one
seemed particularly concerned, although some were nauseated
at the sight and smell of blood when more wounded soldiers were
brought aboard. Down below deck, the medics were busier than
ever. Four amputations were performed in quick succession. There
was considerable anger over a report that a German prisoner had
asked for a different kind of soup than that which he had been
given. Peculiarly enough, the feeling against him was strongest
among the men who had not gone ashore. The American
wounded, who lay nearby, expressed no bitterness. They did voice
great praise, however, for an RAF flier in the same bay, who, with

a foot almost gone, asked that attention be given the other men before he was cared for. I saw his foot—a nasty mess it was—and his tense, sweating face as he bit his lips to keep from crying out. The navy personnel assigned to assist the doctor were inexperienced and slow, although they worked with a will. Since most of them were very young, they seemed more like children playing doctor than corpsmen in a sickroom where men died or were saved from death.

Later in the morning more German wounded were brought abroad. The new men looked at them curiously, without hatred, until it was reported that one carried a grenade, which he had failed to surrender, and immediately there was a hot wave of lynch feeling, so intense that it was noticeable in the air.

My most interesting interview on the second day was with a corporal of the 299th Engineers who had gone in with the 1st Division. Twenty-one years old, a Texan by birth, he had spent two years in the army. He had a wife and a three-month-old baby, whom he expected to see by Christmas because of the bad wound in his side. He grimaced as he told me of the hole made by a mine explosion, but grinned at the thought that they would have to send him home.

From him I got the first criticism of the air force for its failure to clear the beach gun positions, and he told how the German pillboxes took a heavy toll of his group. He related how he had seen two boats with thirty-five men each burn as they neared the beach, while men died in agony or dropped overboard screaming into the sea. Others were heavily hit as they moved across the beaches, but they had reached the top of the bluff in an hour. Captured Germans told them that an attack had been expected on 20 May, but that they were totally surprised on the sixth.

Thursday, 8 June (D+2)

We are being held on board to let LST's with more valuable cargo go ashore.

The interview with the engineer was my last aboard the LST, since at 7 P.M. we began to debark on a Rhino ferry. Resembling a slab of concrete run by a motor at one end, the Rhino furnished transportation for most of our trucks and jeeps. We spent thirty minutes winding our way in through the naval craft around us as we went into the beach facing the exit on Easy Beach, leading to Saint-Laurent-sur-Mer. (This road served as one of the chief exits. Today it comes out by the American cemetery that is maintained on the hill).

On our slow ride in we had a chance to see what had happened to this, the bloodiest of the invasion beaches. Dozens of DUKWs and small craft were destroyed at the water's edge. Ships were already bringing in pieces of the artificial port that was to be towed into place. All along the beach, boats were disgorging their great stores of ammunition and supplies. To our right, the engineers were busy blowing up mines and barbed wire, filling in the antitank ditch, and leveling off the beachfront. Others were deepening the foxholes that had been started the first night. Up on top of the hill, men hastened to build an airfield. Nearby was a hospital overflowing with patients who were being picked up and sent down to boats waiting to take them to England. Also nearby was the cemetery, our first in Normandy. We saw fresh corpses neatly piled in front of the hospital tents; over in the minefields a few of the men who had been killed there still lay grotesquely. It was still too dangerous to bring them out. The soon-to-be familiar German signs with the words *Achtung Minen* and a death's head proclaiming the nearness of death were all around.

Nearby buildings were mere shells, as we had imagined they would be when we first saw them from the beach. The hills were pitted with shot, and numerous pillboxes on the bluff were smashed. Over to the left of E-1 exit, set in the hills, were several still-intact gun positions. Near the entrance to the exit was an undamaged pillbox, which had become the chief headquarters of the beach command. The beach was not as littered as I had expected, but that was probably due to the cleaning effect of the tank dozers, which had pushed obstacles out of the way and shoved battered pieces of human flesh into ditches nearby.

Our jeep was put off in shallow water and had to "wade" the last few yards to the sandy shore. This was possible because of a snorkel-like pipe attached to the exhaust that stuck up out of the water, and because of the paraffin waterproofing which covered the engine. Once ashore we nearly bogged down as the wheels

Omaha Beach in a familiar state of disarray. Wrecked artillery stands silent in the foreground, as Naval craft unload additional supplies.

The E-1 exit road, which led to Saint-Laurent-sur-Mer.

spun in the wet sand, but a vehicle behind us pushed us forward and we bounced across the uneven surface of the beach road, which by then had heavy netting for us to drive on. We worried about mines, paying careful attention to the white tape that marked the areas that had been "deloused." However, we felt somewhat secure because our jeep had a layer of sandbags on the floor. In front of the radiator was a heavy steel bar intended to cut any wire that might be stretched across the roads. At the edge of the beach we joined an ever-growing line of traffic winding through heavy dust up a hill toward Saint-Laurent-sur-Mer.

As we moved up the bluff we noticed at the side of the road, almost crushed by the dirt, several poppies in full bloom. I picked one and pressed it in my notebook.

Chapter 5

The Lieutenant John Spaulding Interview

9 February 1945

The best account I got of the advance from the water's edge was that of Second Lieutenant John Spaulding, a lawyer from Owensboro, Kentucky, who led one of the first groups to the bluff overlooking Omaha Beach. Below I have given the story as he gave it to me:

"We loaded into LCVPs from larger ships at 0300. The companies were divided into sections and each LCVP had thirty-two men, including a medic, plus two navy men. I was leader of the first section of Company E, 16th Infantry, 1st Division, and we were scheduled to go in on the first wave. My assistant section leader was Technical Sergeant Philip Streczyk, East Brunswick, New Jersey. The sergeant was the best soldier I have ever seen. He came into the army as a selectee and worked his way up to platoon sergeant. He was in on the landing at Oran and in Sicily. If we had more men like him, the war would soon be over.

"We unloaded into LCVPs in a very rough sea. It took us much longer to land than it had during the practice landings, because of the rough water. After entering the LCVPs we went an undetermined distance to a rendezvous point. Here the navy crew took us around and around, getting us soaked to the skin. Many of the men got sick immediately and others got sick as we went in towards the shore.

"About 0400 our boats lined up in a V formation and headed

towards shore. As we went in we could see the outlines of other boats around us and overhead we could hear a few planes. Between 0545 and 0600, we saw the first flashes from the shore. We didn't know whether they were our planes bombing, as we had been told to expect, or whether the flashes were from German guns. We caught sight of the shore about 0615. We also saw a few of our fighter planes. About 0630 the rocket ships began to fire, but most of their rockets hit in the water.

"In the meantime the navy had been firing and the dust from debris on shore plus the early morning mist made it difficult to see the coast. There was a very good reason for the navy crews to fail to hit the right part of the beach.

"As we came in there was considerable noise from the shore and the sea. En route to the shore we passed several yellow, rubber boats. They had men in them, but we didn't know who they were. They turned out to be personnel from the DD tanks which had foundered.

"About eight hundred to one thousand yards out we began to receive machine gun fire from the shore, but it was not effective.

"As we neared the shore we came to the line of departure and here the odd numbered boats swung out abreast on one side, and the even numbered went to the other side. In this formation, the boats came in to shore.

"Our instructions were to land to the right of the house at [grid coordinates] 677900; this house was to be the left boundary of my position. We were to go across the antitank ditch near the E-1 entrance and scale the seawall. Once this was done we were to send patrols into Saint-Laurent-sur-Mer, where we were to contact E Company of the 116th, which was supposed to land to our right, and then push on to the high ground behind the town. It was assumed that the air forces would have destroyed the beach defenses by that time and thus we could land without any great opposition.

"About 0630 we hit the line of departure; someone gave a signal and we swung into line. When we got about two hundred yards offshore the boat halted and a member of the crew yelled for us to drop the ramp. Staff Sergeant Fred A. Bisco (Harrison, New Jersey) and I kicked the ramp down. Shortly before this a navy man had mounted the machine gun in the rear of the LCVP and had started to return fire. We were now receiving not only machine gun fire, but also mortar and some artillery fire (the men said it was 88[mm gun] fire but I am doubtful).

"We had come in at low tide and the obstacles were noticeable. They stuck out of the water and we could see teller mines on many of them. No path had been cleared through them, so we followed a zigzag course in. It is difficult to know if the navy could have taken the boats in farther. It is possible that they would have stuck on the sandbars. I am in no position to know whether they could have done any better.

"Because we were carrying so much equipment and because I was afraid that we were being landed in deep water, I told the men not to jump out until I had tested the water. I jumped out of the boat slightly to the left of the ramp into water about waist deep. It was about 0645. Then the men began to follow me. We headed toward shore and the small arms fire became noticeable. We saw other boats to our left, but nothing to our right. We were the right front of the 1st Division. We had seen some tanks coming in, but we didn't know what they were.

"As we left the boat we spread out in a V formation about fifty yards across. There was soon a noticeable decline of sand beneath our feet and we were soon over our heads, so we tried to swim. Fortunately when I pulled the valve on my life belt it inflated and saved me. I lost my carbine. We lost none of our men, but only because they helped each other or because they got rid of their equipment. There was a strong undercurrent carrying us to the left. I had had experience with the strong current of the Ohio River near my home when I used to go swimming there, but this was much stronger. Sergeant Streczyk and the medic—Private George Bowen of Haldeman, Kentucky—were carrying an eighteen-foot ladder, which was to be used for crossing the anti-tank ditch or any other purpose which might arise. They were struggling with it in the water just about the time that I was having my worst trouble staying afloat. As the ladder came by, I grabbed it. Streczyk yelled and said, 'Lieutenant, we don't need any help.' But hell, I was busy trying to get help, not give it. I told them to leave the thing, so it was abandoned in the water. About this time we were able to put down our feet and touch bottom; the water was about up to our mouths. I had swallowed about half of the ocean and felt like I was going to choke. We pulled out

Private Edwin Piasecki (Chicago, Illinois), who was about to drown. About this time Private First Class Vincent Di Gaetano (Brooklyn), who was carrying a seventy-two-pound flamethrower, yelled and said, 'I'm drowning, what do you want me to do with this thing?' Streczyk told him to drop it, so he did. In addition to the flamethrower and many personal weapons, we lost our mortar, most of the mortar ammunition, one of our two bazookas, [and] much of the bazooka ammunition. However, the men who kept their weapons were able to fire them as soon as they came ashore. It shows that the M-1 is an excellent weapon.

"As we were coming in, I looked at the terrain and saw a house which looked like the one we were supposed to hit, so I said, 'Damn, the navy has hit it right on the nose.' Later, I found that we had landed near another house about a thousand yards to the east of where we were supposed to land.

"Our first casualty came at the water's edge. Private William C. Roper, rifleman, of Piedmont, Alabama, was hit in the foot by small arms fire just as he hit the beach. He kept trying to get his legging off, but couldn't reach the lacing, so I helped him. Just after he got ashore, one of my BAR men, Private First Class Virgil Tilley of Dayton, Tennessee, was hit in the right shoulder by a shell fragment, which drove a hunk of the shoulder out towards the back but did not come all the way through.

"By this time, I noticed a number of my men on the beach, all standing up and moving across the sand. They were too waterlogged to run, but they went as fast as they could. It looked as if they were walking in the face of a real strong wind. We moved on across the shale to a house which was straight inland. The first place we stopped was at a demolished building; there was some brush around. We were halted there by a minefield at the first slope. My section was spread out—the men in accordance with orders had deployed the moment they hit the beach. They had been told to get off the beach as soon as possible. They walked on across because nobody stopped them.

"Down near the water's edge we ran into wire. Staff Sergeant Curtis Colwall of Vicco, Kentucky, blew a hole in the wire with a bangalore. We picked our way through. I personally didn't see the gap he had blown, but I was still in a daze. I didn't see any mines on the beach except AT [antitank] mines.

"As we went across the beach my runner, Private First Class Bruce S. Buck of Mitchell, Nebraska, came over to me. I tried to get contact with company headquarters with my [SCR] 536 radio. I took the 536 off my shoulder, worked the antenna out as I walked across, and tried to get contact, but it didn't work. I looked down and saw that the mouthpiece was shot away. Although the radio was useless and I should have thrown it away, training habits were so strong that I carefully took the antenna down as I had always been taught to do and put the radio back on my shoulder. Your training stays with you even when you are scared.

"When we got up to the rubble by the demolished building we were built up as skirmishers and were returning what fire we could. Streczyk and Private First Class Richard J. Gallagher of Brooklyn went forward to investigate the minefield. They decided we couldn't cross it. There was pretty heavy brush around here. Streczyk and Gallagher now went to the left to a defile (apparently a little stream had washed it out at one time) and tried to work their way through. In the meantime we were getting small arms fire. One burst from a machine gun left a series of dots along the wall in front of us (at some places the demolished wall was one and a half to two feet high and we were hiding behind that and the brush). Private First Class Lewis J. Ramundo of Philadelphia was killed here—the only man from my section killed on the beach.

"To our left we had bypassed a pillbox from which machine gun fire was mowing down F Company people a few hundred yards to our left. There was nothing we could do to help them. We could still see no one to the right and there was no one up to us on the left. We didn't know what had become of the rest of E Company. Back in the water we saw boats in flames. I saw a tank ashore about 0730 to 0745. After a couple of looks back, we decided we wouldn't look back any more.

"About this time Gallagher said to follow him up the defile, which was about four hundred yards to the right of the pillbox. We were receiving terrific small arms fire but few were hit. About this time (Lieutenant Spaulding couldn't be any more specific than this) we were nearly to the top of the hill. We returned fire but we couldn't hit them.

"When Gallagher found the way up, I sent word back for my men to come up to the right. Sergeant Hubert W. Blades, Seaford,

Delaware; Sergeant Grant Phelps, Camden, New York; Sergeant Joseph W. Slaydon, Pelham, North Carolina; and Private First Class Raymond R. Curley, South Orange, New Jersey, went first. I went next; Sergeant Bisco followed me, and the rest of the section came along (those not already mentioned were: Sergeant Clarence Colson, Leon, New York; Sergeant Kenneth Peterson, Passaic, New Jersey; Private First Class Walter Bieder, Cleveland; Private First Class Stanley A. Dzierga, Adams, Massachusetts; Private First Class Warren S. Guthrie, Lafayette, Ohio; Private First Class Richard Rath, Altoona, Pennsylvania; Private First Class Alexander J. Sakowski, Norwich, Connecticut; Private William B. Brown, Chicago; Private Donald E. Johnson, Kent, Ohio; Private Robert E. Lee, Camden, New Jersey: Private Raymond L. Long, Westminster, Maryland; Private Carmen M. Meduri, Morrisville, Pennsylvania; Private James C. Renfroe, Cedar Grove, Tennessee; Private Charles Scheurman, Molsy, New Jersey; and Private Richard Simms, Butler Springs, Kentucky). I couldn't take my eye off the machine gun above us, so Sergeant Bisco kept saying: 'Lieutenant, watch out for the damn mines!' They were a little box-type mine, and it seems the place was infested with them, but I didn't see any. We lost no men coming through them, although H Company came along the same trail a few hours later and lost several men. The Lord was with us and we had an angel on each shoulder on that trip.

"Trying to get the machine gun above, Sergeant Blades fired his bazooka and missed. He was shot in the left arm almost immediately. Private First Class Curley was shot next. Sergeant Phelps, who had picked up Tilley's BAR on the beach, moved into position to fire and was hit in both legs. By this time practically all of my section had moved up. We decided to rush the machine gun about fifteen yards away. You may ask why hadn't we hit it; I don't know. As we rushed it the lone German operating it threw up his hands and yelled, 'Kamerad!' We would have killed him, but we needed prisoners for interrogation, so I ordered the men not to shoot him. He was Polish. He said there were fifteen Germans in the area, that they had been alerted that morning and told to hold the beaches. They had taken a vote on whether to fight and preferred not to, but the noncoms made them. He said the others were in a trench to the rear of his machine gun.

A path leading uphill through a minefield.

He also said he had not shot at Americans, but I had seen him hit three. I turned him over to Sergeant Blades, who was wounded. Blades gave his bazooka to Sergeant Peterson and guarded the prisoner with a trench knife. We moved Curley, Blades, and other wounded into a defile and the medic, Private Bowen, gave them first aid. He covered the whole beach that day; no man waited more than five minutes for first aid. His action did a lot to help morale. He got the DSC for his work.

"Coming up along the crest of the hill Sergeant Clarence Colson, who had picked up a BAR on the beach, began to give assault fire as he walked along, firing the weapon from his hip. He opened up on the machine gun to our right, firing so rapidly that his ammunition carrier had difficulty getting ammo to him fast enough.

"At this point Lieutenant Blue of G Company came up and contacted me. He had come up our trail. His company had landed in the second wave behind us. Just a few minutes later, Captain Dawson of G Company came along. We still saw no one on the right. Captain Dawson asked if I knew where E Company was and I said I didn't. He said it was five hundred yards to my right, but he was thinking in terms of where they were supposed to land; they were actually five hundred to eight hundred yards to our left. I later found they had lost 121 men. Dawson said he was going into Colleville and told us to go in to the right. He had about two sections. He said he had just seen the battalion commander. This was about 0800.

"I went over and talked to Lieutenant Blue about the information we had gotten from the prisoner. I asked him to give us some support where the fifteen enemy troops were supposed to be. As we went up in this direction, we hit a wooded area. We found a beautifully camouflaged trench which ran along in a zigzag fashion but we were afraid to go in. We went along the top of the trench, spraying it with lead. We used bullets instead of grenades, since we had very few grenades, and we thought bullets would be more effective. We did not fix bayonets at any time during the attack. We turned to the right and hit a wooded area; got no fire from there, so we yelled to Lieutenant Blue to shove off and he started for Colleville. Then I stood there like a damn fool and waved him a fond farewell. We were headed for Saint-Laurent; G Company went on into Colleville. H Company came up next and went into Colleville under Lieutenant Shelley.

German trenches atop a hill overlooking Omaha Beach.

"We were on top of the hill by 0900. We advanced cautiously. We were the first platoon of the 16th [Infantry Regiment] to hit the top. We now had twenty-one or twenty-two men in the section. We had spent more time at the rubble than anywhere else, and had taken up some time with the prisoner.

"As we went inland we heard rifle and machine gun fire to our right. Streczyk and Gallagher volunteered to check on the situation. Our men were spread out over an area of two hundred to three hundred yards. They located a machine gunner with a rifleman on either side of him. Streczyk shot the gunner in the back and the riflemen surrendered. The two prisoners were German and refused to give us any information. With them in tow we started west. We still saw no one to our right. We were now in hedgerow and orchard country. We were watching our flank and to the front and scouring the woods. We tended to send a sergeant with three or four men to check on suspicious areas. We usually set up someone with an automatic weapon to cover them (we didn't have any machine guns at this time, however). We crossed through two minefields—one had a path through it which looked like it had been made for a long time. When we got through it, we saw the 'Achtung Minen' sign. No one was hurt; we still had an angel on each shoulder.

"We now found a construction shack near the strongpoint overlooking the E-1 draw. If you will examine the defense overlay, you will find an almost exact duplicate of what we saw. Sergeant Peterson fired his bazooka into the tool shed, but no one came out. We were about to go on when I spied a piece of stovepipe about seventy yards away sticking out of the ground. I formed my section in a semicircular defensive position. We were now getting small arms fire again. Sergeant Streczyk and I now went forward to investigate. We discovered an underground dugout. There was an 81mm mortar, a position for a 75[mm gun], and construction for a pillbox. All this overlooked E-1 draw. The dugout was of cement; had radios, excellent sleeping facilities; even dogs. We started to drop a grenade in the ventilator, but Streczyk said 'hold on a minute' and fired three shots down the steps into the dugout. He then yelled in Polish and German for them to come out. Four men, without arms [weapons], emerged. They brought out two or three wounded. I yelled for Colson to bring five or six men. We began to get small arms fire from the west. I yelled for Piasecki and Sakowski to move forward to the edge of the draw. A firefight took place. The navy now began to place fire on the draw; this was about 1000. Piasecki deployed six or seven men, shot several Germans, and chased a number down into the draw, where they were taken care of by navy fire. (The 81mm was not manned; they had beautiful range cards and lots of ammunition).

"When Colson came over, I started down the line of communications trenches. They led to the cliff over the beach. We were now behind the Germans, so we routed four out of a hole and got thirteen in the trenches. The trenches had teller mines, hundreds of grenades, and numerous machine guns. They were firing when we came up. We turned the prisoners over to Streczyk. We had had a short fight with the thirteen men; they threw grenades at us but they didn't hit anyone. We found one dead man in the trenches, but don't know if we killed him. If we did, he was the only one we killed. Several of us went on to check the trenches. I did a fool thing. After losing my carbine in the water, I had picked up a German rifle, but found I didn't know how to use it too well. When I went to check on the trenches I traded the German rifle to a soldier for a carbine, but I failed to check it. In a minute I ran into a Kraut and I pulled the trigger, but the safety was on. I reached for the safety catch and hit the clip release, so the clip hit the ground. I ran about fifty yards in nothing flat. Fortunately, Sergeant Peterson had me covered and the German put up his hands. That business of not checking guns is certainly not habit forming.

"We next took out an AT [antitank] gun near the edge of the draw. There was little resistance. We now had the prisoners back near the dugouts. We had split the section into three units. We got a little ineffective machine-gun fire from across the draw to the right at this time. We tried to use the 81mm mortar, but no one could operate the German weapon. For the first time I saw people across the draw to the west. I supposed that they were from the 116th [Infantry Regiment]. They seemed to be pinned down.

"About this time two stragglers from the 116th Infantry came up. I didn't ask what company they were from but just took them along. We went back and checked trenches since we were afraid of infiltration by the Germans. In the meantime I sent seventeen to nineteen German prisoners back with two men the way we had come. I told them to turn them over to anyone who would take them and to ask about our company.

"At this point I saw Lieutenant Hutch of Company E, who had commanded the section which had been directly to my left in the boats. I pointed out the minefield to him and told him there was a sniper near me. We had sniper fire every few feet now and we were getting pretty jittery. We sent off our last yellow smoke grenade to let the navy know that we were Americans, since their fire was getting very close.

"About 1045 Captain Wozenski of Company E came up from the left. He had come along practically the same route we had used. I was very happy to see him. We had been ordered to contact Major Washington, 2d Battalion executive officer, just aside Colleville. Our objective was changed; there were to be no patrols into Trevières that afternoon as we had been told originally we would do. We never crossed the E-1 draw. Instead, we were to swing in the fields to the right of Colleville.

"Lieutenant Hutch and I now had about thirty men; he was in charge. Three of our section leaders had been killed on the beach. About 1300 we contacted Major Washington near Colleville, and he told us to go to the right of Colleville and guard the right of the town. We found that Lieutenant Knuckus of G Company, with about fourteen men, had the right flank, so we reinforced him. In this area we set up a defensive position. We selected a place where no digging was necessary, since we were able to use drainage ditches. We were now in the orchards and hedgerows. We moved cautiously, since we didn't know where anybody was. About 1500 we got German fire. Di Gaetano was hit in the butt by shell fragments; we told him he was too big to be missed. Sergeant Bisco was killed; rifle fire hit him in the face and throat. Only one round of artillery came in; we thought it was from one of the ships. It exploded about three hundred yards from us; it made an orange and yellow flame.

"As we looked back towards the beach we saw several squads of Germans coming towards us. We had no contact with the battalion. Just as a G Company runner started over to us and got to the edge of our defenses, they opened fire on him. After he fell they fired at least a hundred rounds of machine-gun ammunition into him. It was terrible, but we do the same thing when we want to stop a runner from taking information. Of course, we didn't find out what he was coming to tell us. We fired until we were low on ammunition that afternoon. I had six rounds of carbine ammunition left. Some of the fellows were down to their last clip. We were still surrounded. We called a meeting of Lieutenants Knuckus and Hutch and Sergeants Streczyk and Ellis and myself. About 1700 we decided to fight our way back to the battalion. We were overextended and about out of ammunition. We sent word for the men to come to us in the ditch where we were; we were several hundred yards south and west of Colleville.

"At 1900 or 2000 we set up automatic weapons to cover us as we crawled down the ditch back towards Colleville. Lieutenant Hutch went in front. We got back to battalion and ran into C Company of the 16th Infantry on the way to reinforce us. We didn't know where we were. We found Major Washington in a little gulley at the west of town. He said we were to go back to about the same point with C Company in support. We took up a defensive position about five hundred to seven hundred yards from our original positions. This was closer to Colleville. We were still in the hedgerows; we guarded the roads and avenues of approach. I think that part of the company area bordered on the road into Colleville. We now had machine guns (I believe from Company H). This was about 2100, nearly dark. It was quiet except for some air activity. We had heard American machine guns earlier in the afternoon; it is possible they drove the Germans towards us.

"We spent the night of the first day in the positions near Colleville.

"Of the thirty-two men in the first section, five got DSCs, awarded later by General Eisenhower. They were given to: Lieutenant Spaulding, Sergeant Streczyk, Private First Class Gallagher, Private Bowen, and Sergeant Peterson. During the day two were killed and eight wounded."

Chapter 6

First Days in the Field

Friday, 9 June (D+3)–Sunday, 11 June (D+5)

Our first home ashore was at the V Corps command post in an apple orchard to the east of Saint-Laurent-sur-Mer, along the bank of a small creek, which the French maps dignified with the name of the Ruquet River. Spread out in eight or ten fields in the shadow of the hedgerows and under the apple trees were the vehicles and tents of the corps. As we looked out a few thousand yards away to the barrage balloons over the ships in the harbor, we felt little security, since we were still so near the water's edge. The planners had said that the main attack by the enemy might come on D+2, and that this was the day, and we were only just barely ashore.

Too tired to worry about the possibility of an attack, however, we dug perfunctorily at our foxholes and most of us pitched our pup tents and went to bed at dark—11:30 P.M. those days when we used double British summer time. Going to bed was a simple matter of dragging a blanket roll into the tent and crawling in. We kept on our coveralls and shoes because of the cold. Before the night was over, however, I was acutely aware of the discomfort of wearing impregnated shoes and socks which permitted no "breathing" of the feet, and the torture of coveralls over trousers over heavy underwear that literally "scalded" the body. Sleep, when the night was otherwise free of disturbances, for the first week was gained mainly by gradually clawing off shoes, leggings, and other articles of clothing, while trying not to crash into one's tent mate, and then by trying to find methods of avoiding freezing when partially disrobed. Nearly every night my dog tags awakened me, either lying on my chest like a cold iron or tangled around my neck so that I imagined myself being garroted. At other times, I rolled about trying to rearrange my money belt, which, bulging with a wad of small invasion notes, managed always to slip around my midriff and get in the small of my back.

But there was little chance to sleep that first night anyway. At midnight, the Germans, in accordance with a little habit they had formed in Italy and brought north with them, would send over two or three reconnaissance planes—"Bed-Check Charlies" they were called—perhaps to discover our dispositions, but we felt mainly to attract fire and keep us awake.

I had pitched my tent at dusk near the hedge, unaware that a few yards away was an antiaircraft gun. Just as I dozed off, the proverbial "all hell" broke loose as a plane flew into the ten-mile zone that we held, which extended five miles in and five miles out to sea. Ack-ack guns on land and sea along the V Corps front cut loose—just as they had the night before—as soon as the first gun opened fire. Using tracers to locate the planes, they began to illuminate the sky with 4th of July like flashes of angry lightning,

An apple orchard in Normandy.

pursuing the aircraft across the sky. The steady pom-pom of the guns made the night hideous with noise. Then machine guns joined in along the front, and shortly afterward aroused and startled GIs poured out of their tents and began firing at the planes, thousands of feet up, with rifles and carbines. Suddenly the furious outburst of flame and shot caught one plane and a flash indicated that it was hit. At first the plane fell slowly, as the pilot apparently kept control, and it seemed as if the flier had merely turned on his lights. But then a tremendous explosion and sudden disintegration of the plane returned us to darkness. Having tasted blood, the guns seemed to increase their intensity and soon a second plane was hit. Then again the great light that had burst upon us was put out, and the guns were silent, and we returned to our tents. But throughout the night guns in the distance located other craft and continued their deadly game.

Friday, 9 June (D+3)

Next morning I began with a new routine—the task of shaving without hot water. In the marshaling area, we had learned to use the somewhat greasy second rinse water for this purpose, but here as yet there were only K rations and no need for water in which to wash or rinse our mess kits. Impressed by army talks about how shaving kept up morale, and having more time than most GIs to shave, I managed to go through this ritual every morning but one during the war. Despite the cold, I also managed to huddle at the door of my tent and take a sponge bath from my helmet. This was something I did not continue as conscientiously, but there had been no water for bathing during the six days aboard ship, and I felt that I had to get rid of some of the gas-impregnated smell that had soaked through into the skin. My pair of lime-coated socks had by now become slimy in their nature, but they and the overalls had to go back on since there was still believed to be a grave danger of a gas attack. I got no encouragement from Captain Johnson, who said that an order had been issued to the effect that such clothing must be worn for the first thirty days.

Breakfast was an individual affair. We each had been given a K ration and sterno kits with which to heat water for coffee and to warm the canned food. I managed to get the canteen cup of water hot, but the process was so slow without a proper kettle that I made no attempt to heat the chopped eggs and bacon and managed to wolf that down, even though unheated they were a cold and greasy mass. The biscuits didn't seem palatable. Fortunately, there was always the D ration. Even if extremely concentrated chocolate is no treat in the morning, it is food, and then the piece of candy in each ration helped, too.

During the breakfast period I hunted around for the rest of our party. We were in a field with cows that wandered around placidly by the tents and trucks, occasionally menacing some soul in a foxhole. Off to the right of the field I saw Captain Digby and his driver. The captain had stepped out into the bracing air, divested himself of pajamas (the only ones I saw in the area), and took a vigorous cold-water rubdown. The example did not impress Trooper James, who set about learning to eat an American K ration, which he contrasted invidiously with British rations, without benefit of absolution.

Breakfast finished, I went over to the G-1 area to find all hands at work digging trenches for office personnel so that we could tumble in if planes attacked, and personal foxholes—a rule that applied to everyone from lieutenant colonels down. The sergeants took turns digging a hole for the colonel while he fussed at McKnight and Fox for not getting started on theirs. I spent much of the afternoon digging my foxhole, learning what I had often been told before: that much of one's time in the army is taken up with the fundamental tasks of housekeeping.

At this point only the minimum amount of canvas had been spread, so that the G-1 section, to which we were attached, consisted of an office in a trailer for the G-1 and one of his assistants, while three sergeants, Major McKnight, Fox, and myself were in one wall tent that had just enough room for three men to get behind a table. Next door was a small tent large enough for two people which sheltered the documents. Some ten people were expected to use these quarters, but that just couldn't be. On good days most of us tried to work outside, but when it rained—and when didn't it?—we had to stay inside. Or we sat in our pup tents, typewriters on our knees, our necks craned forward so that we could get our heads under the low-lying canvas while we stuck our feet out into the wet. What a place for a claustrophobe!

During the first week, I learned the value of staying near the motor pool if I wanted to get information. Here were the drivers who went out twice daily with the liaison officers, who went often to the beaches, who overheard the officers talking about the new plans, and who knew the new drivers who had just brought in Bradley or Montgomery or some other VIP. By making friends with this group, and later with the MPs, we found invaluable allies in getting leads to our stories. Sometimes they knew about impending moves before all the colonels knew.

It was on D+3 that we heard the stories of our weakness and we were in a jumpy state by supper time. We had just opened our rations when we saw groups of people shouting and running and then we heard the dreaded sound of a gas alarm. Nearly everyone was caught off guard since we had dropped our masks near our tents while digging foxholes or had gone to the latrine without them. The big brass seemed to have been the most unprepared, and the fat supply sergeant had wonderful stories of colonels who came up pleading for extra masks. The MPs were also caught badly out, and we estimated that if the thing had been real we would have lost most of our strength. In this case, my own mask was several feet away, and I remember that as I scrambled for it, I forgot all the rules about holding my breath and applying all the other things I had been taught to do. All idea of putting the mask on by the numbers went out of my head and I had all the usual trouble of a rookie adjusting the thing. A second report of "gas" reached us while we were still scrambling, and we went through a sprightly drill. The affair was amusing, but it was our first chance to get an idea of the awful fear of war—we had been shaken by this experience in which we were caught helpless and naked in the face of overwhelming disaster—and for one startled moment we could almost feel the choking vapors of death. Then, of course, we vented with the sheepish laughter of those who caught the joke after being almost frightened out of our wits.

Latrine rumor attributed the scare—which was repeated the length of the front in a few minutes—either to a heavy dust cloud that appeared to look like gas, or to an oversensitive group of soldiers who had been told on landing they might be hit by a gas attack. Some special scent—like hay or geraniums—hit their nostrils and a cry of "I smell gas" set off a number of rifles giving the report—and panic swept along the front. For a while at least, we kept our masks at hand.

By the end of my second day ashore I was beginning to realize the awfulness of living forever in the open while trying to carry on civilized pursuits. At home one was accustomed to occasional moments of discomfort or inconvenience when downpours occurred. However, in the field, when one lives almost constantly in the open, a downpour causes not only momentary annoyance while it is coming down, but it wets the ground, one's food, one's clothes, and makes one's life generally unpleasant. If it is hard, it drenches one, leaving no chance for a change to dry clothing, and if it is general, it forces one into the narrow confines of a pup tent or the overcrowded pyramidals. Although this was said to be the driest spring since 1893, there were several showers daily that got everyone wet, put out fires, and wet bedclothes. When it was not raining it was unpleasantly cold, so although I clung to my heavy undershirt and field jacket, I found myself shivering all morning.

Saturday, 10 June (D+4)

Skies overcast. Rained sporadically.

The fourth day of the invasion, 10 June, saw liaison planes and C-47s landing on the Omaha Beach airstrip and the easing of ammunition shortages. Master Sergeant Macaulay of the corps Ordnance Section, looking like a Mexican bandit with his bristling beard and rows of cartridges crisscrossed across his chest, reported that ammunition which had been held back because of landing space and inexperienced crews was beginning to come in. He pointed out that there had never been a crisis in 105mm and 155mm shells, but that their use had been restricted because of the need of keeping a reserve supply.

Lieutenant Fox and I spent most of the day working on our task of coverage of the landing. We were helped by the appearance of a V Corps directive calling to the attention of division commanders the fact that we were combat historians attached to the corps under a plan approved by First Army, and that our purposes were:

1. To insure the preservation and completeness of all sources of materials on operations
2. To prepare specific monographs on certain key operations for immediate publication by the War Department.
3. To prepare an overall campaign study of V Corps's part in operations.
4. To advise and assist unit historians in gathering and preparing unit historical material.
5. To assist and advise commanders and staffs in preparation of reports on operations.

The directive added: "The combat historians under the direct supervision of G-1, V Corps, will be given all possible cooperation in contacting persons and obtaining access to records in order to obtain first-hand information and eye-witness accounts, by section chiefs of this headquarters and unit commanders to the extent that they shall not interfere with the carrying out of any operational mission assigned this corps."

Units were further instructed to gather information that would tell of enemy dispositions, factors affecting actions, and actions that took place.

During much of the day, however, we spent our time talking to persons who wandered into headquarters and watching the constant stream of traffic that passed our camp. We had learned that even as jeep drivers and MPs yielded information, so too did the liaison tent. Personnel in the G-3 operations center had found that to keep the swarm of liaison officers and visitors out of the operational office, it was necessary to have a place where liaison officers could be briefed on the current situation and where they could await orders to take back to their units.

At the supply tent, where a wandering soldier could pick up a K ration, we found the lost soldiers from other units who had become separated from their outfits during the D-Day confusion and were now trying to find their way back. A number of soldiers of the 1st and 29th stayed lost from their units during the first week, fighting alongside the first unit they met, and helping to swell the missing lists of their parent organizations during the early days. Thus it was that we bagged several of the rough looking Rangers and I got my first interview with a paratrooper. The latter, dressed in the distinctive garb of an Airborne man, was one of seven men from the 82d who had landed across the Vire River from his unit and had found his way to us. His particular group had left a point eighteen miles from Nottingham at 2:15 on D-Day morning. They had started fifteen minutes late and had been delayed by bad weather. Instead of landing in an area where it would be possible to get a fighting force assembled within the allotted time, they had become scattered in their drop and had landed amidst German elements. They had fought their way out as best they could, but estimated that their losses were 60 to 80 percent. (I wrote "An estimate likely to be proved completely wrong," a judgment in which I was right. He, like all the others, assumed that everyone else had been killed or captured. This kind of fog of war was responsible for terribly exaggerated casualty estimates, although those at their worst were still well under the pre-D-Day fears).

Tales of discouragement faded during the day when we saw passing our hedgerow the continual movement of the 2d Armored Division tanks. We knew, of course, that the 2d Infantry Division was ashore and that the 4th Division on Utah and the British on our left were advancing. But there were still gaps between the three corps and there was always the possible German counterattack to dread. We were still not ten miles in, and Anzio was too recent a memory for comfort. Now here was the 2d Armored with names on their vehicles that brought laughter to our lips. I amused myself while trying to dodge the dust that clouded in from the road by leaning against a rustic fence and writing down the names of a number of the vehicles. They included: "Porky Pig," "Elyse," "Yonkers," "Penna.," "Espoir," "Ruth," "Ettabele," "Some Fun," "Extra," "E Venetta," "Eddie," "Donna," "Lend-Lease," "Agnes Scott," "Marie," "Baboon," "Bloody Bloke," "Move it Over," "Rec," "Churchill," "Certain conflict, and the dreadful three," "Awful," "Spooky," and "Eternity."

One lieutenant of the 175th [Infantry] burned a house with snipers in it. Road very dusty.

Sunday, 11 June (D+5)

Sunday was no day of rest. Instead we left for the 29th Division, going through Saint-Laurent, Formigny, Longueville, La Cambe, Vouilly and La Forêt. Our trip was delayed by the lack of bridges. At one point where the engineers had hastily thrown up a one-way bridge over a stream, I got my first look at the elusive Bailey Bridge, which I had looked for so often in London. We found that it took considerable dexterity to guide the jeep in the two steel ruts that constituted the floor of the bridge. The people of the region had not moved out of the area, despite the warnings we had given before the attack, and they came out to greet us. One girl pelted Lieutenant Fox with roses.

After losing several hours, we found the 29th Division in an orchard near La Forêt, almost ready to move, their fifth such shift in as many days. Trucks were loaded in the field, but one of the office tents still stood and several officers stood around discussing recent actions. They talked of the trek of the 116th from Vierville to Grandcamp-les-Bains over a five-day period virtually without rest. They declared that the Ranger Battalion attempt at Pointe du Hoe had failed, but didn't mention what we discovered later: that the worst problem the Rangers faced there was an attack from elements of the 29th who thought they were Germans.

Later in the afternoon, Fox and I, now joined by Lieutenant Colonel Jones of our ETOUSA section who was on a roving mission, were asked to go with a CIC lieutenant and two sergeants to a nearby château and help them interrogate a French woman who purportedly had information concerning the Germans who had been billeted there. We found a pleasant chateau with German signs still on the doors indicating the private chambers and the waiting rooms and game rooms. Volubly the woman poured out her story of German officers and their lady friends in the area, of her devotion to France and the Allies. Unfortunately, she was somewhat vague and our CIC lieutenant was unable to follow her story. He turned to me and said, "Doesn't it beat hell; I was commissioned because of my college French, and I can scarcely understand a word she says." I agreed with him. Fortunately, he didn't always have to depend on people he stopped along the road, because he later got a sergeant who had formerly studied at the Sorbonne to help him in his chores.

As we moved along the road beyond the Vire, we noticed various gun emplacements of the 2d Armored units and Airborne groups. We finally passed several antitank positions, but continued on toward Carentan, which we had been told earlier was held by Airborne troops. However, as we became aware that American units were no longer in sight, we turned back to the last gun position we had seen. They told us that we had apparently driven past the last American position and that the Americans did not hold Carentan. We quickly turned the jeep back toward Isigny and confined our search for Germans to an observation of the manner in which the soldiers dealt with a newly arrived prisoner. Some eight soldiers had him under their guns, while two or three took away his possessions and distributed them among several individuals standing about. It was our first view of "liberating" possessions, and, although the young German had a sullen, cocky look that angered his captors, our original reaction was one of shame.

Near Isigny we stopped at the south of the road to examine a German observation point overlooking the valley of the Vire. The guns faced toward Carentan, for it was from that direction they had expected an invasion if it should come in Normandy. The fortifications were built of logs and I found that the leaves on some of them had not yet withered. There were older fortifications back of an old building on the top of a nearby hill. The structure was a windowless, ancient affair, and from the doorway the French owners peered out at us in a manner that caused the two GIs who had gone with us to hold their fingers on their rifle triggers as we passed the house. They were sure that the people were either Germans in French dress or German admirers who had fired on Americans. They favored burning the house.

An underground network led for some distance away from the fortifications, and we suspected that some of the passages led to the river, but we did not care to search them as they had not been tested for mines. To the north of the road, a set of concrete works overlooked the beach and the marshes toward les Rochers de Grandcamp. The papers of the Germans who had been there were scattered in the ditch. We wanted a roll of maps that lay nearby, but a wire ran through them and we decided to pass up the souvenirs. However, I found a set of orders written in German and Russian and containing the names of a number of Russian soldiers. The commander had been Lieutenant Malikow, formerly of Voronezh. He had taken his job seriously, for we noted his Russian-German dictionary and a series of exercises in translation he had been writing out. More interesting was a series of field exercises for the first weeks of April in which defense against landings at Cherbourg and at the mouth of the Orne was to be practiced. The script for the affair indicated that the battle had been a hard one, but that on the fifth or sixth day the Allied forces had been thrown back into the sea.

After 7 P.M. we completed our inspection trip by visiting the beach—our first real look at the place. We proceeded through Vierville-sur-Mer, down along the beach road that had seen the bloodiest losses by our people, eastward to the E-1 exit, and then went out near Saint-Laurent. At some points the beach was not very wide, and it was evident that the enemy had been well dug in. The water obstructions looked formidable. In front of the E-1 exit we could still see the eight- to fifteen-foot-thick mass of barbed wire which sprawled along the beach, the tank trap twenty-five to fifty feet long and fifteen to twenty feet deep, and fifteen to twenty feet more of wire. All this was backed up by mines, 88s, machine guns, and riflemen. After estimating the toughness of these barricades, I wrote, "Add landing on the wrong beaches, inability to cut wire, fact that some engineers and infantry landed at the same time, landing in deep water, panic by some of the naval crews, loss of most artillery and vehicles and you have the picture."

At Easy Beach, we found the historian of the beach engineers, Captain Ian Frazier, who had been with ETOUSA in London. He was assisted by an artist, Sergeant Crystal, and two former newspapermen, Privates Williamson and Jones. Frazier showed us some German gun pits covered by manhole covers in which riflemen had waited for the approach of the Allies. Around the walls of the circular pits were murals which gave a view of the beach, together with the setting range for the rifle to cover any part of the beach on which an American might be sighted. For the first shot, he needed only to set his range, wait for someone to cross his line of vision, and pull the trigger. Little wonder the surgeon's report said that a large number of dead had neat holes through the head. They had seemed to have a preference for shooting at the high-ranking officers and men whose insignia was painted on their helmets. In addition, every officer had on the rear of his helmet a vertical white stripe, visible for some distance, and the noncommissioned officers had horizontal ones. After being exposed to sniper fire for a while, frontline men applied mud liberally to the markings on the front and rear of their helmets lest in the lottery of death they rank first.

Considerable laxity of discipline prevailed near the beach, but Brigadier General William Hoge of the beach engineers was striving to stop the looting which, he declared in a conference, had been denounced by the French as being worse now than when the Germans were there. He found that the infantry had been too busy to do much damage but had been forced to order the arrest of seven navy personnel (navy and merchant marine) who had been caught looting. We got further evidence that evening when the beach MPs asked us to take two drunken soldiers back to corps. They had not been accused of looting, but both of them showed us various articles that they had found in an unoccupied house. I accepted as a souvenir a postcard they had found which German soldiers had used for writing home. On them was written Hitler's admonition: "It is not essential that we live; it is necessary that the German Folk and Germany live."

While we sat on the hill, whose sides were being honeycombed with foxholes, we could see the heavily encumbered beach below, and could look out to sea where the Mulberry—the code name for the artificial harbor—was taking shape. Ships were being sunk as breakwaters, piers were being constructed, and steel pieces were rapidly being put into place. Roads were being broadened and improved. Even now this was not the beach we had seen two days before, and another month would change it completely. I urged Sergeant Crystal to make a terrain study of it so we might know what the beach had looked like shortly after we landed. He assured us that it was not fun working there, as there were numerous air alerts each night and a dump had blown up only the evening before.

We left the beach at 10:30, almost at dark, a habit we had which irritated the drivers, who didn't like to drive late at night. The task of getting home was complicated by the fact that the corps had moved since we had left that morning. As we drove to Trevières and beyond Rubercy, trying to remember the instructions of an MP who may have been mistaken, we began to think of the perils of the night. We were now in the true hedgerow country, going down narrow lanes, surrounded on either side by century-old hedges standing above our heads and almost meeting above us, shutting out any light which might have come through. As we thought of Colonel Jones's story of Germans who had been captured in the area that morning two days after their units had withdrawn, we readied out pistols for firing. At length, speaking as casually as I could, I borrowed the driver's rifle and sat Daniel Boonish in the backseat, listening for any step that might be Germans. It seemed, as we turned down a side road, that we had not seen any Americans for at least fifteen minutes and we recalled how, that afternoon, we had driven very close to the German lines. Perspiration gathered on my forehead, but I said nothing, and the others kept silent. Just as we were about to reconcile ourselves to captivity, we heard a preemptory challenge and saw ahead one of our corps MPs, who waved us into a nearby orchard. As I got out I noticed that buried nearby were two German soldiers, aged eighteen and nineteen, who had died on 8 June. "It is not essential that we live," their *führer* had said.

Chapter 7

First Interviews in the Field

Monday, 12 June (D+6)–Sunday, June 18 (D+12)

Monday, 12 June (D+6)

Lieutenant Fox and I started our first real interviewing on the twelfth. Previously, we had been junketing about and gathering general impressions, but doing little else. We first visited the 116th Infantry, which had come in at H-Hour and had lost heavily at the edge of the beaches. The men had now rested a little, but they were still tired from almost continuous fighting since the landing—haggard cheeks, sunken eyes, leaden feet, dearth of spirit seemed to characterize them as they waited in the fields for an order to move out again. They griped in a mood of self-pity and wondered desperately, "When in the hell do we get some relief?" They recalled promises—no one was certain who made them—of rest and rotation once they had established the beachhead, and they said, "What's the Big Picture, Sarge, when are they goin' to take us out?" Seeing no purpose in sugarcoating the story, I asked, "Did you ever see a coach take out his first team after the first quarter of a tough game?" They grinned at the compliment, but growled, "Hell, let the rest of them get bloodied."

We got very little else specific that morning, because the men were ordered to move to Cartigny-l'Épinay to aid the 115th Infantry, which was having trouble crossing the Elle. Fox and I followed them awhile, discussing the strangeness of war. Five miles back, we had left corps headquarters, with everyone moving tidily about his business, everyone carrying weapons, but virtually without fear, the war remote. Two miles back we had passed division headquarters, more alert, but unruffled; one mile back regiment; nearby the battalion. Here we were following platoons as if they were on a road march in the States. Then they began to deploy into the woods on the south of the road, and we stopped to watch them as they worked their way steadily forward toward the river, hidden from sight by the trees. Not like deadly soldiers, but like hunters, intent on sport, as they walked forward. All the while, we who were privileged to be spectators—protected by the one thousand or two thousand yards we could stay back and the option of stopping when it got dangerous and of returning to relative safety and comfort—sat there at the bend of the road, waiting for the sounds which would indicate the beginning of the fight. As they disappeared from sight, Fox got out to talk to some officers in the reserve battalion, and I wrote my first letter home since I came ashore. While sitting there, I could hear the sound of machine-gun fire coming from the firefight on the Elle.

Exercising our option to depart, we turned from the Elle after a time and went to the new 29th Division headquarters at La Folie. We drove through Lison, railway center for the section, and found that this little village had paid heavily because of the importance of the railway to the Germans and us. The yards were smashed and the small houses round about were rubble. The rail line seemed dead, and one felt that grass would soon claim it. The town itself seemed deserted when we stopped, but in a moment a party of French inhabitants came out, waving their arms, bestowing flowers on us, and telling of Germans who only the night before had threatened to cut their throats. We cast apprehensive glances about, since they said the woods still held "les Boches," but the sight of patrols searching out the prey reassured us. And all the while, the battle for the Elle, three miles away, continued fitfully. (It will not do to romanticize this firefight merely because we saw its beginning and knew the men in it. The push that took the river came that night, when we were safe in bed—or foxholes—at regimental headquarters, after a heavy artillery pounding which cleared the way for the infantry).

In the evening, while history was being made on the Elle, I

listened to another story of Omaha Beach, told me by Captain R.E. Walker, assistant S-3 of the 116th Infantry. Walker, who came from Council Bluffs, Iowa, was a graduate of Creighton, where he had played football. His was one of the best accounts I had received of the week's developments. Others added their bit, a Lieutenant Cravens of Kentucky, a Lieutenant Parker, and Sergeants Yahres and Chase. Still others came and went, sometimes pausing to add something to the conversation. Walker emphasized particularly the heavy losses the regiment had taken in officer casualties. In one week, of the 1st battalion, A Company had only one officer left, B Company had only one officer at the end of D+2, C Company had its commanding officer wounded and all but one officer killed, and D Company all but one officer killed. By the end of the same week, the 2d Battalion had three company commanders killed and two wounded, E Company had no junior officers left, F Company had only one or two junior officers, G Company had only two junior officers, and H Company had only two or three junior officers. In the 3d Battalion, I Company had had all but one officer killed or wounded, and K Company's commander was killed.

The conversation later passed to various things: The universal cry of no support; the belief by infantrymen that they were being hit by their own artillery; the feeling that the battle was going too slowly against inferior German troops; a report that further on the Germans were getting tougher, that we were being pulled in where we would have to fight on their own terms, that the Germans were tunneled in along the river and they kept popping up every time you thought they were licked.

All our talk would have been frightening, but we realized that we were but telling ghost stories that the coming of daylight would make us forget. I left the group, not from a pleasant fireside of festive board around which such tales are usually told, but from a crowded liaison tent where we had eaten beans from a C-ration box, in time to find a spot in a deep ditch along the hedgerow, hacking away at vines which grew about, and scraping the place a little deeper, hoping all the while I need not take seriously someone's shouted warning "that part of the field has not been checked for mines." The night was beautiful, but near dawn the rain splashed unpleasantly in my face.

Tuesday, 13 June (D+7)

Spent morning at 29th Division getting notes in shape. Cloudy and overcast, visibility O.K. Planes absent. . . . Rained in the afternoon.

The thirteenth was the anniversary of the first week the Allies had spent ashore. I went to division to find Fox, stopping for a moment to talk to a Frenchman who was working nearby. He told me that Germans had been in this area of Normandy since the beginning of the occupation, but that Russian and Polish troops had arrived only six months before. He indicated that the Germans had used French labor in building fortifications. He could not understand how we had gotten in over the beaches. He had not heard that the British were also ashore. He was not bitter against Pétain,[1] but disliked Laval. He knew of de Gaulle, but had no opinion about him.

A few minutes later I met a sentry who had been with Company K back in Cornwall. A tall, slow-spoken West Virginian, he looked much the same as I had seen him two weeks ago except for a heavy beard. He had become separated from his unit and had found his way to the Division command post where, to his great disgust, he had been put on guard duty.

While we were talking, three correspondents who had been at General Charles H. Gerhardt's war room, walked by. One was a familiar looking little man, sparse and gray of hair, kind and tired of face, dressed in coveralls that threatened to engulf him; another was a be-mustached, correspondent-looking type; and the third looked a little like a schoolteacher. The sentry, not recognizing them, but seeing the Press patch on their arms, called out: "Hey fellers, what's the news?" Ernie Pyle, for it was that likable champion of the GI who had come to get a story, came over and said, "That's what we are trying to find out." He waved his companions over, introducing the bewhiskered one as Jack Thompson and the other as Don Whitehead. They asked our names, and when I gave mine, Ernie asked if I were a relative of his New Mexico neighbor, Captain Jack Pogue. I had to disclaim kinship, but recalled that several friends had sent me clipping of Ernie's columns in which he discussed Pogue's capture in Italy. Don Whitehead asked my home address, and when I told him that it was Murray he asked if I knew his brother, Kyle, who had once taught in the college there. We talked for a while about what I had found out from the Frenchman, and his colleagues finally urged Ernie on toward his jeep. As they walked away, I revealed his identity to the sentry, who stared and said, "I'll be damned." A lieutenant who had come up near the end of the conversation, also startled, ran after the party and came back with Ernie's autograph.

In the afternoon, I went to the 115th Infantry headquarters and talked for a time with a pleasant, red-haired lieutenant, Chester B. Bise, of Herald, Virginia, who was executive officer of Headquarters Company. Bise was eating C rations with his men at the entrance to the underground headquarters of the regiment. He and his men had had a relatively easy landing on Omaha Beach, but an exhausting march during the days that followed. Since the landing, they had had their shoes off once, and they had gone two days with two K rations and a D ration. They had walked through a flooded area with water varying from knee deep to waist deep; some ditches were filled with water over their heads. They said they were so tired that they were no longer hungry. This was their first real rest since D-Day, and they picked listlessly at their food as they prepared to go to sleep.

Even their night of rest was denied them because soon after dark the sound of planes was heard. Then flares lighted the sky, looking at first like far-off parachutists coming Martian-like to disturb our peace. A wave of sudden fear went through us and we stared fascinated. And then it was clear they were flares, but the disquiet was not gone, because we knew that planes used them to locate spots for bombing or for shelling or for infantry attack. We watched with wonder until at last the lights went out and left the protecting darkness.

Wednesday, 14 June (D+8)

Talked to Corporal Reece of signal outfit. Has married an English girl. Anxious to get to England and then home.

In the morning I talked to the owner of the house near the regimental CP. His was a three-roomed stone house, aged and bleak. Across the road was a similar house behind which the regiment had its mess. Across a hedge was the latrine with its back facing toward the road, and on occasion the people passing by would stop and speak politely.

One neighbor worked for the railroad at nearby Lison. Because of his trade and his four children, he had been deferred from the army. He and his wife and larger children had remained at their home during the shelling of Omaha Beach. Despite all the damage the war had inflicted, he was still glad we had come, because only a few days before he had been scheduled to go to Germany as a railroad laborer.

In the middle of our conversation, four of the railroader's friends arrived, shaking hands pleasantly after the French fashion. One had fought at the side of American troops in the Verdun area in the first war. In honor of his remembrances and the new enterprise, he brought a stone bottle of cider, sharp, vinegary stuff, and I was invited to take the first drink. I gave them a toast and they thanked me profusely. They passed around the bottle again and we talked of their life under the Germans. Some of their fellows had sniped at the enemy, but for most of them the main heroism lay in staying alive during the period. They were not members of the Gaullist movement. They felt sorry for Pétain, but they spat at the name Laval and cried out *"Salaud!"* (swine). At this point an officer from headquarters interrupted our talk. He asked that I tell the man's visitors to go home and the man and his family to stay in, since the house was directly in front of the regimental message center. So, shaking hands gravely, the French and I parted.

The message center—now that the day was dry and the area comparatively safe from enemy fire—had been brought out of its former underground shelter and placed in the open. It consisted of a table and two telephones and a box of messages under an apple tree. This message center, and those I was to see hereafter, fascinated me. To this one came the messengers from the battalions, bringing the real news of the front to regiment. Other messengers came from division with the big picture as seen there and at the higher headquarters. The pieces of information they brought were placed on great white sheets of acetone which, stretched over the base maps of the area, were marked with red (for the enemy) and blue (for the friendly troops) to show how the war was pro-

Sergeant Pogue speaking with residents of war-torn Normandy in June 1944.

gressing. For most of the army it was such maps as these—kept diligently at each headquarters and back to the Pentagon, based on periodic telephone messages and the corrections made by liaison officers—which showed the war as it was known to most of the troops. The slow advances of units through so many hedgerows became slim blue lines on the map boards, while withdrawals were erasures and victories were sudden surges of the oily crayon on the virgin surface of the white map. The score was kept each day by G-1 as the first sergeants and the sergeant majors totted their lists and said: 3 KIA, 12 WIA, and 4 MIA. How like a drugstore when getting the latest ball scores or an election headquarters when returns are coming in. A jeep arrives and the sergeant copies bits of information from the liaison officer's map board and gives him the latest dope from the other areas. The telephone rings and company says: "We have advanced forty yards—now on map coordinate 461892." And the new result is posted. Yet, for the most part, there is no strained tension. Instead, the CP often is listless and the movement on the front is commented on only slightly.

To the message center came that morning the proprietor of Château Sevigny to ask for a permit to go through American lines to his property. Dressed in knickers and wearing a jaunty Tyrolean hat with a feather, he looked like a city gentleman down for the hunting. I translated for him, but the map-keeper revealed that the Germans still held his property. He grunted softly and said: *"Je demeurais ici"* (I used to live here).

My stay at the message center had been occasioned by a lack of transportation. In the late morning, however, a Signal Corps captain, starting out on reconnaissance for his wire-laying teams, asked if I wanted to come along. We went to Saint-Marguerite d'Elle and then, turning left, drove about a mile until we were stopped by a tree the Germans had placed across the road. The driver, with rare discernment, concluded that no wire was needed there and started backing the jeep before the captain could suggest that we turn back. We doubled back, took the next road out for about a thousand yards and, voilà, here was the front line again. I had always thought of the front line in terms of dug-in positions and a sight of the enemy in the distance. Instead, we found a deserted road with no one in sight except a young soldier

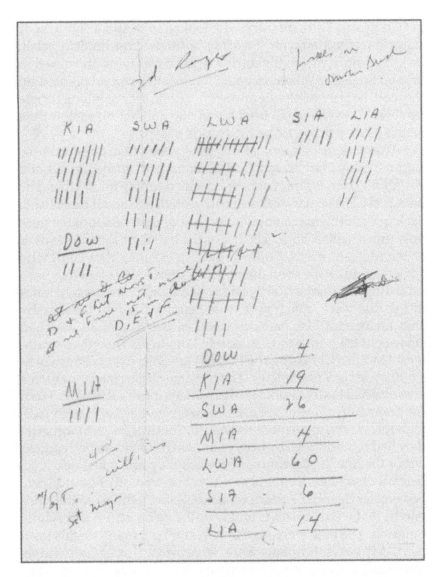

G-1's casualty score card, which was updated daily with battalion messenger reports.

of I Company, 115th Infantry, who looked to be about eighteen. A snaggle-toothed lad with "Frenchie" written across his field jacket, he got up slowly from the ditch where he was lying and asked in broken English, "Where ya goin'?" When the captain pointed up the road, he grinned slowly and said, "No sir, they're killing people up there." Two men had been killed and another hit a short time before as they drove along the road in a jeep.

After this second look at the great war, where one could see the intangible front line and feel its menace, we turned back to 1st Battalion, 115th Infantry, where I decided to stay for a while. The battalion CP, like many others I had visited, was about three fields back from the main road under the natural camouflage of the trees now green with foliage. The S-3 of the battalion turned me over to the sergeant major, Philip L. Russ of Easton, Maryland, who gave me a quick fill-in on their actions since D-Day, together with estimates on casualties. They had walked some twenty-eight miles in the first week, much of it cross-country through the marshy area Lieutenant Bise had described earlier. They had marched cross-country from Saint-Laurent to Longueville and then southwest to Canchy, crossing the flooded area between le Fournay to a point west of Colombières. They had met little resistance in this area and had taken a number of prisoners, mostly Russians. From the area south of Colombières they had begun to hit regular German forces who gave more resistance. South of Saint-Marguerite they had been stopped by heavy German fire and had been pulled out of the line. In the course of a week they had taken nearly 25 percent casualties, losing nearly two hundred officers and men. For greater details, Sergeant Russ suggested that I go to the companies that were nearby, C and D in the fields, and A in a school building. The men were glad to talk and I got many details from them. My best informants were Sergeant W. Cox of Cambridge, Maryland, C Company; Lieutenant L.E. Dunleavy, Jackson, Minnesota, Lieutenant R.W. McGee, Seattle, and Sergeant C.E. James, Waterproof, Louisiana, D Company; First Sergeant James L. Osborn, Hagerstown, Maryland, and Staff Sergeant George J. Bromwell, Baltimore, B Company; and First Sergeant Alton E. Shaff, Frederick, Maryland, and Sergeant John Barrett, Lowell, Maryland, A Company. They corroborated, at length, the story I had already received from Sergeant Russ.

The methods I used in interviewing these groups were fairly typical of those followed during the next eleven months. Starting first with the unit commander or someone in authority at battalion or company level, I would show my credentials and then ask for an outline in broad detail of the unit's experiences on a particular day or during a specific period. I frequently asked for a statement of the mission of the unit, so that I could check it with the next higher headquarters. Of a particular action, I was supposed to get such things as the weather during the fight, the nature of the terrain, the amount of artillery or tank support supplied, the major difficulties the unit encountered, how it overcame them, the condition of the men before and after the engagement, the performance of weapons, what should be changed if the battle were to be fought over, which men did well, and other questions which developed in the course of the discussion. If specific mention was made of the fine work of some individual I would ask to see him or, if he was not available, some other soldier who could describe the action. Often the individual being interviewed, desiring to check his story, would call on various members of his unit until he would have as many as twenty men gathered around. Before leaving a unit, I would ask for casualty figures—preferably from the first sergeants. In the early days these estimates proved our best sources for losses. More than once, the first sergeant pulled an envelope or beat-up notebook from his pocket and slowly began to reconstruct his casualty report. He would say: "We have had fifteen missing since the sixth of June. They found Private Blank's body yesterday near the beach, then two men found their way back here last night. Since then two men in the second platoon have been wounded by mines, and the first platoon says that they lost a man on patrol this morning."

In the course of interviews all of us learned a great deal about army organization and tactics that we hadn't known before. We picked up each new item casually, tried it out cautiously on the next interviewees, and if it worked, we then demanded information about the particular point from the next officer we met.

The one and one-half days rest that the men in this unit had enjoyed since they entered these fields speedily showed its good effect. The haggard looks were gone and they had lost the deadened, vacant looks they had shown the day before. They still wanted to know, however, when they would be relieved and seemed to think they were being held in the line only because the general wanted to win glory for himself. "Why, he has actually asked for the privilege of taking Saint-Lô," some of them said in horrified tones.

Harsh talk came only from those officers whose duffel bags, which had been sent in for the frontline troops after the assault and were awaiting transportation on the beaches, had been slashed and their boots and kits taken. "I'd like to lead a party against that beach gang right now," one lieutenant muttered in a murderous tone. Here was the beginning of a series of incidents that were to set the infantry against the rear-echelon units. Five or eight miles back was the beach, but there was the margin of life. Here, men shared their blankets; there the men on the beach were looting and selling their spoils. At least, so it seemed to the men at the front, and it was useless to remind them that some of the beach groups spent sleepless nights trying to unload the cargoes and build the artificial harbors to support the infantry's advance.

I found in the general talk that always accompanied the interviews that rumors were continuing to spread. Norway, they had heard, had been evacuated, and southern France had been invaded. However, the second week ashore marked the appearance of mimeographed newssheets that found their way about and substituted some fact for rumor. I saw one man reading a copy aloud to another while he dug away on a foxhole, and the digger would stop occasionally to discuss the news. It seemed to be a peaceful spot, where one could relax and read. But five hundred yards away (the estimate is the captain's, I would have thought it nearer) was the rat-tat-tat of the machine gun. Occasionally a spent bullet would rustle in the brush near us.

During the afternoon, I passed back through Saint-Marguerite d'Elle. At Monsieur Fernand's place, which was officially closed to soldiers, an old crone poured out red wine—twenty francs for a canteen cup full, thirty to forty francs for filling a bottle, and 180 francs for Bordeaux. I selected a cup of the *vin rouge ordinaire*— cool and sharp in its taste—since I had no bottle and was not disposed to pay $3.60 for the Bordeaux. They had had bread and butter for sale that morning—twenty francs for a loaf of bread and forty for a pat of butter—but it had gone earlier in the day when "le general," under whose orders technically the shop was placed "off limits" to prevent general inflation for prices such as that we were then experiencing, and his staff had stopped by. The bistro continued to do a wonderful business as the soldiers came up, poured out the water from their canteens, and had wine poured in, splashing its red color and fragrance on their clothing. When I came by at dusk, Monsieur Fernand's was tightly shuttered, and I had to translate for five disconsolate GIs as the neighbors explained the *madame* still feared the shelling and went into the woods every night to stay. We could see little groups of frightened old ladies and little children, carrying their bed clothes with them to the woods more than a mile away, looking for all the world in their patient weariness like the old ladies and children I had seen two months before in London.

When I had bought my wine, an hour before dusk, I had walked along the road south of Saint-Marquerite d'Elle to talk to two members of a bazooka team who lay in a ditch at a bend in the road. I gave them some wine from my cup and they chided me gently for walking so near to the front with my stripes on and the white splotch on the back of my helmet clearly visible. They waved me to a safe spot in the ditch, explaining that now and again a machine-gun bullet whistled overhead and that it was close enough for a sniper to get in his work.

While discussing the dangers of frontline life, we were all shamed by the confident bearing of three little sisters—Iselle, Genevieve, and Jacqueline—who greeted us with all the English they knew: "Good morning" and "Thank you." We had an English lesson in which they learned "good afternoon," and they gave me a lesson in Norman geography and economics. It was only a few kilometers to Saint-Lô. Prices were high. Eggs were five francs each, butter thirty francs a kilo, and wine eleven francs a liter (I contrasted this with the twenty at Monsieur Fernand's).

The dirty-faced, four-year-old Iselle smiled prettily when I called her "*mignonne*" (darling) and showed that already she was a coquette (sophisticated). I asked her when school was out and she referred the matter to her sisters, who said that they had been dismissed on "*Samedi*" (Saturday) last when there was news that the Americans were approaching, and that they didn't know when school would start again. I gathered they were not unhappy about the difficulties of the invasion.

My full day over, I went back to regiment to my foxhole and my one blanket. The night before I had felt like a rugged soldier, but still a bit ashamed because my one blanket was more than the rest had. Tonight their blanket rolls had been brought up by truck and I was the Spartan one. But they found me a good, deep hole under a tree (they were generous in their selection since the front-line infantry had dug in deep there several nights before and had gone deeper than regimental headquarters personnel usually did). I picked one in which I could just stretch out, dressed in my rain-coat, rolled up in my blanket, and had one of the guards throw down branches and grass on me. I slept pretty well except when the coldness of the Norman night struck through my clothing or heavy artillery fire shook me in the foxhole.

I was impressed by the wonderful friendliness of the men, the easy manners of the forward echelons, the minimum of salut-ing, and the comradeship of the men and junior officers. But, af-ter all, they slept in neighboring foxholes and their C rations came out of the same kind of can and were warmed by the same fire. The troops were already giving food to the children, although no one asked for any. A Kentuckian, who greeted me fondly as "Ken-tucky" when he found we came from the same state, handed over to some Frenchmen his banjo—which had lost some of its strings—when they expressed their admiration of the instrument. We were puzzled over a French name for it, and banjo meant nothing to them.

I had no luck in catching a ride on the fourteenth, so I walked the half mile to Ste. Marguerite, determined to converse with Frenchmen if I could not carry on my interviews. Still looking for a jeep going my way, I stood at the crossroads and talked to the policeman and assorted countrymen as they passed by. Very apolo-getically, the young, stockily built gendarme asked for a cigarette, saying, "I don't like to beg, Monsieur, but we cannot get them." As he puffed at his Fleetwood (that was still all I had), he told me that the Germans had requisitioned all the leather and metal early in the occupation, but had taken no food until recently. At the moment, however, they had little bread, milk, or wine. He told me that the town, out of its six hundred had contributed fifty-six men to German labor parties. Five additional men had gone later so that five prisoners who were ill could return, but none had come back.

A bespectacled schoolboy next approached me and told me that school had ended with the debarquement. His question was one asked frequently by Normans those days: "Monsieur, can the Allies hold what they have taken?" That was always the fear among these shrewd, crafty folk. That and the question of "When will there be food?" The shy old lady who charged us outrageous prices for wine while calling us *capitalistes* always wanted to know when there would be flour and chocolate and bonbons.

A disreputable old man wearing GI shoes came up next to ask for a cigarette. When I asked about his shoes he said they were the first leather ones he had had in three years, but gave no other information. Nearly everyone had wooden shoes, although German corpses were beginning to furnish boots to someone since nearly all the dead Germans I saw were barefooted. French orders threatened death for looting. There were also warnings against touching German dead. But one grisly tale was related to me of a greedy trio—two men and a woman—found mangled over a booby-trapped German corpse. Their hands were found full of spoils and their pockets filled with Allied invasion money. Our fellows cursed at that, but others said: "Well, the dead can't spend it."

The scene at the crossroads became properly storybookish when an old man came by with two cows of the "skin and bone" variety and wanted to know where he could get payment for two fine animals which had been killed by American shells, by an old man who struck his daughter and ordered her home when the soldiers began to congregate around her, and by another oldster who screamed "Boche" at a pert young miss as she walked along the road. "She slept with the Germans," he explained, as he continued to shout *"putain"* (whore) at her.

Across from us stood the town church—its towers still intact, an oddity in this section, where towers were observation posts and artillerymen looked for a chance to send a shell just below the bell-rest. We had taken this one for our observation post. It was quiet and only the mass of wire going into the vestibule and up the walls indicated what was happening. I stepped inside the church and found that only the tower was at war—at the high altar were the priests celebrating the miracle of the Prince of Peace and in front of it a few soldiers, carrying their rifles, had knelt to pray.

Despairing of catching a ride, I ultimately walked out on the road to les Cables where the 2d Battalion, 115th Infantry, had its headquarters. It was a lonely road, and I was glad to see the men in the fields. One party came to the roadside, bringing me a drink of cider and a handshake, and warning me that Germans were in the woods not far away. There was also an old woman who asked if it would be all right for her to stay at home that night. And there was also the pretty cyclist who stopped to ask if I would go to examine a grenade the Germans had left along the road. Not wishing to dabble in the equally dangerous trades of the civil affairs people and the bomb disposal unit, I referred both the old lady and the young girl to the American commander in the village.

Near les Cables, once more in an orchard, I found Major M.G. Clift of Cambridge, Maryland, executive officer of the 2d Battalion. A deliberate-speaking southerner, fairly tall and spare, he impressed me as being very careful and conscientious as he told me the story of his unit since D-Day. This interview was typical of many I had during this period, because the major had his chores to perform. He would ask my pardon and then turn to take a patrol's report, to send out new patrols, to change a company commander, to appoint a communications sergeant, or to send a detail to guard a captured German tank. Here was the housekeeping part of a unit technically at rest. The toil of advance was stayed, but there was still work to be done, and even as he recounted the story of the past week for the history books, he dealt with the things that would help to make up the success of the coming week's actions.

This was my first sight of patrols at the beginning and end of their day's action. A sergeant and three men came back from a walk along the Elle. The sergeant, after saluting, sat on the ground by the major and traced his path, while the others took a pull at their canteens and showed little interest in the report or us except when they were asked for information. Here they had crawled a hundred yards, there they had hidden behind the trees, here they had worked their way around a German machine-gun position. They had seen evidence of a few enemy troops, but they had little of consequence to report. The major nodded his approval and called up another sergeant to start another patrol. The route to be followed was outlined and the object made clear. These were not the normal patrols of reconnaissance, but actually the means of establishing a front line, of denying to the enemy an opportunity of reoccupying any part of the front they had left or of reconnoitering it with impunity. Here I learned why I had seen no one on our front, and how battles might go on for days with only members of patrols seeing the enemy. It was these parties going up and down every few hours that guarded against chance attack, gave information on the activities and position of the enemy, and forced the Germans to be on their guard. Less important than in earlier wars, since the liaison planes we frequently saw above us did much of the reconnaissance work, they still played an important role—particularly in the hedgerows where it was easy for the enemy to hide in the undergrowth.

Sometimes, I suspected that the patrol leaders went only a short distance on dark nights, and I imagined that the two fronts were mutually safe because the patrols on either side kept their peace. I talked to enough men to believe the *Stars and Stripes* tale of a German and an American patrol which spent several days under a gentleman's agreement visiting a wine cellar in no-man's-land at discreet intervals. I like best the story of a patrol, not in the 29th Division, told me by the leader of a group which reported itself cut off by the enemy for three days while they enjoyed the favors of two buxom French girls in a farmhouse.

But the stories of the dalliance of some patrols must not be allowed to obscure the important and dangerous work they did. Nothing so angered men who were at the mercy of larger enemy patrols or well-concealed machine gun or mortar positions as a communiqué that read, "Only routine patrolling took place during the day." It was a well-established fact that if you went on patrols too often you rarely kept your health. Men were wary of volunteering for these duties, and they usually made clear when it was not their turn to go. If the reader is one who dislikes going down a darkened street late at night or even going through the friendly halls of his home at night without a flashlight, let him imagine the feelings of a soldier who is awakened at two in the morning and told that without any light or noise he and four or five others are to go several thousand yards in a westerly direction, to establish whether or not the enemy is still nearby, and then return with a whole skin and the information. Along the way and the return, there might be Germans on a similar mission, or Germans armed with machine pistols who were expecting such a patrol. Of course, there was sometimes excitement in being told to capture a German for questioning, and I have heard men chortle with glee when told they were to bring in a live "Kraut." But this sport could be dangerous and occasionally the resistance was so strong that on an army front no prisoner would be taken in a single day.

When he ceased each job, Major Clift would turn back to his account of the past eight days. The companies of the battalion had landed on Easy Red (instead of Dog Red) about 1100 D-Day. Their casualties were relatively light, sixteen in all, but of this number six were officers. They came up the hill rapidly and were on top of the hill overlooking the landing beaches in about twenty-five minutes. They assembled with the other two battalions of the 115th Infantry near Saint-Laurent-sur-Mer. The 2d Battalion moved out from here on the seventh, but had to pull back a short distance that evening.

About midnight of D+1 the 1st Battalion began a march along secondary roads to a point south of Longueville, which they reached about 0200 the following morning. In the meantime, the 2d Battalion was moving on the town. Little opposition was met as the group moved up astride the road west of the town and set up defenses. The 3d Battalion was ordered into Deux-Jumeaux.

On the night of D+2 all three battalions moved toward Canchy. From this point on the following morning they began crossing the inundated area formed by the tributaries and canals of the Aure Inferieure between Canchy and Colombières. Crossing in reverse order with the 3d Battalion going first, the battalions did not complete the task until 1200. Men waded water that averaged two to three feet deep, but had to have engineer boats in crossing the canals where the water was too deep to wade. The average company took about one hour to cross the one and one-half mile expanse of water. The groups crossing the flooded area met no fire, although it had been expected. Potential opposition had been destroyed by a foray of a platoon of E Company under Lieutenant K.C. Miller. This platoon had crossed the night before and had surprised the enemy in Colombières as they awakened the next morning. They were credited with killing forty to fifty Germans. They took eighteen prisoners, wrecked some vehicles belonging to the enemy, and rejoined their company the following morning. They had three wounded. When the 2d Battalion entered Colombières the following morning, they found it clear of the enemy and a report that some two hundred Germans had withdrawn to the south. The 1st Battalion followed the 2d across and went south of La Basse Riviere, while the 3d went into the woods north of Colombières.

But the relatively easy advance was to be followed by heavier opposition and disaster. The 2d Battalion was next given the task of clearing the Bois de Calette. As they moved westward toward this forest, they encountered Germans near Vouilly. Entrenched in the hills and aided by bicyclists armed with machine pistols, the enemy put up a spirited defense. Artillery fire was laid on the German positions, but resistance continued and it was decided to establish a defensive position at le Carretour. The battalion passed through Vouilly and turned southward to Castilly, where resistance ceased. At this point they turned off the road by error and went to Mestry (Major Clift indicated that this was due in part to an error in the maps, which were not very accurate in regard to secondary roads). By the time they had retraced their steps to le Carretour it was 0230 of D+4.

When the battalion reached le Carretour, the soldiers were exhausted, having marched some twelve miles and having fought much of the way. This point was stressed as an explanation for their failure to make proper reconnaissance of the area to determine whether or not enemy units were in the area. No enemy forces had been met south of Castilly, and there was nothing to indicate that the armor they had heard moving south from the Bois de Calette earlier in the day was German.

The battalion halted near the crossroads at le Carretour and the leading three companies—F, G, and H—went into the field on the right, just south of le Carretour. Company commanders posted light security guards and the heavy weapons company set a platoon of machine guns around the perimeter of the field. Six mortars were set up to complete the defenses. While that was being accomplished, Major Clift moved to the rear of the column to get Headquarters Company, E Company, and the medical detachment into the next field. Just as he arrived, he met the supply officer, Lieutenant Tucker, with two jeeps full of rations. At that moment they heard a noise that sounded like that of a Weasel. Lieutenant Tucker asked for the password and went to the road to challenge the vehicle's driver. As he called halt, a machine gun or machine pistol was fired and he fell. By then it was clear that German tanks, supported by infantry, were advancing down the road. The E Company commander was ordered to get his troops off the road before the Germans discovered them. In order to discourage an enemy reconnaissance party, a sergeant from E Company was posted to fire antitank grenades at anyone who approached. He complied with his instructions and scattered the first group sent down the road. In the confusion, the men of E Company began to seek cover. An effort was made to find bazookas and mortars, but in the one case ammunition was missing and in the other no tube could be found for the mortar, since the carriers were taking shelter in the hedgerows in a nearby field. A soldier was sent back to direct the fire of a mortar that was already set up, but he was shot before he could reach it. At that point the Germans began firing with two machine guns and with machine pistols and tanks, and German infantry began to move down the road between the fields in which the men of the battalion were sheltered. Major Clift estimated there were eight tanks and more than a company of men in the German column. The tanks fired broadsides into the hedges and the infantry fired into the fields. About 350 yards after opening fire, the tanks stopped and opened up with all their guns. The men of the battalion returned fire and killed some of the Germans (Major Clift estimated there were a hundred German casualties).

The Germans reportedly called out the battalion commander's name, saying, "Surrender Warfield." But the colonel made no reply; he had been killed while trying to organize resistance. Also killed in the fight were the battalion S-3, Lieutenant Peter C. DiGagni, Lieutenant Miller of E Company, who had led the patrol into Colombières, Captain Angelo W. Onder, commander of

Company H, and Lieutenant E.B. Tucker, the supply officer. Two officers were wounded and four others reported missing. There were 129 enlisted casualties—ten killed, twenty-one wounded, and eighty-eight missing. Enemy fire created such confusion that it was impossible to organize a defense. However, Private First Class Armbruster of G Company fired a bazooka that hit one tank, setting it on fire.

Finding the position untenable, the men began to disperse while the executive officer started back to Bricqueville to notify the regimental commander of the situation. Meanwhile, reports reached division that the battalion had been wiped out or had surrendered, as small isolated groups turned up saying that they were sole survivors. The commanding general of the 29th Division, Gerhardt, came down to the fighting area and found most of the men gone. He said that the battalion was a disgrace and sent a new battalion commander, Lieutenant Colonel Arthur Sheppe, to reorganize the unit. Some 110 replacements were also sent in the next day. On the afternoon of 10 June the battalion was put back into the line with the objective of holding a position north of Saint-Marguerite d'Elle, and on the following day the battalion was ordered to move down to the Elle. A German force that had crossed the river hit them, but they managed to push the enemy back. Meanwhile, the other two battalions had failed in their efforts to cross the Elle, and the 115th was told to hold to its positions north of the river while the 116th went across.

After getting these details, I went from battalion headquarters to Company E some distance away, passing on the way three U.S. tanks about fifty yards from each other which had been knocked out by German fire when they moved up to aid the 115th Infantry's attempt to cross the Elle. The German weapon, an 88, was concealed in a little road to the right. A bazooka had knocked it out, but it had done its work. The 747th Tank Battalion, which had lost these tanks, complained that it was being ruined by the piecemeal commitment of its tanks. "The infantry thinks we just have to send up a tank to get rid of the Krauts," the officers argued, "but instead we just get them knocked out that way." The tanks liked the hedgerow country, I gathered, about as much as a great ship likes fighting in the reefs of a narrow sea.

Company E was welcoming replacements—the first that we

had seen. Their clean uniforms, shaved faces, and bewildered looks made their newness at the front evident, and the week-old veterans treated them like "recruits." The old-timers assured me that the new bunch was awfully stupid, and to prove it they put one of the new men through his paces. He was trying to find his platoon area, which he had left only a few minutes before. "Where were you?" "Down the road and over in a hedgerow." "Who is your squad leader?" "Well, he's a little fellow." "And your platoon leader?" "I ain't sure." "There you are," the veterans said triumphantly, "He won't last a week against the Germans." But they learned—if they lived—and the veterans soon ceased to laugh at them. Instead, they nurtured them and taught them their tricks, because the coming of these replacements-reinforcements helped to restore the odds, still short it's true, that the old-timers might live to fight another day.

I went back to regimental headquarters hoping to get a ride back to V Corps, but had no luck. However, I spent the time talking to Sergeant Norman Overmiller about the girl he intended to marry when he got back to Easton, Maryland; to Corporal Joseph Rieser of Philadelphia, who had married an English girl just before D-Day, and to Private Moon, a nineteen-year-old rifleman from New Jersey, who planned to study law when he returned home. As we talked about his future, although he was garbed in olive drab and watching airplanes through the binoculars he had found on a dead German, he might have been one of my freshmen asking for advice. And I was helping to plan his courses. Meanwhile, he gave me the count of 292 planes which were flying back from a mission—Spitfires, Thunderbolts, and Mustangs, none of which I was ever certain I recognized—and remarked casually, "I guess the Germans caught hell."

It rained during the night and the dust in my trench became mud. My blankets got wet and my filthy clothes stuck to me and the morning was dismal. My state of mind was not helped by the sour smell that came form my uniform. I had changed underclothes but once since 23 May, and my outer garments not at all, and I had slept in all of my clothes the two weeks since 1 June. But I had had a chance to shave and take a few sponge baths, so I was almost effete in the company I met in the field.

Thursday, 15 June (D+9)

Continuing the question of how we live. We sleep in foxholes or hedgerows or bedrolls under vehicles rolled up in 2–4 blankets. Sometimes we improvise bedrolls with blankets put in a shelter half. Twice so far I've pitched a pup tent with another fellow. At Corps I have started to stay at the motor pool because I pick up considerable info from the drivers and sometimes I get some wine they pick up. Our driver got 4 cases of Burgundy and 5 gallons of cognac. I still hang around with ——— Richards and the troops.

Stayed at 115th. Only one blanket, so I had to sleep in raincoat; was rather cold but I made out. Was awakened from time to time by hard shaking from barrages.

Waited for a ride without success. Around noon I walked to Ste. Marguerite (only a 1/2 mile, but no one likes to walk alone this near to the front).

After finding out that morning that XIX Corps was taking over the 29th Division that day, I caught a ride back to the division headquarters with a lieutenant colonel. There I got my first talk with a colonel who had just been relieved of his command. He was sitting out along the road with his belongings beside him, waiting for a jeep to take him to the rear. The day before he had held the destiny of three thousand or more men in his hands; now he looked almost like a mendicant. Interviewing these people was a cruel sort of business that I had always held against newsmen who probed at people's grief. Now here I was prying into a man's vitals when he was dazed, forcing conversation when he would have preferred to hold in check a voice he was not sure he could control. But for us it was an excellent time to get the exact story. Still angry and hurt, they would talk freely, whereas later they would be inclined to evade. Too upset to be prudent, they would strike out at others who shared their blame. Later, when they realized that their chances of making a comeback might depend upon the goodwill of the men who relieved them, or on the suppression of some of their mistakes, they frequently would ask us to change their accounts. Since we did not send our interviews back through channels, where they would be seen by their superiors and held against them, we would rewrite the story and include it with the original. Then we would include a note with the original stating the circumstances under which it had been given. (We were allowed to rewrite interviews, but we never destroyed the originals, and we sometimes added some rather biting comments as to the reasons for the amendments).

Just as a newsman must feel sorry for the victim at whose heart he picks, so we felt pity for these officers. A few hours before they had been masters of units, with power over their men, with chances for promotion, decorations, and a good name in the history books. But because they could not take a particular little place on the map, which they had never heard of the day before and would remember only because of their failures, because some subordinates had not been dismissed during maneuvers when it was clear that social charm was no substitute for leadership, because they could not get their troops to perform the task which division or corps said had to be done, then they had to be relieved. It was a rough game through the whole chain of command. In combat, selection was ruthless. In the rear, the inept might flourish for a season, but no frontline commander dared hold on too long to a subordinate merely because he liked him or they had been in the same class at West Point. Even if a man did his best, when the heat was on from above for so many hedgerows, or the crossing of a stream, or the taking of so many little Norman houses, a commander had just so many hours to deliver the goods or he was relieved. If he had really done his best, as in this case, and he had the respect of the man who relieved him, there was usually a friendly call from division or corps to the next higher headquarters and another spot was found for him. But the sickness of heart was there, and the look of tired, beaten, exhausted helplessness could not be effaced.

Friday, 16 June (D+10)

Raining when I got up. Rained until nearly noon. Very dismal; blanket wet and clothes damp. (They are also filthy. I have changed underwear once since May 23 but have not changed outer garments.) Caught ride with Lieutenant Colonel ———. To Division in the rain. Learned that XIXth Corps had taken over. . . . Got ride with Captain O'Bryan of Div.

I Corps. There I found Lieutenant Fox had been to Rangers. I found my 3 blankets were lost at Division.

I reached V Corps in time to receive the first mail I had gotten in a month. There was no word from home, but reassuring news from one of my brothers in New Guinea. I was dismayed to find my duffel bag and musette bag in a foot of water in a foxhole. The former had stood the test, and the clothes were dry, but my papers were soaked and one of the one-pound candy bars I had bought in Newfoundland was ruined.

Soon after arriving, Major McKnight, who was eager to do some observing for the War Department, invited Lieutenant Fox and me to ride to the beach. We found that we didn't rank very high in the estimation of the motor pool when they sent us a command car—an impressive looking piece of machinery with a high silhouette that was originally intended for field grade officers in the field. We were still near enough the front that the high brass preferred and got the lowly jeeps which were less likely to draw fire and easier to get out of in case of attack.

We drove slowly over the narrow, muddy roads, packed with traffic, stalled for many minutes by the double lanes of vehicles going to and from the beaches. MPs sweated at the crossroads as they tried to get order into the columns. At one point a helmeted figure yelled at me and I shouted, "Indiana." He was a Hoosier crapshooter who had bunked next to me at Fort McClellan in February 1943. We both said, "How are things," and "Take care of yourself," and saw each other no more.

The jeep made its way with difficulty through Trevières, which had been smashed by the guns of the ships we had seen firing on D+1. This town of 870, second largest yet taken in the V Corps's area, was the pride of the 2d Division, which had marched directly from the beach to capture it. They were to suffer many losses in harder battles before they spoke as proudly of their later victories as they did of this one. At the threshold of the partly smashed and burned Hotel de Ville, I found a heavy key, scorched and rusted. For days thereafter, Major McKnight teased officers of the 2d Division when they boasted of the taking of the town by saying, "How can you claim it, when a sergeant in our outfit has the key to the city?"

The old lady who was concierge of the Hotel de Ville had been in the building during four shellings. Fortunately, the part of the structure she was in had not collapsed. On the front walls, which were still standing, could be seen German placards. On the announcements by the mayor, who had fled the day before our arrival, was the countersignature of the *oberleutnant* of the area and the German seal. Lists of all males over eighteen in the town were posted on a bulletin board through whose wire covering I managed, at the loss of a little skin, to extract one of the announcements. Here was Pierre, aged eighteen, three days of labor; Jean, excused because of illness; Fernand, with four children, only one day required; and so on for several pages. And what was their job? To set posts in open fields to bar the landing of Allied gliders, and to guard the roads. What was their pay? Fifty to a hundred francs (pay for ordinary work was about thirty francs per day). And the penalty if they didn't work? No bread tickets for the man and his family, and perhaps forced work without pay. It was just a German employment list.

The people were not bitter over the shelling of the town, although they spoke with grief of their sixteen dead and thirty-one wounded. They had not been warned to flee, they said, as had the people near the beaches (the planes had strewn fields and small settlements with leaflets warning of the initial attacks). They shrugged their shoulders, however, and said, "*C'est la guerre.*" Their question was an old one by now: "Can you hold what you have?" They did not want to be overrun again, particularly after they had been friendly to the Americans. Our relations with the townspeople were aided by the American hospital that had been set up across from the Hotel de Ville and to which injured children and oldsters were being brought to have their wounds dressed. A sign on the Hotel de Aignonville spoke of *soupe populaire gratuite a tous heures*, while another offered milk for children. Nearby were *affiches* that proclaimed General Eisenhower's instructions to the French people, the new laws, and the latest war news. The old mayor, who had been brought back, signed the proclamations. This time he placed his name on papers held before him by an American officer, just as he had once signed for the *oberleutnant*—although perhaps more cheerfully now.

Outside the city hall, the bulldozers were at work pushing

wrecked houses out of the street. Groups of soldiers strung telephone wires to a conveniently located pole or tree or left the cables
along the roadside.

Every place our party stopped that morning seemed to become a center for the gathering of part of the population. Finding
that someone spoke French, they pressed about to ask questions
and to furnish information. Major McKnight amused himself taking my picture "electioneering" with the good people of Trevières.
They spoke of the rampant black market and then they cursed
the Germans. One lovely young lady told me that her husband
was one of twenty-six forced labor prisoners who had been taken
from the town. She said that the number would have been larger
but that most of the remaining young men had fled.

The people here claimed to be Gaullists, but, as elsewhere in
Normandy, they hated Laval but not Pétain.[2] They had listened to
clandestine radio reports and knew of Allied preparations to cross
the Channel. They had collected or made French and American
flags to welcome us. The latter must have been made for the most
part, since many were of a crude sort, with the wrong number of
stripes and stars.

Sergeant Pogue (left) and Lieutenant Fox with a map of Normandy, discussing
the historical team's coverage of the war.

Some of the town was still habitable. It was possible at a few places to get a black market steak, and the correspondents wrote happy stories about the excellent drinks set out for them by a former barmaid from the Ritz.

That evening, as we returned to corps, Fox and I found our historical team boss, Major O'Sullivan, waiting for us. He had come to Normandy a short time before with elements of First Army headquarters, and then had spent some time with 1st Division, which Fox had not had a chance to visit. We laid plans for coverage of the campaign. In honor of the occasion, we shared a bottle of Chauvenet burgundy, loot that Corporal Richards, who drove a liaison officer, had brought back from the well-supplied VII Corps. Wine and cheese, the latter of the K-ration variety, made up our supper.

Saturday, 17 June (D+11)

O'Sullivan, Fox, and I drove next morning to the beach to see Captain Frazier and his crew and to get a better view of the beach defenses. We drove the length of the beach by jeep (I was enormously amused in the fall of 1946 when I revisited Omaha Beach and was told by the caretaker of the cemetery that it was still mined) and saw that it had changed completely in appearance since D+2. The hastily buried bodies at the foot of the hill had now been taken to the top of the bluff and carefully interred. Bulldozers had leveled much of the area back of the beach. However, it was still possible to get an idea of what the invaders had faced, and I begged that someone get the engineers to do a careful set of measurements. Meanwhile, I spent several minutes pacing off the distance from the seawall to the top of the ridge just to the west of the E-1 exit, which led to Saint-Laurent. Taking the long strides which Kentucky farmers use in "laying off" land, I found it to be eighteen paces from the seawall to the house facing the road, twenty-five paces to the end of the low ground, and 120 paces more to the bottom of the first ridge, which seemed about twenty feet high. On the slightly level top of this ridge, it was thirty-six paces to the point from which the second ridge rose. This one seemed to be about fifty feet high.

Sunday, 18 June (D+12)

Up late. Spent afternoon discussing plans for week and in writing up notes. Looked through some journals of the first day.

My first exposure to artillery fire aimed at the area in which I was standing came on 18 June. I had gone to 116th Infantry headquarters that morning, but was incorrectly directed and ended up about noon in the woods near Couvains, where several companies of the 2d Battalion, 115th Infantry, had stopped for chow. It was a quiet enough looking place—secluded woodland spot, sylvan charm, and all that—ideal for a picnic. I told the driver, Private McGowan, to join the chow line in the next field and that I would go along as soon as I got some other directions. The captain to whom I addressed my inquiries was pointing out the 116th's location on a map he had laid on the ground when artillery opened up on the area. McGowan had just reached the fence thirty yards away and was starting over the "stile block" when the shells began to explode. As we hugged the ground, I was pleased to hear someone yell from a nearby foxhole that there was room for me and I ran for it—to find that the friendly occupant was Private Moon, with whom I had talked a few nights before. Once there we felt safe enough to swap yarns, and he told me of some souvenirs, including a German rifle, which he had saved for me.

We sat there discussing what he had done since I last saw him while 3 more shells dropped (each one farther away). I had no sense of fear, since the shell made less noise than our own shells fired nearby and since I was some distance away from the men who were hit. I could not visualize the danger.

When the shells finished exploding, people began running toward the next field where the missiles had fallen in the chow line, hitting some nine men. My driver, who had seen the whole thing, had lost his appetite. I had survived the first shock from ignorance more than any lack of fear. However, when the bloody and maimed soldiers were brought out for first aid, I was sobered by the sight of the ugly holes made by shell fragments and by the thought that another two minutes would have found me in the line. The more experienced soldiers of the companies soon recovered their composure, but some of the newer men clung to their foxholes and gave every indication they would spend the afternoon there. Everyone relieved his pent-up feelings a few minutes later by shouting angrily at a tank that came chugging up the road, looking for all the world like a frightened animal seeking shelter. The driver was sworn at roundly for inviting fire from the 88s.

After the excitement had died, and as soon as we could decently leave—one always felt a certain delicacy about leaving too quickly a hot spot and turning toward a rearward sanctuary—we went back to the 116th Infantry command post. There I talked with Major Howie, the man whose body was carried some days later into Saint-Lô. Our talk was interrupted, however, by the storming presence of "Dutch" Cota, the assistant division commander, who wanted to know why the regiment was so slow moving out. The major winked at me and suggested I come back another day.

Chapter 8

The Last Weeks of June

Monday, 19 June (D+13)–
Mondy, 3 July (D+27)

Monday, 19 June (D+13)

Rained all day and was very cold. Pretty dismal.

While sleeping with three others under a command car in the motor pool, I was awakened by rain that found its way through a hole in the car. It had wet my head and shoulders, and had run underneath my blankets to make them soggy. And then it was cold. My clothes were wet, I shaved in a downpour, and the food, which we still ate outside (I noted pettishly in my diary that the officers had eaten under canvas since the first week), got wetter and wetter. I sat in Fox's pup tent all day, trying to type out my notes, but the rain wet my feet and legs and spattered in on the paper. My general disgust at the French climate was lessened somewhat at night when Private Radin, one of the drivers who had been getting eggs and cream from a nearby family, asked me to go over and translate for him. We took them some of our K-ration cheese, which they praised highly, and that in this land of milk and good cheese, and they furnished us with cider. They talked of politics, saying they preferred us to the English. With some reluctance, however, they added that Britain and Russia had fought the good fight when others were not yet in the war. They indicated some lack of faith in de Gaulle.

Tuesday, 20 June (D+14)

Tried to clean my field jacket. . . . Cool and dark all morning. Turned warm and bright in afternoon. Heavy barrage after midnight last night. Great excitement around midnight when a group saw a barrage balloon descending and shot it down, thinking it was a parachute.

Major McKnight and I again went to the beach. On the way, he told with indignation an ugly story concerning awards. He and several other officers had been sent out a few nights before to get the names of a number of men for decorations. In order to hasten the process, because it was felt it would help morale if a list of awards could be announced soon, recommendations were to be signed in blank, living men were to be preferred in the selection because of publicity value, and the main details of the decorations were to be written out at corps on a basis of the oral accounts given at the lower units. One officer had complained angrily of cases where men of great courage had been omitted because the first name or serial number was not readily available.

I was properly incensed at the account, but was later pleased to find that General Gerow, on hearing of these incidents, had ordered a second list made to correct these injustices. Unfortunately, it was not always possible for a general officer to be on watch, and there were cases where fine men were overlooked because no one pushed their cases, or because their officers were too hard-pressed by vital duties to send in citations, or where an officer, who knew the details of an individual's bravery, died before he could write a citation. Often, too, there was a tendency of the higher headquarters to assume that all recommendations were rated too high and to give a lower medal than the one suggested. Too often, the higher headquarters said that frontline men were merely doing their duty in actions recommended for Bronze Stars, while giving out similar awards (I got one) to men from the rear echelon merely because they went forward on some occasions.

Here is a description of the beach as I have seen it on five occasions.
D+2—went in on Rhino ferry, drove off in shallow water not up to the hubcap; hit wet sand which stalled car in front of us. Went through E-1 exit off easy Red beach. Road was curved and fairly steep. To the left was

a long ravine and across it was high ridge equal to or greater in height
than that to our right. The ravine was about 1/8 to 1/4 mile long and
covered with vegetation. To our right were remnants of a pillbox and to
our left in the face of the ridge was a bigger gun emplacement. The ridge
took on new features and appeared much higher.

On 11 June—Beach was a great mass of foxholes; kitchen in a
pillbox. Scattered with debris. Looking up at commanding ridge it is
obvious that the climb up was considerable. Roads are at a sharp grade
and ridge guns and emplacements in face of ridge could put cross-fire on
several beaches.

On D+11—went over the hill along ridge. Saw Mulberry project
from ammo dump near Vierville, above Dog beach. Here I got an idea of
the beach for the first time. The ridge is 40–50 feet high above another
ridge, which is 20–30 feet high. It covered several beaches with fire. A
great line of concrete blocks have been sunk to provide breakwater and
two great piers have been built. It is said they will take as much material
as at Cherbourg. Beach crews march on 12 June to Vierville; place being
cleaned up.

D+14—Beach doesn't look same. Nearly flattened out between
seawall and beginning of ridge. Beach cleared of obstructions and craft
being handled to seawall. . . .

At no time did I see much evidence of air or naval fire on beach
except for beat up houses along shore. In the towns back of the beach, I
saw a number of hits on towns. Man who came in D+2 tells of disgust at
seeing a pilot near Red Cross sign dressed in pinks and wearing oxfords.

Some sleeping around today.

Work last night was by an Aladdin lamp. It flickered, but wasn't like
working by candlelight.

Weather better at night. Sun shone in late afternoon.

Wednesday-Thursday, 21–22 June (D+15–16)

A great gale hit the Channel on 21 June. To us several miles inland, it was marked by a heavy wind and a cold, gray sky. High
waves lashed the artificial ports, destroying the U.S. breakwater,
and it was decided to abandon it. We saw some of the damage
from a distance on the twenty-second as Major McKnight, Chaplain Dempsey, and I went to Pointe du Hoe. The cliffs there are
very abrupt. The heavy bombardment from the ships failed to

destroy the fortifications, but their massive iron doors were warped from the explosions. The ground in this area was the nearest thing to a World War I battle area that I was to see in 1944–45. It was churned up enormously and there were deep shell holes in profusion. The German headquarters near the hill had been thoroughly smashed. Little remained of the French home in which it had been located save for a number of photographs of French generals of World War I that had been scattered over the fields. We found a number of boxes of wooden bullets in the area and were able to establish by the simple expedient of translating the labels—which plainly said "For practice purposes"—that the stories of wooden dum-dum bullets were a myth.

Shortly afterward, I heard the story of how on D+1, when the Rangers at Pointe du Hoe were cut off, a Major Street took a party with food and ammunition to relieve them. He found Lieutenant Colonel Rudder wounded but unwilling to leave. When Street left, he found Rudder ready to send out several large patrols, keeping only fifteen men at Pointe du Hoe. This story prompted navy lieutenant Elzey, who was gathering history on the naval action for Captain Morison, to tell an account of Admiral Bryant's efforts to aid the Rangers one day when the 743d Tank Battalion, mistaking the Rangers for Germans, fired on Pointe du Hoe. The admiral, who had taken a paternal interest in the Rangers since his ship was supporting them with fire, noticed the signs of shelling. Thinking he might help, he radioed Rudder, "Are you being fired on?" "Yes," came the reply. "Do you want me to put fire on them?" "No," was the reply. The admiral thought that one over and said, "Are you being hit by friendly fire?" "Yes," came the laconic response.

In the course of the Pointe du Hoe trip, Chaplain Dempsey, a popular priest from New York, said that he had talked to a number of German prisoners. He had heard the confessions of several wounded men who had shown him the "R.K." for *Römischer Katholik* in their *soldbuchs* (pay books), and had seemed pleased to have him at their bedsides. Dempsey said that a French priest at Trevières had told him he had had as many as two hundred German soldiers at church and that they had been pretty well behaved in the village.

The end of the second week of the invasion found the Allied

forces getting all their services ashore. Adequate telephone lines, traffic cops, the *Stars and Stripes*, mail, promise of PX rations, and electric lights, run by a generator, instead of electric lamps. It was a rare spot that didn't have an MP, not only to direct traffic but also to put towns off limits.

Heaven knows the MPs were needed on the roads. With great lines of vehicles going back and forth to the beaches for ammunition, fuel, food, and equipment, and with new units pouring in constantly, the roads had become frightfully jammed. The vehicles were driven faster than in England, now that traffic again went right, and the traffic directors were going crazy. Even with additional help, the MPs found it difficult to give accurate directions. It was easy to get lost in a countryside in which narrow shady lanes, hedges, and orchards all looked alike. Most command posts were hidden in the hedgerows and orchards near a farmhouse. When one asked the way to one, he was given a map coordinate which might take you there if there had been no typographical error on the map, or if the person who gave you the coordinate had read it correctly from the map in the first place. Then, if you turned down the right road, didn't confuse one Cerisy with another, and the units hadn't moved since you last heard where they were, and if an MP didn't direct you down the wrong road, and if someone didn't understand you to say "Dakota" when you meant "Danger," you might find your way. And that was by day. By night, subtract lights and add confusion.

Visited I Army headquarters.

Talked to 3 (of a crew of 10) American aviators who bailed out over our lines after being hit by flak near Paris. Had been hit at 20,000 feet; started burning near here. Dropped 19,000 feet.

In moving up and down the roads during the day, we noticed, as John Hall was soon to tell his readers in the *London Daily Mail*, that jeep names have begun to lose their English tinge and take on a French flavor. "Allon-zi," "Oui, oui, mademoiselle," "Oo-la-la," and "Tous la France," showed the new trend, although "Bouncing Lil," "Hallucination," "Hepcat," "GI Jimmie," "Jane Baby," "Calamity," "Dixie," and "Baby Chick" had a familiar sound.

We have had strafing the last three mornings and one afternoon. Several men have left tents and vehicles for ditch. I still don't have enough sense to duck. We have awakened the past two mornings under strafing, although the guard reports trouble.

Weather beautiful, although cool all day.

How to win war—Major Hamlin—"Keep your sense of humor and the infantry in front of you."

Friday, 23 June (D+17)

On returning to the corps CP I found twenty-five letters dating all the way back to April. Unfortunately, my pay for March—which I was told in another letter had been mailed from London—had not arrived. It never did. (Some months later I applied for it; thirty-two endorsements later the letter came back saying that I could not be paid again. One year after the check had been issued, I received a letter asking sternly why I hadn't cashed my check, so the army could clear its books. When I explained it was lost, I was asked why I hadn't said so before. The money was finally paid to me in April 1945.)

Saturday, 24 June (D+18)

Beautiful day. Everyone working and taking baths.

Best story of day—on day of heavy storm when ships not coming in, one Captain on shore called for boat to take him out to a ship for a shower. . . .

Officers now eat off of plates.

Work was more or less suspended when the sun shone brightly. Everyone took baths from helmets and put out washing, or rather rinsings, since we had only cold water, and put the clothes out on the grass to dry. The day was otherwise rather typical of this static period when the units on our front were still pecking away at the Saint-Lô defenders. We checked at the liaison tent and saw that the pins had moved very little on the map. Fighting was proceeding on the British front toward Caen and on the VII Corps front toward Cherbourg. There was a little excitement in the G-1 section area in the late morning when one of the cows which inhabited our front yard, an unmilked creature whose udders were swollen with milk, ate the camouflage off a lieutenant's pup tent and knocked it down in the bargain.

The Germans still had enough airpower to send over a few planes every day, and the twenty-fourth found several of us scurrying for cover. There were already several coarse stories in circulation about colonels caught with their pants down at latrines and chuckles over the Rabelaisian possibilities which might develop if they found no "better 'ole" available.

A number of children were wandering around the area. Most of them wore wooden shoes, probably not because the Germans took the leather but because they were accustomed to wearing them in this region, and black (and dirty) smocks. Many were bareheaded, but some had acquired U.S. service caps, lavishly decorated with American insignia. They had picked up English easily and tried patiently to teach us French. They seldom asked for anything, except perhaps "cigarettes for Papa," but they were amply rewarded by the food and other articles they were able to scavenge in the area. I doubt if they cared for the lemonade powder and malt tablets which were tossed at them by nearly everyone, but they dragged away canvas bags full of them—together with other items that were more pleasing. Orders were issued every few days to keep the children away from the mess tent, but the soldiers paid no more attention to these warnings than they did to the prohibition against shooting at airplanes.

Captain Grimson, former assistant attorney general of North Dakota and newly appointed corps historian, entertained us during the day with his story of the replacement company (newcomers were still called replacements, although shortly afterward as a morale measure orders were issued that they were to be known as reinforcements) of seventeen officers and 750 men. The army, happily, had overestimated the number of casualties during the first few days of combat and had ordered a thousand replacements sent in daily to make up for the losses. Someone forgot to shut off the flow, and the rear area was soon filled up with newcomers. The army had arranged the replacements in packages, with so many cooks, bakers, riflemen, interpreters, typists, and the like, apportioned on the basis of rather intricate mortality tables, and had assigned them to special personnel centers where they could be drawn on when needed. Unfortunately, if no demand was made for a specially trained man in his specialty, he was assigned to his second, third, or fourth capability. The *Stars and Stripes*, which was beginning to creep in at the rate of about two papers per section, told of an ASTP graduate, one of twenty-five men trained in the Korean language, who had been sent to the ETO for duty. When it developed that the forces in Normandy had no overwhelming need for an expert in that field, the man was put on permanent KP. I would have been inclined to dismiss all of these stories as exaggerations had not Colonel Lee, the corps G-1, told us that replacements were being very poorly handled.

Sunday, 25 June (D+19)

> *Cleaned my field jacket and washed some things. Day absolutely cloudless, until after 6. Out of field jacket for first time, although it is cooler tonight and is usually around 40 at night. Landscape looked like a Corot painting last night.*

Lieutenant Fox and I were visited during the day by Lieutenant Blackwell, USN; Captain Frazer, beach engineer historian; and Captain Ferriss, the newly arrived XIX Corps historian. Blackwell was collecting information on beach demolitions and wanted to know what we had found on the subject. He admitted, in answer to our questions about the D-Day landings, that the navy crewmen did not always know where they were going, laughingly remarking that it was proverbial in the navy that men good for nothing else were assigned to landing craft details. However, he pointed out that much of the trouble on the beaches was due to the fact that some of the men in the early waves clung to the beach until kicked out of their places. This tended to confirm a similar story by Captain Lee of the engineers who said that some of the beach engineer people had moved only when threatened with pistols. He attributed their reluctance to move to a lack of training, although others said that the beach engineers had been briefed to wait until the infantry had cleared the enemy from the beach before beginning their work.

During the course of the day I managed to get part of the D-Day story as it looked on the *Ancon*, the V Corps command ship. Master Sergeant Peter Shain, who had helped keep the journal on the *Ancon*, showed me copies of teletype messages that had come in and been flashed on one of the *Ancon*'s three screens. Much of the news was fragmentary until Colonel Talley had been able to take a small boat equipped with special radio apparatus close in to shore and relay communications from the units there.

Monday, 26 June (D+20)

Captain Ferriss of XIX Corps asked me to go back with him to the 29th Division, which was now under his corps. We were joined by Lieutenant Tucker Ervin, the division historian, and went together to the 175th and 116th regimental headquarters. At the 175th's CP we talked to the S-2, Major John C. Geiglein of Westminster, Maryland, and Second Lieutenant Martin P. Alexander of Middletown, Maryland, leader of the regiment's Intelligence and Reconnaissance Platoon. Major Geiglein was shaving when we arrived, and we talked to him while he completed that ritual. He said that the prisoners were a pretty poor lot, but that reinforcements consisting of better troops were arriving. Their food supply was all right, he added, noting that they had recently captured two trucks and ten trailers containing Argentine beef, good wines, and some fair bread.

The major was full of praise for the spirit of the men in his regiment. One of them, who had been captured by a German and twelve Russians, had succeeded in persuading the Russians to make their noncom a prisoner and then to come in and surrender. Lou Azrael, a Baltimore newsman who was with the 29th Division several months before D-Day and had been with them through the Normandy fighting, at this point called to our attention a forty-seven-year-old soldier who, just after Pearl Harbor, had given up a newsstand in Baltimore and had enlisted as a private. While one of his sons was serving in a rear-echelon supply unit, the old man was constantly on the road between regimental headquarters and the battalions. Another old soldier was pointed out who had refused to take his pay for a year on the grounds that he didn't need the money.

After giving us details of the fighting which his unit had engaged in during the past two weeks, the major showed us weapons and trophies taken from the Germans. He said that if anyone wanted a Luger he would have to shoot the German himself and catch him before he fell. (Major McKnight had told us a few evenings before of seeing a sailor at the beach pay $135 for a Luger and later of hearing another offer $250 for one.)

We reached the 116th regimental CP in the midst of a downpour. While Captain Ferriss talked to officers there, I went down to the 2d Battalion. There, the battalion commander, Major Sidney V. Bingham, of Dallas, Texas, invited me to come into his foxhole, which was partly sheltered by a piece of canvas stretched over four sticks. Despite the covering, the water stood in puddles around the blankets on which he lay. To keep my paper dry, an orderly held a raincoat over my head, but still the rain came through, making great tearlike splotches on my notes.

When I finished the battalion story, Major Bingham called for runners from Companies E, F, and G, three of the first companies ashore on Omaha Beach, to take me to their CPs. Among the men I interviewed were First Sergeant John W. Baughman of Virginia, E Company; Sergeant W.T. Dowdy, Farmville, Virginia, and Private First Class August Bruno, Esmond, Rhode Island, G Company; and Technical Sergeant Walter R. Wilborn, South Boston, Virginia, and Sergeant John Thaxton, F Company. In going from one company to the other, the runners and I ran as fast as we could through the mud, spreading out so as to avoid possible mortar fire which, together with 88 fire, plastered the woods in which the men were billeted. The trees helped to make the foxholes drier than the one where Major Bingham was located.

Because of the high incidence of casualties among company officers, the sergeants were the only ones available to discuss the D-Day landings. They and the men who were called in for supply details were eager to talk, although there were all too few left of those who had landed on D-Day (E Company, for example, had lost its commander and ninety-three men in the landings, and F Company had none of the officers who had landed on 6 June). They were bedraggled sights, covered with mud, many with four-day beards, and all looked tired. Only their rifles remained in something like good condition, for they had tied rubber contraceptives over the barrels and working mechanisms of the weapons to keep out the rain, a practice which was to bring more than one severe directive from the harassed services of supply, which complained of the inordinate use of these commodities at a time when the supply was scarce.

The men, as they told their stories of activities since D-Day, huddled about in small groups, hoping, it seemed, to get a little warmth since their raincoats were of little aid against the rain and none against the cold. They spent much of their time urging me to list the names of their buddies who had received no awards but who richly deserved them. Most of them asked that I get the story of their efforts back to higher headquarters so that they could be relieved. Their morale did not appear bad, but they, like nearly every soldier I talked to, felt that they had done most of the fighting and wanted to be pulled out of the line.

Back at XIX Corps later in the evening, I talked to a Lieutenant Parker who said that special efforts were being made to deal with the terrible problem of the hedgerows. Colonel Freese of the 747th Tank Battalion had proposed that special tank-infantry-engineer teams be used for this purpose. Engineers were to blast the hedges, tanks were to come up and spray the hedges, and then the infantry would exploit. Mention was made of experiments in the 2d Division with a special hedge cutter made of the steel obstructions found on the beaches. This device, attached to the front of tanks, later proved extremely effective in punching holes through the hedgerows so that tanks and infantry could pour through. (After the war, General Eisenhower revealed that a Sergeant Culin was responsible for this device.)

That evening I saw Dave Garth for the first time since May. He was in his sleeping quarters, the bottom of a ditch up against a hedgerow, with a shelter half suspended like a canopy from branches of the hedge above him. The heavy rain had turned his bed into mud, but he threw down some branches for me to sit on. He had an extra D-ration chocolate bar, so we had our dessert and swapped yarns, stopping now and then to drool over our first meal together in O'Donnell's in Washington some three months before.

Later in the evening Garth introduced me to Major Ray Craft, a California newsman who was aide to Major General Charles H. Corlett, commanding general of XIX Corps. Craft was putting out a corps newspaper—*Le Tomahawk*—signed each day with a new editorial title: Ray (the poor man's Scripps-Howard) Craft, Ray (he never stops) Craft, and the like. Craft had great contempt for the pretty-pretty gush that characterized many editorials and advertisements in American publications of that period, and he put out some savage imitations that were reprinted back in the States. One, satirizing an advertisement which said the men were fighting to get back to mom's blueberry pie, said that the soldiers were fighting to get back to the beauty of cow drippings in their own barnyards and for the right of old Shep to have pups in her own way.

Craft pointed out to us the Marquess of Weymouth, a tall Britisher who had attached himself to the XIX Corps as a sort of liaison man. He gained a reputation for eccentricity because of some of his trips through the German lines and his habit of leading two ducks around on a leash.

General Corlett joined us while we were talking. He had a heavily furrowed face and a stern manner, but he was very considerate and gracious. When he found out I was from Kentucky, he asked about mutual friends at the university, and we talked at some length until Major General Leland S. Hobbs, the 30th Division commander, arrived for a conference.

Tuesday, 27 June (D+21)

I had intended to return to the 29th Division, but the day was taken up with attempts to define our status at V Corps. The G-1, seeing that we were of no value to them and that we took up room which they needed, proposed that we go back to the rear echelon at the next corps move, now that we were far enough in to have both corps forward and corps rear CPs. The corps chief of staff, finding that we were not instructed to write V Corps history, had appointed two captains and a corporal to handle the work. The G-1 suggested that we share a tent with these three and that we report to the adjutant general. I drafted a statement on our status and discussed with Fox a more complete memorandum that he might give to Colonel Matchett, the chief of staff.

That evening we had our first movie since coming ashore. The beach units had seen it five days before, a fact that we noted with indignation just as, no doubt, units forward of us received the news that we were seeing movies. Bing Crosby's *Going My*

Way had been chosen for the night's entertainment. The screen was set up out in the open. Since it was still light, we saw little of what was happening on the screen, but we enjoyed the music. It was growing dark toward the end, and I walked the mile and a half to the motor pool in complete darkness. I went through all the routine that Fox and I had followed several nights before when we thought we were lost, except that this time I actually went a half-mile too far and had to retrace my steps, fearing both a shot from a German straggler and trouble from a trigger-happy sentry who might not expect anyone on foot from that direction at that hour of the night. (Nothing really is much more likely to make one's heart jump into his mouth than a sudden challenge of "Halt!" in the dark, particularly when one hears a quality in the sentry's voice which makes it clear that he is afraid.)

Wednesday, 28 June (D+22)

> *Worked on story of landing. Had talk with Lieutenant ——— of ———*
> *———, Lieutenant Colonel Gamon of G-2 and Lieutenant H.C. Gold-*
> *smith of G-2. Goldsmith, a University of California professor of French . . .*
> *gave me dope on French forces in this area. Valuable material. Is very*
> *careful in statements. He thinks Germans in this section had developed*
> *——— mentality. Most early info came from underground group.*

Thursday, 29 June (D+23)

This was a day for several firsts. We saw baked bread for the first time. The cooks didn't let any out of the kitchen, but we saw it just the same. We were especially unhappy that day because the hard K-ration crackers were difficult to get down without lots of water or coffee. That day also saw our first green vegetables—not dehydrated carrots, but onions and beans from the local market. We also drew our first ration of fruit drops, chewing gum, tooth-paste, and razorblades. The army had worked out a wonderful system for distributing toilet articles. Since the rations were being given away, there was no means of knowing which persons would want razors, toothbrushes, and the like, so they ended up decid-ing that each week one out of ten would get a toothbrush, one out of ten a razor, and so on. They figured that American barter methods would get the commodities into the proper hands. Until Christmas, this style of operation was in vogue.

> *The whistling from ———— ———— guns nearby [?] make me tenser [?] than enemy shells landing nearby. One gets fairly well used to artillery firing which can be heard throughout the day. Sometimes unusually heavy barrages will wake one up at night.*
>
> *Rain during parts of day.*

Friday, 30 June (D+24)

> *Rained. Spent morning discussing our set-up with Lieutenant Fox. Both of us bemoaned the fact that no one has a definite program for us. We are trying to work out something for ourselves.*

Fox and I were called back to First Army by Major O'Sullivan to discuss the policy for the coverage of history. Cherbourg had fallen the day before and Sergeant Bromberg, a battlefield artist who was helping the major at the moment, had brought back from that city some excellent white wine, canned chicken, and two upholstered chairs. The First Army cook, with whom he had gone, had brought back wine and cognac for the messes. White and red wine appeared that evening at the enlisted men's mess as we sat at tables, on benches, and under a canvas roof. Gravel was scattered around so that we would not have to stand in the mud. But there were penalties for this soft living in the form of stricter regulations than we had found up at the front. A mess officer met us at the garbage pail both to make sure that we had eaten all we had been given and that our mess kits were clean. When he saw the dirt on the cover of my kit, he said, "Sergeant, do you know how to get that off." I answered, "Yes, sir, with steel wool." Thinking I was being insubordinate, he said, "I meant sand or rocks." "But I have steel wool," I replied. "Don't talk back to me and get that dirt off," was the clinching final argument. We received news on the thirtieth of Dewey's nomination. I had been in favor of him for some time.

Saturday, 1 July (D+25)

Major O'Sullivan held a big pow-wow of all the First Army historians. Ruppenthal, Lieutenant Harris, and Sergeant Lange were there from VII Corps, Lieutenant Blair Clark from the newly arrived VIII Corps, Ferriss and Garth from XIX Corps, Bromberg from the artists' section of ETOUSA, Fox and myself from V Corps, and Colonel Jones from ETOUSA. We sat around in a circle and each one presented his special problems. The discussion was extremely serious at the outset, but when several of the officers who had just come from Cherbourg started to pass around brandy and liqueurs the tempo began to change. Lieutenant Harris produced a bottle of Cointreau which, in the absence of special glasses, was passed around and drunk out of the bottle as if it had been cider. When that was gone, Colonel Jones, who had entered the citadel of Cherbourg just after it surrendered, produced a bottle of 1893 Armagnac, "compliments of General Schlieben."

At conference found that others thought we had done better than they. All the others had been saddled with special duties in sections, which we never accepted. . . . We seem to have interviewed more people than the others.

As Fox and I started to leave for V Corps that evening, Ruppenthal, who felt sorry for us because we hadn't been to Cherbourg for supplies, gave us a bottle of champagne. It was dark when we returned, so we decided to open it before we went to bed. As the cork popped out with a loud noise, we suddenly heard a gruff voice say, "You are under arrest for having liquor in a combat headquarters." We were a bit shaken until Major McKnight, for it was he, laughed and added: "unless you give me some." So we shared the spoils of Cherbourg with him.

Sunday, 2 July (D+26)

Slept fairly late.

Major O'Sullivan invited Fox and me to go with him to Cherbourg. We left in the early morning in a command car, driven by a nineteen-year-old West Virginia lad named Venable, who had been in the army only nine months and ashore only two or three days. He was properly awed by this trip which took us through Isigny, Carentan, Saint-Mère Eglise, Valognes, Montebourg, and Cherbourg—all of which had recently become part of the American legend and history.

Isigny, now universally pronounced "I see ya," even as nearby La Meauffe was pronounced "Murphy," had changed greatly since 11 June. The debris that had choked the streets then had been pushed away. The streets were now jammed with two lanes of traffic that poured into Isigny, the link to Cherbourg, Utah Beach, Omaha Beach, and the roads leading to St. Lo. At times we didn't move a block in twenty minutes. The people were out in their Sunday best and they waved at us as heartily as if the town had just been liberated. The traffic jam made it possible for the passengers in vehicles to talk with the passersby, and the conversation books furnished by the army were put into use. (The books were not as useful as the daily lessons in the *Stars and Stripes,* one of which had been "My wife doesn't understand me.")

We inched along from Isigny to Carentan, glancing uneasily at signs that still proclaimed, "60 yard intervals—this spot under observation," and the bridges named for men killed during their construction. The country in the peninsula was pretty. From Isigny, the highway gradually went up higher grades until we hit steep hills near Cherbourg. Some of the roads were unusually straight uphill and down dale. Near Saint-Mère Eglise we saw fields still filled with broken gliders. Montebourg and Valognes proved to be badly wrecked. Three or four miles outside Cherbourg we saw fortifications, wire, and mines stretching one or two miles to the right and left of the highway. The guns in this area were strongly encased in concrete and we wondered how the Germans were driven out of those positions.

Overlooking Cherbourg to the right was a great steep cliff atop which was Fort du Roule. This cliff and the smaller hill to its right were scarred from shells. Cherbourg itself did not at first seem hard hit, but we could see great damage as we visited the arsenal and then moved toward the harbor. Most of the warehouses were smashed and several ships had been sunk in the harbor, making it useless for some time.

Later, Fox and I visited the former Todt Organisation[3] headquarters at the Hotel Atlantique and found numerous pamphlets and books in the recreation room. I was struck by the fact that in nearly all of them was the theme of the glory of death in battle. Special monthly bulletins had pages filled with designs of simple monuments that could be erected at battle cemeteries and used to play up the nobility of war. There were also sample memorial service programs and books of quotations emphasizing Germany's greatness and the beauty of war. There was little anti-Allied propaganda here except for several copies of an anti-American book entitled *Das Land Ohne Herz* ("The Country without a Heart"), which purported to be a carefully documented story of life in the United States. Drawing on American writers popular during the depression, it described and showed pictures of breadlines, contrasts of tenements and mansions, attacks of police on strikers, and the like.

The driver and I ate supper outside the Hotel de l'Etoile et de la Normandie, whose neat signs forbade enlisted men to enter one of the few places in the city selling wine (rather ordinary sauterne was 180 francs a bottle). However, the food outside and inside was the same, one K ration coming up. A block away from the hotel at *numero vingt-cinq*, some seventy-five to a hundred soldiers (white and black) were lined up before a house of prostitution formerly run by the Germans. A Frenchman, who noticed my three stripes and may have made the common mistake of assuming it was the same rank as the French captain, said, "You should tell your men to be careful when they are there. The Germans have left much disease." I asked him if many French women had carried on this trade with the Germans. He said that some did for food and some for money, but that the number was not great. I thought of de Maupassant and wondered if there were any like "Boule de Suif" or the girl in "Bel Ami."

The entrance of American troops into Cherbourg had permitted former French soldiers and sailors to appear in uniform for the first time since 1940. Two French naval petty officers who came by stopped to talk of their gladness at being free again. They said they had attempted to hide their service records lest the Germans put them into their navy. They were bitter at the British and made clear that they were glad that we instead of the British armies had liberated them. But they gave the chief credit for our victory to the Russian armies. "Two years ago," they declared, "Germany had 500,000 men in France." You could not have landed against that number. But Russia has bled the Germans white. When the Germans came to Cherbourg, they had vehicles like you have, but now they are vanished toward the East."

In the early days of the occupation, they continued, the German troops had been given great quantities of French money and they had bought nearly everything in the French shops and sent it to Germany. They had thus sent up prices, which made it easier for them to persuade the French to help work for wages on the beach defenses.

I noted that the city seemed well to do. They pointed to mass evacuations of the city by the Germans in 1940 and 1942 that had reduced the population from 40,000 to 6,000–7,000. However, in the three days since the liberation, some 7,000 had come back, and they expected the population to double again within a week. One of the officers, who had traveled widely in France since 1940, said that France was not to be judged by Normandy. "We are rich, but in the cities and in the Midi, there is much misery."

The Frenchmen spoke of considerable Gaullist sentiment in Cherbourg, and added that he would stand up to the British (I assumed from their tone that they meant to the Americans as well). Laval's followers had left with the coming of the Americans, although a few Germans, in civilian clothes, were believed to be still in the city. "They will not be hard to find," they insisted, "he cannot hide his face, because he remains always the German." They added that the Germans had tried to make friends in Cherbourg by giving popular concerts on market days, but everyone had left when the band began to play.

The petty officers hoped that the peace settlement with Germany would be dictated by Russia. "She is not too easy." And they hoped that this was the last of German aggression. "Is there a chance for them to come back?" they asked anxiously. They hoped, and this was a common hope which we heard often expressed, that the war was finished for France. They were sanguine over the chances of Paris's liberation by September, and they believed this might bring the end of the war since the city meant so much to the Germans. They thought that the Germans were good soldiers, but without imagination. Here in Cherbourg, they noted, all their guns pointed out to the sea.

One of the petty officers, accompanied by his wife, had been in Paris a month before the invasion. The Eiffel Tower still stood; Maurice Chevalier was no collaborationist.[4] The main part of the city was intact, but from Montmartre one could look out on desolation where the great factories of the suburbs had stood. In Brest, which they had also visited, B-17 Flying Fortresses had destroyed nearly everything. Many people had finally decided not to go to their shelters, preferring dying in their beds to suffocation in their cellars. Food in the cities was very scarce, and many people lived only by going out in the country to seek food.

After the Frenchmen had gone on their way, I walked about a bit in the city, examining some posters the Germans had left behind. One out-of-date one showed a map of Italy with British and American forces located near the boot's heel. A snail was shown slowly crawling up the boot and written above in English it said, "It's a long way to Rome." Unfortunately for them, Rome had fallen even before they left the city. The most effective poster I saw was one showing a pitiful mother holding her child, who had been killed by American bombs, and saying, "They who commit these outrages shall be paid back in kind."

Our people had not bothered to take down the posters, but were beginning to substitute some of our own. Our most popular handout at the moment was not propaganda, but a small newspaper giving in capsule form *Les Dernières Nouvelles de Guerre* (most recent news from the war).

Monday, 3 July (D+27)

Rained most of the night. Awakened to find myself in mud. Got wet and muddy crawling out from under truck. Rained most of the morning.

The trip to Cherbourg, which ended in pouring rain that soaked us on our way back to corps, ended the first phase of our combat history gathering ashore. Until that time, we were without real guidance and without real mobility, since no organic transportation was available at army or corps for us and we were forced to rely upon the goodwill of the units and the availability of their transportation for our means of getting about. Some of our historians had been seized on eagerly by their units and had been set to work doing various jobs of the sections to which they were assigned. Lieutenant Fox and I had held out against such assignments, but had been somewhat divorced from the sections to which we were attached. Because of the relative freedom which we had, we did succeed in getting a number of interviews, so that by the end of the month we had a number of fragmentary stories to form some basis for a story of D-Day and the period just following. In our meeting at First Army on 2 July, we found that our own jeeps would soon be in Normandy and that we would be in a position to carry on our work in a more systematic manner. It would be less interesting for us, since we would not have as much opportunity to hang out at the crossroads and talk to passersby or to wait around the liaison tents and hear the rumors and gossip that were brought in, but it meant that we could do far more serious work on the task of collecting material for an integrated history of the battles.

Chapter 9

Writing History for a Change

Tuesday, 4 July (D+28)–Monday, 17 July (D+41)

Tuesday, 4 July (D+28)

Up at 10:30. . . . Worked all of the afternoon on records. Lieutenant Colonel Jones came up. Bromberg and I had a long talk about Daumier, and others.[5]

Heavy barrage at night. New attack began the day before along VII and VIII Corps front.

On the eve of Independence Day, Major O'Sullivan sent a jeep for me and asked that I come to First Army for several days to write a preliminary history of the landings on Omaha Beach. He felt that I could be spared from interviews on current actions because the American forces were in an almost static position in the Saint-Lô area. Stubborn German resistance in the hedgerows limited our advance to what seemed yards each day, and the horrible weather made effective air support impossible. So the time was taken in piling up supplies near the beach and in planning an air-ground offensive that would knock a hole in the German lines near Saint-Lô and permit the U.S. First Army, which would be joined later by the U.S. Third Army, to swing south to Avranches and then westward into Brittany, while other units prepared for a drive eastward in company with the British. The major had sent for me that day his newly arrived jeep and driver. The latter, Private First Class José Manuel Topete, was to become one of my best friends and was to work closely with me during some six months of the war.

Born in Mexico, Topete had come to California while still in high school and had later gone to the University of California at Berkeley to study Spanish literature. He had completed his master's degree and was working toward his doctorate when he had the choice of returning to Mexico or of entering the American army. He had chosen, as he put it, the privilege of fighting. The army, having no use for a Spanish-speaking expert, had found him a place as a tank driver. He had come to England as a replacement, waiting for some armored unit to call him for combat duty. While at the replacement center, he heard that Headquarters, ETOUSA, was looking for historians. Since he had done research in Mexican documents for the history department at Berkeley, he applied for a transfer. When he arrived in London, there were no spots immediately vacant, but there was a need for jeep drivers and Topete, on the strength of his tank driving, was assigned to Major O'Sullivan in Bristol. On his first drive, he took some curves rather fast and showed other signs of unfamiliarity with jeep driving. On interrogation, it was found that he had never been instructed in that subject and that, indeed, he had never driven a car. The major hastily assigned Captain Howe the task of teaching Topete this new art—a task which was described in several reports of the First Army historical team to ETOUSA. At the end of two weeks Topete was officially declared to be a jeep driver and he set out for First Army with his new jeep—which he christened *"La Cucaracha."*

Wednesday, 5 July (D+29)

> *Moved to new location near Vauilly. Got set up by three P.M. Washed clothes—first time I had changed trousers since leaving London April 28. The trousers hadn't been cleaned since I left Memphis in March. Took a bath (in ice cold water)—an event. We are in another apple orchard. We have the tent well underneath it and I have my desk out in front.*
>
> *The Major got some brandy which we helped him drink. It cost him 260 francs ($5.20) for a bottle.*
>
> *Lieutenant Fox and Topete came up at night.*

After a few days at VII Corps and First Army, Topete came to us at V Corps, where he was to stay until the end of the war. During that time he became adept at driving, without knowing the fundamentals, in the way some people become fluent in a language without knowing its grammar. He allowed me to criticize his driving because, at his worst, he did better than I, who could not drive at all. I know he must have driven well because we never had an accident. But he drove with his characteristic individualism well in evidence, not caring whether he was on the side of the road intended for him, whether he was observing the rules concerning the use of brakes at certain points, or whether he was keeping his hands on the wheel when driving and talking rapidly. He would have been most at home in Paris, where the emphasis is on the horn and not the brakes, and where a fine command of language substitutes for the finer points of knowledge on how to conduct a *"voiture."* Topete never openly resented any of my remarks about his driving, but once, when the two of us were riding in a jeep with another driver at the wheel, he noticed that I was being very nonchalant and roared at me, "You are not holding on to the windshield." Yet during the awful period of the Bulge when there was ice and mud, and drives through darkness in rain, wind, and snow, he managed always to get home. So well was he known and liked by the MPs that he would hail them in the dark as we came in from some late drive, and they would say, "Pass Pete," without bothering to ask the password. He had trouble with some of the cooks, but made a friend of the mess sergeant who saw that food was saved for us when we went out on a long trip. As for the motor pool, he played a politicians' game. He collected cigar rations from the three nonsmokers in our section and handed them on to the motor pool sergeant. It thus was not difficult to get a needed tire or some extra help in doing the repair work on the jeep, although technically First Army and not V Corps was responsible for the vehicle. Only once did the system fail. Once, when on the road between Naumburg and Leipzig, we tore up a tire so that it could not be fixed, he hitched a ride back some ten miles to the corps CP to get help while I remained with the vehicle. It was growing dark and cold. Topete found that the regular sergeant had gone forward to a new CP, leaving behind someone in charge for whom he had done no favors. When the chap refused to give him a tire, Topete adopted the coldly formal air he sometimes assumed, and said, "I regret that I have to pull rank, but I have promised Sergeant Pogue I will bring back a tire and I intend to do it." So he called a major, and with some embellishments explained our plight and the importance of our mission (I am still not sure but that he told them I was carrying the message to Garcia), and got an order for the motor pool attendant to bring out a tire to the jeep. Later, Pete saw to it that the man bore no grudge.

One quality that made enlisted men like Topete was the high hand he took with officers and the top-grade sergeants. There was one occasion when, with colossal gall, he told one of the two captains with whom he was working, "I hereby appoint Captain ———— my boss, and I will take no orders from you." The thing was so colossal that it worked. Yet the captain in question saw to it that Topete was promoted on two occasions when a vacancy came up. One prank he played on a group of officers nearly disrupted a court-martial when a colonel and four other officers one day took over our office for the trial of a soldier for indecent exposure. Just before he left the office, Topete arranged on the desk which the colonel was to use four statuettes of the little boy of Brussels who is famous the world over for doing there in public what the soldier was charged with doing in another Belgian city. The sight of the statuettes nearly destroyed the decorum of the trial, and we always believed it responsible for mitigating the sentence of the soldier.

But Topete most liked to needle me into saying things to people who tried to get difficult in interviews. Knowing that I still had orders which I had brought from the Pentagon, he would sometimes whisper in my ear when an officer proved recalcitrant about answering questions, "Intimidate him with the War Department, Pogue." There was the occasion when a white-haired colonel, hearing me ask one of his officers about his casualties, had said testily, "I'll tell the sergeant the facts of life." He had then lit into me and similar parasites, making it clear that he had a war to win and no time to fool with a bunch of nonsense like this, when Topete said, quite audibly, "Sergeant, you don't have to take this, let's go." Inspired by his angry statement, which had jolted the colonel for a moment into shocked quietness, I said, "Yes Colonel, I am here under orders and I am required only to get the information or to report to First Army why I did not." The colonel, who was angry at the moment because he felt that his unit was being badly handled by higher headquarters, said calmly, "Sit down, Sergeant, and I will tell you what you want to know." And for nearly an hour, to the amazement of his staff, he did just that. And then there was the time in the Huertgen Forest when a colonel had virtually thrown us out of his CP and we had gone a week without attempting to get his account of the action. Finally he came to the room where we slept and told Topete, who was standing in a pan of warm water trying to get some feeling back into his cold feet, that he had some interesting information on the action we were covering. Topete grinned and said, "Shall we take his story, Sergeant." I told him yes, if he wanted to, and he, with the grand air that one of his ancestors (he said that he was descended from a General Topete and from the Spanish admiral of the War of 1898, Pascual Cervera y Topete, Marques of Jerez and Santa Ana) might have used, condescended to take the colonel's story. Later, at the end of the war, when Topete saw the colonel again, the latter shook Pete by the hand and told his staff, "Give this man what he wants." Topete responded by bestowing on the colonel one of his peppers.

Of course, I never undertook to control this remarkable driver, a fact that officers and men of corps headquarters readily understood. Once, when we had been arrested for speeding in a ten-mile-an-hour zone, I was taken before the corps commandant for punishment. When he asked who was driving and I said "Topete," he took a lenient view of the whole case. After asking if I was going to the movies that night, and I replied in the affirmative, he told me that I was ordered to go to the theater and prevent fires from breaking out. He solemnly wrote across the notification of my speeding offense the words, "Proper company punishment imposed." I told Topete that the commandant had said that he considered riding with him punishment enough.

Topete had an eye for a pretty girl, but his chief affection was for *La Cucaracha*. He had a scholar's aversion for manual labor and a masterly dislike of dirt. But for *La Cucaracha* he would work in grease and grime—unless, Tom Sawyer-like, he could persuade the motor pool men to do the messiest jobs by pretending he couldn't understand the directions on how to perform first-echelon maintenance. He had great confidence in the jeep and would talk to it soothingly when he got stuck in mud or deep snow. Topete's interest in the war never seemed the same after the end of February 1945, when for a time we had to lend the jeep to Joe Webber. He got her into tough scrapes, got three shots into her, and brought her back dirty, limp, and uncertain on her tires. But she made a magnificent comeback and was with us at the finish. Few jeeps had so proud a history. In on Omaha Beach in late June; a close student of the roads of Normandy and Brittany; into Paris for the liberation parade; early into Belgium, Luxembourg, and Germany with V Corps; frequenter of the Ardennes and the Huertgen Forest; in the hands of a borrower an early visitor to the Remagen Bridge and the east bank of the Rhine; and present at the link-up between the American and Russian forces at Torgau. What a history she had! Wound stripes, her wheels wet with wine if not with blood, reliable and trustworthy, *La Cucaracha* deserves a fair tribute.

Topete never had trouble finding information in a new town. Through his friends the MPs, who at least on one occasion even dug a foxhole for him, he knew everything that was going on. I saw him in Paris two days after he got there and found that although there were only a few bistros open past 9 P.M., he had discovered them all.

Topete was the type of soldier on whom army legends are built. When he swung his carbine carelessly over his shoulder and jumped into the jeep, which he drove with a flourish, one could imagine that here was a *caballero* come to life. There was the tradition of the *caballero* in the way he collected weapons: a carbine, a rifle, and two or three pistols. Bromberg said once when he was taking photographs of German prisoners that Topete turned up in so many of the shots, it seemed for a moment as if Franco was furnishing men for the whole German army. One day I found him giving my caramels to German children who had presented him with Easter eggs and saying, when I looked at him accusingly, "Hell, you can't hate kids."

I arrived at First Army in time for the Fourth of July. In honor of the day, every gun in the field fired one round. The day was filled with speeches in liberated cities, and our sound trucks went about playing "La Marseillaise," "God Save the King," and "The Star-Spangled Banner."

Much of the Fourth for us was taken up with preparations for a move. So far, at corps, Fox and I had missed all the headquarters' moves. But here I had blundered in on a worse one. For an army is more trouble to move than a circus. First there had to be mimeographed orders of movement, with lines of movement sketched out so that we would not block supply routes and lines of march. Staggered hours were arranged for truck loading, areas set up for assembling, and the like. To make matters worse, we had to wait much of the day, since we were to move with the rear-echelon units. We shared with psychological warfare and chemical warfare a place in the rear and the dubious honor of having been given a derisive nickname. For the three were now known as "pizzological warfare," "comical warfare," and the "hysterical section." The fourth member of our group, the chaplain's section, did not receive any special title.

In the later days, when we had a truck to ourselves and it was possible to throw in the section tent, half folded and tied, it was far simpler than now. We were sharing a truck with two other sections and it meant that the wet and heavy tent had to be carefully folded and squeezed until it took only a small part of the truck. Since we were shorthanded, Bromberg having gone forward, Jerry (the major) and I were faced with the task of loading the truck by ourselves. Fortunately, in the days preceding the move, Jerry's Irish brogue had attracted a group of friends—"the Russians" he called them: Kelly, Sullivan, and perhaps an O'Reilly. When they saw the major struggling away with ropes and canvas, they pitched in and we soon got the truck loaded.

The last minutes at an old camp were taken up with filling in foxholes, sewage sumps, and latrines. In the latter case, signs were erected with the name "Latrine" and the date when it was filled. *Stars and Stripes* got the laugh of the week with a yarn about a group of Frenchmen, seeing one of the grave-like mounds with name and date on it, had decorated it with flowers.

Once the trucks were loaded they went to assembly areas, from which at specified times they moved toward the new area. To aid the unwary, signs labeled "MASTER MAIN" pointed the way. Many times, instead of putting them up, headquarters personnel merely hung the signs around the necks of the MPs, who thus were made to look like pickets.

Parties had gone ahead to put up signs in a convenient orchard in sites chosen for the facility with which they could be hidden, for their nearness to roads, and for the space they provided for tents. This move took us to a point near Vouilly. We were back in the orchards again—the blossoms had now disappeared and small, green, knobby apples were beginning to appear.

Bromberg had preceded us to stake our claim to the site, which had been marked out for us. It had become clear from other movers that if someone else could get his tent up on your site, he could always claim he had misread the map and was unlikely to be forced to take his canvas down again. We were located in the center of a field next to the chaplain, with the result that the major was frequently mistaken for him. Nearby we dug our trenches for shelter in case of bombing. White-taped lines indicated the places to walk so that no one would fall over tent ropes in the dark. The tents were erected so that they got as much coverage as possible from the trees, and we then spread the heavy, smelly camouflage netting over the canvas. Our location was not the best in the world, but we were only three minutes from the Lister bag, so we did not have far to carry water very far. Ultimately, the major's "Russian" friends volunteered to bring him a five-gallon can of water each day.

In the course of the move, a found a five-gallon water bucket someone had thrown away. So, near dark, I heated water and washed my trousers, the first time I had changed them since leaving London on 28 April. I had saved the clean pair on the mistaken assumption that there might be an occasion when I would need them for an important interview.

Lieutenant Fox and Topete came up in the evening and we shared a bottle of brandy the major had bought that day for $5.20. Fox entertained us with the story of the exchange of German nurses taken at Cherbourg. Captain Quentin Roosevelt of the 1st Division had made part of the arrangements. In accordance with the agreement, three officers and a noncommissioned officer had come to division headquarters under a flag of truce. The sentries they met waved them on to the tent where the nurses were. When they arrived, the German officer in charge asked if he could send for enlisted men to carry the luggage. His request was granted and he waved his arm, at which signal four soldiers came out of concealment. The next morning, two of the Germans surrendered. They said the stories the nurses told had convinced them they would be treated well. They added that the nurses had spoken so well of their treatment by the Americans that they were at last shut away from the enlisted men. The two deserters pointed out to our G-2 officers machine-gun positions that had been set up to hit U.S. patrols. They indicated that our uniform was easily seen and that we invited ambushes by patrolling at the same time each day.

The major and talked late into the night after Fox and Topete went back to corps that evening. We had moved our blankets into the office tent that day and did not return to the pup tents during the remainder of our stay. The arrangement was conducive to late-night conversations.

Jerry and I were pessimistic about the postwar world. We agreed that, barring a miracle, the countries of the world would be more statized than ever after the war. We were also fearful of new totalitarian movements in the United States and elsewhere. We dreaded the effects of another great depression, particularly when we had many former high-ranking reserve officers and noncommissioned officers who had learned what power was and who would not be content to beg. It was clear that it was not just former officers who might make trouble—after all, Hitler had been only a corporal in World War I. We thought that the GI Bill of Rights might cushion the postwar readjustment.

We were also worried about England's weakness, her lack of reserves, her dangerous economic position, and the possible effect that this weakness would have on international politics after the war. Jerry was more realistic than I when it came to Russia. He predicted increased power and greater totalitarianism in the Soviet Union, and warned that the Russians would supplant Hitler as the greatest menace to the West. I was not as worried as he because I thought, as many in higher places did then, that Russia would be too weak to cause trouble for at least twenty-five years.

In talking about the possible disillusionment among those who might argue that we had set up a group of ideals to fight for and then had not achieved them, we agree that there would not be the same basis for this that there was after the First World War, since the administration and the army had deliberately avoided stressing the idealistic approach that in 1920–25 gave rise to jeers over "make the world safe for democracy." Arguing with the major, whose Irish background led him to say it looked as if we were fighting to save the British again, I pointed out that we were fighting because it was not in our interest to let any power, in this case Germany, become preponderant in Europe. We had come to a balance of power position just as the British had before us.

After scaring ourselves to death for two or three hours, we finally went to sleep.

For the next ten days I wrote on the history of the Omaha Beach landings while ducking frequent showers that were doubly annoying because much of the time there were no lights for the tents and I had to type on a little camp desk under an apple tree. However, I had the comfort of an armchair looted from Cherbourg and did not have to sit on a water can. The first night we had lights, I worked so late that I failed to notice it was after blackout time (about 2330) until the telephone rang and I was reprimanded for violating security regulations.

The major and I continued our evening sessions, one night sitting over a bottle of cognac the chaplain had given him and discussing the Crusades, the Renaissance, popes, and great professors of history.

Thursday, 6 July (D+30)

Worked all day on material for narrative on Omaha landing. Washed clothes.

Friday, 7 July (D+31)

Intermittent rains.

Saturday, 8 July (D+32)

. . . Howe is to go with Ruppenthal; Lange is to come back here. Lieutenant Colonel Taylor is to work on records, Lieutenant Colonel Marshall is

to gather small details; I am to work ahead on Omaha Beachhead with hope of getting a Technical Sergeant rating.

Typed along steadily, grinding out 25 pages on the narrative.

Talked late with the Major. Rained intermittently all day; only one day in the past week that it hasn't rained some.

Showers have been set up.

Headquarters had been set up in a chateau, and there were rooms for officers according to rank. The major enjoyed telling a yarn about the first night this new arrangement had been set up when a crusty full colonel called the commandant and said, "There's a lieutenant colonel in the house, get him out." The new bunch, Jerry said, was getting tough about uniforms, saluting, and the like. They had begun to bring in housekeeping detachments to wait on officers, and were bringing in many extra items of issue of officers and men. This was the first of many explosions I was to hear from him and others about "the rear echelon," "SOS," and so on. Always the plaint was the same: "We do the work and they get the gravy." We had noticed some differences between corps and the beach parties, three miles away, after the first week, but until Cherbourg fell every unit was so near the front that nearly every unit shared the common danger to some extent. Now it seemed that part of the units were far enough back to enjoy the war.

Sunday, 9 July (D+33)

Skies overcast.

Monday, 10 July (D+34)

Cloudy and apparently ready to rain again. We escaped the rain but the sun stayed in. . . . Worked away on Omaha story.

Tuesday, 11 July (D+35)

Overcast. Sun tried to come out. Word that Caen has fallen.

Wednesday, 12 July (D+36)

Sun shown rather brightly at times. Got some washing out. Somewhat cool.

My work was disturbed from time to time by the appearance of a character who had attached himself to an officer of our acquaintance. His experiences were so amazing that we all talked of them and, sometimes unkindly, cited his case as an example of the errors made by the army. The officer in question had been before a reclassification board in England and was all set to be sent home, but was given two days in which to find another spot. He was lucky to find a lieutenant colonel who needed a vehicle and driver, and who offered to take the officer to Normandy if he could find a jeep and act as chauffeur. The junior officer hitched a boat ride to Omaha Beach and then set about looking for a vehicle. According to his account, which he repeated frequently as if it were a good joke, he found a navy jeep chained to a log. Since it appeared to be jettisoned, he persuaded a guard to help him break the chain, and he got paint from someone else and erased the navy's markings from the bumper—just in case they hadn't actually thrown it away.

He and the colonel scoured the countryside on inspection trips in the newly requisitioned jeep. Contrary to orders, they billeted themselves in a French home and soon became favorites of the family, receiving eggs, fresh raspberries, and chicken in return for sugar, coffee, and other commodities which the junior officer drew from ration depots for a mythical company he claimed to be serving with. This was in the early days, when an officer or high-ranking sergeant with a combat patch and a positive look could draw provisions simply by demanding them. The colonel said that the other officer was most successful in stoking the larder, and the junior officer said that anything was yours as long as it was not tied down and that it was yours if you could get a guard to help you steal it. The colonel had been a good officer in the First World War and had worked hard as a civilian, but he seemed now to be interested mostly in enjoying the war, so with an officer driver, a stolen jeep, requisitioned rations, and an elastic assignment, he found life in the French chateau where he lived, as he put it, "*très soigné.*"

But such a good life could not always last for the junior officer. The time came when the colonel's jeep and driver arrived from England, and the question came up as to what should be done with the officer driver and the stolen jeep, which now, for the first time, weighed a little on the colonel's conscience. While the colonel and other officers discussed the matter, the junior officer disappeared and brought back several cartons of cigarettes and other hard-to-get items, which he handed to the colonel. Later, the colonel declared in the tone one would use in speaking of a smart retriever: "He knew we were talking about him, so he went off and got those things from somebody's tent." He agreed that the junior officer should be kicked out, but felt it wrong to use a man and then get rid of him. So he then asked a lower-ranking officer in his organization to use the man awhile and, "When he gets so you can't stand him, I'll take him again."

The major and I waxed indignant over the affair, since the man was getting officer's pay for procuring commodities. We spoke of the colonel's new driver, a corporal, who was a good high school teacher, but no scrounger. But the colonel had said that no matter what his former driver was, he was an officer, and we should treat him with courtesy. In my anger, I wrote that day: "Surely the meek have inherited the *earth*; the others have bedrolls, cots, and orderly service."

Thursday, 13 July (D+37)

Rained last night and early this morning. Sky overcast.

Friday, 14 July (D+38)

Sun tried to shine a little, but it still got cloudy. Wrote all day on story of the 115th Regiment.

Saturday, 15 July (D+39)

Beginning to get tired.

Sunday, 16 July (D+40)

The usual routine was broken on 16 July by a visit from Hal Boyle of the Associated Press and John Hall of the *London Daily Mail*. They thought we were the historical monuments group and had come to ask what had become of the Bayeux tapestries. Since we had no information on them, the newsmen asked about our historical program, which I outlined. I reminded Boyle of the stories he had written while in North Africa, where a friend of his had put up signs reading, "Vote for Hal, the Arab's pal," and "Vote for Boyle, the son of the soil." Boyle wrote some of the most honest accounts of the fighting, and Hall, in the early days at least, wrote some of the most complimentary stories published about American soldiers. These two correspondents, in common with Ernie Pyle and Don Whitehead, had the reputation for going where the news was and in asking for no special favors.

On the sixteenth I completed the hundred-page summary on the landings and was told I could go back to corps in order to collect material on the breakout which was expected in a few days. The trip back was very roundabout because Topete, Fox, and I had to go to VII Corps, near Katz, to get the major. We visited Ruppenthal, who was covering that corps' history. He told us that the corps, commanded by Major General J. Lawton Collins, was in the throes of preparation for a great drive around 24 July. We left near dark, piling four people in the jeep along with three bedrolls, two duffel bags, two boxes of documents, and some musette bags. The major, Topete, and I squeezed in the front seat, while Fox rode in the rear on the debris.

Monday, 17 July (D+41)

Weather beautiful. Wrote all day and into night on material for operation report on first 14 days of V Corps.

R E S T R I C T E D

HEADQUARTERS V CORPS
APO 305

17 July 1944.

CIRCULAR)
)   HISTORY OF V CORPS
NO....39)

1. Section 1, Circular No. 20, and Circulars No. 34, 36, and 37, this headquarters, current series, are rescinded.

2. The attention of all commanders is directed to AR 345-105, and changes
thereto, pertaining to Histories of Organizations.

3. Two Combat Historians have been attached to this headquarters, from
Headquarters, ETOUSA, and G-2, War Department, in accordance with a plan approved
by the Commanding General, First U.S. Army, for the purpose of assisting in the
gathering of material relative to the operational history of V Corps and subordinate units. These historians are 1st Lt. WILLIAM J. FOX and Sgt FORREST C.
POGUE, Jr.

4. Two Historians have been appointed in Headquarters V Corps, assigned to
the G-3 Section, and attached to the AG Section, for the purpose of gathering and
preserving unit historical material and preparing a V Corps Operational History.
These historians are Captain LYNN G. GRIMSON and Captain LESTER K. BORN.

5. The purposes of the historical program of the War Department, Headquarters
ETOUSA, and Headquarters V Corps, are:

    a. To insure the preservation and completeness of all sources of
material on operations, including adequate journals, written orders, the recording of oral orders and decisions, maps and overlays, estimates of the situation,
notations of informal conferences, and other such pertinent items.

    b. To prepare an overall Campaign Study of V Corps' part in operations.

    c. To prepare special monographs on certain key operations for immediate
War Department publication in a series of pamphlets desired by the Chief of Staff
for distribution to men participating in these actions.

    d. To assist and advise commanders and staffs and unit historians in
preparation of Reports of Operations, Battles and Engagements and in gathering
and preparing unit historical material.

6. Unit Historical Officers will be designated as follows:

    a. Separate battalions will designate one officer; regiments and lar-
ger units will designate officers as they deem necessary, but will appoint at
least one officer. The historical officer is to act as such in addition to his
other duties. His duty will be to assemble and submit all historical matter
pertinent to his unit, including a short running account of unit operations, with
small unit activities of human interest value included. Names of these officers
will be submitted to the Historical Section, Headquarters V Corps.

- 1 -
R E S T R I C T E D

Sergeant Pogue's orders from V Corps.

Chapter 10

The Breakout at Saint-Lô

Tuesday, 18 July (D+42)–Sunday, 30 July (D+54)

Tuesday, 18 July (D+42)

The long awaited fall of Saint-Lô took place on 18 July, but my diary bears no mention of it. We heard firing a few miles to our right during the day, but no report that the town had been taken. Since the 29th Division was no longer in our corps, there were at our headquarters none of the periodic messages that would have told of the steady advance of the special task force that pushed into the city.

Good weather.

Special service group came in during night. One was Jack Hieful—a former student from Astabula, Ohio—and another was Howard McClain from Murray (I gave his commencement address in 1936). Worked away on material for report.

Wednesday, 19 July (D+43)

Cloudy. Talked about fact that Germans haven't attacked convoys. Spoke of fact that Germans may draw forces back from ——— France and prepare for attack east of Paris.
Saw list of divisions. British have 5 and we have 4 corps. They have 14 and we have 16 divisions over. We have destroyed 6 German divisions. They have 26 divisions opposed to us.

The nineteenth was extremely busy because corps headquarters, angry at conflicting instructions on combat history issued by Headquarters, ETOUSA, and First Army, had canceled its circulars on the matter. Headquarters, ETOUSA, was requiring journals to be sent in by units promptly at the end of each month, while army and corps headquarters were requiring after-action reports that required the use of journals. Thus the day was taken up with efforts on the part of the corps historians to placate angry divisional chiefs of staff and adjutants general. Captain Grimson and Captain Lester K. Born, a newly arrived colleague of Grimson's, handled most of this burden. Fox and I helped some, but we weren't of sufficient rank to deal with angry colonels on the telephone. The matter was finally resolved by an agreement that the divisions could keep their journals a few days in order to write their reports. Many of them ultimately solved the matter by keeping a duplicate journal.

Thursday, 20 July (D+44)

Cloudy all day. Rain at night. Rather warm in the P.M.

During the day, we got a chance to look at recent casualty figures which indicated what the war was costing us and the enemy. It was estimated that we had destroyed six German divisions, while suffering on our side ten thousand dead, fifty thousand wounded, and four thousand missing. The 79th and 4th Divisions led the casualty list with six thousand to eight thousand each, and the 29th Division came next with five thousand. We were upset by reports that the British had lost 131 tanks against forty-six Germans tanks in the day's fighting. In the course of discussing these statistics, we recalled that ten days before there were supposed to be a million men ashore, and began to estimate how many riflemen there probably were at that time actually firing at the enemy. Our figures were likely full of errors, but our process of reasoning showed vividly the small number of men who actually fire rifles in the army. We began by subtracting hundreds of thousands of rear-echelon personnel in headquarters, supply units, service units, postal units, quartermaster dumps, water purification units, guard units, psychological warfare units, and a dozen others. Then out of each corps we estimated that at least one of the three divisions was in reserve, that out of each of the divisions in the line there was likely a regiment in reserve, and of each regiment a battalion, and of each battalion a company, and of each company a platoon in reserve. Subtract from the companies the mortars and automatic weapons, the aid men, the supply men, the mail orderlies, and the dead, wounded, and missing, and it seemed likely that of one million men ashore on 8 July there might have been seven thousand with rifles in their hands prepared to shoot at or shooting at the enemy.

At night we went to First Army to see Colonel Taylor, who was making an attempt to straighten out the matter of historical records. He told us that the historical section was now established firmly in the army by a special order that organized us into service units, attached to army groups, with our own tables of organization and tables of equipment. It meant that we could now have tents and jeeps and typewriters by right and not by sufferance, and that perhaps there might be some promotions.

While we were at First Army, Captain Ferriss arrived with news of the Saint-Lô battle. He also told us the touching story of Major Howie. The major had said that he was going into Saint-Lô and when he was killed leading the way into the city his men had taken him in and placed his casket on the rubble of the cathedral of Saint-Lô. Later I saw this story, in much this form, become a legend. One correspondent wrote after the war that the major, leading his men to the outskirts of Saint-Lô was killed during a heavy fight, and that his men, fired up by his example, had driven into the city, carrying the body of the major with them. Later, Dave Garth wrote the official story, based on interviews, division telephone journals, and reports. It is clear that the major was killed shortly after a conference as he stood talking with other officers on a little hill near Saint-Lô. His men were not inspired to take the city, because the men who took it were from a different unit under the command of Brigadier General Norman Cota, who was wounded in the fight. The body of the major was being evacuated in the usual way when the commanding general of the division, General Gerhardt, a man with a flair for the dramatic, demanded that the body be found and taken into Saint-Lô. Then, after the first units were in the city and it was secure, the major's body was taken in by ambulance and placed on the rubble of the cathedral where the men who passed it saluted it and threw flowers upon it. Told in its true form, it was a good story, a fine tribute to a fine soldier, and worthy of the tribute in the *New York Times*, which read, "in the manner of the Cid of old, the body of the major was taken into St. Lo."

Friday, 21 July (D+45)

The most disgusting weather I had experienced since D-Day was on 21 July. We had had rain regularly, but this time our cup ran over. And, to make it worse, I was especially prepared to get the worst of it. I had inherited a cot at First Army from Lieutenant French, who was on his way to England, and Topete had been good enough to set it up in a nice hedgerow under some bushes. I went to sleep, thinking how pleasant it was to get out in the open again after sleeping in a tent. When I heard it raining, I worried about the people who were sleeping on the ground. But soon I realized what the cot had done to me. The canvas caught the water as it hit the foot of the cot and funneled it evenly underneath my blankets so that I was thoroughly soaked when I awakened. It was my first experience in gaining consciousness in about six inches of water. When I put out my bare foot it met mud, and then there was the problem of dressing under dripping hedges. Fortunately, my trousers, which had served as a pillow, were dry. But by the time I stuck my muddy feet into them, I had to change again. I found that everyone had the same experience. Captain Born cheered us with his story of finding two inches of water in the seat of the jeep when he got in it to go to the morning briefing at the forward CP. The driver was not perturbed, however—he calmly handed the captain a bulky army manual to sit on. Born looked at the manual's subject: Waterproofing.

Saturday, 22 July (D+46)

And the next day it rained! The blankets were still wet, and I had given up my cot to sleep on the ground with a shelter half under me. And what a night's sleep! At first I was wet and clammy. Then, as the heat from my body developed steam, I roasted and awakened clawing at the blankets, which began to smell like a stable. It was more than a week before the sun shone enough to dry them, so every night it was a matter of choosing the least wet blanket to put next to me, and then going through the process of steaming and roasting again.

We moved that rainy morning to a new location south of Balleroy and the Forêt de Cerisy. The country began to change in appearance. There were fewer hedges and orchards and the area was more densely forested and marked by higher hills. The Forêt de Cerisy had been impressively marked on our maps with a great green blotch. It had worried the invasion planners, as they feared that it might hide reinforcements and great stores of ammunition. They had insisted repeatedly that the air forces burn these woods, until the airmen made clear at last that the project was hopeless. Happily, the forest had hidden only small forces and stores, and these had been bypassed by rapid thrusts of the 1st Division. But our artillery had taken no chances and a great center had been chewed out of the woods. By the time we reached there, we found in the midst of splintered trees a traffic circle where convoys from Bayeux toward Saint-Lô and from Vire to Trevières and the beach converged. Six days before there had been Germans here; now there were smartly appearing MPs directing the heavy traffic that rolled past.

In the afternoon we put up our pyramidal office tent, a great, heavy affair of canvas and camouflage netting. The ground was slippery and the poles and tenting cumbersome for our small gang to handle. Fortunately for the enlisted men (Topete, Corporal Kelly, and myself), we had the aid of Captain Born and Lieutenant Fox. Born, a two-hundred-pound Ph.D. who had once taught Latin and then worked with OPA before going into the army as a reserve artillery officer, and Fox both lent a hand. Born did the heavy work on the center pole lifting, and Fox later climbed the tent to do the work of attaching the ropes to the pole.

Once the tent was raised, we ducked out to dig our foxholes. I didn't have the MPs to "Tom Sawyer" into digging me a hole like Topete did, so I sweated away. Despite the new directive that said we should dig deep holes, cover them with a log or branch roof, and then cover that with two or three layers of sandbags, we worked rather slowly. However, after about an hour, enemy artillery opened up on the forward CP and hit some nine to eleven people ("these statistics strictly rumor" says my diary). Mindful of the fact that we were about as far forward as the forward CP, we got busy and dug on through gravel to a four-foot level, with deeper digging promised on the morrow. Torn-up K-ration boxes furnished linings for the holes, branches of nearby trees furnished the covering, and I found that newly cut hay from the field we were in when put inside my gas protective coveralls made an effective, though odorous, substitute for a typical army straw mattress. The big story of the night came from Captain Born and Lieutenant Fox, who were digging their foxholes when the shells fell nearby. When the scare was over they found that they had grabbed their helmets and hastened to put their feet into the four-inch deep hole they had just finished digging. The immediate effect of the shelling was an order requiring us to stand two yards apart in the chow line. We were able to reflect on the fact, while waiting for food, that part of us could get fed if the others were hit.

Sunday, 23 July (D+47)

> Slept late. In afternoon completed writing material for Colonel Taylor on D-Day manuscript. Took it up at suppertime to Master. Colonel Taylor was very complimentary. Helped the Major drink some rum which he had acquired. Home late with Lieutenant Fox and Topete. Very dark and Topete exclaimed loudly about having to drive under such circumstances.

Monday, 24 July (D+48)

> Overcast skies. Better weather later in the day.

The day after we got our tent up, I paid a visit to the French family which lived one tree and a narrow fence away from our office tent. Captain Born wanted to get the dirty clothes washed which he had been accumulating since D-Day, so I took them over to ask if the woman would do them. She and her husband gave me cider, the same vinegar-like mixture we had been getting all along, and he showed me numerous coins and souvenirs the Germans had given him. He added, with a grin, that they had left a number of little souvenirs throughout the neighborhood. His seven-year-old son pointed to his recently born brother, André, and said, "There is a little one." But his mother said, "This is no German souvenir, this is a French one." There were four children, seven years old or under, so the father pounded his chest and said, "You see I am doing my share for France." The chief outcome of the visit was that we were asked to get the G-5's permission for the mother to take André to be christened. Since the church was outside the two and one-half mile limit in which the inhabitants could circulate without permission, we had to intercede with the authorities. The military records of G-5, which I saw some years later, have noted solemnly for history that the Historical Section asked and received permission for Madame X to take André to be baptized.

The twenty-fourth was chosen initially for the execution of COBRA, the operation to break the enemy line west of Saint-Lô and get the American forces moving in the direction of Brittany. It was not hoped at the time that the great sweeping move to the east could develop almost automatically out of the breakout attack. At least we were told of no such ambitious plan; we were informed that a drive to get us out of the hedgerows was to come Monday afternoon, 24 July. There were many rumors because Patton had been sighted, and we had seen Lieutenant General Lesley J. McNair at the corps CP the day before. The British had moved in on our left, so that sometimes we passed through their lines in going to the beaches. The chief effect of the announcement was that we were ordered to dig our foxholes deeper and to cover them with at least three layers of sandbags. All this was to guard against any of our bombs that might fall short. We heard bombing and firing at 1 P.M., but the overcast skies had prevented the full-scale attack from being launched, and we were told that the show would take place the next day instead.

V Corps still not very active; only has 2 divisions (2 and 5) and only one to be active at a time.

I dug a foxhole at night. Very tired but can't sleep much because of exhaustion and almost continual air alerts.

Tuesday, 25 July (D+49)

Weather overcast.

Beginning at 9 A.M. on the twenty-fifth, the preliminary bombing began for the great breakout which would not end until we had reached the German border. I slept late that morning because I was almost sick from digging the night before. I didn't awaken until the first wave of an estimated three thousand planes had gone over and dropped their bombs. They were not too many miles to our left and front, and I experienced for the first time the so-called bouncing in a foxhole that follows nearby bombing. Without leaving my place in the hedgerow, I could see wave after wave of planes coming over and dropping bombs, the odd blobs of smoke from German antiaircraft guns, and the occasional sight of an Allied plane dropping quickly to the ground in flames.

Despite the attack, or perhaps because of it, Topete and I headed over to ARMOR (XIX Corps) to get information on the 29th Division. We noted with pleasure that the headquarters commandant at XIX Corps had arranged barrels of hot water for the use of all personnel, and that the cooks had improved on the K and C rations by tumbling the meat out of the cans and heating it a bit. At our corps, there was still no hot water for shaving except that out of the greasy water in the last rinse can at the mess hall (I have often wondered if that grease contained lanolin), and the cooks furnished a can of boiling water into which we could put the meat cans for heating.

Discovering that units of the 175th Infantry were out of the line, I went to visit my old friends from Company K, whom I had last seen going aboard an LST at Helston. I found that of the company officers who had been in Cornwall, all but two had been wounded or transferred. The captain, a Yale graduate, who had seemed a bit too academic to the men, had been shot while leading his men across the Vire west of Isigny. The first sergeant, who had seemed to be a perfect model of the tough army topkick, had been evacuated the first week as an extreme combat exhaustion case. One of the twins who had made up a BAR team was dead. It really seemed that only Corporal Gideon was going strong. He helped me get some good stories on the work of the company in Isigny and on the fight along the road toward Carentan.

Company K's story of the landings and Isigny action were related to me by Lieutenant Paul Condon, Sergeant George Rauscher, Corporal William Gideon, and several other enlisted men who took part in the action. Their story follows:

"We landed on June 7 at 1730 from a Rhino ferry on Dog Red Beach. It should have been Dog Green, so we had to go out and come back the second time. We hit a sandbar offshore and were put off the boat, having to swim with full field equipment for about ten yards. No one was lost, but we did lose some equipment. We went out the D-3 exit at Vierville. We stopped short of our objective, which was the assembly area south of Vierville. We left the battalion area at 2230. The 1st, 2d, and 3d Battalions marched out in that order. We moved up, supported by tanks, on the road towards Enlesqueville, where the 1st Battalion came under fire. There we stopped for a short rest.

"About 1030 on June 8 we started on the road which runs to Isigny. The 3d Battalion was in the rear as we passed through La Cambe. We had the job of cleaning out the houses to the left of that town. We captured three prisoners, wounded one, and killed one. We had one casualty, Sergeant Oscar Dunn, who was wounded. After taking the houses, we remained in the vicinity until 2030 and then left for Isigny.

"Supporting tanks moved so fast that the 1st and 2d Battalions moved off the road so they could pass. Naval artillery had completed its shelling of Isigny before we came up. Some artillery was present, but our supporting fire came from the battalion's 81mm mortars. We moved up the road in a column of platoons with thirteen tanks, about sixty feet apart on an average. K Company was leading, with Sergeant Ervin Clancy of Baltimore leading the company. The company's order was 3d Platoon, 2d Platoon, mortar section, headquarters personnel, and 1st Platoon. We had the normal rifle company rifles with 60mm mortars. We were marching in this order when we reached the first road junction outside Isigny. The enemy had mined this area, but the tanks rode through the mine belt, losing one tank in the action. The infantry rested at this point about two hours. This was about 0200; up until this time we had killed about twelve Germans since midnight the night before. We had lost one killed, Private Albert Mattia, and two wounded, Private Herman Gray, hit in the shoulder, and Private Gordon Jones, hit in the hand. All were hit by small-arms fire. We were now about seven hundred yards outside Isigny.

"On the morning of ninth we jumped off about 0400, moving into Isigny. Sergeant Clancy was still in front. The tanks advanced up to the bridge in Isigny. Machine guns were emplaced on the other side, and our tanks opened up on them with their guns. (We didn't see the tanks after that.) We moved in behind them to hold the bridge with one squad under Sergeant Charles A. Claypool of Kiska Valley, Pennsylvania. We held the bridge while the rest of the 175th went through. Then we came down the road and went to the right of the main church. The main road, to the left of the church, was covered with rubble, so we took the alley to the right and came out to the road behind the church. We were held up at the road junction when we saw four Germans come up toward the church. Sergeant Clancy killed all of them with a BAR (the Germans fear the BAR more than any other infantry weapon). At this time a company was ordered toward Auville-sur-le-Vey to protect the regiment's right flank as it turned south. Isigny was still full of snipers, but units behind us caught more trouble than we did. We saw a 37mm or 57mm knocked out in the street. We had no losses in Isigny. There was a general firing into windows by our men.

"At the outskirts of Isigny, Sergeant Clancy killed two more Germans with his BAR. Private Louis Stabile of Luzerne, Pennsylvania, killed at least two. Just as we got outside the town, we saw Germans by a large hedgerow on the right, looking over the hedgerow and saying in English "don't shoot." Captain King yelled in German for them to come out. They came out, but one started running down the road and everybody shot the poor guy. The others were sent to the rear. We moved up the road toward the Vire and were told by Lieutenant Bradford that we were to take the bridge. We walked down the road several hundred yards and we heard horses and wagons in the woods at the right of the road before you reach the railroad crossing (there was a big V sign at the left side of the road). We saw emplacements which were obviously German. Captain John T. King III, the company commander, estimated the group as too great for us, so we went back up the road and spent the night. We put roadblocks out and occupied the field on the left-hand side of the road. The defense was put up by the 3d Platoon.

"Next morning, Colonel Reed, the regimental commander, said we had to take the bridge. The company commander, who was always second in line, moved out with the 1st Platoon in the lead at about 0800. This was followed in order by the 2d, 4th, and 3d. During the night we picked up one platoon of Company L under Lieutenant Edward Bean. The L Company platoon followed the 3d Platoon and up the rear guard. We moved down toward the river on the road without opposition. We then moved to a big house overlooking the draw above the railroad (the house was on the left on a hill—gun emplacements behind it and across the road from it). The German dugout across the road was empty. There was .40-caliber machine gun there, but we didn't look too closely. We moved down the draw about two hundred yards this side of the bridge, which was burning. About a hundred yards this side were two Germans with a 44mm gun. They stood with their hands up. We took them prisoner, but believe now they were bait to get us to move up. We moved forward to see if we could cross the river, and intense fire hit us from machine guns, snipers, and mortars. All but two squads were where they could be observed. Mortars started firing on the railroad track and came straight up the road. The 1st Platoon dropped to the ground. The first casualty was Private Howard Cooney of New York City, who was hit by a shell fragment. The 1st Platoon counterfired and the others went back to the side of the road. The 3d Platoon and the L Company platoon went back to protect the rear. The 1st Platoon was pinned down. Captain King sent 2d Platoon to the right to hit snipers in a house armed with machine guns. A squad led by Sergeant Sanders set the house afire with antitank grenades fired by Sergeant Stell. We had one man hit by a machine pistol in the affair—Private Beeler.

"We deployed mortars on the right of the road and tried to get the men out; we were pinned down about three hours. The company commander asked for a volunteer to go back and ask for support from the rear echelon. Staff Sergeant Cyril Whitworth went back and contacted someone from regiment, possibly Colonel George. After a time we heard a tank coming down the hill (this was about 1330). It was a beautiful sight. While pinned down we had had two men killed—a paratrooper who had joined us and Private Rogacki—and eight wounded. Two more tanks came down to help our withdrawal up the hill. A platoon of E Company also came up. The captain now ordered the first sergeant and two others to start the withdrawal, with platoons in reverse order (1st Platoon holding). Five wounded men remained in a hole at the right of the road since they could not be carried out. We withdrew under cover of tank fire and with support of platoons from E and L Companies and took up positions around the house at the top of the hill. the 2d Platoon was sent in to get the wounded. Second Lieutenant Bradford and Second Lieutenant Conway went down and got Stabile and Spatz. It was the first taste of enemy fire for the company as a whole.

"We took up defensive positions on top of the hill, got chow, took care of the wounded, and rested. General Gerhardt came up and said that the bridge and the town beyond would have to be taken. Captain King made an estimate of the situation. The 29th Reconnaissance Squadron had joined us about 1500 and was to give supporting fire. Captain King began to plan the attack, supporting fire, and the route of attack. He made his plan, gave it to the platoon leaders, and contacted the tank commanders and the reconnaissance troops. Captain King, with the supporting fire of the 29th Recon, two tanks, and with 81mm mortars attached, started the attack. We went in on the left side of the bridge, two platoons abreast, followed by the next two, with one platoon in serve. The mortars were left behind. We jumped off about 1800. Engineers had made wooden rafts for the river crossing if they were necessary. These boats would hold about a half squad (six men). We finally sent Private Scott Roese, who volunteered, out to see if he had to swim the river. He found the water only up to his waist, so they decided not to use the rafts. The tide was not in. we jumped off at the left of the bridge. There was no one on it, but machine guns were across the river at the left of the bridge. One machine gun fired under the bridge and hit Captain King through the tender part of the back part of both legs (Captain King had taken the position on the exposed side of the platoon) and killed Private Icard and two other men. Captain King, after being wounded, dragged himself out of the water, refusing help, and directed his men across. He sent back for his executive officer, Lieutenant Dennis, and put him in charge. Technician Fourth Grade Harold O'Connor was brought over to take care of the captain, and the medic bandaged his legs while under fire; he got the Silver Star for the action. (The captain should have gotten a Silver Star, but there was no one around to recommend him for it.)

In crossing the canal, the 3d Platoon was on the right with a platoon from E Company on the left. The 2d Platoon was behind the E Company platoon, and the L Company platoon was behind 3d Platoon. We were held up by barbed wire on the other shore. One man had his hand blown off by a booby trap (the first one we had seen). The 29th Recon gave great support with its 37mm guns from across the river. Tanks moved through mines up to the bridge and fired. The canal (or river) was about forty yards wide at high tide. The tide was out, so it was less. The whole group crossed in ten minutes. Two platoons crossed and the firing stopped for a moment. The next two came over under cover of the advance platoons. They fired on the creamery place. One sniper was in a tree nearby; everybody fired at him until he fell out. We move forward to the line of houses, shot into the houses, and moved through the town and up the road to the junction. The E Company platoon was given the task of taking the little bridge five hundred yards outside Auville-sur-le-Vey. They went too far and were almost wiped out; this gave rise to the report that K Company had sustained about forty casualties. We took up the defense of the town and remained there all night, covering the engineers who worked all night putting up a bridge. When it was in, the 29th Recon came across. With their aid, we took 120 prisoners, mostly Russians and Poles. We had lost two more men by then. We were relieved on the next day by elements of the 2d Armored Division and went on to join the regiment near Lison."

We had supper with the company outside an old farmhouse, and then slipped away when they were summoned to a movie, which was being shown in a nearby barn.

On our way back, we got off our road at Couvains and were proceeding blithely along on the assumption that we were headed toward the rear, when we spied a column taking up skirmish positions. When Topete asked them if they were on a practice march, they pointed across the hedgerows and indicated that they were getting ready to go into positions nearby and that we were almost in enemy range. They pleasantly invited us to join them, but we didn't want to attract fire with the jeep, so we turned back towards corps.

Three miles from corps, at Bois d'Elle, we were stopped by an embarrassed American sentry who asked if we spoke French. Nearby were several other soldiers, all looking sheepish, and two French women who were sobbing loudly. He had stopped them because they had no safe-conduct passes, and in their absence of any knowledge of English and his lack of knowledge of French, they had concluded from the words he said that they were going to be shot. Every gesture he made to indicate that he meant no harm was interpreted as a threat. When he brought up other troops, they thought it was a firing squad. We managed after some talking to calm the women, and then went on to Cerisy, where we found a Civil Affairs sergeant who said that he would take them where they wanted to go.

The first news that reached us at corps on the attack near Marigny was that there had been a tremendous bombing but no breakthrough yet; there was great enthusiasm about the possibility of the early end of the war.

Wednesday, 26 July (D+50)

Weather warm and rain in the afternoon. Rumors of early peace continue to circulate.

An artillery attack started about 5:30 on the twenty-sixth and shook us in our foxholes more than we had been the day before. But the war was not on our front, so I spent the day with Captain Grimson visiting Major McGuire of the 5th Division and Lieutenant Colonel Woods of the 2d Division in order to explain what we were trying to get in the way of history. Our visit to the 2d Division was interrupted by the arrival of Lieutenant General Courtney H. Hodges and members of a Russian military and naval mission accompanied by several American officers. They were taken through the underground war room, which was strongly reinforced by several layers of logs. We seemed safe in the midst of the heavily wooded part of the forest, but splintered branches

testified to the heavy shelling they had sustained around the headquarters the preceding day. The Russians seemed most interested
in U.S. activities, but we were told by General Gerow's aide, Captain Jock Thames, that they had stiffened perceptibly when, in
answer to their questions about the quality of the first prisoners,
someone had answered: "They weren't very good; they were Poles
and Russians." We were told that General Hodges now preceded
the visitors and warned the hosts, "Don't say anything about
Russian prisoners to them." The members of the delegation were
very striking in their red-striped trousers and golden epaulettes.

Thursday, 27 July (D+51)

Rainy during the morning. Became better in the afternoon.

Although we were within a few miles of Saint-Lô and Marigny,
we didn't get news of the death of General McNair until two days
after he was killed. Most soldiers had never heard of the great
work he had done as chief of the Army Ground Forces, although
most of them had undoubtedly sworn at some of his rigid rules
for physical conditioning and realistic training. It was not until
the thirtieth that we heard that McNair was perhaps killed by
American bombs that fell short. Naturally this lack of news was
due not so much to the failure of communications as to the need
for security. But even on the matter of the advance some fifteen
miles to our right we knew only that things were going well
around Coutances and that we were not doing well on the V Corps
front. The rumor was that General Gerow was angry because the
divisions were losing too many men without getting results, and
that the division commanders were relieving their subordinates
who did not show progress. Likely, these were unfair statements,
because we weren't supposed to be going anywhere much, as the
right wing was intended to pivot on us and the British.

*I have seen an account of Germans and Americans raising fire, so medics
from both sides could remove their wounded.*

During the last week of July an APO was set up near V Corps
and we visited it to find that it was jammed with company clerks

buying thousands of dollars worth of money orders and sending canned cable messages for men of their units. Mail delivery had been speeded up by this time, and I had received letters written as late as 17 July, although letters from home written at that time indicated that they had received no mail since 1 June. I got a heavily water-soaked copy of the *New York Times* on the twenty-seventh, the first copy of mine to come through, telling of the fall of Cherbourg and of the Republican convention nearly a month before. Some of the earlier copies of the newspaper, which had been forwarded to me from Fort Myer, continued to arrive in no particular order until that winter.

My diary for the last days of July has a number of entries from various proclamations put up by civil affairs officers. These called for such things as the collection of eggs for hospitals, the requirement of special authorization to operate motorcars, a ban on the movement of cider, and the requirement that all members of the French merchant marine and all French fishermen report to the nearest Hotel de Ville. I also noted that I was indignant at news that a Red Cross club had been opened at Cherbourg but was "off limits" to all personnel save the SOS men stationed in the city. It was another opening wedge between the forward and rear echelons. I reacted by writing, "I have seen several Red Cross girls up here, but no doughnuts." I am sure that they had passed out coffee and doughnuts to men several miles in front of corps positions, but I wasn't inclined that day to be generous.

During this period, we were visited by a colonel from our organization who wanted to see something of the war before it was over. Too old for field duty, he had tried to get a vicarious touch of battle by insisting on personal accounts of the action we had seen. We had last seen him in the pinks of the dress uniform, especially fitting for teas and cocktail parties in London. But now he was proudly dressed in field garb, which not only didn't fit him but also made him conspicuous by being more "frontlinish" than the clothing worn by most officers at corps headquarters. He insisted on being taken up to see "The Real Thing," and we took turns taking him from division to division. No one cared to run the risk of getting him killed, so he was kept a comfortable distance back. But he could hear the guns and an occasional rattle of what might be a burp gun, so he was happy. Everywhere he went he had tales to tell of the excitement at the last headquarters and the near brushes with death he had encountered. The excitement or the outdoor air worked wonders for him, and he walked with a firmer step and his face showed a new gleam of life when he had completed his week in Normandy and went back to the perils of London.

Friday, 28 July (D+52)

Except for the visit, there was little activity on our immediate front. I managed to find time to complete Robert Sherrod's *Tarawa*, the only book I had read in Normandy, and we visited the area to our left where we found tanks, later to be used in the push against Falaise, being massed. Airstrips were springing up everywhere. There seemed to be thousands of MPs bringing order out of chaos, although they were furnishing a number of men daily to the casualty lists because of enemy interdictory fire on road centers. The road system had been much improved by the laying out of new thoroughfares, the mending of old ones, and the introduction of one-way traffic. Despite the almost constant rain and the heavy and continuous movement to and from the beaches, the maintenance crews had kept the roads in reasonably good shape. Of course, a sleepy rider in a jeep or truck needed to be on his guard at night against sudden jolts that were enough to throw him out.

We spent the afternoon of 28 July at 35th Division headquarters discussing means of covering history with the historian, Lieutenant J.E. Judson, and his assistant, Technician Fourth Grade Leon Rosenthal, a lawyer from Philadelphia. The lieutenant added to the horrors of war by ladling out generous portions of calvados. In an earlier entry I had mentioned calvados as an effective antidote against snakebite, but did not elaborate on its peculiar qualities. Soldiers acquainted with the special attributes of "Jersey lightning" always complimented the stuff as having characteristics in common with their local product. Having never been addicted to Kentucky "white mule," I was somewhat handicapped when it came to finding an adequate comparison. I had once tasted calvados fine, aged ten to twelve years, in Paris in 1937, and had found it to be drinkable apple brandy. So I was not prepared for the fiery liquid that was handed to me at 35th Division headquarters. Fortunately, it had aged a few days and was not in the same category as the warmish variety sold straight from the vat which almost made its imbibers blind. This merely shocked the linings of the stomach and made the drinker aware of the virtues of water. One canteen of water to a thimbleful of calvados was a proper degree of dilution. Russian propaganda had made people think that vodka was one of the hottest and strongest drinks known to man, the French later put forth the claims of marc and mirabelle, and the Germans supplied steinhager, but it is likely that few Americans who fought in Normandy will ever agree that anything else can be classed with calvados for fieriness.

Unfortunately, the drink was not strong enough to make me sleep through the biggest ack-ack fight I had heard in July. This was not just a bang-bang party against a lonely Bed-Check Charley, but was directed against several planes that were apparently attracted by the activities of the past few days. Instead of the desultory firing we usually responded with, missing Charley so he could pay us a call another time, this was more serious. The guns some ten miles away opened up and others joined in as the planes came across our front. It was all Hollywood with plenty of noise and a touch of disaster. But the movies would never have dared show all the guns along the First Army front blazing away at four or five planes and consistently missing them! Just about the time we thought they would all get away, one was hit and immediately flared up. He was not on our side, so we reacted as if he were a fox at a chase. It was not a person but another item marked off the list. The fire lighted up the others, but they rapidly flew out of sight. Apparently, they later met with bad luck because three "kills" were claimed the next day. One didn't burn and there were souvenirs.

Saturday, 29 July (D+53)

The twenty-ninth was wet in more ways than one; it rained in the morning and the first regular liquor ration for officers was delivered in the afternoon. Any officer who had been in the corps at the time Cherbourg fell got a bottle of wine and a bottle of cognac (or reasonable equivalent) from the stock taken in the city.

Also in the day's "in" basket was a memorandum from theater headquarters saying that the Expeditionary Forces Institute offered one bottle of whiskey and a half-bottle of gin a month for eighty-five francs. Naturally, the enlisted men were not included, but the officers in our section were generous. Topete and I helped Fox and Howe drink their Bordeaux and Cointreau. We were properly indignant because they, as mere lieutenants, had been done out of their cognac.

Sunday, 30 July (D+54)

Pretty day. Wrote letters until 2:30 in the afternoon.

My last days in July were spent in going over Hill 192 where the 2d Division, after a hard fight, had taken this hill overlooking Saint-Lô and dominating the road from Bayeux entering Saint-Lô from the east. Topete, Kelly, and I made the first trip with a lieutenant who had been relieved during the last day of the attack. Like many of the men in his plight, he was much upset and inclined to talk at length about the factors that led to his relief. The battle conformed more to our notions of what a real fight should be like than any we had yet seen. Instead of stretching over many miles, the hill and its approaches covered an area less than half that at Gettysburg; instead of men firing away at an enemy thousands of yards away, these were close enough to hear the Germans talking.

The Germans were on the top and south side of the hill, while the men of two regiments of the 2d Division came up from the north and occupied hedgerows on the side of the hill. For two weeks they held hedgerows halfway up the north side, a field away from the Germans who tried vainly to blast them out of their foxholes with mortar fire. Peculiarly enough, although the Germans had covered the hillside with tank, artillery, mortar, and rifle fire, there were very few shell holes, and houses just to the east and west of the main battlefield were undamaged or just barely touched. Trees in the area showed the intensity of the fire, however, and the hedgerows were clipped by fire and shattered by the special hedge cutter that had been put to good use by 2d Division units here.

Companies had come from near Colleville to the north and had moved to a point near the bottom of the hill. They advanced two hedgerows and then dug in for about two weeks. On 11 July, corps and divisional artillery laid down a covering of fire a hundred yards ahead of the infantry moving slowly up the hill. Then the tanks went along, and, with their special hedge cutter, lifted the hedge out by the roots so the infantry could go through. Meanwhile, the tanks acted as cover for the foot soldiers. They found the enemy well dug in, with deep holes scooped out under the hedgerows, with passageways so that a rifleman could stand concealed behind the thick hedge and fire, and then duck and run along the passageway to get up and fire again. It repeated the pattern of the "diggingest army" that we ever saw; the Germans filled the hedgerows and high-banked roadsides throughout Normandy with their deep burrows.

A few days before our visit, a letter was taken from the body of a German soldier from 10th Company, 3d Battalion, 9th Parachute Regiment, who had fought at Hill 192 on the eleventh and twelfth of July. It had been written just before the breakthrough of the twenty-fifth, and he died before he could mail it. It described the Hill 192 action as follows:

"For the third time I am trying to get in touch with you by letter. I hope that it will reach you. Some time ago when I left the 6th Group, I arrived by way of Gardeleben in Wittstock where I made my 10 jumps. Then I came to my regiment in France and to my company. We were stationed in Brittany near Brest. When the invasion started we moved out and marched approximately 30–40 kilometers daily, but only at night. During the day American fighter-bombers controlled the area. Then we were put into the line east of St. Lo approximately five kilometers away from the town. When we were committed our company strength was 170.

"Then the 11 July arrived and the most terrible and most gruesome day of my life. At 0500 our Company sector got such a dense hail of artillery and mortar fire that we thought the world was coming to an end. In addition to that the rumbling of motors and rattling could be heard in the enemy lines—tanks. It scared the pants off us. We could expect a very juicy attack. If we thought the artillery fire had reached its climax we were disillusioned at 0530. At that time a tremendous firing started which was continued until 0615. Then tanks arrived. The movement of tanks, however, is somewhat difficult here in Normandy. As we at home have our fields fenced in by wire and wooden fences, so the fields over here are lined with hedgerows. They are almost 5 feet high and have the same thickness. These hedgerows are winding crisscross through the terrain. We dig in behind these walls and the Americans do the same. It is a regular "hedgerow war." Well on that 11 July the tanks were rolling toward us. They shot with their guns through the hedgerows as through cake dough. Sharpshooters give us a lot of trouble. You must know, however, that the Americans are using H.E. ammunition, which tears horrible wounds. Around 1000 the order came to withdraw as the position could not be held. I had one wounded in my machine gun position. When I wanted to get him into my position with the help of someone else, a shell landed 2 yards away from us. The wounded fellow got another piece of shrapnel in his side and the other fellow was also wounded. I, however, did not get a single piece of shrapnel. Anyway, on that day I escaped death just by seconds a hundred times. A piece of shrapnel penetrated through the leather strap of my machine gun and was thus diverted from my chest. I could name several similar instances.

"At 1135 I left the platoon sector as last man. I carried my machine gun through the enemy lines into a slightly more protected defile and crept back with another fellow to get the wounded. It was time to get them, for tanks were moving 30 yards away from us.

"On our way back we were covered again with terrific artillery fire. We were just lying in an open area. Every moment I expected deadly shrapnel. At that moment I lost my nerve. I chewed up a cigarette, bit into the ground, and acted almost like a madman. The others acted just like me. When one hears for hours the whining, whistling, and bursting of shells and the moaning and groaning of the wounded, one does not feel too well. Altogether it was hell.

"Our company had only 30 men left. In the meantime it was reorganized to a certain extent. We are now located in a somewhat more quiet sector, i. e., what we call quiet. We are expecting a new attack supported by tanks today or tomorrow.

"I have been recommended for the Air Force–Ground Force

Badge, on account of the hand to hand fighting on 11, 12, and 13 July."

The tanks and infantry and artillery had finally smashed the tanks and guns we found at the top of the apple orchard, looking down at the men who were coming up. There were no bodies now, but the evidence of what had happened was still there. We found bloody bandages in the scooped-out hole which had been a first aid station; we saw scraps of clothing, pieces of food containers, empty shell cases, scattered books—one of them titled in German "Dancing Death"—and a group of wooden crosses with German helmets on them.

On our way back from the hill, we stopped at a little house just to the east. It was undamaged, and a cow and some chickens were nearby. The building had not been hit, but it was wrecked inside. Soldiers of the two armies had stayed there, their cast-off clothing and meat cans mingled together on the floor, along with French wine bottles. They had not broken the china, but they had pulled down all the clothing in the house and had walked back and forth until everything was in shreds.

We were coming out of the house when a woman and her small son appeared. They had been told by the Germans on 11 July to leave the house, and had gone to her sister's some ten miles away. Now, two weeks later, she was the first of the people in the neighborhood to return. I had seen many dispossessed people returning to wrecked towns like Trevières and Isigny, but this was the first time I had seen an individual returning to his own home. It was extremely moving because we saw the trouble of war reflected in these two persons, and our presence seemed to make us accomplices in the damage and the uselessness of the destruction they found in the house. The boy managed to find an unbroken toy, which he held on to grimly as if he feared we might take it. The mother, stunned by the waste around her, merely stood and gazed at the damage the passing troops had left.

Chapter 11

Restless Days at the Rear

Tuesday, 1 August (D+56)–
Saturday, 26 August (D+81)

Tuesday, 1 August (D+56)

With the end of July, my carefree days of wandering around the front by jeep were temporarily brought to a close. On 1 August I was sent to Valognes to work on an account of the Omaha Beach landings. Colonel Taylor, the War Department representative, was there preparing a pamphlet on the subject for the army, but I was told to write something of a different nature which fit into the plans of the Historical Section, ETOUSA. Because the difference in interpretations of writing history still existed, I duplicated for a number of days the work Colonel Taylor was doing without helping to speed up a project that the War Department wanted. Nothing could better illustrate the way in which different sections of the army could sometimes work at cross purposes. I was particularly perturbed because I had been briefed on the War Department program by Colonel Taylor in Washington. Ultimately, I decided to help as I could with the pamphlet, but much of my time was wasted.

At AD SEC, I met for the first time Captain William Knowland, head of the AD SEC Historical Section, who was to become a U.S. senator from California. Also there were his assistants, WAC sergeant Eva Spencer of South Dakota and Russ Jones, an old friend from London. With Colonel Taylor was Sergeant John Hall, who was cataloging the first after-action reports coming in from the units in the field.

Valognes, as a place to live, was a dream in comparison to what we had been used to at V Corps. Here we lived in pyramidal tents and slept on cots. We still washed out of our helmets, but they were placed on wooden stands and we could have all the water we wanted! Besides, the latrines not only were surrounded by canvas—even at corps we had grown effete enough to have canvas to keep out the curious—but a covering overhead to keep out the rain. Besides, there was no work at night. But there were several large flies in the ointment. All the peacetime rules were enforced. Beds had to be made properly with no bulges in the blankets, rifle inspection once a week, and reveille at 6 A.M. But there was less strain and it was fun to tell lies to the rear-echelon lads. It was also pleasant to be doing research with Colonel Taylor—like a seminar with a fine scholar.

We stayed only a week at AD SEC, during which time we listened avidly to radio news of the activation on the Continent of 12th Army Group under General Bradley, the commitment of Third Army under General Patton, and the start of the great drive south of Marigny toward Brittany. Although I had been within a few miles of the front as late as 31 July, I found myself on 3 August listening as if I were in another country to Captain Ruppenthal of VII Corps tell how Fighting Joe Collins's troops were going. Lieutenant Morris and Sergeant Ludden of the newly arrived XX Corps came by the same day.

Wednesday, 2 August (D+57)

> *Up at seven and walked to tent in afternoon.*
> *Worked all day on material for beach obstacles, underwater obstacles, defenses and German forces.*
> *At night went for a long walk with Colonel Taylor. Talked to some of French.*

The French 2d Armored Division was now on the Continent, and its men were greeted wildly by their compatriots. Morris and Ludden said at some points Frenchmen, noticing that the two Americans were dressed in the same uniform as the French, asked why the U.S. Army didn't get "a uniform different from ours." This reaction was to continue throughout France, to the great anger of the GIs, until buttons with French design were substituted on the uniforms for buttons with the American eagle. The effect of the story on me was that I wrote in my diary: "Seems a pity to start arming Europe again, since Hitler's fall would mean disarmament of all save Russia, U.S., and Britain." The XX Corps historians had brought stories of Patton's boast that he was tired of this delay (although he used a four-letter word) and that in eighteen days he would be in Paris, and that he had said he would drive his men, leaving little time for food or rest, stressing action to the point that even in rear areas the men would stand retreat.

Thursday, 3 August (D+58)

> *Good weather but windy. Up at six for reveille. To work at 8.*
> *Worked all morning and part of afternoon on story of enemy defenses on Omaha Beach.*

We listened on the radio to Congressman Andrew J. May, a Kentucky Democrat, guess that "Old Blood and Guts is leading the advance," and while giving credit to Patton for dash and bravery, we felt it unfair to take credit from the First Army infantry which had paved the way. The hole in the German line at Marigny had been made by American air and exploited by the infantry of First Army's VII Corps. They were on their way at the base of the Cotentin when Third Army's armor was turned loose.

4 August (D+59)–10 August (D+65)

> *Worked writing most of day, patching up holes in material on beach defenses.*

From the eastern front came word that the Russians were near Warsaw, and rumor had it that the Germans were letting them through, so that they could make a deal with them. It pleased us though that they were moving and there was much optimism about the war ending in October. I became worried lest it end before I got back forward again.

The war, save for the bits of news brought by visitors, British newspapers, the *Stars and Stripes*, and censored bulletins on the radio, seemed far away. We were now in the grounds of the Château le Rilly, which became Riley at once. The château was built in the style of the time of Louis XIV. Its owner, a *vicomte*, was said to be living with his family in the gardener's house beside the château, which served as the central headquarters building.

Armed, helmeted men passed back and forth between the tented billeting area and the château over a lovely canal in which swans floated. What appeared to be a spring-fed stream flowed over a waterfall near the entrance to the château. Great trees, reminiscent of the Orangerie in Strasbourg, formed an arch over the roadway. Some tropical trees were planted on the lawn, and roses were abundant in the garden.

But the beauty of the grounds was to us nothing as compared to the dining places—under tents and with chairs. And, of course, luxurious showers, gallons of hot water, and dressing rooms. Then too there were WACs in profusion, carefully guarded while off-duty, looking not too beautiful in their ill-fitting field slacks. The fine-looking characters of the area were some newly arrived army exchange lads from London, dressed in beautifully pressed clothes, low-cut shoes, and neckties. Although a rear-echelon Joe myself when I went down to the companies, I found myself feeling that I belonged to a different army, particularly when they complained about the food. C rations, it's true, but warm.

In an effort at cleanliness the army overdid itself. To curb diarrhea among the troops, the mess officers made strict regulations for the careful washing of mess kits and an extra can of hot water was put out for washing. Instead of helping matters, the cases of diarrhea rose rapidly. The culprit was too much GI soap in the wash water.

Omaha beachhead stories failed to keep me interested on 6 August when I heard of the advance on Brest, the resistance at Saint-Malo, the fight at Rennes. I wanted to get on back to V Corps since it seemed we were completely out of the show. Time was taken up the following day by another move, this time only a few miles away, to the grounds of a Monsieur Ledoux. The château, rather gloomy looking on the hill, had many aspects of a feudal manor house, with great stables and an outdoor laundry under the side porch. At the same time, its great gates, long lanes bordered by arched trees and thick hedges, and formal gardens, now neglected, with blackened and rather ugly classic statuary, brought to mind nineteenth century neoclassic styles. Major General John C.H. Lee, head of the Communications Zone, had one of his several headquarters here. The main building also served as residence and headquarters for some members of the staff.

Beyond the château, farther up the hill, in a field pocked by shell or bomb holes, was the tented officer area. Colonel Taylor told me that the tents for some colonels had floors, rugs, and bookshelves, and that the tenants complained because of lack of comfort. Our own tent city was about one and one-half miles away near the mess hall, which was reached over newly cut roads which by turns were muddy or dusty. The WAC tents were in a field on top of a rather high hill. As usual, guards stood along the road. Our office buildings—yes, we now had prefabricated huts for offices, a fact which angered men who came in from the field because they felt that the craft that had brought in this material could have been used to bring in necessary items for the fighting men.

John Hall and I liked our building, which was far too large at the moment for the records we had to store in it. So we—and later Bill Harnett of Cleveland, Colonel Taylor's typist—took advantage of the fact that the move from our last headquarters made it impossible for the first sergeant to know where we belonged and slept in the office. We thus escaped reveille and inspections. To avoid detection, I went for some time without PX rations since I didn't want to get my name on the company books by asking for a ration card. To my amazement, when I finally left the place, I discovered that no one knew that I had ever been there since I had arrived on VOCO, and I had considerable difficulty in getting my name on travel orders so that I could get away from the place when we moved to Paris in September.

Our particular hut was hidden carefully under the densely wooded side of a slope just above a large spring-fed stream that ran through a large field, bordered by large trees. So dense were the woods that we had to use electrical lights throughout the day and the heat at midday failed to reach us. The great advantage was the crystal-clear stream that served as laundry basin, a shaving place, and bathing pool. Always cold, it was still invigorating, and we luxuriated in a bath every day at the end of work—never disturbed by the parade of milkmaids who came by every night about that time to drive their cows home. Russ Jones and I built a log bridge across the stream and set up a shaving stand that soon attracted a great gang of bathers, shavers, and casual visitors. To our disgust, the great group of visitors was officers who aroused our special ire when they occupied the pool at milking time.

To me, the great virtue of the stream was the chance to wash my clothes. By this time I had lost all my shirts but one and had no chance to get another. With the stream nearby, it was possible to wash my shirt after breakfast, wear my jacket closely buttoned up, and put the shirt out in the sunshine, which was usually hot for three or four hours each day. If we could keep the wandering cows away, the laundry was ready for wear by evening. All in all, I was in much better shape for clean shirts than during my first two weeks in Paris.

Our move left us cut off from news for a couple of days. We heard of the counterattack at Mortain at a time when we were mainly exercised about the fact that we were having to stand in the chow line for two hours every day. The trouble, of course, was the steady influx of ETOUSA personnel from London. It seemed that the mess officers were never able to estimate the increase enough to take care of the newcomers.

The period was also marked by entertainment, the second USO show in the area. My diary for this week speaks of Dinah Shore and Spike Jones and the great response they had from the crowds of GIs sitting around on a hillside. It speaks also of a rustic hut—a summerhouse—across from our office, which reminds me of something from *Paulet Virginie*. And I wrote again of the Corot-like atmosphere that surrounded the trees, of the arched roadways, the rustic causeways, and the substantial wall, covered with ivy and marked by a grim sign saying that dogs are set *"en liberté"* at night.

Major Hugh M. Cole, a War Department historian who had come in with Third Army at the beginning of August, brought us a breath of the war on 10 August when he arrived from Brittany with stories of disagreements between Patton and his corps commanders over the former's habit of rushing armor ahead and leaving infantry the heavy job of cleaning up pockets. The Germans, we learned, were still fighting hard, withdrawing slowly. Our tanks had been badly chewed up, and we were not completely set for a drive to Paris. But he was optimistic about the future and predicted that before long Third Army would have the French capital. Cole had become well set-up at Third Army and was permitted to attend Patton's briefings each day. He kept a careful diary during that period, and later showed me Patton's statements when he got ready for the drive that took him to Paris. He told his staff that there were only ten battalions of Germans in front of his army and added, "but don't tell the press."

Cole, who I was not to see again for some months, was looked upon by many of us as an ideal combat historian. With a firm knowledge of military matters, using a checklist which he himself had worked out for coverage of military actions, with historians which he had picked or had retained out of those sent to him, he had aggressiveness and the ability to get people under him to produce results.

Friday, August 11 (D+66)

Fired by talk of the front, I got Colonel Taylor's consent to go back to V Corps to sign the payroll and see something of the fighting front. Russ Jones, John Hall, and I set out by jeep on 11 August for a point near Vire. Leaving at 8:30 A.M., we followed the battle route of VII Corps from Valognes to Saint-Sauveur le Vicomte, Lessay, Coutances (concerning whose beautiful cathedral, Colonel Taylor, good medievalist that he was, wanted a report), and Avranches. The fields were filled with craters, roads jammed with supply trucks moving forward, and pipelines being laid. There were still dead cattle marking the route of war. A truckload of stiffened corpses was parked along the road. Near Avranches, we found the road still lined with wrecks of German vehicles, and the road itself packed with a steady line of trucks going up with supplies, convoys of new units, lines of tanks, and motorized columns.

At Avranches we decided to follow Third Army's westward push sufficiently to see Mont Saint-Michel in the distance. Returning through Avranches, we stopped long enough to ask an

MP the best route to Vire. After the usual "it beats the hell out of me" answer, we found from some passersby that the road to V Corps was open despite recent fighting in Vire. We took the Villedieu-le-Poele road and proceeded to get lost. But we were not sorry as it took us by a primitive army rest center that fed us without question—good meat, fresh bread, and some cookies, with apologies because the better food was gone. After eating and getting back on our road near Saint-Plois, we started again for the corps. Near that town we suddenly heard shells from American guns passing over a small ridge that rose at the side of the road. On stopping a sentry we found that this so-called safe road was being shelled from time to time by remnants of a German artillery unit which was in the woods to our front, and that our artillery was trying to silence it. They were the last of the Mortain counterattack force in that area. This was part of the group which had retaken Vire two days before, leaving it burning still, with their dead still at the side of streets through which we passed. We didn't tarry too long in the area, although I stopped along the roadside long enough to pick up a copy of *Life* that had Robert Capa's D-Day photographs.

The VICTOR Rear CP was finally located near Étouvy, not far from Vire. Here I signed the payroll, got a K-ration box full of NEPTUNE papers for Colonel Taylor's use (these were some of the same BIGOT papers which I had seen at Taunton; they were now downgraded to Top Secret; several years later I had difficulty trying to get permission to see them in the historical files section of the Pentagon), gave instructions about the proper care of my souvenirs to Kelly and Topete, got the latest dope on V Corps plans, and set off again on the sightseeing tour.

We returned through Saint-Lô, that fabulous city which I had often approached but never entered. The streets were still choked with rubble, save for a small area cleared by bulldozers so jeeps could get through. It had been fought over in the belief that it would serve as the main road for an attack toward Paris. But the bombings and shelling had obstructed the roads and the battle had swung to the south and east so quickly that Saint-Lô was to live in legend because of the heavy losses near it rather than for its contribution to the pursuit. Actually, it will be best known because correspondents, already accustomed to its name and struck perhaps by the ease with which it fit into a headline, used the name Saint-Lô breakout for the great breakout attack of 25 July, which was actually much nearer Marigny. We stopped briefly by MASTER Rear headquarters near Canisy and then came back through Perriers, whose cathedral had suffered badly, and then back by Lessay and La Haye du Puits, feeling that we had been near the war.

It was clear from the trip that in ten days the whole nature of the war as I had seen it in June and July had changed radically. We had gone from inch-by-inch battles in the hedgerows to a great battle of maneuver with the whole of Normandy and Brittany for the battleground. The Germans had brought on the quickened pace by a desperate effort to cut through our supply lines at Mortain and had left their forces too long in an extended position. While Field Marshal Günther von Kluge begged Hitler to relax his order to stand and fight, the columns of First and Third Armies turned to the east and pushed the enemy units in toward British and Canadian forces coming southward from the Caen area.

12 August (D+67)–23 August (D+78)

But I was to know little of these battles until later. We spent the next few days picking up what information we could from news bulletins at the mess tents. My diary speaks of fights with the Norman bees, which developed a great appetite for the orange marmalade the army provided in great quantity, and of a volunteer hillbilly quartet that serenaded us during meals. Some of our WAC friends had discovered an excellent cider supply, and Eva Spencer told us it was always possible to get an escort to the place where it was sold. We had just about kidnapped her from Captain Knowland's outfit by this time.

It was a period of visitors. Captain John Westover, who won his Silver Star in North Africa, had arrived from Washington for an assignment, and Lieutenant Herbert French and Lieutenant Yarmon from the 4th Port Command, who were writing the story of the opening of Cherbourg, came to see us. Now the ETOUSA historians began to arrive, with Major Wood Gray, Captain Bob Healey, Lieutenant Harris, and Captain Greenwald arriving almost simultaneously. In addition to these, we had engineer, ordnance, medical, and other technical service officers who, hearing that we were collecting records, came to examine them in order to start special studies that would help them make "on the spot" reports to Washington.

One visitor was a Free French colonial, Bir Cacen of Oran, who was a member of a French unit at nearby Château Chevrival. In mid-August, he was wearing his heavy GI overcoat. After five years in the army he had served at forced labor for the Germans, had escaped from Germany and returned to Oran, only to get wounded there when our forces landed. His unit had come to the United Kingdom in mid-May and to Normandy around the first of August. His ambition was to cut German throats. This talk with the first French soldier I had met on the Continent coincided with news of the Allied landings in southern France and the report of a German rout beyond Alençon and the "rapidly closing gap." Only a day or two before, on the fourteenth, General Eisenhower had spoken of an unparalleled opportunity that lay close at hand and called on everyone to make an all-out effort to grasp it.

Our most important visitor of the period, Colonel S.L.A. Marshall, arrived on 18 August. He had been in Normandy shortly after the invasion but had returned to the United Kingdom with the 82d and 101st Airborne Divisions to conduct the type of mass interviews he had made famous in the Pacific. Marshall, who was ultimately to become our chief in the theater, was already a legend among the combat historians. A native of Texas who had been commissioned an officer in the first war while yet in his teens, he had gone into the newspaper business after the war and combined a knowledge of sports and military affairs into an unusual newspaper career. At one point, while with the *Detroit News*, his main activity was promoting polo matches, and then at other times it was building reader interest in military history and the development of the army. A friend of British military historians like Major General J.F.C. Fuller and Captain B.H. Liddell Hart, he had helped to make their writings known in the United States and had attracted the favorable attention of the army by the late 1930s. He was an observer for a time of the Spanish Civil War, and early on became interested in the effect of airpower and "the new mobility" on warfare.

With the outbreak of war in Europe, his writings as a military editor on the *News* became nationally known. His books *War on Wheels* and *Blitzkrieg* pounded home the lessons of the new style of fighting. In 1943 he was asked to go to the Pacific—in uniform—as a combat historian. In several of the battles he developed a system of mass interviews, mentioned earlier, in which he attempted to interview entire units at a time. His interviews on the battle of Kwajalein, conducted in this fashion, were the basis for his volume *Island Victory*, which was widely cited.

"Slam," as he was usually called, was short of stature, nattily dressed, and cocky in manner. Equally ready with a good story or a quick decision, he was a type who attracted or angered people quickly. His characterizations of individuals who crossed his path could be withering, and he could upbraid people who failed to carry out his orders in a most caustic manner. But he practically never used strict discipline on his subordinates, and his executive officers complained that he was constantly letting people off the hook who should have been severely punished. He was extremely kind to the enlisted men and, when we later came under his direction, saw to it that provisions were made for our comfort.

Marshall's great interest in the war was in the work of the airborne troops. Not only did he conduct exhaustive interviews on their work in Normandy, but he also followed their actions in Holland, and his book on the 101st in the Ardennes helped to add to the legend of Bastogne. Words that he wrote of that battle are now preserved around the wall of the monument in that town. We who worked with the infantry were often inclined to think that Slam overplayed the airborne story, but it was easy to understand why he liked the paratroopers. Not only were they something new, but they also fought many individual actions, filled with heroism and close-in fighting, and it was possible to get a hundred wonderful stories with blood and fire. The newsman in him liked that. His interest in the individual soldier was to show through the great book *The River and the Gauntlet*, which he wrote about the Korean War.

Colonel Ganoe, aware of Colonel Marshall's standing with the War Department, gave him broad powers over the men in the field. This was to give rise to a somewhat anomalous position later, when First Army continued to try to cover history according to the directive that London had laid down, while the rest of the historians were following the War Department policy as outlined by Marshall. Not until Colonel Marshall finally became the theater historian early in the following year was the situation firmly resolved.

Slam was eager to get into the field, so he set off with one of the First Army jeeps. Captain Westover served as his driver, and the two rapidly sped through Brittany and most of Normandy, and arrived in Paris in time for the liberation parade.

Each day now brought news of fresh victory. On the twentieth there was word that Patton had reached Versailles, and that many of the Germans at Falaise had escaped the trap. This slight damper to our elation was modified by the report that more than a hundred thousand prisoners and most of the German armor and vehicles had been seized in the trap which had been closed a few days before at Chambois by units of the U.S. and British forces. Tank men of the V Corps and of a Polish armor unit under a Canadian corps had made the linkup.

Falaise as it looked after the fighting in late June 1944.

On the twenty-third the great news was flashed that Paris was in the hands of the Resistance forces. Earlier there had been news of an uprising by French police in the city, but we had feared that the Germans might quell this resistance or that they would force us to destroy the city before they would surrender it.

Thursday, 24 August (D+79)

Skies overcast. . . .

I'm as mad as the devil because I'm stranded here and V Corps is over towards Paris. Our jeep was taken yesterday and there is no way for me to get to V Corps and they naturally won't come after me until this advance stops.

British papers called this the best day of the war.

And now came a spate of good news. The twenty-fourth was described by the papers as the best day of the war with announcement of Rumania's surrender, Marseille's capture, the Maquis's wresting of control of the Haute Savoie from the Germans, and the approach of V Corps, which now contained the French 2d Armored Division, to Paris. The latter announcement was surprising in that a few days before, V Corps seemed to be out of the race for the French capital. Some preinvasion plans which I had seen in May had shown V Corps in the southern part of Paris and British forces in the north, but that had seemed long since outdated by events as Patton's forces had appeared almost in the city. However, in a sudden maneuver, General Gerow and a small staff were suddenly taken from command of their units and brought up near Paris to assume command of three divisions previously under Third Army. This action can be explained on the basis of the need to straighten out the lines of the American forces, which had become amazingly tangled as the First Army had turned due north across the British front and the Third Army had turned part of its forces also northward across the front of First Army. The shift of units from Third to First Army put Patton's forces on a straight eastward course south of Paris and left that French city to First Army and V Corps. To Third Army it was merely an attempt to do General Patton and his forces out of an honor rightfully theirs.

Friday, 25 August (D+80)–Saturday, August 26 (D+81)

Weather not bad. Sun shines most of these late days, but it gets cloudy too. Really hot in late afternoon.

Like any other soldier, inclined to interpret all developments in the light of the way they affected him personally, I was heart-broken because the corps with which I had spent the rainy, dull days in June and July was now, in this month of beautiful sun-shine and great victory, going into Paris and I would not be along. It seemed that the end of the war was not far off and I was miss-ing the whole show back at the COMZ, a thorough rear-echelon soldier, knowing less about the war than I would have in front of a good radio in the United States.

While I cooled my heels and fumed at my misfortune, I caught up with the British newspapers, copies of which our recent arriv-als had brought from London. I noted that columnists, particu-larly in the *Daily Mail*, were concerned lest the Americans should claim they won the war. One writer said that Eisenhower was not responsible for control of the battle and that neither side could claim the victory. They pointed out that the Allies had contrib-uted equally to the landings, and that although the Americans now had a ratio of 2:1 in men, the heavier burden was on the British, who had the tougher front. They added that since the Americans had more armor, they had made the more spectacular gains. Even the London *Times*, which tended to avoid headline brawls, said that U.S. gains in southern France had been due in part to the work of the Maquis and that Paris had liberated itself.

Don Iddon of the *Daily Mail* insisted that someone should be court-martialed for intimating that "Monty had been sacked" when Bradley's coequal command was announced. He added that the Americans were very adroit in publicizing their contributions. By using the white star on all Allied equipment and trucks throughout United Kingdom and Europe, the impression was spread that the Americans had furnished everything. He felt that for the sake of opinion in the Dominions at least, the British should have their own distinguishing mark. I was amused at this out-burst because some American papers at this point, noting that all Allied vehicles used the white star, grumbled because there was no way for the Europeans to know we had supplied a great many of them. Also at this time the *Washington Times-Herald* was charging that the British were running the war with Eisenhower as a stooge. My feeling was that such argument over the spoils and credit for victory, while childish and ridiculous, indicated at least that the war was going well.

My diary, at a point when it seemed that the war was won, showed that I was thinking hard about the laurels of victory:

"Without doubt the British pulled their share of the load in the landings. But as Churchill has said, the British share would have to diminish after that. They will only be able to spare 18 divisions, according to some reports. They have made up to an extent by full use of their shipping and by naval and air support. The fleet in the Pacific is considerable. On the other hand, there has been a tendency in the more sensational British press to do what our same press does back home—to write accounts in terms of Monty's men and in playing up the work, naturally, of the British forces. . . .

"Unfortunately [for the British] nothing can stop our people from claiming the victory. They believe the British slow, they overemphasize our total contribution. They rub in on the British the total contribution we've made. The British are bound to feel like country cousins.

"There really is going to be a considerable amount of snide remarks [about us] after the war is over. We are likely to get blamed for very low morals, because of our promiscuous sex habits (something that has just called forth a very hot blast from SHAEF warning against advances to respectable women, leaving of contraceptives in public, improper actions in air raid shelters, etc.) Undoubtedly some of our men have taken too strongly the stories from the last war that any French woman they meet can be picked up. Cases against soldiers on this score date from the very first day.

"The British will never get full credit for [their part in] winning the war, since their greatest glory was in holding on in the 1939–42 period. This was a negative type of fighting and will fade. Dunkerque, like Corregidor, will be dismissed for more substantial victories. Montgomery will probably salvage more credit out of the North African campaign than anything else. The British Air Corps undoubtedly will get and keep considerable praise. Russia will be played down, perhaps, in later years at home. . . . Hers was the positive sacrifice that broke Germany and made the landings possible. However, ours was the voice and the helping hand that encouraged England to keep fighting, that replaced the terrific losses of materiel suffered by the Russians, and that furnished the extra manpower to overwhelm the enemy. If England had not held out, there would have been no war to fight. We would have had to go on a war footing [alone] and to have stayed on that footing against Germany. Without Russia's sacrifices which, even in retreat, strained Germany's resources, Germany would have won for at least 20 years. There was a period in which we were hitting our stride in which what England and Russia did was crucial. We shouldn't forget that, but we will. They should not and will not forget, although they may try, that the 50 destroyers helped win the battle of the Atlantic, that Sherman tanks helped to turn the battle in North Africa, that American supplies played a great part on the Russian front. It must be remembered that Roosevelt and others took their political lives in their hands to support the war in Europe over the Pacific war. On our side we must remember that equal to the Air Force in importance in breaking Germany has been the Russian Army. If Germany had been able to mass her armies in the west, we could not have come ashore. Without a landing, Russia could probably have crossed the German frontier (this assumes our Italian front and Lend-Lease aid.)

"There is enough glory for us in the Pacific (the lion's share) plus a proper share of the European gains. German reports indicate clearly that our infantry is still green. We have played fast and loose with some of our training rules—camouflage discipline, gas security, proper cover and concealment—but like a strong football team which can run no bad plays, we have been able to take chances and win against an opponent disorganized by our air force. . . . We must praise the infantryman (I claim to be one) who suffers the greatest casualties and the horrors of war. [The Siegfried Line and the Ardennes were still in the future when I wrote this.] . . . I have been told by too many company and battalion leaders that they have never been opposed by anything remotely approaching their strength. When our men have been cut off or forced to fight against great numbers they have done nobly, have shown themselves resourceful and capable."

Chapter 12

Liberated Paris

Wednesday, 30 August (D+85)–
Sunday, 3 September (D+89)

In the days just after the fall of Paris, when the Allies were speeding toward the German border, Seventh Army was marching rapidly northward from the Mediterranean, Bulgaria was leaving the war, and V Corps tactical headquarters was being set up near the Hotel des Invalides, I was reduced to such diary entries as: "Had first chicken in France—a wing but well cooked." I fumed about not being able to see Paris, and my irritation was increased because there was a First Army vehicle assigned to us but neither John Hall nor I knew how to drive.

Finally, Colonel Taylor, fine gentlemen that he was, saw the stew I was in and agreed that I could go to V Corps to draw my pay and perform several errands for him in passing. Then Hall and I went to work on Russ Jones, who needed no urging since he was anxious to visit his friends at *Stars and Stripes*, which was opening up in Paris. We needed only to get the approval of Captain Knowland for Russ to go, and that was soon forthcoming. At the last minute, two of the newly arrived ETOUSA officers, possibly desirous of using the jeep for such a trip themselves, told Colonel Taylor that I could draw partial pay at Valognes without making a trip. I was sure that he was aware of that, and, inspired by what seemed a last-minute upset in our plans, I eloquently told the officers in question to mind their own business. Colonel Taylor stuck by his bargain. To make the trip legal, he directed Hall to stop at First Army to check on records and he accompanied us as far as Omaha Beach to conduct interviews with the Rangers. I have always thought of his action in staying behind as a study in self-abnegation and of the painful duty which responsibility imposes. The colonel had done much study in France and wanted mightily to make the trip with us, and would have gone had he been in our place, but he felt that there was no excuse for his going. So he took vicarious pleasure in our trip. In his place, I think I would have done the same, but at the moment I reveled in the fact that I was an enlisted man who could leave my conscience to someone else.

Wednesday, 30 August (D+85)

Russell Jones, John Hall, and I left for V Corps. Took Colonel Taylor to ——— CP; arrived at noon there. Left at 12:30.

We had sandwiches at Omaha Beach, the two boxes of K rations we were carrying in the rear seat, and then set out for Paris by way of Bayeux and Caen. The area was a madhouse of activity. The beaches, particularly the British artificial port at Arromanches, were pouring traffic into the main highways from Caen to Paris and Caen toward Rouen. We were stuck most of the day behind convoys. Traffic discipline was rather strictly enforced by motorcyclists who rode in and out through the traffic making sure we didn't get out of line. The big MPs at the "circuses" and "roundabouts" were much in the cop tradition and gave us severe verbal lacings from time to time. Steady rain added to our troubles, as did craters in the roads, and rubble in the streets of cities like Caen.

The great cathedrals of Caen were still standing, but much of the rest of the city was badly smashed and the smell of death was there. The fields round about and the smaller towns showed the great pounding which the long battle for this key city had brought. From Caen we took the road to Lisieux, finding the newer cathedral hit, but the older one in relatively good condition. (Colonel Taylor didn't feel too badly about the new one when we told him). Near here we had a slight accident when we slid into the back of an English truck that had stopped suddenly on the wet road. The soldiers were solicitous and told us where to stop for maintenance.

We were rather worried for a time since we thought we would need special papers of authorization (in those carefree times we didn't even have a trip ticket). To our delight, the unit was made up of Canadians. The head mechanic, a huge sergeant, virtually bent our damaged radiator back in place without tools and with a little help soon had it in good shape. On top of the bargain, they fed us, taking advantage of our company to throw insults at the "bloody British." One of the soldiers had worked on a horse farm in Kentucky, and another in Detroit, and they sounded more like a group of American soldiers swearing at the Limeys than they did men in British jackets.

We went on to Évreux for the night on the assumption that it was still held by American troops. We found virtually no troops in the city, and a blackout that restricted movement. Some Frenchmen finally directed us to a civil affairs detachment that consisted of an American and two British officers and ten British "other ranks." These people knew of no nearby American troops and invited us to spend the night—making us ashamed of having listened tolerantly to the Canadians a short time before. We shared the room of a Sergeant Francis, an engineer in civilian life, who, with Sergeant Major Cox and the remainder of the troops, was billeted in a hotel that had been beautifully refurbished by the German officers who had lived there. Cox had a room he said had been occupied by General Dietrich—a large room, done in a dainty blue. The Germans had departed hurriedly, and had left behind them nude pictures, ladies' wearing apparel, and a few ladies.

Sergeant Francis was a good host, producing a bottle of Cointreau that we drank with K rations, while arguing amicably about the war. Cox and Francis felt that U.S. bombing was more destructive than theirs, since they believed that our pilots were unwilling to come in close enough to do the precision bombing of which they were capable. They defended the British record at Caen, pointing out—and we agreed—that they had borne a heavy part of the fighting during the first weeks. They were full of praise for the U.S. supply organization, declaring that we had the job done while the British were talking about it. They told us a number of good war stories, my favorite being one of a British soldier who had stolen a DUKW and started for England in it, finally being headed off by a destroyer.

Thursday, 31 August (D+86)

Day is beautiful.

We started at 0900 and headed for our destination. Before leaving, however, we learned what the British meant when they said that the best mess in the army is the sergeants' mess. (The thirteen men in the detachment had three messes: one for the officers, another for the sergeants, and a third for the others). I am sure the sergeants' mess was the best. They had found an Italian displaced person who could cook marvelous dishes, and they had supplemented their ration with eggs, milk, and other items which the countryside afforded, so that we had one of the best breakfasts available in that part of the country—all washed down with scalding hot black tea. It was not only one of the best breakfasts I had ever had but one of the few I had had on the Continent, since there was seldom any inducement to get up for chopped egg from a can even if warmed, and no inducement whatever to get up for the powdered eggs usually served in the rear areas.

Refreshed by the morning feast, we set off for Mantes-Gassicourt, where the civil affairs people thought we might find some Americans. We proceeded to get lost and wandered around for an hour or two not knowing whether or not troops had been in that vicinity. On the side roads we were traveling, the war had passed with little effect. For some miles, we saw no soldiers, no wrecked tanks, no prisoners. Only when we hit the towns would cheering groups of Frenchmen or a member of the FFI, wearing a characteristic armband and carrying a nondescript weapon, give some indication that the armies had come that way. As we neared the Seine, however, we began to see knocked-out tanks and vehicles, and to meet elements of American units moving up. Several times we overtook tank columns, moving slowly, and we were forced to stay behind them on the narrow roads, which left no room for passing.

At Mantes, we found that XIX Corps was in a nearby château some thirty miles from Paris. Knowing we could find friends there, and get a line on the First Army historians and their whereabouts, we hastened in that direction. We arrived in time for lunch, running into Dave Garth as he came up to the chow line. We were fed, given extra K rations, some gasoline (now a precious item), and were told that V Corps's forward headquarters was at 8 Rue des Invalides.

We scarcely stayed long enough to say "thank you" to our hosts before we started off in the direction of the Pont de Neuilly. The roads were jammed as usual and dust was thick. We decided to pull out briefly near Neuilly. Accustomed by this time to finding bars and restaurants off limits to troops, we stopped the first MP we met and asked if it would be possible to go into any of the business places. The first one we asked replied: "Yeah, the town's off limits, what do you want. I'll watch the jeep for you." So we went in for a glass of beer, becoming acquainted with that extremely watery stuff which was to be a familiar beverage to us in the days to come. No near beer of Prohibition time ever had as low an alcoholic content.

We were told that the bridges were in over the Seine in the Neuilly area, and were soon on the broad, smooth highway leading into the city. As we neared the city we were seized by a wild sort of excitement—a type I had not felt since I was a child riding a Ferris wheel or a roller coaster. My first visit to Paris had not affected me this way. We began to giggle, to sing, yell, and otherwise show exuberance.

At 2 P.M. we hit the Étoile. Although the city had been liberated for six days and the grand parades held for the 2d French Armored and the 28th Division, the people were still in a mood to give a delirious welcome to anyone in uniform. The Metro was still not running, so people in holiday garb filled the streets. The Étoile was surrounded by American sightseers like ourselves, and they were surrounded by the French. A truckload of German prisoners was being driven around the Arc de Triomphe and some of the crowd jeered at them. Only two or three weeks before, some of these men may have participated in the daily parade up the Champs-Elysées to the Arc, or they may have been stationed one and one-half blocks away at the Hotel Majestic, which was now serving as the headquarters of General Lee's Communications Zone headquarters. Behind the hotel still stood the damaged tank that had attempted to stand off the Allied troops.

Much as I wanted to go directly down the Champs-Elysées, I determined to keep a resolution I had made weeks before. Since I had known I was going to Europe, I had said that I would go first in Paris to 15 Rue Mesnil, to see if the Comte Paul de Lassus, my old landlord in 1938, had lived through the war. As a child in 1871, he had seen the Germans enter the city, and had been there when they nearly came back in the First World War, and had been living in Paris, I knew, just before the German occupation. So we turned from the Arc, went down Avenue Foch to Place Victor Hugo, and then to the old apartment house. Monsieur de Lassus had been sent away to a rest home a few weeks before, but his daughter, the Comtesse Brabant, and his maid, Rose, were still there. Mademoiselle de Lassus had died during the war—in 1941—but the old gentleman, at eighty-three, was still living. His son was an officer in the FFI, and Rose's son, an old-time Alpine Chasseur, was somewhere with the Maquis.

I left soap, cigarettes, and rations and went back to the jeep. We were far enough off the beaten path to be an object of curiosity, and children and grown-ups surrounded the jeep. They asked for cigarettes, candy or chewing gum, or were satisfied to look at an American soldier. Between handing out presents, shaking hands, and giving autographs, we found difficulty in getting away.

With my sentimental pilgrimage accomplished, I was ready to get an idea of how the city had fared under the Germans. Traffic was not too heavy, since only a few thousand of the thousands of Americans who had recently passed through remained. The city was almost totally denuded of French traffic, since the Germans had taken nearly all the buses and taxis with them. So we got in on some of the same sort of wild acclaim the first troops received—particularly in those parts of the city which I picked out to visit. We had learned long since to expect flowers, but this time we would pass groups who would count one, two, three and break into applause, as if at a game.

Down the Champs-Elysées we went, Russ driving slowly so John and I could imitate some of the stately dignity that some GIs in a nearby rented carriage were showing. Instead of heading first for Montmartre or Pigalle, we turned south at the Place de la Concorde, which still was marked by barbed wire barriers and Belgian gate obstacles such as had been used on Omaha Beach. Not far away were wreaths marking the spots where the last Resistance leaders had been killed in the battle for liberation.

Knocked-out tanks stood at the entrance to the bridge leading to the Chamber of Deputies—the same bridge that French mobs, seeking to attack the Daladier Ministry in 1934, had tried to cross. The bridge had been hit by random shots, and the Palais Bourbon showed damage done by fire when the departing Germans had fired records in the French lower house. Down the Boulevard Saint-Germain by the Carnegie Foundation where I had attended classes in 1937–38, by the Cafe aux deux Magots, where I had once discussed French politics with Alexander Werth of the *Manchester Guardian,* Italian politics with a follower of Mussolini, and drunk some white wine with Glendal Harper and other students of the Quarter. The church of Saint-Germain des Près, one of the most ancient edifices of the city, was still undamaged. The Cafe de Flore showed no signs as yet of the Existentialists.

We turned off the Boulevard Saint-Germain at the Boulevard Saint-Michel, and followed the route up by the cafes and bookstalls I had known best, including the spot where a booth had stood during the Christmas of 1937 and I had knocked down six tin cans with a baseball to win a bottle of cheap champagne and the plaudits of some Americans and British in the crowd, by the Luxembourg Gardens, to the Pantheon, by the Faculty of Law, where I had been enrolled, by the Bibliothèque, where I had waited for hours to get books, and to the church of Saint-Etienne du Mont. As we stopped for a moment to get a view of the church, we were approached by an old woman who offered us three wizened apples, which she wiped carefully on her apron. We had no cigarettes or rations opened at the time, so we demurred, saying that we had nothing to give her. But she insisted, with a slight touch of hurt in her voice, "But messieurs, I wish to give you this to say thank you for having our city back again." That answer, and a few similar ones, were to stay with us when we met people later who merely wanted what we had to give.

I had still one more sentimental journey to make—this time past the Lycèe Henri IV, past the pension at 3 Rue de l'Estrapade, where I had stayed in the fall of 1937, and then in quick succession down Rue Clovis, by Rue le Cardinal Lemoine, past the Botanical Gardens, down along the Seine, back to the Pont Neuf. We got a good view of Notre Dame de Paris, where de Gaulle had been shot at a week before, and by the Palais de Justice, where the police had staged the first step of the revolt which drove out the Germans. We then crossed the Seine, came down by the Louvre, whose gardens, strangely enough, held tanks pointing their ugly gun barrels out at us.

We went northward, then quickly to Montmartre and back by Boulevard Ney to the Étoile. From there we came to the Place Washington, where one could see undamaged the monuments to Washington, and to the American members of the Lafayette Escadrille, and the Herrick bust, thence across the Pont d'Iena and to the Hotel des Invalides. We found the V Corps TAC in the process of moving out of Paris, and the people we wanted to see were in one of three places: either south, north, or east of the city.

With all sorts of directions to pick from, we set out on the grand tour. First to Saint-Denis by way of Boulevard Sebastopol-Strasbourg, Magenta, Barbes, Ornano, to the Porte Clignancourt. I had last visited this workers quarter in 1938 over the objection of Monsier de Lassus, who warned that I might suffer violence from the Reds there. We were stopped near Saint-Denis by the press of the crowd, and found a group taunting a girl who had been friendly to German soldiers. Her head had just been shaved and Free French soldiers were escorting her down the streets while the crowd hooted. She, and sister sufferers we saw later, got our sympathy no matter what they had done. For their look, in the hands of their tormentors, was that of a hunted animal. It seemed to me that nothing made a person look so naked to the world, nothing was so overwhelming brutal in its humiliation, than this forcible shaving of heads. Rather to be pilloried all the day or be ridden through the crowd than this. Neither did I like the placards on nearby shops that said "here is the house of a Boche," or "supplier of the Boche." It smelled too much of the "Here is a Jew" signs I had seen in Germany in 1938.

We stopped but seldom on our journey, since each stop brought requests for cigarettes. At one point a well-dressed man, who begged our pardon in perfect English, said he was dying for a cigarette for which he was willing to pay. The newspaper l'Aube at about this period had a cartoon depicting the national password. A Frenchman made the V-for-victory sign to an American GI. The soldier returned the salute and the Frenchman followed it with two fingers to the mouth—without a cigarette. The soldier handed over a Camel and the Frenchman gave a proper V sign with a cigarette between the fingers.

At Saint-Denis, near the old church where the kings of France were once buried, we found a detachment from V Corps headquarters located in a girls' school. Captain Grimson was on hand, but he told me that the historical section was in the process of moving to Moussy-les-vieux, beyond le Bourget, two miles off the road toward Soissons. Unfortunately, when we got there, V Corps elements had not arrived so we headed back to Sceaux, south of Paris, where Victor Rear was said still to be.

Returning, we stopped at the church of Sacré Coeur. We had to slow up as we neared the summit, and this was a signal for the growing crowd of children that was following us to jump on the jeep. As we reached the terrace in front of the basilica, we were overwhelmed by about fifty children who clambered aboard, demanding souvenirs, presents, autographs, or just plain handshakes. One nice lady came up with a postcard for each of us—for which she refused a proffered gift. Her card, bearing a photograph of the church, was marked with this message in English: "Today 25 August 1944. Remembrance deliverer of Paris. Welcome at to Allied."

John at this point made the tactical error of opening a K-ration box to get the small package of cigarettes that each one contained, and we were nearly trampled by children. When we started to leave, we became the center of an inundation of gamins, all of whom wanted to ride. Two or three six-year-old ruffians teetered precariously on the hood, pushing each other, while others climbed over John and me, searching still for other K rations. Only by appealing to nearby adults to drag the children from the jeep did we get away without hurting anyone.

Friday, 1 September (D+87)

Rained at intervals.

Not daring to brave any more crowds, we drove on to Sceaux, stopping only to take on agents de police who, in the absence of transportation, were hitchhiking rides to their posts.

At Sceaux finally, we found Topete, Captain Born, and Lieutenant Graney, who was sharing quarters with the Historical Section at the time, established on the second floor of a girls' school. Finding that Fox and Howe were now in Paris, and would know where First Army's historical section was located, we got Topete to take *La Cucaracha* and lead us back to the city. This time we headed for the Hotel Scribe, headquarters of the correspondents, where Russ could find *Stars and Stripes* representatives. We also found that the bar there was one of the few open at night; electricity was still off in most of the city and the few places that were open were illuminated by candlepower. Prices were still not high, and it was possible for an enlisted man to get a table in the private room of the bar, where we celebrated by ordering champagne—Mumm's Cordon Rouge at 235 francs and Veuve Clicquot at 350 francs a bottle (or $4.70 and $7)—just half what it cost the following evening. A soldier who had already celebrated too freely aided the cause by donating a bottle he had just bought but could not handle. It was amazing to be sitting in this rather swank bar, only a few steps from the opera and the Cafe de la Rue de la Paix, being served champagne in fragile glasses by white-coated waiters. We were not well dressed for the occasion. My field jacket had a huge grease stain down one side, and we were wearing helmets and sidearms. I had taken off my hunting knife and canteen, but still had my pistol and compass on my gun belt, and Russ was carrying his grease gun. (By the next evening, the war had progressed far enough for the private dining room to be reserved for colonels, wine and champagne had doubled in cost, a woman correspondent turned up in evening clothes, and some of the male correspondents turned up in pinks. Ernie Pyle, who was about to leave for the United States, turned up in his usual battered battle togs).

When the bar closed, we went to the billeting office at the Place de l'Opera and found that we could get a room in nearly any hotel in town without showing any credentials. Rooms were available not very far away in the Hotel Edouard VII, a fairly nice hotel with accent on stone. There was no electricity and no hot water, but we were given separate rooms, immaculately clean, and baths. We were almost overcome by the prospect.

As inviting as the prospect was, we accepted Topete's offer to guide us to one of the nightspots still open. In the blackout, which still prevailed in Paris, and without car lights, he managed to find a small underground nightclub of sorts near Pigalle. We were warmly welcomed at the door by a rather buxom lass who left her glowering companion to give each of us an enthusiastic kiss. She was not hospitable to Topete who, it seemed, owed them about twenty dollars, but I explained that he would be paid the next day and the rest of us had money, so she let him in.

Several members of the FFI were swaggering around the bar. One was carrying a British revolver with which he claimed to have killed seven Germans during the liberation. The proprietor, who had once lived in New York, talked pessimistically of possible trouble in the city, but hoped that de Gaulle would lend an authoritarian hand and establish a stable and efficient government. I soon found that the old bitterness against Jews and labor remained.

Saturday, 2 September (D+88)

As pleasant as Paris was, we had not done any of our errands, so we set out fairly early next morning for First Army headquarters. We were told at the Hotel des Invalides that they would probably be at Versailles. There, in a mad affair only the army could match, American elements were moving in and out of areas near the Château of Versailles, setting up kitchens and latrines along the regular rows of trees, within sight of the elegant grounds of Louis XIV's palace. But the First Army headquarters had not arrived. Some of the advance party said undoubtedly Major O'Sullivan, whom we sought, would be back at Rambouillet at the Château Rothschild. There we found that the Historical Section was supposed to be thirty-five miles away. We went there and found that the major had left sometime before for VICTOR Rear, where we had been that morning. When I returned to Sceaux, I found that the paymaster had already gone on to VICTOR Rear, which momentarily was ahead of VICTOR Forward. So we hit the road again for Soissons.

This time we found the major sitting on a stump in a field while tents were being put up around him. We talked at length about my project, but he was unable to heed my pleas to return to Corps, saying that it appeared the war would soon be over and it was important to complete the study on the landings. No pay was forthcoming because someone had failed to get the payroll. So, I didn't get my pay until several weeks later, when V Corps was in Luxembourg and Captain Fox drew it for me and sent it to Paris.

We wanted to check on records next, but First Army was still moving and we suddenly were faced with the fact that gasoline was running short. V Corps was just about out, so they could spare us only five gallons and advised us to get some from trucks we met on the way back to the beaches. I attempted to call Colonel Taylor to explain our problem. On the theory that the COMZ headquarters, the communications center for all U.S. forces in Europe, would have contact with the beach, I wandered into the bedlam that was the switchboard center of Paris. In addition to dozens of officers demanding to be put through on some vital, top priority call, the place was besieged by Frenchmen trying to locate their families. The GI operators were aiding French operators trying to merge the two systems and trying to work out some mixed patois. I shall never forget the pitying look a sergeant gave me when I asked for a line to the beach. He informed me that he couldn't locate people forty miles away. Many weeks later I learned that for several days during the period the War Department could not get in touch with the Supreme Commander.

Apparently because we had been good customers the night before, the billeting office gave us a better hotel the second night. This time we stayed at the Hotel Palais Quai d'Orsay. There we found the clerk and porters in frock coats. There was electricity downstairs and the elevators worked, but in our wing of the hotel we had to be conducted by light from candelabra. Again we got a room apiece. Apparently because I spoke French, and there were few other comers, I received a large suite, complete with baroque clock. Despite all the swank, there was no breakfast. When we asked the next morning, as we tripped lightly down the grand staircase, if we might have coffee, members of the staff said, "But yes, if you will be so kind as to give us some of your Nescafe."

Somehow, the idea of no coffee in a French hotel seemed impossible. Yet during the previous day we had been made aware of food shortages in the city. Long queues stood in front of bakeries and butcher shops. Rationing seemed to be very severe, although trucks of food—we had seen several marked "Food from Britain" in French—were pouring into the city. Stores had little for sale. The city had not been hard hit by planes, but there was evidence of bombings around some of the rail centers. Damage had been especially heavy north of Saint-Denis, at le Bourget, and near Versailles, where we attempted to cut rail lines and hit airfields.

One commodity in great supply was newspapers. The underground had started printing its wares opening as soon as the city was liberated, and these were quickly joined by many others. Most of them were rather small two- or four-page affairs. Very few paid any attention to British or U.S. victories but laid heavy emphasis on the work of the 2d French Armored Division and the French forces coming up from the south. It was pointed out that General Gerow's statement that he was pleased to hand the city over to General Pierre Joseph Koening was merely a gesture since Paris had liberated itself.[6] (Corporal Kelly had already shown me V Corps correspondence showing that U.S. forces had entered Paris when General de Gaulle indicated that there was danger that the Germans would prevent the liberation from succeeding). The newspaper *l'Aube* sounded a word of warning to the various groups in Paris, pointing out that it was folly to scramble for place and appointment, and cars, that the equality of defeat should not be swept away in the moment of victory.

Flags were everywhere. We were struck by the evidence of many red flags. The American flag was just below the tricolor on the Eiffel Tower.

Sunday, 3 September (D+89)

We reluctantly started back to Valognes on Sunday by way of Versailles–Dreux–Verneuil–Argentan. We followed many American and British trucks filled with French refugees on their way home. People still waved at us along the way, but we scarcely looked at them because we were watching for gasoline trucks. Only in the proverbial nick of time did we meet a gasoline convoy. Fortunately, the driver of one of the vehicles was very helpful, filling the tank for us, and tossing away the jerrican when he emptied it.

Between Argentan-Falaise, as we went down a narrow road, we were suddenly stopped by a tree which toppled and fell across the road, narrowly missing a truckload of women and children. A group of FFI and American and British troops on the various trucks coming and going piled off and began running toward the point where the tree had fallen. We were alarmed as we saw three or four other trees also toppling. They had been sawed through, and the French said that the work had been done a short time before by Germans who were still in the woods beyond a nearby hill. So, without any thought, all of us charged the hill and began to run toward the woods. Russ had his grease gun, which I doubt he had ever used. John was struggling with a jammed carbine and ultimately lost his clip, and I had my .45, which was perfectly harmless in my hands at more than ten feet. The French began firing frantically at the woods. We decided that discretion was the better part of valor and retired to the jeep, not wishing to be killed either by the Germans or the FFI. I gave my clip of bullets to one of the men on the firing line as I retreated.

By this time a tank had been brought up and it pushed away the fallen tree. A priest tried to get order among the truckload of refugees who feared that they were returning to more war.

From Argentan to Falaise, we saw what the tardy withdrawal from Mortain had done to the German forces. Hundreds of smashed vehicles marked the roadside, tanks were disabled in the fields, dead horses lay beside the wagons they were pulling, papers were spilling out on all sides from overturned boxes, prisoner cages were overflowing, and wooden crosses were seen everywhere.

Once we got past Chambois, we made good progress. We returned to the beach in time to get Colonel Taylor and to return to a quiet and peaceful dinner in the grounds of the pleasant château, now far away from war, near Valognes.

Chapter 13

Last Days in Normandy

Monday, 4 September (D+90)–
Sunday, 10 September (D+96)

While in Paris, I had actually lost sight of the progress of the war. There were many papers there but very little news. I spent the day I returned to Valognes reading the papers and army periodic reports. British forces were now in Belgium and U.S. forces were beyond Verdun. The Canadians had wiped out the Dieppe disaster by taking that port. The British papers for 3 September were beginning to scold their leaders for not advertising British efforts more. They stressed the fact that the battle for Normandy was won at Caen, and that the plan was Montgomery's. Dispatches from SHAEF gave lame explanations for denial of an earlier story that Bradley was now equal in power to Montgomery. To offset British criticism that Montgomery was being demoted in the 1 September move by which Eisenhower became commander in chief in the field with Montgomery and Bradley as his coequal army group commanders, Churchill announced that Monty was now a field marshal.

On the evening of our return, we were told that a special entertainment was to be held nearby. Bing Crosby and Fred Astaire had just arrived on the Continent and COMZ had arranged for them to give a show near Valognes. Thousands of GIs brought from many parts of the Cotentin Peninsula were seated in a large field where they could observe the performance. The show was largely spontaneous and filled with the type of ad libbing for which Crosby is famous. The two men appeared without their wigs and proved to be extremely bald, a fact that served as the basis for many of their jokes. Astaire showed his age when, after some of his more exacting dance routines, he had to struggle against the speechlessness brought on by his exertion. Although the two men appeared without makeup, special microphones, and the like, they were an uproarious success.

The show was accompanied by an incident that made for bad feelings between enlisted men and officers. The early buses that came that evening to take men from our area to the show were marked "For Officers Only," and the men got angry before trucks appeared to get them. When time came to return, however, a number of us had to walk back because the officers would not wait for the buses only they could ride and took our trucks instead. In talking of this incident on the two-mile hike back, stories of several such incidents were repeated. A few nights before, a soldier just out of the hospital was given a seat by a truck driver. An officer hitched a ride and obviously expected the soldier to move to the rear. Finally, with ill grace, he got into the backseat, but on leaving made some nasty cracks to the driver. This story was matched by one by an MP who said that he and several soldiers had been on a bus a few evenings before when several officers entered. There were no seats for them, so two privates got up. When the MP kept his seat, one of the officers said, "Don't you know your military courtesy, soldier?" The MP said, "Yes sir," and, in accordance with sound army practice, kept his seat. Another had a story to the effect that recently in the finance office, an officer had pushed in ahead of him. But the sergeant in charge had refused to pay him first, much to the officer's disgust. My diary comment on all this was: "These incidents, which happened here, seem to bear out the EM's grudge against SOS littleness and pettiness. Officers at the front seldom display this kind of attitude."

By 6 September, the rain was getting more and more disagreeable and the weather was colder. We were anxious to see the last of Normandy, although we hated to leave just as the apples that we had seen bloom and mature were about ready to be picked. The headquarters people had begun to leave for Paris at the first of the month, and we were anxious to join them. The war seemed near an end, as the newspapers reported a 210-mile advance in six days and indicated that Allied forces were in Holland, Luxembourg, Saarbrücken, Brussels, and Antwerp. News of stiffening resistance near Aachen should have tempered the optimism, which was shared by nearly everyone from the frontline infantryman to SHAEF, but until mid-September the intelligence estimates all along the lines were marked by almost hysterical optimism.

Our unit was left almost to the last in the COMZ moving plans. Our task was increased enormously because the London branch of the Historical Section, not wishing to be left out of the war, was beginning to fly over and establish offices near Valognes. Only by tall tales of snakes, bombs, and the like did we manage to keep most of the WACs away, although just before the move one or two of the more buxom types, resplendent in form-fitting slacks, arrived. Many of the files came our way, but with little extra help to move them. They had barely been unloaded when we had to load them again. I was extremely angry since Colonel Taylor, Hall, Bill Harnett, and I had already moved our stuff. Now we were pressed again into service. The junior officers of the London branch outnumbered the enlisted men and were not inclined to help. I was particularly irate because a warrant officer who had been a corporal the week before and was easily the largest man in the group stood around checking off boxes from his list, while poor little Abie, weighing about 130 and standing five foot six, helped me load a field safe. I had no argument since I weighed over two hundred, a fact that was to get me in on many moving details, but I was not mollified until Colonel Taylor, seeing the situation, came forward to help. I got some solace from talking to the Negro driver of the truck we were loading. A graduate of Columbia University, he had been with the truck company for more than two years. He claimed that his white officers considered him a troublemaker and, therefore, unfit for any other assignment in the army. He was quite bitter.

Sunday, 10 September (D+96)

A beautiful day but cold.

We were up at 4:30 and loaded into trucks soon afterward. Wrapped in blankets and huddled together for warmth we waited, although not patiently, for more than an hour until someone had his coffee and we could move out. Having never had the experience of riding a "40 and 8," I will hold on to this ride as one of the most unpleasant I had during the war. The seats were narrow and the roads bad, so that one was constantly threatened with being thrown to the floor, where three or four hearty souls were trying to sleep. During the first part of the trip the trucks were covered with canvas, which came so low on the sides that one had to bend forward in the truck, a posture that was very tiring. Add to that cold feet and cold that seeped through the blankets and one has a picture of temporary misery. Later in the day, however, when it was warm enough to roll up the sides of the canvas covering, the trip went better.

In an attempt to avoid crowding the roads, our group (we were mixed in with trucks from the chaplain's, finance, judge advocate, and other rear-echelon sections) was split into several convoys. Ours went by Coutances, Vire, Tinchebray, Flers, Seés, and Versailles. At first we saw little of the countryside, but about midmorning, when we stopped for the inevitable "rest call," we rolled up the canvas on the side of the truck. The fighting troops had passed that way more than a week before, but people still in a holiday mood greeted us warmly along the way. Inspired in part by a desire to get cigarettes and other gifts, they lined the roads and waved or called greetings. It was clear that they were pleased to see us, with or without presents, and they swarmed around the truck every time we stopped. Often they embarrassed us when we stopped for a "rest call" and they ran up before we were ready to see them. The *Stars and Stripes* cartoon strip "Hubert" made this situation famous with its sketch of troops who are dismounted from trucks and lined up along a road facing the fields when an aged grandmother and her son come riding along on bicycles. She asks, "What is it that the Americans are always looking for along the roadside?"

We did our best to play the role of liberators, and we finally hit on the device of wrapping up two or three cigarettes and a piece of candy in paper bundles and tossing them to people along the road. I went into my supply of Fleetwoods, now rather battered in my duffel bag, and got rid of several cartons that way.

We reached Versailles at 11:30 P.M., but were misdirected on how to proceed toward Paris and went around in a circle for a while. We sat for a time in the courtyard outside the Ecuries, the former royal stables of the château and later offices belonging to the French Ministry of War, where some of the enlisted men of SHAEF were now billeted. Someone finally put us on the right road and near 2 A.M. we reached the newly built Lycèe Claude Bernard in suburban Paris and were assigned quarters. We were bedded down at four, just about twenty-four hours after we had been awakened in Normandy to start our trip.

Chapter 14

Watching Paris Come to Life

Monday, 11 September (D+97)–
Friday, 10 November (D+157)

The Lycèe Claude Bernard was a new school building on the outskirts of Paris which the Germans had used as a billet for their troops. The lights were still off, so we wandered about the huge halls by candlelight. We were pleased by the large shower rooms and the prospect of modern plumbing, but the water was cut off and the showers and water closets did not work—a fact which did not prevent some of the men from using them.

The Germans had left in great haste, leaving books, pieces of uniforms, toilet articles, and notepaper scattered over the floors. We were intrigued by the murals that decorated the walls. One room had quotations from Hitler's speeches and writings, done in imposing German script. The squad room had photographs of German generals and scenes of Germany. Above the latter were branches of faded flowers. Elsewhere were cartoons of Pluto the dog and other Disney characters. In the recreation room, a German soldier was portrayed receiving a hearty kiss from a rather portly wench. Our favorite was a huge mural covering the entire wall of one room. It showed members of a German column proudly goose-stepping beneath the Arc de Triomphe.

A kindhearted officer or first sergeant let us sleep until eleven the first morning. No orders had been received about the Historical Section. Our records were still on the way from Valognes and there was nothing to do for the day at the office. We wanted, therefore, to be out seeing the city. We were kept for some three hours behind the gates around the school, and we feared that we would remain there for the day. As we went out by the sentry, we had the sinking feeling that life was going to be much more restrictive than in the field. Inspections had already been promised for the next week, with demerits for improperly made beds. (Ever try to make up a bed on a canvas cot?)

Near the Lycee was the Auteuil Metro stop, and close by the stadium and racetrack. Because of the lack of electricity, the Metro ran only a few hours a day, stopping at eight on weekdays, and not running at all on Sunday. Yet our eating places were at least two miles away on the Boulevard des Ternes, in the Rue de Berri, and on the Champs-Elysées. But we didn't think of inconveniences. The war was suspended for the moment. Hall, Billy Harnett, Melvin Richards of California, and I took the Metro to the Étoile, and from there went for a walk that brought us finally to Notre Dame.

Paris, to a considerable degree, was as dead as we had seen it nearly two weeks before. The streets were blacked out at night and bicycles furnished the chief civilian means of transportation. Persons who had stayed out late sometimes used the vele, a bicycle with a sidecar usually propelled by a rather thick-limbed Parisian. Now and then one saw a horse and carriage. But the prices were astronomical and usually only persons so befuddled by drink that they were unworried about prices ever used them. There was practically no coal for heating. Lights were turned off in homes and offices between eight and ten in the evening. There were no movies open, except one showing films of the liberation. All in all, the City of Light was dead as late as mid-September 1944. I had first seen it at the height of the Great Exposition of 1937 and had left it just as the city was polishing up for the visit of the King and Queen of England in 1938, and it contrasted painfully with the old days. No bread without a ration card, very little to eat or drink and that terribly expensive, the streets drab and dirty, no life. Many of the people were poorly dressed. The lack of soap and warm water for many months showed itself in terrible sores on the legs of many people one saw in the streets. Malnutrition was evident in splotches on the arms and faces of children, and in their pinched faces. That was to be the picture of Paris for several weeks. But little by little it stirred, and by the time I left in late November it was again alive.

Our new office, it developed next morning, was to be in the headquarters building, the Hotel Majestic, located on Avenue Kléber, a few minutes walk from the Étoile. Our mess was in a swanky cafe at the corner of the Champs-Elysées and the Rue de Berri. There was little to eat for several weeks, but we sat at tables with clean tablecloths, while French waitresses brought plates of Spam and C rations, with extremely unpalatable GI bread and great mounds of peanut butter and marmalade. After a time, an amateur GI orchestra played from the music stand on the second balcony. Meals were served on all three floors. It took some 350 employees to run the place. Such elegance was disturbing when contrasted with conditions at the front, and I always winced when I took there some visitor who had just returned for a day or two. "Jesus," they would say, "women to wait on you and an orchestra."

Our first day at work was fairly typical of the first ten days in the city—during which time it appeared that we were all on a sort of holiday. I spent the morning helping to unload boxes of records from a truck, and then went with Joe Bierstein, who had just changed from master sergeant to warrant officer, to find some cognac with which he could "wet down" his bars. In the afternoon, I went with Captain Healey to the large reception room of the Majestic to a reception held by Archbishop Spellman. I found out why he was called a statesman of the church. Modest and unobtrusive, he had a politician's memory for names and places. When I told him that I lived near Paducah, Kentucky, he asked about its recovery from the great flood of 1937 and inquired about several people who lived there. Later in the afternoon, four or five of us went to one of the sidewalk cafes along the Champs-Elysées and sampled the weak beer, while trying to imagine what Paris looked like when it was full of tourists. Now the place was crowded with GIs, most of us rather grimy in soiled jackets and trousers, since there was no cleaning and pressing service as yet. (My grease-stained jacket continued to embarrass me as I wore it for a week or two to various receptions. I took it to a cleaning establishment and was told that no fluids were available, but that they would try vinegar as a bleach. It removed the grease stain, but the white splotch showed up strangely against the remaining dark background). In the evening we went to the Place de l'Opera and then to the Hotel de Paris, between the Opera and la

Madeleine, which was newly converted into a Red Cross club. We had fruit juice and listened to a three-piece French orchestra feebly trying to pretend to be an American "combo." Later, back at the Lycèe, we emptied a bottle of burgundy that Harnett had acquired in a deal involving three packages of cigarettes.

When the Metro was running, we were allowed to ride free. The army had offered to have us pay, but the feeling was that since the Germans had refused to pay, we should not be required to. A vignette in one of the papers told of an old lady who cried *"scandale"* when a soldier offered to pay and the money had been accepted. It was really a frightening experience to ride the Metros at this time, because at any time of day or night, they were like the worst of the rush hour in New York. The conductors literally applied their arms and knees to the backs of passengers in order to get the doors closed. When GIs sometimes pushed a bit, the French were inclined to mutter imprecations. Increasingly, there was the tendency to say *"pire que les boches"* (worse than the Germans) at the GIs.

Our records were slow in arriving, and the feeling continued that we must celebrate our holiday. The business of going back to the sidewalk cafes to watch the traffic—particularly pretty girls wearing rather full skirts and riding bicycles and causing traffic snarls when GI drivers turned around to gawk at them—was continued. On our third day in Paris, after a morning of moving furniture, I went to the Sorbonne to get the addresses of some of my former professors and then went to a nearby bistro. The clientele there were mostly laborers, and I wondered what my reception would be. They were extremely friendly and all offered to buy drinks. Soon afterwards, I ran into a couple of soldiers who were anxious to see the city. I guided them around the Châtelet, the Quai de l'Herloge, the Sainte Chapelle, the Sorbonne, Palais du Luxembourg, the Odeon, and the like, getting all of the kick an old citizen gets in showing off his town to a visitor.

I got a great deal of fun that day out of an attempt to get directions for a soldier from a Frenchman on the Metro. We were so packed that at least a dozen participated in the discussion and nearly everyone suggested something different. After a time the best guides were ten- to twelve-year-olds who, learning that grateful Americans were soft touches, would soon hang around

Metro stops and ask in pretty good English if they could give directions.

On our way back to the Lycèe on the evening of the thirteenth, we could not find our way easily from the Metro, and we accepted the aid of a sixteen-year-old student who walked with us from the Porte Saint-Cloud to our gate. He was a refugee from Le Havre and told us of having heard of the D-Day landings on a hidden radio and of the great difficulty he and his family had in suppressing their elation in front of the Germans. After our landings, the Germans had put SS troops in his Lycèe, their first attempt to interfere with teaching.

On our way to the Lycèe, we stopped outside a bistro where a large crowd was gathered and men were gesticulating wildly. We found that there were reports of small bands of German soldiers in the woods outside the city. Some of the men wanted to take guns and look for them. Others dissuaded them, saying there were probably also many Germans in civilian clothes still in Paris, and that it was best to leave them to the army. We went on our way after a time. As we turned into the gate of the Lycèe, an old lady said in English: "Good night, sleep well. God bless you!" We thanked her, a bit self-conscious in the face of her gratitude.

Meanwhile, American forces were moving into Germany. V Corps had gone into Belgium, intending to push for Coblenz, and then had been sent to Luxembourg City. From there its units pushed across the Luxembourg frontier, with elements of the 4th Infantry, 28th Infantry, and 5th Armored Divisions claiming to have been the first into Germany on 11 September. To the north, VII Corps crossed the next day and began an attack on the Siegfried Line near Roetgen. Patton's forces to the south had been brought to a near standstill in the Metz area by increased German resistance and a shortage of fuel. Deliveries of gasoline were being made to some units by planes. On the thirteenth I had met a pilot dressed in pinks who was grumbling because he had been taken off his regular bomber run to deliver gasoline. However, like others I was to meet, he had timed his return in such a manner that when he got ready to fly back to England he was told that it was too late and he would have to spend the night in Paris. Not all the pilots disliked the fuel run. Later there were stories that sometimes, when they brought fuel to Third

Army units, a case of champagne would be brought to the pilot "with compliments of General Patton."

One of my pleasant visits while in Paris came on 15 September when I went to the home of Prof. André Siegfreid, famed French historian and publicist and a former instructor of mine at the Institut des Hautes Études Internationales. We talked for more than two and one-half hours during which time we ranged over the whole field of the political situation of France and spoke of his personal situation while the Germans were there. Siegfried had not been treated badly by the Germans and had continued to teach his classes. On two occasions they had tried to persuade him to give his backing to a book made up of quotations culled from his books on the United States and Great Britain to prove that those countries were decadent. On his second refusal, the German officer who had summoned him to Gestapo headquarters had screamed out: "Good God, man, don't you want to help Europe?" Siegfried had actually managed to continue writing for *Le Figaro*, which was published in unoccupied France and distributed clandestinely in Paris. While he had never been bothered, he said that from 1940 to 1944 he never heard the front doorbell ring late at night or early in the morning without the thought that perhaps the Germans would be there.

As I was leaving, I asked if I might get something for him, thinking of cigarettes or coffee. But he asked only for American journals and copies of the *New York Times*. I took him all the magazines I could find on several occasions after that and Douglas MacArthur II[7] of the American embassy saw to it that a copy of the *Times* from the embassy's pouch was delivered to him daily. Professor Siegfried was to do many favors for me afterward. I attributed this to the fact that I was one of the first Americans to visit him and that I had been a student of his. But in part, I think it was due to the fact that he had been a sergeant in the First World War, that he resented his army service, and that he wanted to do something for another professor turned sergeant. When, several days later, I took Prof. Crane Brinton of Harvard, then on OSS duty in Paris, and Colonel Taylor to see him, he said as they were ready to leave, "If you care to come back again, get in touch with Sergeant Pogue, he has my private telephone number."

The seventeenth was my thirty-second birthday. I had celebrated it the night before by spending the night in Paris. Finding that the Hotel de Paris, with private rooms and baths, was being opened by the Red Cross as a billet for men on leave, but discovering that men in fighting units were not yet permitted to come into Paris, I had registered for a room at forty cents a night. I could not have had a finer present. (I managed to stay on there until 1 October, when Captain Ierardi, who was more or less in charge of the discipline of our group, told me to return to my regular billets. The order was expected, since I had seen that morning a statement that Paris was now open to troops on leave and that all other persons would have to give up their rooms. But it had been pleasant while it lasted).

My decision to stay in Paris had been based in part on my desire to go on the seventeenth to Notre Dame for a special high mass to be said by Archbishop Spellman. Since there was no Metro service on Sunday it meant that I had to walk to the cathedral, and I preferred to do that from the Madeleine than from Auteuil. The mass was to a great degree the American official celebration of the liberation of Paris. Notre Dame was packed with soldiers. French and Allied flags were in evidence. I thought, as I stood in a side aisle, of the many Te Deums that had been celebrated there in honor of the French victory. The service was made especially thrilling by the great organ at the conclusion of the service, when it pealed out the "Star-Spangled Banner."

On the following day, the enlisted men of our section moved from the Lycèe Claude Bernard to the former Austrian embassy at 15 Rue Beaujon. The members of our artist section were already installed there. We were to have our billets in the great ballroom of the embassy, and a few days later our offices were moved there as well. The building was not pretentious, but, like most of the Parisian buildings, entered through a gate that was opened by the concierge. Our gatekeeper was of White Russian extraction. He always seemed in a bad mood and tended to scowl at us when we came in late at night. The building had been used by the Germans as a headquarters for the German agency that dealt with the property and holdings of French Jews. I found a number of interesting files on French companies that I picked out of the debris on the floors and put away as souvenirs. Some weeks later,

French officials came by asking for any documents we might have seen and I was able to hand these over.

The office seemed also to have been a storage place for German propaganda because the closets were filled with copies of Hitler's speeches and bloodcurdling attacks against the Americans. These proved to be very helpful that fall and winter when thousands of them were used in the fireplace to keep us warm. I found a complete file of the *Pariser Zeitung,* a German language paper, and was amused to discover an issue that came out just before D-Day in which a correspondent who had just returned from Normandy told of the impregnability of the fortifications, and how the Allies would be thrown back into the sea. It was fascinating to read the issues for June and July, as they tended to discount our victories and to say that the tide would soon turn. Even in early August there was still hope that the war would end in favor of the Germans. As our armies came closer to Paris, however, German "successes" on the eastern front and Japanese "victories" in the Pacific were given big play.

The ballroom proved to be particularly bad for a bedroom. Our cots were lined up in rows across the room. Overhead was a ceiling mostly of glass, which was splendid for letting in the light but terrible for letting in the cold air. As a result, I slept with as much cover there as I did later in the field. On one score, that of nearness to work and to food, we had no complaints. Three seconds away from our desks and three or four blocks from the place where we ate, we were better situated than we had been anywhere else on the Continent.

At the Rue Beaujon I met a number of new men in the section who had recently come from London. The one I was to know best was Royce Thompson from Amarillo, Texas, and Detroit. "Tommy" was a librarian by profession and had served for several years in that capacity on the *Detroit News.* Colonel Marshall had suggested Thompson as an assistant to John Hall in keeping track of the voluminous records that were now beginning to flow into the headquarters from all the units in the field. We were to become close friends and after the war, in Washington, to work together in the army's Historical Division. Many of the jackets that held the records of the European campaigns still have the scrawled numbers and descriptive titles which he and John Hall put on them in Rue Beaujon, and later at the former Gestapo head-quarters on Avenue Foch and at the Château Hennemont in Saint-Germain-en-Laye, which the Historical Section occupied in 1944.

Occupying the top-floor rooms with their studio-like skylights were the battlefield artists. This group included Lieutenant Arnest, and Sergeants Dows, Manuel Bromberg of Cleveland, Harry Dix of New York (who had married a former student of mine), Pete Deana of Washington, Stanley, and Albert Gold of Philadelphia. The artist group was somewhat unhappy with its lot, and with good reason. They had earlier been promised commissions and a well-organized program. Instead, they had been pushed around from one headquarters to another until they were finally assigned to us in the spring of 1944. Much of their work can be seen today in the halls of the Pentagon.

The artists normally did not accompany units, as did the combat historians. There were exceptions to this rule, and Dows got far enough forward to capture several platoons of Germans in Normandy, thereby wining a decoration from the infantry unit to which he was attached. For the most part, they were sent to battle areas shortly after a battle to take photographs and make sketches from which their later pictures were made. In some cases the combat historians would go back to point out some important point of the terrain so that they could make a study of it. For our historical purposes, the work was never satisfactory. We wanted, of course, studies that could portray for us scenes the camera could not get. They, true to their training, wanted to do sketches that told a story. Their history consisted of interesting sketches of old churches battered by shells, a vignette of a tank silhouetted against apple trees, or a weary soldier propped against a fence.

We had similar difficulties with the army photographers when we tried to get real battle photography. They had thousands of photographs of generals shaking hands, of men getting haircuts, of mascots, of presentations of medals, of tanks moving up, of muddy roads, but little of the particular battle scenes we wanted. As a result, army films on campaigns made since the war tend to be heavy on photographs of prebattle coverage but detailed on narrative when it comes to the actual battle. There was a good reason for this, and there were some notable exceptions, but for the most part the army did not get what it wanted in the way of battle shots. Naturally, the difficulty lay to some degree in the fact that modern battle does not often lend itself to portrayal by the lens of a single camera. It is too diffuse; the troops are too spread out and camouflaged too well to be captured on film.

Life in September, October, and early November consisted of work from eight to six on the story of the landings. Colonel Taylor and I sat across a table from each other and plowed through V Corps plans, 1st and 29th Division field orders, and the after-action reports and journals of those units plus the 16th, 18th, 26th, 115th, 116th, and 175th Infantry Regiments, the Rangers, the special engineer brigades, special tank battalions, and the like. Day in and day out we tried to reconstruct the story from the records and from the information we had gathered in interviews. We found that in the periods when war moved the fastest the information was the most meager in the journals.

One of the great problems in interviews was the pinning down of times that certain actions took place. We learned early in the game not to suggest a time because the soldier would seize on it and say "that was when it was." Or he would ask when they were supposed to go in, and then say that was it. Some of them were candid enough to say, "Hell, I had other things to do besides look at my watch." So, we adopted the method of asking them to locate the time before or after some event that we could establish.

Not only did the fighting men fail to remember time, they were not sure where they had gone. They would say, "Well, after the firefight we went along a couple of miles until we came to a turn in the road at a little town and then we went east for a mile or so." Yet they could tell you precisely whether fire from an old barn came from their right or left, and who was hit by it.

The great problem always was establishing the nature of the firefight they got into. Nearly always it was "sharp" or "heavy" or "intense" or "considerable." But how sharp was sharp was something else again. Sometimes it boiled down to a machine gun or two burp guns or three rifles. Nearly always, if we didn't watch out, there was 88 fire. After a week of hearing about 88 fire we began to ask, "Could it be mortar fire?" We found that indeed it could.

The testimony was especially unreliable when it came to the question of the support the unit had from the companies or platoons to its right or left, or the backing it got from units to the rear. In perfect good faith they would say that the "no good jokers" to their right had failed utterly to come up. The average infantry-man was nearly always certain that everyone else had quit the war except his platoon.

Then there was the task of trying to tell what the battlefield was like from the maps and from our recollections of the areas we had visited. Noting the changes that had come in the invasion beaches two days after the landings, we sympathized with those historians who try to reconstruct the description of the battlefield at Marathon or Hastings by a look at the present-day terrain.

And the problem of casualties was most difficult to establish. Because of the confusion of units landed on wrong beaches, the D-Day statistics were quite heavy in the number of the missing. Colonel Taylor finally suggested that I go to the Central Machine Records Unit in Paris, and try to get their totals. This unit suppos-edly had the best personnel statistics in the theater. On my initial visit to the headquarters, I thought I had found a break because the first officer I talked to was someone I knew from Second Army in Memphis. He sent me along to a major, and I was passed along over a period of several days from one officer to another—each one saying he thought the next man had the information. After ten days of this, I finally came back to one of the first officers I had seen. I said, "The merry-go-round stops here; who do I have to see to get the information." Then the major said, "The dope you want is too hard to get together; you will have to have some-one who can outrank our chief, Colonel Blank, to get the work done on it." Since Colonel Taylor had only a silver leaf, we de-cided to leave it to Washington. When he returned there in 1945, he managed to get the information for his book.

Part of our days were taken up with callers from various agen-cies of the army coming by to say hello or to get information. In late September, Captains Emrich and Price, historians of the SHAEF staff, came by to see Colonel Taylor. Emrich, an expert on western folklore, and Price, who taught history at the University of Glasgow, were then engaged in writing a history of COSSAC, the predecessor of SHAEF, which had made the early plans for the invasion. I had no idea when I talked to them that day that a little more than a year later I would be given the task of completing the short history of SHAEF they had begun and that two years later I would be back in Paris gathering material on the complete, official history of SHAEF under a personal directive from General Eisenhower.

Another visitor of this period was Colonel Goddard, historian of the Seventh Army, who had been appointed before the invasion of southern France but who wanted, now that his army was under ETOUSA, to conform with its practices. A personal visitor of the period was Colonel Beebe, chaplain of the Mediterranean theater, whom I had known when he was chaplain of the Second Army. He had come up from Rome for a visit with Father Tiernan, our theater chaplain, and, finding I was there, had called me up.

Two new historians, Captain Condren and Dello Dayton, arrived in September and, after a short period of briefing, were sent out to the armies. Shortly thereafter Condren and a Sergeant Dorsey who was with him on a field trip were badly injured when they stepped on mines in an area they were visiting. Condren was so badly injured that he lost a leg, and Dorsey was in the hospital until late in 1945. Later in the year two of our historians in Ninth Army were killed while visiting a unit command post when it came under fire. Our fifth casualty was suffered near the end of the war when Lieutenant Kiley of the Medical Corps's historical staff was killed when the jeep in which he was riding hit a mine.

Of our various visitors, the one we shall likely remember longest was a WAC officer who came often to work in some of the files. So unobtrusive was she that we finally forgot that she was there. One day, Colonel Taylor, to whom "Gosh" was a fairly strong expletive, was teasing Billy Harnett, our typist, about several asterisks in copy that contained Taylor's interviews with the Rangers. When Billy asked what they had said, the colonel read the original, which, much purified, said that a Ranger who had been narrowly missed by an enemy bullet stood up and reflected on the German's ability to hit a bull in a vulnerable spot with a bass fiddle. John Hall, who was sitting where he could see the WAC, was trying frantically all this time to catch Colonel Taylor's eye. He succeeded only after the damage had been done—just in time to embarrass the colonel profoundly. He said later, however, that he had been stopped just before he read the next line, in which the Ranger had cast various obscene aspersions on the German's ancestry.

The evenings, my diary reveals, was seldom spent in the billet. The USO, Red Cross, French reception committees, and various French institutions were busy trying to make life interesting for the men of the rear echelon. Some of these efforts were later to be extended to men on leave, but for the moment they were mainly for us.

Near the end of the month, the figures of the French entertainment world joined hands with USO and ENSA, the British counterpart of the USO, to present at the Olympia Theater one of the most fabulous entertainment's ever given in Paris. With Fred Astaire as master of ceremonies, these organizations presented top French entertainers. Les Folies Bergeres, Casino de Paris, and Bal Tabarin sent many of their girls and comedians, while private clubs sent singers, instrumentalists, and dancers. One of the great favorites was Django Reinhardt, who got encore after encore.[8] We were told later that the list was very full because, in addition to the performers who wanted to appear before the Allies, there were dozens who had been marked as collaborators who hoped by these means to remove the stain on their names.

In a few weeks, many of the great motion picture theaters along the Champs-Elysées and near the Étoile were taken over by the British and U.S. organizations for movies, and two music halls offered the best in vaudeville. The other well-known French theaters were in operation, but they were for the most part unheated. The Folies Bergeres and Casino de Paris continued to show the same performances they had been giving while the Germans were there, although the Germans were now the butts of the jokes.

The Red Cross club at the Hotel de Paris was joined soon afterward by an enlisted men's club in the Rue Elysée. It had been used as a club by German airmen. Earlier, I think, it had been a private residence and then a very swanky private club. Located not far from the presidential palace, the building was very elegant, with a swimming pool, a private garden, billiard room, ballrooms, and the like. But the food was still standard Red Cross sandwiches, doughnuts, and soda pop.

Later, under the sponsorship of Lady Tedder, wife of the

deputy supreme commander, an Allied club was opened at the Grand Hotel near the Opera, and Glenn Miller's band, without its famous leader, played nightly for French, British, and American GIs.

Constant efforts were made by the clubs to make life pleasant for soldiers on leave from the front. All messes set up for them served wine and a glass of liqueur free to men who asked for it. After the war's end, a long-felt need was filled by the establishment of a club where a GI could not be admitted unless accompanied by an officer, or an officer unless accompanied by a GI. There was also a special hamburger place just off the Champs-Elysées where a GI could not be admitted without a girlfriend. Soldiers, liking to take a dig at the WACS, used to say that it was the only place where the girls were willing to go with them. Paris Post Number One of the American Legion also made friends and got some members by offering hamburgers for sale and limited quantities of American bourbon at reasonable prices.

By late September, the Red Cross club at the Hotel de Paris had asked various French student groups to organize receptions for American soldiers. Mademoiselle Suzanne Pannier, a student of art and political science, was active in this work. Early in the organization of this program she enlisted the aid of Sergeant Jay, who was in psychological warfare, Sergeant Wash, a literature major, and myself. Our job was to help suggest things soldiers might want to do and then to drum up groups of soldiers who might attend various receptions. The results were not always happy. On one occasion she complained to me that Red Cross workers had asked two soldiers if they would like to have dinner with a French family and they had said yes. Unfortunately, their host was a professor who had hoped to discuss American politics and literature over some fine old wine; the GIs were high school graduates who had been interested only in the professor's cognac. I was almost as unlucky in choosing soldiers to go to dinners given by the Institut Catholique. After several weeks of taking along people who were interested in the Institut because of its connection with François Mauriac and Jacques Maritain, Mademoiselle Pannier asked if I could please take one Catholic; thus far I had taken only Jews and Protestants.

This problem of Franco-American cooperation continued to

have its amusing sides. Later in the year, the wife of the librarian of the Sorbonne told me that since she had once taught at Wellesley she thought she should help the American clubs get French hostesses from good families for some of their dances. On the evening of the first dance, she told the director of the club to have transportation at the main door of the Sorbonne at eight o'clock. The group waited until 8:30 and then nine and was ready to leave when, at 9:15, a befuddled driver drove up and asked if he was at the Sorbonne dancehall, saying that he had been sent to take them for the GI dance. He explained that someone had told him to come to the Sorbonne, that someone else had told him that was a college, but that when he asked for the college, he had been directed to the College de France. After much difficulty in trying to explain his problems to the first person he met, he was ultimately sent to the Sorbonne. He had played it safe by asking for the dancehall. Since he got a truckload of girls from the place, he probably still has a highly unusual concept of the purpose of that institution.

Mademoiselle Pannier, a onetime Communist who had changed her views after studying for a time in Russia, was extremely active in her work with soldiers who wished to meet various personalities of Paris. When she heard that a few GIs would like to see Picasso, she arranged for an interview.[9] This proved so popular that she finally set up regular visits—limited to fifty persons a visit to the painter's studio. Instead of being angered by being treated as a curiosity, Picasso turned the visits to his advantage by asking for cigarettes and coffee. Later, the Red Cross added Gertrude Stein and Alice B. Toklas[10] to the list, and the former had great fun in lecturing the soldiers on various notions that came into her head. She proved to be as much of a favorite as the painter.

In addition to Mademoiselle Pannier's activities, Monsieur Jean Rouelle, who had studied in the United States under the same exchange program that had brought me to Paris in 1937–38, arranged for special receptions for former American teachers and university students among the armed forces. At the same time, various French institutions, acting on their own, began to issue invitations. For one who spoke French and was interested in meeting people of the city, it was a great opportunity.

Through the efforts of Professor Siegfried, the Ecole des Sciences Politiques had two or three receptions each month, combined sometimes with talks or discussions, and ending always with pleasant chats over wine and sandwiches. One of the nice things he did for me personally was to ask me to a dinner given by the faculty of the Ecole des Sciences Politiques to which five Americans were invited. The others were Harold Callender of the *New York Times*, Douglas MacArthur II of the American embassy, one of the chief Red Cross workers of the city, and an officer of the SHAEF staff.

The Institut Catholique, as I mentioned earlier, was one of the first institutions of the city to hold regular dinners for visitors from the American army. It was here that I had the first meal I felt was in any way comparable to the prewar meals I had known in Paris. The groups at the Institut were always interesting, made up, as they were, of a few older people who were somewhat pro-Pétain in their views, and a younger, liberal group who had been most active in the Resistance. They were dynamic in their approach to France's problems and had a fresh approach to politics that made me hopeful then about France's postwar development.

One of my most interesting evenings was arranged by Monsieur Rouelle with students of the Ecole Normale Superieure. A group of students who were interested in American literature and politics invited me to take part in a bull session in the rooms of two of the students. I was particularly struck by the fact that they had just discovered many of our writers like Hemingway, John dos Passos, and William Faulkner, and were reacting to them with all the enthusiasm that American students had for them in the 1920s and early 1930s. It was hard to realize that they had not really known of these writers earlier, and it was a little difficult to take when some of them began to interpret them to me. I saw no signs at the moment of the cult of Sartre and Camus. Actually, a year later when Tim Hadsel asked me if I knew of this fad of "existentialism," which his wife wrote him was reported in New York to be sweeping Paris, I had to admit I had barely heard of it.

One of the receptions arranged by Rouelle was that given by Monsieur Bonnerot, librarian of the Sorbonne. We were served tea and then shown through the building. Later one of the actresses of the Comédie Française entertained us with readings from *La Fontaine*. They were done in the grand manner, and she ran a risk that some of the audience would laugh at the wrong places. However, she was expert enough at her art that she held the attention of the group. I met several American ladies there who had remained in Paris throughout the occupation, suffering no greater inconvenience than going to appear before the police once a month to report their whereabouts. Among others present were M. and Mme. Raymond Pannier, old friends of mine from 1937–38. She had gone to school in the United States and later was secretary of the American University Union, which administered the fellowships held by American students in Paris. After Dr. Horatio Krans had left Paris on the coming of the Germans, she had remained for a time at her post, and had later taken the documents with her to the American Church, on the Quai d'Orsay. Her husband, a former teacher of French and a staunch royalist, who had regularly gone out on Jeanne d'Arc's birthday with members of the Camelots du Roi to riot with antiroyalist forces, had been active in the Resistance during the war and was now a captain. They told me that they had remained passive until the Germans had occupied the south of France.

Several nights after the meeting at the Sorbonne, the Panniers took me to dinner at Prunier's on Avenue Foch. That famous restaurant was still as fashionable as it had been before the war, but rationing had caused it to fall on evil days. Our meal was a sort of meatloaf surrounded by potatoes, the salad was meager, the bread was the half-bran type of commodity I had seen in Normandy, and the dessert was applesauce. The wine was more than adequate. This meal, which the poorest Parisian restaurant would have been shamed to serve before the war, cost Monsieur Pannier between eight hundred and a thousand francs—or some $16 to $20 in our money. They had insisted on taking me to this place because I had given them two cartons of cigarettes and, despite the cost of the meal, insisted later on giving me one of their last bottles of prewar cognac so they wouldn't feel they had robbed me.

A week or so later, the Panniers invited me to their apartment, which was located on the Quai de l'Horloge just above the Conciergerie where Marie Antoinette and other prisoners of the Revolution were held in prison. During the occupation, the Germans made use again of some of these cells, and on one occasion when Monsieur Pannier was arrested on suspicion, he was actually in jail under his own apartment. They ultimately had to move to another part of the city and live there under assumed names when it was discovered that Mademoiselle Pannier had once worked for the American University Union.

I spent a number of pleasant evenings visiting Monsieur de Lassus, who in October came back to Paris from the nursing home where he had been staying. Still full of vitality and wit despite his eighty-three years, he had many stories of his past to tell and re-tell. His grandfather had been an official in Louisiana when the French handed that territory over to the United States in 1803, and he had stayed on in the territory. Monsieur de Lassus's father lived in the United States until the 1840s and then returned to France with a Negro servant whose influence could still be seen in some of the Creole dishes still prepared from her recipes for the old man's table. As I have noted earlier, the old man had seen the Germans enter Paris in 1871, had heard their guns as they neared the city in 1914, and had seen them return in 1940. He detested the Boche with a passion. He also hated the Jews. As a royalist who had once represented his party in the Chamber of Deputies, he was strongly opposed to most governmental leaders, and he held against the church the fact it had put *L'Action Française* under the ban. He used to say that he had been born, confirmed, and married in the church, and would be buried in it, but beyond that he would have nothing to do with it. But the old man was unlike many of the other Rightists I met in the 1930s and now. He still loved France and he detested anyone who would hurt her. He detested Blum but honored him for his fine brain and writing style; he sneered at Herriot, but thought him an excellent speaker. When he found that I could not tolerate the anti-democratic jibes of some of his friends, he would make clear to them that they were offending a guest. In short, he was still a fine old gentleman. He had fallen on evil days as a result of the tobacco and coffee shortages, and he would sit and puff at an empty pipe and wince as he tasted his "national" coffee. I ultimately took all of my tobacco ration in pipe tobacco and gave it to him, and had some powdered coffee sent from home. He would immediately hide it, saying that he hated to hoard, but that his friends and family would beg for it if they knew he had it.

As he sat biting the stem of his pipe or puffing it with relish he would relive the days of the late 1890s and early 1900s. He had seen them carrying the Prince of Wales away from a party where he had drunk too much, a handkerchief thrown over his face; he had later seen him as king, riding down the boulevards as a visitor to France with the crowd, which liked his Gallic spirit, acclaiming him. *"Bravo, mon vieux Edouard,"* a man called out from the crowd, and Edward VII had graciously acknowledged the salute. The old man seldom went out since his legs had failed him, but he would recall the period when he often attended to the opera and the art galleries. His name was still on the lists of those invited to the opening of special exhibits at the Louvre, and he would get out his cutaway and high starched collars for those events. He could remember where certain pictures were hung in the Louvre, and, when I told him I was going to see a particular opera, he would hum the tunes of some of the arias. He liked to tell scandalous stories of some of the great painters, writers, and political leaders of his time, but he was offended by the plain language of *Lady Chatterly's Lover* and thought that it should be banned.

As he sat there recalling the days of old Paris, I fancied that the old man summed up in his person the plight of France. Full of wondrous memories, of happy and cultured living, of esprit, mockery, a rich past, and a bitter empty future—that was his lot, and, he feared, the lot of his beloved country.

It was well that he could not go out very much, for Paris would have shocked him now. What would he think of the U.S. Army trucks parked in the Tuileries gardens, of men billeted in the Petit Palace, where great exhibitions had been held in the past, and with a great "PRO [prophylactic] STATION HERE" sign posted outside the door? He would have been shocked at the great sale of Henry Miller's books in Paris bookshops, and at the spectacle of soldiers chasing women up the boulevards and of soldiers lying drunk on the sidewalks in the Place Vendôme.

He and many other Frenchmen were shocked by the soldiers' behavior. We were told that the Germans had not even permitted their men to smoke in the streets, and that they were not allowed to go out without their uniforms in perfect array. Of course, these well-mannered gentlemen had sometimes been responsible for atrocities, and plaques on some of the newly named streets made it clear that the person for whom the street was christened was a victim of German tenderness.

General Lee made some effort to make his soldiers orderly. Avenue Kléber, in front of his headquarters, became known as Avenue de Salute, and he sent out field officers to walk up and down the streets to take the names of soldiers who did not salute. Sometimes he too took a hand in these proceedings and negligent soldiers would suddenly see a three-star general, his hand raised to his cap brim, yelling, "Soldier, return that salute!" The GIs back from the front on leave became furious at these measures, and sometimes ignored the admonitions of officers or MPs whose splendidly pressed uniforms contrasted strongly with their own battle-stained garments. Their attitude was perhaps best expressed by a Canadian soldier I saw after the war in London who, when told by a smartly dressed English MP to button his jacket, said, "Make me you cease-fire son of a bitch. You never heard a shot in anger."

And what of Montmartre and Place Pigalle, where thousands of soldiers gathered each night? Tourists seeking a little excitement had known the nightspots of Montmartre for years, but the war had made it and Pigalle—known to the soldiers as "Pig Alley"—a byword for vice. Here was the Piccadilly of Paris where France's and, indeed, it seemed all of Europe's, prostitutes swarmed. The soldiers soon discovered that no French was needed, since the *filles de joie* had either learned the necessary words of invitation or were expert enough in sign language to make clear what they meant. The area became particularly bad when the number of men from the front on forty-eight-hour passes began to climb to ten thousand and above a day. Many men would head for Pigalle on their arrival and remain there until the last few minutes of their leave expired.

In certain underworldish spots of Montmartre there could be found deserters who had joined with local gangsters to run the black market. Kings for a day were the army truck drivers who discovered that a truck and its cargo of blankets, gasoline, or food would bring $5,000—enough to live well with the pick of the prostitutes for several months. Or one could use the stake to go into the wholesale black market and add to the original investment.

Some of the members of this group, to the shame of the American army, in the first days of the liberation, before the MPs could get matters under control, had parked their trucks near the Arc de Triomphe, in sight of the eternal flame which marked the resting place of the Unknown Soldier, and had auctioned off items to the highest bidder. Some of the deserters who "holed up" in Montmartre became so active that by war's end they had won for Paris the name of "Chicago-sur-Seine." This title seemed particularly fitting in 1946, when several gun battles were held between American MPs and the French police and some of the deserter-gangster band. Notable was the battle in front of the Opera when a deserter fired at an MP and hit a Frenchman. He was almost torn to pieces by the mob before he was taken into custody. A general told me after the war that during the 1944–45 period, a member of the French Ministry of Interior had quoted to him statistics on the monthly assaults, rapes, and murders committed against Frenchmen by members of the armed forces. The official had said, "I realize that you can't do much about the rapes and assaults, but could you reduce the murders by one or two a month?"

The black market, of course, was fed by many sources. One that became notorious before it was crushed in the winter of 1944 was a railway supply company that took so many cigarettes and put them into French channels that the cigarette ration had to be sharply cut. An investigation showed that sergeants of the company had put officers on an allowance in return for protection against arrest. In early 1945 some of them went to jail, and the commanding officer, a former railroader, was permitted to resign. I later met one of the officer's defense attorneys, who complained bitterly that the man would never have been forced to resign if Eisenhower hadn't personally demanded that the court-martial take drastic action.

Another channel of supply was the American PX through the individual buyer. One factor in this was the absurd overvaluation of the franc by which officers and soldiers were paid in invasion currency valued at two cents a franc, when it was quite clear that the franc was worth less than half that. The result was that everything was terrifically high for the soldier. Wine was $3 or $4 a bottle and champagne $20. The French were aware of this situation and offered various solutions, short of changing the value of the currency, to remedy it. After the war, under pressure from the army, they at last arrived at an overall sum that they estimated the soldiers had lost by the unfair difference in currency. So every officer and man who was on duty in France got a special check for $17 (or was it $14?). Meanwhile, many officers and men, realizing that cigarettes that cost a GI $1 a carton would sell for $10, made their own private readjustments in foreign exchange. The soldier's musette bag was used so often to transport black market items that it was universally known as "the black market bag."

The situation became embarrassing when COMZ set up its main PX on the Champs-Elysées, one block from the Arc de Triomphe. Hundreds of men stood in line there every day, and Frenchmen gathered to intercept them as they came out to offer them the prevailing prices for their surpluses. Some became so bold that they would interrupt old friends in the line and indicate special objects they wished them to buy.

A little less embarrassing were the beggars and entrepreneurs who waited beside the chow line as it wound its way down the Champs-Elysées into the cafe on the Rue de Berri. Ragged old men and women waited patiently to fight for every cigarette butt that hit the ground. No matter how small the fragment of cigarette, it was seized on avidly and stuck into a bag brought for the purpose. Later the paper would be removed, the tobacco dried, and it would be sold in bulk for pipes or "roll your own" cigarettes. The packaged article was broken open, since few people could afford twenty at a time, and sold one or two to a customer.

Stars and Stripes ran a story on an incident in which a soldier, noticing an old man watching him open a package of cigarettes, tantalizingly offered him one and then carefully dropped and stepped on it just as the Frenchman reached for it. The old man picked it up anyway, but as he did, a young French girl, crying, "Have you no shame?" knocked it from his hand and crushed it with her heel.

The mercenary spirit showed itself in many ways. Just after we reached the city, we found prominently displayed on a board along the Champs-Elysées a large picture of the American flag. Around it were words saying, "Soldiers, such-and-such a company welcomes you." The French newspapers twitted us about this fine piece of American enterprise. The sign not only brought protests from Americans, but from British business people who complained that American businessmen were coming into Paris in uniform, while the British had to stay out.

The French were not without blame. Guards had already been assigned to the pipeline running back to the beaches to prevent liberated Frenchmen from tapping it for gasoline. Others helped to loot trains carrying supplies between the beaches and Paris. Particularly revolting were the vultures who had lived high while the Germans were there and who, now that a new set of conquerors had come, quickly joined the new victors. In their fine homes, they made a special play for anyone who might serve their purposes. I recall one evening when one of our officers, who had been seen often with members of this group, persuaded the girlfriend of one of the men in the group to come home with him. When she pointed out that her friends knew where he lived, he calmly brought her into a room where several of the enlisted men stayed and used an empty cot for lovemaking the rest of the night. The men were not amused.

In contrast to this sort of living were some of the quiet little cafes where ordinary people came for their cup of frightful coffee, their glass of weak beer, or their glass of wine. Here one could listen to an accordionist or violinist, playing some "new" American tune that had come out before 1940 or talking about France before the war or under the German occupation. In one such cafe I helped the old lady who kept the cash register translate a long piece of doggerel that welcomed the Americans to Paris. She said the thing was to be set to music and sold as a ballad. Of course, ladies of the street could invade even these places. One evening, while talking quietly to the woman behind the bar, two soldiers interrupted to ask if I could find out what prices two rather demure looking girls drinking fruit juice in a corner were charging. When they were outraged at the fee, I turned the conversation over to Madame, who arranged matters on a satisfactory basis. Another evening, Dave Garth and I were having a chat in one of the better places when two heavily painted hefty types came in and beckoned to us, saying, "Come along, babee, come along babee."

By late October the time for the Metro to operate had been

advanced to 9:30 or 10:00 at night so that the opera and theater could run on something like a normal schedule. One delightful concert given for army personnel was that of the Orchestra of the Conservatory, directed by Charles Munch, with Jacques Thibaud, a French violinist who was to be killed in 1953 in a plane crash while en route to Indochina to play for troops there, as soloist. Among the operas I heard in the period were *Lakme* and *Le Jongleur de Notre Dame,* and I saw at the Comédie Française a wonderful performance by Raimu in *Le Malade Imaginaire.*

During October and early November, as the number of individuals assigned to Paris increased in number and as thousands came back for leave, I saw a number of old friends. I met Preston Ordway, business manager of the college where I had taught, on the steps of the Majestic. Near the Étoile I ran into a Major Buffington, who had interviewed me in 1943 at Fort McClellan and had tried to get me an assignment in Washington. In the chow line I saw James Murray, a soldier from Indiana, who had visited us some weeks before at Valognes and was now doing signal work in Paris. He took me one day to the concrete building where the Germans had had their great communications center and showed me how they had set up a place they believed would be proof against shells or gas.

In addition to my regular work during this period, I was called in from time to time on other duties. I spent one day as a translator for an officer in the Chemical Corps who was trying to understand the nature of a patent a French scientist was trying to sell to the American army. The process was in technical terms that I could not understand, so my job was to turn the French words into English, then watch hopefully while the American struggled with the meanings, and then would suggest that perhaps it was similar to such-and-such a formula. I would bat this back to the Frenchman who would beam and acknowledge that it was something along that line, but it differed in that such-and-such did so-and-so. And so we would go through the business all over again. At the end of a lengthy session they finally understood each other, but unfortunately we didn't need the patent.

One of the most thankless jobs I was assigned while in Paris was to make suggestions on how combat historians in the field could improve their accounts. Colonel Ganoe temporarily gave me this task because of my experience in the field. I trustingly made some rather strong remarks—thinking that the criticisms would go out over his signature. To my embarrassment, several days later I found that they had been sent to the men in the field, nearly all of whom were officers, over the name of Sergeant Pogue. I later got a few sarcastic digs from them, but fortunately the incident was held against the colonel and not against me.

A few days before I left Paris I went to a session of the Consultative Assembly. I had asked at the embassy for a ticket but was told that only two were allotted to them for each session, so I had to use direct means to get one. I went on the morning of 10 November to the Palais du Luxembourg, the prewar Senate chamber, which was being used in place of the damaged Palais Bourbon, and asked if I could have a ticket. I invoked the name of Professor André Siegfried as a friend and found that sufficient to gain admittance. They were debating changes in the rules of the temporary government. Amidst the tedium of changes in the language here and there it was possible to see definite trends of thinking. The Communists and Catholics tended to line up against each other, and it was clear that the church was emerging as a political force. The Catholic group wanted to take social problems out from under the Ministry of Labor, but they were beaten by a left-wing coalition headed by the Communists.

I noted that this body differed from some I had seen in 1937–38 in that it had more decorum, more good speaking, and less violence. The presence of several women members seemed to have a quieting effect, although it did not lessen the time devoted to speaking. Nearly all of them talked, and one of them rose to her feet the third time, only to be admonished by the president of the body: "Madame, I must advise you that under our rules no one may speak more than twice on a question, but for you we will make an exception." There were more young men in the membership than I had remembered seeing before.

The great debate of the day had to do with the punishment of traitors, and I felt that the French Revolutionary assemblies must have been like this when speaker after speaker arose to demand vengeance. Right and Left alike applauded loudly the Communist demand for more punishment. "It is almost two and one-half months," one speaker said, "since Paris was liberated and only one traitor [Georges Suarez] has been shot—and that only the day before yesterday."

The visit to the Assembly was to be one of my last visits in Paris until after the war's end. Word had come from Colonel Marshall in late October that in accordance with my often-repeated request I would go back to my unit in early November. Captain Ruppenthal and Sergeant Garth had come back some weeks earlier to work on War Department pamphlets dealing with the Utah Beach landings and the battle for Saint-Lô, so that First Army was shorthanded. On the tenth of November, just after I returned from the meeting of the Assembly, Lieutenant Jack Shea, Sergeant Ferdinand, and Topete arrived from First Army to say that I was to return to the front as soon as I could complete my project. I received the word with mixed feelings. While I desired very much to be back where things were happening, Paris was daily becoming more interesting and it was hard to leave.

Chapter 15

Opinion and Politics in Liberated Paris

Saturday, 11 November (D+158)– Tuesday, 14 November (D+161)

Paris in the fall of 1944 mirrored the divisions, the hatreds, the despair, the hopes, and the future of France. In 1937–38 I had become heartsick about the condition of France and had gone home to tell my friends that she was no longer the great champion of freedom nor the great leader of Europe she thought herself to be. In 1939 I had given a series of lectures on the warring countries and I had said, incorrectly, that the Maginot Line would protect France but, correctly, that France did not have the will to fight. I had been disturbed by signs of decay, as seen in the growing number of Frenchmen over forty and on government relief, the increased number of fertile acres being taken out of cultivation, the schisms between peasants and urban dwellers, and between labor and capital, the self-pity of intellectuals who felt that France's glory was gone, the anti-Semitism of the upper classes, and the contempt for democracy that marked too much of the intellectual society, the feeling, as one writer put it, that it was no longer to be France's destiny to lead crusades, but merely to supply the leaven that would bring civilized touch and charm to the world.

I had been frightened in 1934 when Frenchmen had gathered by the thousands at the Place de la Concorde and had tried to fight their way across the Seine to the Chamber of Deputies, where they planned to seize the prime minister and his cabinet and throw them into the river. Then had followed France's strange neutrality in the Spanish Civil War, the dazed acceptance of Hitler's marches into the Rhineland, the unwilling alliance with England to save Poland, the happy grasping of the lies of Munich, the half-hearted preparation for war in 1939, and finally the collapse in 1940. What was worse was the next period—the first years of the occupation—when it seemed that France could only regain her self-respect by pulling England down with her.

But there had been a challenge by de Gaulle and other Frenchmen who fled to England, and there had been covert resistance within France by Communists and Catholics, by peasants and city men, by laborers and manufacturers. Some men, called Maquis after the thickets in Corsica where outlaws and men under the ban of the state had once gone to hide, had concealed themselves in the fastnesses of France, had acquired arms—either on their own or from those dropped by British planes and parachutists—and engaged in terror tactics against the Germans. Still others, members of regular Resistance cells under elected or appointed leaders, were organized under the aegis of the French Committee in North Africa or Allied auspices in London. Their task was to furnish information on German action, to carry out prescribed missions against enemy installations, to get Allied fliers and escaped prisoners out of France, but mainly to be prepared against the day when British and American troops should come again to France.

Many Frenchmen had stayed apart from these movements, either from prudence or their distaste for underground activities. More than one Frenchman sniffed disdainfully at the Resistance and Maquis and said, "But they came from rather low society." However, after our landings in the summer of 1944, many young men called for labor service by the Germans left their homes when they received their notices and joined the underground. Others, like my friends the Panniers, who were put under special surveillance as the Germans, grew increasingly jittery and went into hiding.

Then came the great week of liberation and the week or two of celebration. De Gaulle installed General Koenig as the military governor of Paris and moved the French Committee to the capital. France, except for a few ports in the west, was now cleared of the enemy and it seemed to many Frenchmen that the war was over. To many, the chief task was to kill traitors, to dispose of those men who had followed the Vichy line. To many former officers, who had taken no part in the Resistance movement, it was a time to rebuild a disciplined army in France—something which former sergeants and junior officers, now colonels in the resistance movement, opposed. Former Communist leaders like Maurice Thorez, who had left France in 1939 rather than oppose a Germany with whom Moscow had made a pact, and who had become violently anti-German once the Russians had been attacked by Hitler, now were claiming that their group alone had clean hands. In the absence of well-known prewar leaders like Daladier, Blum, Herriot, Reynaud, and others, who were still prisoners in German camps; in the absence of murdered leaders like Mandel, who had perished at the hands of Herriot's or Darnand's Miliciens or the Gestapo; and in the absence of the followers of aged Marshal Pétain, who had played the German game and their own and were now in hiding or in prison, a group of newcomers had risen to power.[11] Most of them had worked in some way with the Resistance groups, and they wished not only a France purged of Vichyites but one purged of timidity and fears. Unfortunately, the violence they had seen and remembered did not always make it possible for them to favor the compassion that France so desperately needed.

When I had been a student in Paris, I had discovered that one seldom got the news by reading one paper. Instead, each paper tended to color its news as it did its editorials. Fortunately, however, the masthead usually carried the name of the paper's political director, and it was possible to determine the nature of the journal's bias. I had known these coloration's in 1937–38 and usually bought four or five papers a day, hoping that I could strike a rough average by reading pages of widely divergent political views. Of that group, the Communist l'Humanité, the socialist Le Populaire, and the conservative Le Figaro were back in business. Added to these were dozens of new papers, among which Franc-Tireur and Combat were particularly popular. For news, one had to depend on Stars and Stripes and the Paris editions of the London Daily Mail and Paris Herald-Tribune.

By mid-September it appeared that *l'Humanité* was making a fairly successful drive to get the biggest circulation in Paris. By choosing good writers, many with good records in the Resistance, by working at circulation, and, so some French opponents said, by getting more than its share of the American-controlled newsprint, it became one of the most powerful newspapers in France between 1944 and 1946.

I found in *l'Humanité* perhaps the strongest feeling of any French paper against giving too much credit to the United States and Great Britain for liberating France. It played up the Soviet Union and continued to follow the Moscow line. It was also the shrillest proponent of shooting collaborationists and it printed each day photographs of eminent Vichyites. It was not satisfied with the dissolution of pro-German newspapers like *Le Temps* and *Paris Soir,* but demanded the firing of newsman on papers like *Le Figaro.* It opposed the disbandment of the Resistance armies, saying that the Right was arming to the teeth and wanted to deprive the people of their chief weapon—a people's army. It also wanted a large national army to help France's Russian allies defeat Germany. In many ways, the paper at that moment was the most militaristic and nationalistic paper in France.

De Gaulle still had a good press in September, although the backing from *l'Humanité* and *Le Populaire* might have been described as lukewarm. His speech of 12 September in which he spoke warmly of Russia and warned the Allies that it would be an error to make peace without France found great favor. All papers and parties were agreed that the French Committee of National Liberation should be recognized as the government of France and that France should have a voice in the Allied councils. De Gaulle promised punishment of collaborationists and seizure of their property, but the Leftist press felt that he was not vigorous enough.

The French press, while tending to leave the impression that mainly their compatriots were fighting the war, was careful in September of American opinion. An article titled "Cher Paris" in *Le Figaro* warned shopkeepers against profiteering at the expense of American soldiers and asked for a fixed price on drinks. Others, protesting against the begging of cigarettes and chocolates, called for an end to a policy of *"les mains tenus"* (outstretched hand) and the substitution of *"le main tenu"* (helping hand). Despite many such articles, there was an overall uneasiness in the press about the duration of America's stay in France after the end of the war, and the expression of some fears about the enormous power the United States would have after Germany was defeated.

As time passed, the French papers became more critical. Again and again they complained that the Americans fed German prisoners in their camps more calories daily than the average Frenchman had to eat a day. At other times they were shocked by the waste of American food. Reports were published of installations near Paris that had thrown away or buried hundreds of pounds of meat and fruit. When American officers explained that it was not up to our pure food requirements, it was pointed out that much of it was above the standard of food then being eaten by the French. As it began to get colder, criticisms were registered of the way in which fuel was being allotted and it was charged that Paris was worse off than it had been under the Germans. As a matter of fact, 1944 was an extremely cold winter and shortages of food made it easy to attack the liberators. Our forces had also requisitioned not only all the hotels which had been used by the Germans, but had added others to the list. As the French army wanted quarters and office space, it, too, began to clamor for better treatment. The press at times, noting the noises made in the night clubs of Paris, sarcastically asked the Americans and French celebrating there not to laugh too loud lest it disturb the fitful slumber of men fighting and bleeding at the front.

But the French were pleased on 14 October when Ambassador Jefferson Caffery of the United States and Ambassador Duff Cooper of Great Britain arrived in Paris to be near the "de facto French government." Ruppenthal and I went to the Avenue Gabriel to see Caffery and his party arrive. Several hundred Frenchmen were on hand, and a group of American MPs, smartly dressed, went through their proper paces, and the band played the "Star-Spangled Banner" and "La Marseillaise."

On 23 October, the United States, Great Britain, and the Soviet Union announced their recognition of the French provisional government. The press indicated French appreciation of the move, but wondered why it had been so long delayed. Among the reasons suggested were: (1) the influence of Chautemps, Bonnet and others in Washington; (2) Russian opposition to a de Gaulle government; (3) personal antipathy to de Gaulle; and (4) fear of France's internal weakness. My own reactions were that some of the following factors may have been more important: "(1) We have been told for years that the French *revanche* policy after the last war made peace impossible. I think we may prefer to keep her out of the peace conference. (2) We may think that a French army makes for trouble in Europe and not for peace. For the first time Europe (save for Russia and Britain) will be disarmed unless we arm France again. (3) If France had to bargain for recognition she may be more amenable to colonial settlements favorable to us or to peace." At all odds, de Gaulle's government has popular support. It needs recognition if it is going to be strong. If we intend to recognize it, it is better to avoid rancor. It appears that the British may be getting the better of the diplomatic handling, so that it appears that we are at fault. Russia has strengthened her own position.

Actually, many of the points which I made and which the papers outlined were incorrect. Careful study of the documents and conversations with General de Gaulle, Admiral Leahy,[12] and others convinced me later that President Roosevelt's personal dislike for de Gaulle and a real belief on Roosevelt's part that recognition of a provisional government might force an unwanted regime on France were the main points at issue in this affair.

Siegfried said that France trusted de Gaulle because it believed he would bring back the republic. The group he led was new and untried, but he had shown a willingness to bring in all elements of the Resistance forces. Therefore, he should be supported. Of Pétain, the professor said scathingly, "He is a 'mean' man, and basically a defeatist." He characterized the old marshal as one ambitious for political power, and as one who took advantage of France's defeat to foist his ideas on the people. He may have believed at one time that he could save France's internal independence by truckling to the Germans, but his basic governmental ideas went back to Clovis. In the case of the schools, the courts, and agriculture, he turned the clock back.

Laval, who was described as a shrewd, low, tricky trader capable of anything, was the real power of the Pétain regime.

Gamelin was intelligent but ambitious and therefore willing

to stay in office at the expense of giving up ideas which he knew to be right. I said that I had heard that Weygand urged surrender to the Germans in order to save France from the Communists. Siegfried said that this might be true, but that it was false to assume that France could have held North Africa in 1940 against a determined German drive. He felt that France had no choice but to surrender. Daladier, Chautemps, and Bonnet he criticized as weak men;[13] Reynaud, once the hope of the conservatives in France, he called intelligent but lacking in moral force.

Of the church under the occupation, the professor held that the Protestants universally acted well. Their clergy were brave; most of the Maquis strength in the south was Protestant. Among the Catholics, the smaller priests did well, some of the bishops were doubtful, and the cardinals dubious. On the whole, however, the church escaped blame. Among his colleagues of the university, the story was mixed. One professor of law had accepted an office under Vichy. Then he had finally consented to set up special courts to try hostages. The Germans had agreed not to execute a hundred Frenchmen for each German soldier who was killed if the Vichy court would condemn twenty, preferably Communists and Jews, and turn them over to the Germans. These special courts performed this task. Another brilliant lawyer had written for the German press, but had died before he could be brought to trial. Another vain professor, noted for the elegance of his lectures, had been flattered into making speeches of a type favored by the Germans. Still another had accepted a university rectorship under Vichy and had lost much standing.

Against these were people like Renouvin, who had stayed loyal to his views; Basdevant, who had resigned a post with Vichy when he saw its trend, who had lost his teaching post, and who had seen his seventeen-year-old son shot as a hostage; and the scholar Bloch, who himself had been shot by the Germans.

Siegfried thought the Rightist parties in France were still 20 percent pro-Vichy, that they wanted what Pétain wanted, and that the poison of fascism was still in France. This group had been taken in by the Germans when they attacked the moral integrity of the state. The professor condemned especially Charles Maurras, who along with Leon Daudet had for years led the royalist l'Action Française group, and said he was the worst intellectual in France.

He thought Croce was right in saying that Maurras was responsible for Fascism in Europe.

My old professor was disturbed about the Communists and about prisoners who might return full of bitterness or who might be tainted with fascism. He pointed to the difference between the Maquis and the Resistance, saying that the former was made up along the lines of the La Vendee and that it had a lawless tradition that might cause trouble. He felt that they must be speedily disarmed. He believed that for the moment France had passed the danger of a civil war, but violence was still possible. He thought that France might have to come to a presidential system to achieve order.

His views contrasted somewhat with the opinions of a manager of a small French bistro—a typical French woman of the careful or grasping type. She felt that France might still have disorder and that de Gaulle lacked the prestige to lead France. Her view was that only Mandel could have done the job, and he had been shot by the Miliciens even as our forces were at the gate. (This story was often repeated to me, sometimes by those who believed the story that Mandel was the son of Clemenceau[14] and had inherited the "Tiger's" ability.) He had been imprisoned by the Germans. When our armies approached Paris, members of the pro-German French guard had taken Mandel from his cell and "took him for a ride." A small marker near Fontainebleau now marks the place where his body was found. The woman feared the Communists; she despaired of French politics and doubted if French unity had been obtained. She, like Siegfried, thought that France would have to copy the American presidential system if she was to be strong.

These views were somewhat at variance with those I heard in the home of a countess I had met before the war. She invited me for dinner to meet several businessmen. The countess had been a strong Royalist when I met her before, and I had heard her friends speak mockingly of parliamentary systems, of labor, and of Jews. I recall one night arguing with two young doctors who complimented Hitler on having solved the Jewish problem in his country by wholesale killings. They and people like them had distributed the literature of Charles Maurras, which spoke of the kings who in a thousand years made France and who alone could retain France's glory again, tracts which preached that thirty Jews controlled France, cartoons of Blum as a spider spreading Jewish influence throughout France, and who chuckled over Maurras's editorial asking that someone take a butcher knife to Blum. They, above all others I had seen in the countries of Europe in 1938, made me the most angry, with their abandonment of intellectual hope, with their abandonment of spiritual faith, and with their complete willingness to scuttle the country if they could hold on to their positions and be comfortable.

Two different Royalists were a man and his wife who had worked for the Resistance. They were still anti-Semitic, but had regained some faith in democracy. They were anti-Communist in feeling, but were convinced the Communists would come to power. "They are the only people with a program, and some part of it pleases everyone," they declared. They described l'Humanité as the best-edited and strongest paper in France. They felt that it and the party were being smart in their nationalistic policy. They divided French Communists into three groups: (1) those who believe in Communism intellectually; (2) those who believe that it worked in Russia and is therefore worth trying here; and (3) those who want revenge and find the Communists handy. Russian victories had proved a potent factor, they believed, in swaying public opinion in their direction. Much of their support, they noted, came from non-Communists who liked the party's promises of local reforms.

In most of these conversations, I sensed the fears and lassitude and despair that I had known in France in the 1930s. But at times I got a different view. This was found particularly in conversations with the students and young businessmen and professional people at the Institut Catholique and the Ecole de Sciences Politiques. One evening at the Institut, I talked to a Monsigneur who defended Admiral Robert and made a case for Darlan.[15] He admitted that the Cardinal of Paris had not been too firm in his patriotism, but said he was not pro-German, and he muttered some words in favor of Pétain. The younger people present, all of whom had worked in the Resistance, listened politely, but later told me that the Monsigneur represented a different generation from theirs. They held that de Gaulle had been right to put the Cardinal of Paris under guard. They were strong against Pétain, and they felt that de Gaulle was the man to lead France.

One of them who was starting a business said that France needed new ideas and that they must study the United States more. He hoped to get more young people into the government and to put the old hatreds in France behind them. He blamed France's financial problems not on labor but on industrialists who failed to see that you must pay good wages to get good work. For fifty years, he continued, we have been told that if you raise pay, the people will stop work. But the United States has shown this is not true. The French, he added, were too individualistic and too theoretical. From this and similar conversations, I got a promise of what France might become. The French, despite their fears of future U.S. power, showed great respect for our form of government and our ability to produce. As I noted before, there was usually some reservation about the fighting qualities of the American army. Again and again, some Frenchmen would say: "You Americans are great producers, but you fight as if you were building a bridge or a railroad. The only great fighters in the old tradition are the French and the Germans."

The presidential election of 1944 naturally attracted great interest in France. Not only were they concerned about the outcome, since they believed that Roosevelt was the better bet as a wartime executive, but they marveled at the way a country fully mobilized for war could undertake an election when its armies were grappling with enemies all the way around the world. As a result, a great deal of the limited space of the papers was given to explanations of the electoral system, to the powers of the president, and the background of the candidates. The results were reported in full. The opinion of the French seemed to be best summed up by *l'Aurore* which wrote, "Let no one speak to us any more of the instability of democracy."

My stay in Paris was about to come to an end. I was told on the tenth to be prepared to go back to V Corps as soon as I could wind up what I was doing. I was nearly through, since I had expected such a message since the first of November. My chief job was to incorporate some material which Lieutenant Shea, formerly General Cota's aide, had written about the fighting in Normandy in June.

I was pleased that the orders to return had not come before the great parade that occurred on Armistice Day. The day was cold, but we were out early along the Champs-Elysées so that we could have a place. Actually, the time of arrival had little to do with the matter because a great rush of the crowd came about fifteen minutes before the procession started, and those in the front rows were speedily engulfed.

By ten that morning, the windows of every building along the great boulevard were filled with people. They occupied every street running into the Champs-Elysées between the Arc de Triomphe and the Place de la Concorde, and they stood ten or fifteen deep on the pavements facing the boulevard. A tremendous French flag was suspended inside the Arc, and planes flew overhead.

There were rumors all morning that Churchill would come, but no one was able to confirm the fact that the British prime minister would join de Gaulle in this, the first Armistice Day parade since 1939. Meanwhile, the crowd grew denser and people began to push and jostle for position. In the midst of the bustle I heard a child crying and looked around me to see a chap of about four, holding tightly to his ten-year-old brother, but running the risk every moment of being crushed in the crowd. After seeing him bounced around a moment or two, I picked him up and put him on my shoulder. During the next hour and a half I had cause to regret my decision. Not only was the sheer weight of the child agonizing as my neck and shoulder muscles and arms ached under the strain, but every unusual movement in the street caused him to scramble up on my head where the scraping of his shoes added to my discomfort and prevented me from getting a good view of the parade. However, people in the crowd smiled at me and clucked sympathetically, and the little boy, at the end, had a shining face that showed he enjoyed it.

At eleven, a cannon was fired and there was great activity around the Arc de Triomphe, where de Gaulle had gone to take his wreath to the grave of France's Unknown Soldier. Almost immediately there were cries of "Shursheell, Shursheell," and it was clear that the great man of Britain was indeed there. In a few minutes the ceremony at the Arc was over and the parade began down the Champs-Elysées toward the Concorde. Before long we could see Churchill, de Gaulle, and Anthony Eden, walking proudly along. De Gaulle, even in this great moment, did not really unbend, but Eden was smiling and bowing, and Churchill was delighting the crowd with his famous V for Victory signs.

De Gaulle, eager to make a show of force as well as to celebrate the victory over the Germans, put on a great demonstration that day. Units from the various services of the Allied forces paraded, with WACs and WAAFs thrown in for good measure. A Scottish group attracted great attention, as did some of the other smartly dressed and soldierly stepping units. There were cries of approval for the columns of tanks and other pieces of equipment, and shouts for the bands and the splendid mounted members of the Garde Republicaine. But the great applause was for the cavalry from Africa, riding wonderful horses and looking properly fierce. The French, knowing what they owed to their troops from overseas, gave their loudest cheers to their colonials.

The parade was a splendid farewell to Paris for me. I was to remain in the city three more days preparing to move, and I had one delightful evening with Harrison celebrating his thirtieth birthday over a bottle of champagne he had brought back with him from Third Army. But the rest was anticlimax. The parade had seemed to signify that Paris was itself again, that the ills of the German occupation had been forgotten, and that the spirit of Nazism had been exorcised.

Chapter 16

Return to the Field

Wednesday, 15 November (D+162)–
Thursday, 30 November (D+177)

Wednesday, 15 November (D+162)

I returned to the front on 15 November after spending the morning at the Majestic talking with Colonel Ganoe, Colonel Marshall, and Colonel John M. Kemper—the last of whom had only recently come from Washington for an inspection tour. Colonel Marshall said that I would probably be summoned back soon to do more writing, but that for the moment I was needed at V Corps to conduct interviews on operations in September and October. As I left, some of the group joked and said that I was fleeing the cold of Paris for better-heated quarters at the front. It was the same sort of jibe men at London headquarters had made in June, when the buzz bombs were at their worst, to those who went to Normandy on visits.

A driver named Trotter from Georgia and I left Paris by jeep at about noon. It was extremely cold, because the vehicle was open and we had to contend not only against the piercing wind, but also against mud and muck thrown up by the wheels. I dragged out my blankets and bundled up, feeling a bit as if I were retreating from Moscow. We turned north before we left Reims and headed for Laôn. The towns showed little signs of battle but many evidences of the liberator. Near every hamlet there were soldiers, mostly from supply units. Quartermaster companies, petroleum

dumps, warehouses of clothing and food, rear-echelon maintenance outfits, replacement depots, rear bases of air units, all the
myriad installations that make the frontline units tick were there.
One had the notion that these men had moved in as inhabitants.
If one stopped at a local restaurant or bistro, there were always
soldiers who obviously had found a home there. Their habit of
going behind the counter for a drink, their familiarity with the
proprietor, or their open overlordship of the owner's daughter
made this clear. The presence of GI articles on the shelves of the
establishment indicated the price of the liaison. Trucks and jeeps
had regular stopping places along the way, and the MPs, who
had made their own arrangements, paid no heed.

Former parks in the little towns had become open-air garages
for the units. The steady traffic and the slush soon gave nearly
every village the same drab, mud-splashed touch. In most of the
drinking and eating places the atmosphere was that of some far
western town of the movies where the men gathered at night to
spice their lives with liquor.

These soldiers, for the most part, had made their deal with
the army. They didn't care for the life, but they proposed to make
the best of it. Their adjustment was no different from that of men
stationed in Paris to the pleasanter life in the French capital; they
worked longer hours and were up at the front occasionally, but
they had found a place to come back to at the end of the day or
their trip. The difference between their routine and that of the
soldiers in Paris was the same as that between the man who goes
home every night and a truck driver who gets home every few
days between trips. Before the winter ended, men as far forward
as corps were to take advantage of the static situation to find similar solaces. Perhaps the men between Paris and the front had it
best. On the move and far enough forward to feel that they were
in the war, and yet far enough back that they could establish a
place of their own.

Thursday, 16 November (D+163)

> *Nice day. Snow for several miles. . . . Saw planes starting an all-out
> attack along front.*

In a little town it was possible to get a sense of belonging that one did not have in Paris. They came to feel that Monsieur Jean or Georges at the local bistro really liked their company as well as the money they spent. And it was often possible, with the agreement of the parents, to sleep with the daughter of the house.

Part of this I saw as I stopped along the way; part I gathered from the drivers I talked to. We reached Sedan that night. It was a city of bad memories for the French—in 1870 the Germans had taken Napoleon III there, and in 1940 the German tanks had pushed through on the way to Paris. The speed with which both the enemy and later the American forces had gone through Sedan had spared it heavy shelling by artillery, but some air bombardment around the railroad yards had left the marks of war. An MP company stationed in the city was our host that night, and we stayed with them in the old people's home where they were billeted.

At Sedan we had seen a spattering of snow, and it became heavier as we went along. Our speed was slowed by the conditions of the roads and the denser traffic that tended to pile up as we approached Liége, one of the great supply centers of First Army. This city, which had attracted the attention of the world in the First World War, had been taken with little effort in the second and had escaped great damage. But lately the German vengeance bombs had been turned against that city and Antwerp, and wreaked greater damage than the two cities had seen in both wars. The bombs, without mind or soul, fell where chance put them, and they struck at hospitals and ammunition dumps with great impartiality. Unfortunately, there were more homes of the poor and defenseless than anything else, and these were frequently claimed, along with their inhabitants, by the weapon technically intended to prevent the supplies of the Allies from reaching the front. From time to time a broken home or place of business spilled down across a thoroughfare and held up American trucks for a few minutes until a dozer could be brought to clear the way. But the chief ruin was to the helpless.

We spent the night at Spa, headquarters of First Army. This once-happy resort town, where Wilhelm I of Germany had a headquarters in World War I, exhibited the same muddy, drab look that I had seen earlier on the way. The parks as always were filled with trucks and jeeps. But for the wearing of weapons, which had disappeared in Paris along with most field clothing in the first weeks of the stay there, the headquarters, only twenty or thirty miles from some parts of the front, might well have been in Paris. True there was more bustle, and the messengers who came in and out had the air of men carrying momentous papers, and the correspondents made it one of their chief clearinghouses, but the war still stopped from time to time, and there was not the same immediacy of battle there as at corps or division.

I was briefed on the current historical program by Captain Dick Shappell, a newspaperman from Flint, Michigan, who was acting at the moment as head of the First Army Information and Historical Service, then installed in the Hotel de l'Universe. I was upset because my promotion to master sergeant—which I had been promised a month earlier—had not come through, and Shappell promised to investigate the matter. Later in the evening, after Sergeant E.P. Patterson, chief clerk of the section, had shown me some of the recent interviews which had been conducted by the corps, Colonel Corpening, onetime West Pointer and later a member of the *Chicago Tribune* staff, showed up and gave us word of Ninth Army, which he recently had visited.

Friday, 17 November (D+164)

Rain.

Captain Shappell, knowing that I much wanted to see my friend Lieutenant Fred Hadsel at VII Corps, drove me the next afternoon to Kornelimünster, where the corps was located. A heavy bombardment was going on some four kilometers to our front and we headed as soon as possible for the Historical Section, hoping they would have a friendly cellar should one be needed. After a little search we found Hadsel, Lieutenant Condren, Sergeant Dorsey, and Sergeant Cooper billeted in a combination barber and beauty shop. A place was made for our bedrolls beside the barber chair in a side room. The racks and shelves that had held beauty lotions were cleared of their supplies, which were pushed into a corner, and the records of the Historical Section were filed under the heading "Eau de Cologne."

Hadsel and I had been at Clark University together in 1938–39, he receiving his master's when I did my doctorate. He went on to Chicago for his Ph.D., which he completed before going into the army. He was in Provost Marshal Officer Candidate School in the spring of 1944 when I went to Washington. At Colonel Kemper's request for the name of possible combat historians, I had suggested Hadsel and he had been assigned to the Historical Service on the day he was commissioned. He and Shappell had come overseas together in July. Hadsel had succeeded Ruppenthal in VII Corps and had done an excellent job. Son of a former professor of Latin at Miami University, a brilliant student with a good knowledge of Europe, he proved to be one of the best men the section had in the field.

Hadsel showed me the VII Corps troop list so that I could get some idea of its present dispositions. Looking through it I saw the name of the 3d Armored Division, and glancing further along the list found the 709th Tank Destroyer Battalion, my brother's outfit. When I asked its location, they took me to the war room at corps headquarters, and I learned that Tommy's unit was two hundred yards forward, outposting the corps. It was dark, however, and Cooper and I made a considerable trip before we finally discovered at the head of a little lane the shack in which the battalion orderly room was located. I had just left the jeep to ask for directions when I saw a tall figure come out of the dark, and it was my brother. He went back with us to the beauty shop, where the hosts had prepared a powerful punch for us. It started as equal parts brandy and Benedictine, and then champagne and, I think, gin was added. In addition to this explosive mixture, which I sampled for the first time, I was introduced that evening to the sound of the buzz bomb as one lumbered overhead sounding like a train.

Hadsel told me that the heavy bombardment of the previous day had marked the beginning of a joint First and Ninth Army attack toward the Roer. The First Army was ordered to take the forest to its front—an area that was known to the army and the public after many days as the bloody Hürtgen Forest, in which the Germans heavily mauled four divisions.

Saturday, 18 November (D+165)

Pretty day.

In the afternoon on the eighteenth the rain of the day before changed to pale sunshine as Captain Shappell drove me down to V Corps Rear. It was located in a heavily wooded area southeast of Eupen and, to my dismay, was still in tents. The large pyramidal office tent, however, had a stove that the officers had bought in Luxembourg, and it was not uncomfortable, despite a coating of ice outside the tent left from an earlier snow. Captains Fox, Howe, Born, Lieutenant Graney, Corporal Kelly, and Private Leone were on hand to greet us. After a time, Shappell started back to Spa and left me to be officially welcomed by my old friends. Hadsel thoughtfully had given me a bottle of champagne when I left VII Corps so there would be something with which to welcome me. This was brought out early in the evening, and the historians opened their "Top Secret" document boxes where we kept such important "records" and brought out their remaining three bottles of Cordon Rouge. The first bottle was opened by the accepted method of swathing the bottle in a towel and banging its bottom against a tent pole until the cork came out. The others, since we were impatient and had no time for ceremony, were opened by the simple method of hitting their necks sharply against a heavy object. We ran some danger of drinking glass by this method, but it was assumed that liberal applications of calvados and other such liquors in the previous spring and summer had given the stomach a proper lining to offset sharp objects, so we didn't worry. In lieu of glasses we used our canteen cups. Mine had not been used for some weeks and there was a coat of dust and grease around the inside, but that did not seem to affect the taste of the champagne. The lack of champagne prevented the evening from being quite as convivial as an earlier one when "Congressman" Graney and Topete had made speeches on politics and love, but they kindly gave excerpts of their earlier efforts and added speeches of welcome as well. I felt, indeed, that I was back with the fighting historians.

Sunday, 19 November (D+166)

Cold—Rain.

It rained the entire first week I was back, but never entirely washed away the remnants of ice and snow on the ground. Kelly and I shared a pup tent. I was not cold because a sleeping bag, which I had bought in Washington the preceding March and had left behind because of weight limitations on the plane, had finally reached me before I left Paris. The issue sleeping bags were rather thin things, made for men of much smaller frames than mine. They were so made that one could get in them only with much wriggling and, if he were a small man, he might take in a blanket with him. Then he struggled to zip up the bag in order to keep in the heat of his body. This arrangement could be made with an expenditure of time and effort and contortion, but woe to anyone who suddenly had to get out of this strait jacket, either to face an unexpected enemy or a call of nature. With few exceptions, a sleeping bag spread on a shelter half kept me warm and dry throughout that winter.

Monday, 20 November (D+167)

Rain.

My first days back were spent reading G-2 and G-3 reports for the period since I had been away from the corps. It added nothing to the broad outline I had received from the papers concerning the progress of the war, but it did fill in a number of fine points. When I had reached Paris in mid-September, the offensive was grinding toward a halt, and would not really be resumed on our front with effectiveness until February 1945.

At the beginning of this period of attrition, Eisenhower and Montgomery had sought to send airborne forces across the Rhine at Arnhem. The 82d and the 101st U.S. and the 1st British Airborne Divisions had dropped at Grave, Nijmegen, and Arnhem. The first two, after some delays, had seized their objectives. The British had established positions north of the bridge at Arnhem, but the armor that was to have come from the south, and the reinforcements which were to come from the air, did not reach them in time. Two-thirds of the division was either captured or destroyed. The two American divisions were kept in the line as infantry until their losses made it necessary for them to be sent back for refitting.

Tuesday, 21 November (D+168)

Rain and colder.

The setback at Arnhem had been followed by an all-out battle to clear the banks of the Scheldt Estuary and make it possible to use the port of Antwerp, which had been captured intact at the beginning of September, but was useless so long as the Germans held the approaches. Meanwhile, First Army units took Aachen, Emperor Charlemagne's city. It was a symbol the Germans had fought for grimly until destruction from planes and guns had made a shell of it. To the south, Third Army waged a slow battle of the type disliked by Patton for the forts that made up the defenses of Metz. The greatest progress at the time was made in Alsace, where the Seventh U.S. and First French Armies pushed toward the Rhine. Although they reached it at Strasbourg, a German pocket remained west of the river near Colmar and menaced the Allies position.

Wednesday, 22 November (D+169)

Rain.

On the V Corps front, an attack had been started at the beginning of November for the little town of Schmidt, which led toward the Roer and in turn toward the Rhine. Just to the south of it—although that was not their mission—was the Schwammenuel Dam, which held back the waters of the Roer and its tributaries and threatened any action to the north of it. Schmidt, approached by a narrow winding road over which it was difficult to send either supplies or tanks, had been taken early in the fight by a regiment from the 28th Division, but a German counterattack had driven them back and they had given up the town. Not until the end of the first week in February were American troops to take back the city. German possession of the town was to make more difficult the fight for Hürtgen to the north and the battle for the Roer dams. Fox and Howe, recognizing the importance of this fight, made it their chief job for November and part of December.

The picture then was one of a sweep across France into Belgium, southern Holland, and Luxembourg and into Germany, and then a sudden halt. The lack of supplies had played their part, as lines, stretching all the way to Omaha Beach and Arromanches, became longer and longer, and as new units came in to increase the demands put upon them. But some blamed the high command and said that if this or that course had been followed, the disintegrating German armies could have been smashed in September and the war would now be ended. That type of talk was more common to the rear than at corps and division levels. So far as the men knew, the war was being handled as best it could, but it was cold and the enemy was still in front of them.

Thursday, 23 November (D+170)

Rain.

We celebrated Thanksgiving in a muddy field south of Eupen. We were in our fifth day of rain and our footing was uncertain. The kitchen was under a tent, but there was no place for us there, so we got our prescribed ration of turkey, cranberry sauce, dressing, etc. all dumped together in one great mass in our mess kit and went out in the rain to eat it. The dreadful raincoats, which we swore at every time we wore them, made us uncomfortably hot and also sprang leaks from time to time. The pouring rain added an extra ingredient to the dressing and cooled the warm mess kit, and the steaming coffee was soon cold. But the turkey was good and enough of the flavor survived the drowning to remind us it was there. When the meal was finished, we went to a nearby tent where a movie was to be shown in honor of Thanksgiving. It was *The Good Earth,* and the plight of the poor heathen in that film was enough to make us feel warm and satiated with fine living. The electric current was not right for the movie sound projector, so instead of getting English voices we got a sort of chatter instead. But since these were Chinese, the vocal mixture did not seem out of character. During the performance the water began to run through the tents and we had to take off our helmets and sit on them while rivulets were formed around our legs. But it was Thanksgiving and we were happy. Besides, the word had come that we were to move into buildings the next day.

Friday, 24 November (D+171)

Cool.

The rain did not let up for our move, and we were faced with the usually disagreeable chore of taking down the clammy, heavy tent again. But since the future promised an end of such shelter, we worked at it willingly. By afternoon we were loaded up, and the tented area where the corps rear had been located since the move from Luxembourg some time before soon showed only a few signs of former habitation. There were stumps of trees that had been cut for firewood, gravelike mounds marking former latrine spots and refuse dumps, and deep ruts where the trucks and jeeps had been. Captain Born stayed behind with one or two others on what he called "the smelling detail" to see that all the trash and debris were buried. They reported this task well done, but as they were leaving they could see slowly moving up in the distance small groups of people with shovels who were prepared to open some of the dump heaps to see what articles of clothing or food the Americans might have left, for we had the reputation for burying articles which most other people would be glad to have.

Less than four weeks later, a few days after the Ardennes attack, I was shown some captured films taken by a German soldier in the early hours of the 16 December attack. The shots showed some German soldiers, some dead Americans, and a sign indicating that an American depot was located nearby. On checking, we found that it was a short distance to the rear of the command post we had left on 24 November.

Our new command post, the best we were to have until the end of the war, was located in Dolhain-Limbourg. This settlement consisted of a small town two or three miles south of Eupen and the remains of a château to the east. Since we were to remain there until the end of February, its history became of great interest. The original château had been built shortly after the middle of the eleventh century, and the dukes of Limbourg had strengthened it against possible enemies. The château had been besieged by Henry IV of Germany at the beginning of the twelfth century; it had withstood a siege by the rulers of Liége in the fifteenth century; and then had fallen victim to a fire at the beginning of the sixteenth century. A Spanish army under Alexander Farnese had seized the city in 1578, the Dutch had taken it in 1632, and a Spanish army had returned in 1635. Later in the century the Dutch reentered Limbourg and were forced to defend it in 1675 against a French army led by the Prince of Conde. The Prince of Nassau surrendered after seven days and the town was given to Spain in the Peace of Nijmegen. The French reoccupied Limbourg in 1701, but lost it in 1703 after one day's fight to the duke of Marlborough. The town was restored to Holland and, in the course of events, became Belgian in the nineteenth century. Fires in 1834 and 1914 had reduced the château to ruins, but a religious order had built a chapter house on the hill, and the town below had flourished as the main center of a farming and small handicraft area.

Thus the town, standing as it did within four or five miles of the German border, was no stranger to war. The people were pro-Belgian in their background and sympathies, but a few miles away in Eupen, which had been taken from the Germans and given to Belgium in 1919 for purposes of frontier security, the people spoke German as their native tongue and were correct but sullen toward the Americans.

The rear headquarters was set up in a school building erected only four or five years before. Unusual for that part of the world, the structure was completely modern. Each room was extremely well lit (our office, which had been a classroom, was on one side made up entirely of windows reaching from floor to ceiling), and a large gymnasium served as the enlisted men's mess. Our special pride and joy was the shower room, which had twenty-four separate showers. Unfortunately, there were only four water closets, and these were divided equally between officers and enlisted men. The resultant waiting line on the side allotted the EM did much to stimulate reading, as one sometimes took an hour moving slowly from one place to another on the benches set around the entrance to the WCs. Army pocketbooks were then available, and everyone kept one in his pocket for the daily reading sessions.[16]

The building was surrounded by a large courtyard, at the corners of which were two buildings. These had formerly served as school buildings, but one now was used as an officers' mess and the other as the MP headquarters. Upstairs were former inmates of a special house run by the Germans, and the women, held prisoners at the request of the Belgians, served under guard as cleaning women. The motor pool was located in the courtyard.

Officer and GI billets were out in the town proper, although our group, being small, was permitted to sleep in the offices. This was a great privilege, because the building, drawing on German coal supplies, was always well heated. Actually, too well heated, because it was often difficult to sleep at night because too much coal had been poured on. I was to have my first colds since I left England.

The move into a regular building made great changes in our living conditions. It was possible to do laundry in the shower rooms or to get clothing washed by people in the town. More important, the cooks, having places for their stoves, and a mess hall, seemed to take new interest in their trade. Bread and meat were cooked in the public ovens in the city, and it was possible by furnishing the ingredients to have ice cream made. The city's moving-picture house, part of which was used as a billet, was turned into a joint recreation hall and theater. After a few weeks, kegs of weak Belgian beer were brought in and movies were shown three times a week. Restaurants in the city were off limits to officers and men, but they were always willing to serve steaks and french-fried potatoes for $2, and they carefully and discreetly saw to it that enlisted men and officers were served meals in different rooms to avoid embarrassment concerning the prohibitions on eating there.

This was the first place in weeks where many of the men had been able to find shops, and they practically bought out the little stores filled with postcards and souvenirs that were crowded together on the main streets. The people were quite pleased to see us at first, and even toward the end were still friendly. Some rivalries developed between the few remaining young men of the town and the soldiers about girlfriends, but most of these difficulties were settled amicably.

Particularly pleasant to the men who had been for weeks in the field were the little bistros. In many of them at first were groups of eighteen- to twenty-year-old lads who reminded one of the gang in a drugstore or restaurant in a small town. They played darts, drank beer, and danced with the barmaids. Occasionally a GI would cut in and they would give way graciously. Many of the young Belgians were of army age and said they would soon be going into the army. Meanwhile they joked with each other, or now and then they would say to some GI who frequented the place, "The only way to learn French is to sleep with a mademoiselle every night." At one I went to several times there was a town fool who would wander about showing off American cigarettes or other things GIs had given him. The manager winked at the crowd when jokes were made, puffed at his cigar, took a turn now and then at darts, and protested in an injured tone when GIs brought back bottles of cognac that had been watered down.

The children of that town were soon terribly spoiled by the soldiers. Some of the poorer ones came each day to the backyard behind the mess hall with their buckets to get food. We had arranged that the nuns of a nearby school could have the garbage to feed pigs they were raising, but when it became apparent that many of the scraps being thrown away contained good meat and bread the children came to ask that the food be put into their pails instead of the garbage cans. For some weeks, until the practice was stopped, most GIs either took an extra helping or left something on his mess kit to go into the buckets. Some of our food found its way to some of the young women of the town, and when the mess officer became suspicious of a shortage of food in our mess hall, he followed one of the cooks down a street one night and discovered that the soldier was taking a ham to his girlfriend.

Some of the GIs taught the children to play tricks on the MPs and officers. The former they would hail with "Mademoiselle Promenade?" saying that these words of GI invitation to girls of the town were what the initials MP stood for. They would also greet officers and sergeants with choice profanity and obscenity, smiling like cherubs and completely unaware of the meaning of the words they had been taught to say.

But for a time, Topete and I didn't see too much of Dolhain-Limbourg. We were assigned the task of getting the story of the 5th Armored Division's initial advance into Germany, and the fight that took place at Wallendorf. Elements of the division were among the first to go into the Reich, and they were the first to withdraw from a position in Germany. We were warned against taking chances, since Lieutenant Condren and Sergeant Doresy had already been badly injured by mines a few days before. We heard again Colonel Kemper's statement that while he wanted live history, he did not want dead historians.

Saturday, 25 November (D+172)

Before starting out on the new assignment I drew a new field jacket to take the place of the one that had been issued me at Fort Harrison in April 1944. It was quite worn and dirty, but I didn't care for the new one—which was of the field green variety. It was laced up around the middle with a drawstring, and unless handled properly gave one the appearance of unusual fullness in the midriff. Several months later, the theater quartermaster issued a memorandum entitled "How to wear the new jacket, field, without looking pregnant."

Sunday, 26 November (D+173)

Cool.

My first important interview was with Lieutenant Colonel F.B. Butler Jr., G-3 of the 5th Armored Division, with whom I talked in his trailer office in a woods between Eupen and Roetgen. V Corps had sent two combat commands of the division from Luxembourg into Germany on 14 September, following a patrol crossing three days earlier, with the idea of taking Bitburg or the high ground in the vicinity. It was assumed that the Germans had no strength in the area and that it would be possible to penetrate the advance portion of the Siegfried Line there. This assumption proved correct and the tanks rapidly bypassed a number of unmanned concrete pillboxes in the first two days of the attack. Several villages were occupied and it seemed that this area west of the Rhine would soon be taken. But while armor can surround, assault, or bypass, it is difficult for it to hold. The infantry, already stretched out all the way back to the Mons area, where V Corps had helped seal the great pocket in northern France, could not be brought forward in time to occupy the overrun area. As a result, the Germans had time to send forces from near Trier. By the evening of the second day they were bringing down fire on the Americans. The enemy was aided by the fact that the 5th Armored's lines of communications ran through a saucer-like area on which it was possible to concentrate damaging fire from the surrounding heights. At the end of three or four days, the losses were such that it seemed best to withdraw. Therefore, on 22 September, one of the first armored forces to enter Germany withdrew into Luxembourg. Colonel Butler, like many others in the First and Third Armies, believed that if more infantry had been available the armor could have rolled to the Rhine. Unlike Third Army officers, who blamed the failure to reach the Rhine on the lack of gasoline, which they felt had been unfairly given to the British, Colonel Butler made no recriminatory remarks. He felt that the tanks had already undergone twice the punishment that anyone believed them capable of taking. His judgment on the failure to go to the Rhine was that the American forces had prepared for a heavy fight in the Siegfried Line; they were not prepared for a pushover.

Monday, 27 November (D+174)

In the week that followed, Topete and I got the rest of the story from a dozen or more major interviews. At Troop B, 85th Reconnaissance Squadron, near Monschau, we heard the account of what may have been the first American patrol to enter Germany in 1944. The squadron on 11 September had moved through Diekirch, Luxembourg, and then north through Bastendorf and Kippenhof to Hoscheid. This part of the advance was easy since the Germans had not blown the bridge at Diekirch. Around 12:30, a platoon was sent to Stalzenburg, north of Vianden on the Our River, which separates Luxembourg and Germany. Three patrols were instructed to try to cross the river and observe German fortifications in that area. One patrol from the 2d Platoon under Staff Sergeant Holzinger, included Lieutenant DeLille, a French officer who was accompanying the American forces as an interpreter, Corporal Ralph Diven, T/5 Coy Locke, and Pfc. McNeil. They waded the river near a blown bridge and walked some four hundred yards to the crest of a hill where a group of farmhouses stood. They noticed an old chicken shed, built around a pillbox, shortly after crossing the river. From the crest of the hill they could count some nineteen to twenty pillboxes. They did not hurry their reconnaissance, so it was after six o'clock when their crossing was reported. It was, therefore, listed after others. The best guess is that they crossed by 4:30 in the afternoon, and probably were slightly ahead of patrols from the 4th and 28th Divisions and from their own squadron. Since all three of the divisions had been instructed to send patrols across as soon as possible in order to get credit for being the first across, all claims are subject to doubt. Since I got the story of this patrol and not of the others, I naturally was always inclined to argue that this was the first. It is a matter of record that all three of V Corps's divisions had patrols across the German border before midnight on 11 September. VII Corps pushed armored elements across in force from Belgium to the area near Roentgen on the twelfth.

Tuesday, 28 November (D+175)

Cold.

On the following day, Lieutenant L.L. Vipond, executive officer of Troop B, went back into Germany with a motorized patrol. Accompanied by Lieutenant DeLille, he inspected the pillboxes that had been reported the day before and found that they had not been manned. Farther to the east, near Bauler, they discovered Germans around only two pillboxes in the area. While they were in one of the unoccupied fortifications they observed some sixty men carrying bundles, boxes, and machine guns approaching from the north. Six to ten men stopped at each pillbox as they went by. By evening, the area was well prepared against an American advance.

Farther south, the battle for Wallendorf began on 16 September. One of the important groups in this action was Task Force Anderson, led by Lieutenant Colonel Leroy H. Anderson. His force consisted of the Headquarters Company and Companies B and C of the 81st Tank Battalion, B and C Companies of the 15th Infantry Battalion, two or more platoons of the 628th Tank Destroyer Battalion, a platoon of the 22d Engineer Battalion, and a medical detachment. Statements by Colonel Anderson; Captain Weldon Wilson, commander of Company B, 81st Tank Battalion; Captain Charles P. DeBevoise, S-2 of the Task Force; and Technical Sergeant Edgar Thilman, S-3 sergeant of the Task Force, helped us reconstruct the important work of the Task Force. A summary of their statements reveals vividly the fighting the armored forces met when they entered the Siegfried Line.

In the week preceding the crossing at Wallendorf, the Task Force had made one or two crossings from Lipperscheid, Luxembourg, into Germany, but found no Germans. On the sixteenth they were ordered south with the initial mission of clearing the five-kilometer gap between Wallendorf and Gentingen to the north. They crossed a ford at Wallendorf about 4:00 in the afternoon, finding the stream to be about sixty feet wide and one and a half feet deep. There was no opposition, so they moved up to Hommerdingen just before dark. Plums were ripe and they ate some.

On the following day, about noon, they went eastward toward Biesdorf and northward toward Ammeldingen to clean up pillboxes in the area. By nightfall they had cleared out some ten pillboxes. Part of these consisted of two large concrete rooms in which soldiers slept on bunks suspended from the ceiling. A small storage room completed the interior. Iron doors, with baffles to stop shell fragments, covered the two entrances. A small annex, entirely separate from the box, had a gun position for an antitank gun, but the Americans reported that they never saw the guns for which these mounts were intended and assumed that they had been removed earlier for the protection of the Normandy beach positions. The larger pillboxes had a large mechanical filter with a hand-cranked rotary pump for purifying the air. The larger bunkers could hold as many as thirty-four people. Smaller boxes had only one room and were sunk about halfway into the ground. The pillboxes were connected with one another by telephones, and in a few cases American soldiers entering a box would hear the instrument ringing as they entered.

Wednesday, 29 November (D+176)

Cold.

Such periods seemed always marked by growing doubts on the part of the soldiers as to the wisdom of the war. In a typical discussion one evening, several of us talked of the listlessness of the American soldier and the fact that he seldom seemed to know what he was fighting for. Some of them argued that there had never been any reason for our coming over; that all the United States needed was a strong navy. I doubted if we could ever make people see what they were fighting for unless they were invaded. I said that most of them in 1942, soon after Pearl Harbor, seemed to think they knew why they were fighting, but as time went on it was harder to show them, and we seemed less certain why we fought.

My diary summarizes part of the discussion:

"Too many people expect the war to settle everything. They think of war as abnormal; they think of disorder, depression, disasters as abnormal. Each generation assumes that it is the mistreated one and that if they can get over this hump they will have peace and prosperity. Unfortunately, difficulties are part of the scheme of life. While none of them is inevitable, perhaps, they are there until something definite is done to remove them. The winning of a war merely means that we avoided the disaster attendant on losing it. It does not mean that we have peace automatically.

"Discussion of tactics. Everyone seems to think that we [V Corps] would have gone to the Rhine with a little more infantry [1–3 divisions]. It seems we were prepared for difficult going, but not prepared for the great success that we had."

The pillboxes were now named Kampfgruppe Appel, headed by an officer who blamed the Americans for killing his brother and carried on a personal vendetta against them. He had personally knocked out a tank with a German bazooka. His unit, from which the Task Force took some twenty-five prisoners the first day, was made up mainly of convalescents from a hospital at Trier. Some of them were "stomach cases" who had to have a special diet; some had seen action on the Russian front (one had frozen hands and one an artificial wooden arm); one had been discharged earlier for "stupidity'" but was now back fighting.

On the eighteenth, the Task Force continued clearing the fortified area, this time between Ammeldingen and Niedersgegen on the Gay River to the northeast. By the 19th they had set up an observation post on a hill looking in on Niedersgegen, Cruchten, and Biesdorf. Meanwhile the rest of Combat Command B (Task Force Anderson and Task Force Gilson made up CCB) was receiving heavy fire south of Ammeldingen. Part of Task Force Anderson spent the day assaulting Biesdorf. The Germans now had moved up some antitank guns, tanks, and additional artillery to hit both combat commands. They attempted to infiltrate troops through the woods south of Gentingen on the twentieth, but they were driven back. Heavy firing, reported to be from four German railway guns, fell in the area just north of Ammeldingen during the day. Our air forces, whose aid was now being called in, ultimately destroyed the four.

While conducting interviews, I recorded the following in my diary:

"The question came up as to the fighting between British and the Greek leftists in Greece, the troubles between the British and Count Sforza[17] in Italy, difficulties with the Left in France and Belgium. One soldier said 'the soldiers don't understand it. Why should we fight people that we just liberated.' I pointed out that each nation fought for certain things—mainly to get the type of Europe and world set-up they want. At first England would have settled for the security of England against Hitler, next for the Empire. Now they want governments in Europe which will not disturb the status quo by precept or example. For that reason England fears Leftist movements in Greece. I dislike to see the situation which is developing there. Apparently Britain got a hint that her policy was okay with the States."

On the matter of Britain, I had noted that a few days before, Sir Oliver Lyttelton, in a House of Commons debate, had said that Britain must give up the air of "the grand seigneur" after the war and become accustomed to a shabby coat. This was attacked by the conservatives and the *Daily Mail*, who said that England didn't intend to be dependent on her rich American relations.

The arguments relative to Greece, Belgium, and France had been prompted by events in November and December in which efforts were made by the Allies to disarm partisan bands. Active against the Germans, they desired to come to power after the enemy had been driven out. Part of the people were following a Communist line, others had risen to power under the partisan regime and didn't want to relinquish power to persons they considered either lukewarm in their efforts during the German occupation or who were inimical to their interests. The controversy in each country became confused with the Communist drive for power. Certainly in France and Belgium, for people who had gone early into the underground movement and who had remained at home to carry on the fight, it seemed hard to hand over their arms and their positions to governments dominated by individuals brought back by the British and American armies. The case was difficult to resolve, and even moderate papers in England and the United States attacked Churchill, in particular, for his course of action. The Left, however, managed to put itself in the wrong by insisting on personal vendettas against individuals they didn't like, by placing the chief emphasis on revenge and a sort of vigilante law, and by refusing to give up arms to the state. When they threatened armed resistance, they played into the hands of the government. The Allied armies could not permit conflict and strikes between factions of the liberated countries while the war was in progress, and they made clear that such would not be permitted.

In a thick fog at daybreak on the twenty-first, an estimated company of Germans, believed to be from the 19th German Air Force Division, approached the Task Force's positions. The Americans were startled, but the Germans, who had been told that the armored forces had pulled back, were caught completely by surprise and suffered some forty killed. Later in the day, a prisoner reported that many of the Germans in the area were willing to surrender if the Americans would not shoot them. A request was sent back for a public address system over which an appeal and instructions for surrender would be broadcast, but it had not come before a large group (one estimate was 150) came out of the woods carrying their guns. Suddenly some of their own people opened fire on them and they, apparently assuming that the Americans were firing, dropped to their knees and began to fire. The tanks killed most of them.

Meanwhile, the attack against the CCR (Combat Command Rear) and CCB was growing stronger, despite the commitment of two battalions of infantry from the 112th Infantry Regiment, 28th Division. Infiltrating Germans destroyed two bridges at Wallendorf on the twentieth and interfered with supply columns. Finally, on the evening of the twenty-first, orders came for withdrawal to Luxembourg. The Germans heard the noise of movement and gave the Americans a scare when they began putting up flares. Fortunately, their attack was light and with small arms. Tension developed later at the Wallendorf ford, which was under interdictory fire, when a large truck stuck near the head of the column and nearly the entire Task Force was stuck bumper to bumper. Fortunately, the fire stopped and only three or four vehicles were lost. One jeep blew out a tire, but this time there was no wait. A tank was ordered to run over it and the withdrawal proceeded. Despite the withdrawal from Germany, the Task Force took some satisfaction from the fact that between 16 and 21 September they had inflicted casualties equivalent to 30 or 40 percent of the German force opposing them. In addition, they had rendered useless many of the pillboxes in the area—some by covering them with dirt, others by dropping charges of TNT down ventilators, others by exploding compartment walls, and still others by attaching explosives to the hinges of the iron doors so that they could not close.

Thursday, 30 November (D+177)

Pretty day.

Similar stories to those of Task Force Anderson were repeated to us as we talked to various officers and men of the 5th Armored Division. One day we went to a farmhouse near Wolheim, Germany, to copy material from the CCR journals. While guns were booming a few kilometers away, and Topete was busy typing, I undertook to keep the fire in the kitchen stove stoked with wood.

Part of the house was in ruins and a piece of the chimney had been knocked down. Even if the fire had burned properly, it would have waged a losing battle with the cold air pouring in from outside. The result was a tableau in which I continued to poke wood in the range, while Topete, gloves on, poked away at the portable. Now and then he would stop to blow on his fingers and then go back to his typing. We spent that night at Kornelimuenster, again at the barbershop, with Hadsel and his people. Lieutenant Tuttle, a new member of the Historical Section, had joined him that day.

Part of the first week of December was spent in putting down the details of the Wallendorf story. This was in accord with existing theater instructions to send back connected narratives as soon as possible to the information and historical teams at army headquarters. There the material was to be coordinated and, when desirable, was sent back to Paris for inclusion in army pamphlets. I usually checked interview material with entries in journals of the units concerned and with corps and army after-action reports, and then Topete made sketch maps to accompany the stories. His maps, based on rough outlines that company and battalion leaders made for us, undertook to show the actual avenues of advance by units of platoon size and larger. To some degree, they were able to sketch in fortifications and points of resistance. The fortification maps were often compared with corps and division G-2 maps in order to determine the accuracy of information.

The period of inactivity or slow progress continued. Jokes were made about our gaining two or three trees daily, and communiqués leaned heavily on "routine patrolling reported." V Corps had started an attack on the Hürtgen Forest near the end of November and was finding the combination of snow, bad roads, and dug-in Germans almost too much.

Chapter 17

The Deadly Forest

Friday, 1 December (D+178)–
Saturday, 16 December (D+193)

Friday, 1 December (D+178)

A little rain. To 85th Reconnaissance Squadron. Saw a Lieutenant
Vipond. Gave us details of the first British patrol to go into Germany on
4 Sept. To Eupen for dinner. Back to V Corps Rear in afternoon.

The Hürtgen Forest is a wooded area in Germany that lies
between the Belgian frontier and the Roer River north of the
Ardennes. During the late fall of 1944 the name was also used to
denote other forest areas to the north in which American soldiers
fought.

When the U.S. First Army moved into the Hürtgen Forest in
November 1944 it was much like the other wooded areas of Germany: carefully preserved by forest masters who saw that the
undergrowth was cleared away and who superintended the cutting of any trees in the area. There was nothing sinister about it,
and there were few, if any, legends connected with it. Within four
weeks after the Americans had entered the forest, their initial force
had been badly battered and the forest itself was smashed. Once-
proud trees were in ruin; blackened stumps remained where great
wooded giants had stood. There were no birds, no sighing winds,
no carpeted paths. There was desolation such as one associated
with the Battle of the Wilderness. An American general who had

fought through one of the battles in the forest offered $5 for every tree his men could find unmarked by shelling and got no takers. Two years after the war, when I returned to see what nature and man had done to restore the area, I found it still bleak and battered. A few people struggled to remove some of the stumps, but their efforts were hampered by mines. Most of the area to the east was being used by the British as an armored practice range.

The town of Hürtgen itself, containing some fifty to sixty houses and lying just north of Schmidt, was taken at the end of the first week of December in a battle in which the 8th Division's 121st Infantry Regiment, elements of the 5th Armored Division, and a battalion of Rangers was involved. On the twelfth Topete and I went down to get the story of the battles for Hürtgen and three other towns—Kleinhau, Bergstein, and Brandenberg—which we had never heard of before.

Rain and melting snow had turned the roads into lakes of cold and slimy mud. The so-called paved roads, once adequate for peacetime traffic, were beginning to give way under the effect of freezes and thaws and the continuous pounding of tanks and trucks. The smaller roads, which at best had only a little stone or gravel on them, were no more. In some cases the engineers had made corduroy roads, but the logs would get dislodged and it was almost hopeless to get going again under one's own power if the jeep slipped off. On roads that were not reinforced with logs or planks, vehicles had a formidable time. Once caught in a deep rut made by a truck, a jeep would soon be caught by the mud so that its tires could not touch the bottom of the track, and it would hang suspended until a vehicle with a winch could pull it out. Worse still were the narrow, winding roads over which tanks and trucks had attempted to move into action.

For the most part, the units we wanted to visit were in fixed positions and it was possible to interview the officers and men without difficulty. We thus talked to more than fifty officers and men in the course of five days and got one of the most detailed accounts we had thus far collected. At the conclusion of our stay in Hürtgen, I wrote the following summary of the action:

"The failure of the 28th Division in November to take Schmidt made it necessary for V Corps to secure another road which would serve as a supply route in the push toward the Roer River. An alternate route was found in the road through Huertgen to Kleinhau. Not only were there several approaches to this road from the west, but possession of the positions around Huertgen would also give the American forces observation for its artillery, while denying observation for the enemy. (Of course, during the battle, the situation relative to observation was naturally reversed).

"The approaches to Huertgen were through a heavily wooded section of the forest. Near the town, however, the area was cleared, so that an attacking force attempting to enter from any side was under observation of the enemy. Both of the roads entering the town from the west had sharp bends or curves in them that afforded ideal sites for strong points. The heavy woods offered concealment during the early days of the attack, but were soon destroyed by the heavy bombardment on the part of German artillery. German defenses for the most part consisted of log bunkers, with machine guns, and heavy antitank and antipersonnel minefields on the roads leading into Huertgen. Heavy concentrations were laid on those areas by German mortars and artillery situated north, south, and east of the town. Attacking forces were interfered with by mud, rain, and sleet. Enemy personnel were not of a high quality. The forces consisted principally of regiments of numerous units that had been disorganized in France. Numerous Kampfgruppe were formed of exceptional young or old soldiers. Little use was made on either side of aircraft, although enemy planes strafed American troops on two occasions. Poor observation interfered with use of artillery by the Americans.

"The original plans for the taking of Huertgen provided for the relief of the 12th Infantry, 4th Division, by the 121st Regiment, 8th Infantry Division, as the preparation for an attack through Huertgen to Kleinhau and to nearby Bergstein and Brandenberg by Combat Command R of the 5th Armored Division. The 121st Infantry, which was to secure the approaches to Hürtgen, was in Luxembourg 107 miles away when orders were given for its attack. It was required to make a hurried move on 20 November, and it closed into its assembly area barely in time for its advance at 0900, 21 November. Officers of the regiment blamed the delays the regiment suffered on this hurried move and the fact that the men had to go into action without rest. The regiment, however, had been reorganized during a six-weeks period in Luxembourg.

It had recovered many of its personnel wounded in the early days in Normandy and Brittany and went into battle overstrength. The regiment was reinforced by elements of the 644th Tank Destroyer Battalion, the 709th Tank Battalion, a company of the 12th Engineer Battalion, and the 56th Field Artillery Battalion. The movement of the 121st was part of a general interchange of areas, unit for unit, by the 28th and 8th Divisions.

"The early attempts of CCR to break through to Huertgen failed because of heavy artillery fire and the mud. It was then decided that the infantry would have to take the town. One battalion of the 13th Infantry was to attack north of the 121st, while elements of the 2d Ranger Battalion were to attack to the south. The 2d Battalion, 121st Infantry, was to attack along the road leading from the west into Huertgen, the 1st Battalion south of the road and the 3d Battalion west of the north-south road into Huertgen and south of the town.

"The heaviest artillery concentrations the regiment had faced hit the various battalions and stopped them with little or no gain. The 2d Battalion made no gain, while the 1st and 3d made between 200–500 yard gains. Company I found a way through the minefield at the east of the road and reached its objective at 1100. During the next four days the three battalions made repeated attacks with little success. Continuous artillery fire inflicted heavy casualties and made movement virtually impossible. The regimental commander was relieved, five officers from one company were relieved or cracked up, all the officers were lost in November, and one platoon leader was arrested when he refused to order his men back into the line after repeated attacks. Attempts made to use tanks to capture strong points were thwarted by mines and mud. Despite the activity of the 12th Engineer Battalion, Germans infiltrated back into the roads and re-laid mines, interfering with tank assaults. In some cases, the bogging down of a tank made it impossible for an advance to continue.

"On 25 November the three battalions made advances along their fronts and brought increased pressure on Huertgen. The 1st Battalion, 13th Infantry, and the 3d Battalion, 121st Infantry, successfully occupied commanding positions to the north and south of Huertgen. On 26 November, Company F, 121st Infantry, was ordered to take the town. It was stopped about 300 yards west of

Huertgen by small arms and machine gun fire. Patrols estimated that 400–700 Germans were in the town. On the following day, the 1st Battalion moved north of Huertgen and tried to advance on the town but, because of greatly reduced strength and heavy small arms and machine-gun fire by the enemy, it was unable to move very far. The other battalions made slight advances to improve their positions.

"At 1200 on 28 November, the 2d Battalion, 121st Infantry, with a platoon of the 12th Engineers and Company A, 709th Tank Battalion, entered Huertgen. The tanks fired into each building in the town, while squads of men drove the enemy from the cellars of the houses. Approximately 250 prisoners were taken.

"On 29 November CCR advanced through Huertgen and took the town of Kleinhau. The 1st Battalion, 13th Infantry, advanced in support of the armor, while the 2d Battalion, 121st Infantry, occupied a trench around Kleinhau. The 2d Battalion consolidated its position, while the 3d Battalion advanced eastward, south of Huertgen, to clear out pockets of enemy troops west of the road running from Kleinhau southward to Bergstein and Brandenberg.

"After CCR took Bergstein and Brandenberg on 2 December, the 3d Battalion was sent to that area to support the armored units and to take German positions east of the Kleinhau-Bergstein highway. Heavy casualties and straggling reduced the companies to the point where on 4 December a morning attack was made with 8 riflemen in one company and 10 in another. The 3d Battalion reached its objective in the afternoon and was relieved by the 1st Battalion on 5 December.

"The phase of the Huertgen Forest battle that closed on 5 December succeeded in giving the Americans control of important supply routes to towns north and southeast of Huertgen. Observation was gained for friendly artillery action. In securing this point, the regiment suffered 1,334 casualties and temporary disorganization; the armored command was also heavily hit in tanks and personnel. 121st regimental leaders blamed their difficulties on the following factors: (1) weather and forest, (2) mines, (3) unsatisfactory equipment; (4) preponderance of enemy artillery and mortar fire. The armored commanders felt that they had not been handled properly, having been committed before the infantry had control of the roads, and having been forced to use their armored infantry like ordinary infantry. Everyone agreed that this fight was the most difficult that they had met."

This rather restrained account fails to give the reader the true picture of the difficulties the infantry and armor faced in the Hürtgen Forest. A better concept of the problems they faced may be gained from extracts from accounts by several of the officers and men who took a leading part in the battle.

One of these interviews was given us by Lieutenant Jack R. "first on the objective" (as his executive officer mockingly called him) Melton, who commanded Company I in the attack south of Hürtgen. Company I had its headquarters in a pillbox, camou- flaged by a barn, at Kleinhau, just east of Hürtgen. The runner who took us from regiment told us to leave the jeep at the last house in Hürtgen since the area beyond that was under observa- tion from the south. The belief was that the Germans would not waste ammunition on one or two men, but they would fire at a jeepload of men. So, hoping that this theory was sound, we left the jeep behind us and ran, trying to zigzag a bit as we bent over.

The lieutenant was lying on a bunk when we entered the pill- box and told us to come on over. I laid my notebook and map on his chest and another lieutenant held a flashlight over my shoul- der so that I could see to write. Meanwhile, the men, who were supposedly resting, were eating their noonday K ration and think- ing wistfully of the hot meal they had been served the day before. Rest and rehabilitation at that time consisted of being taken by truck a mile or so back to a warm tent where they could get clean clothing and change their socks and eat a warm meal. A kitchen unit was moving up so they could have one hot meal a day, brought to them in great cans by the regimental mess personnel.

Melton's story, condensed and slightly rearranged, follows:

"We left on 19 November from Diekirch, Luxembourg, by truck. About noon the following morning, I was told to pass through Company K of the 12th Infantry Regiment, which we were relieving. The exposed four hundred yards to their com- mand post was covered with 150mm and 170mm fire, so we could not contact their commanding officer at once. So we went to a point about one thousand yards from their command post—to the southwest—and put men on the reverse slope where there was no mortar or artillery fire. At this time we had an overstrength in personnel (198 men and six officers). I went back near Germeter to talk to the battalion commander of the 12th Infantry." He said that since they arrived there they had made seven different attacks, with an advance of three hundred yards. They had been stopped by concertina wire, and by machine gun, 150mm and 170mm fire. They were covered from three different azimuths (50, 90, and 150). In six days they had received about eight thousand rounds of artillery fire.

"On the 21st of November, we were to cross the line of departure at 0730 (about daybreak). We were to attack in a column of platoons northward toward Huertgen. The main line of resistance was along the forest south of the town. We knew we had to cross at least one minefield. Concertina wire was in front of the mines and the mined area was covered by automatic weapons and artillery.

"We advanced with twenty yards between squads, echeloned to the right. There was no right flank protection. Company K of the 12th was just to the south of us. We did not relieve them; we asked permission too, but it was not allowed. We needed to advance eight hundred yards. If we didn't take our objective, it meant we had to go back fifteen hundred yards under artillery fire. We got artillery fire from the north, east, and south. However, my company was made up of veterans; there were few replacements and these were excellent men.

"The 2d and 3d Platoons were in a sawmill at the right of the road leading toward Huertgen; the 1st in a house to the west of the road. One of the first men to come out of the house was killed by a 75. Our men rushed seventy-five yards from the house to the sawmill, a squad at a time. They then went by rushes toward the minefield (there was about a one hundred–yard clearing between the sawmill and minefield). Jerry had no clear observation and there was an early morning haze. We bypassed the first wire although we later lost men in the same field. We sneaked through without preparation. I kept the 2d platoon with me until the SCR-536 radio (this was one of the two times it worked during the whole fight) reported the others had passed through. Then we crossed by rushes, more or less Indian fashion. We did not fire; if we had, we would never have been permitted to go through. We managed to get through before artillery fire was laid down. M Company weapons platoon was held up by artillery concentrations and could not come up until night. The enemy was drop- ping fire beyond the first minefield. We were in a nice wooded area, but it was nearly all knocked down that night.

"At the second field we ran into trouble. Two men were killed almost at once. A sergeant from the 2d Platoon, two scouts, and a platoon leader, armed with tommy guns and an M1, attacked some Germans nearby. Going to their aid another platoon leader stepped on a mine and was killed. Shortly afterward still another solder was killed by a mine.

"The 1st Platoon was pinned down at the second field by ar- tillery fire. The 3d Platoon came up and was also pinned down. The support squad of the 3d Platoon now made an envelopment to the rear of the Germans and captured about forty German sol- diers and two officers (this was probably the strength of an entire German company). The 3d platoon moved to the right. As soon as the two platoons cleared a place through the minefields, we brought up the support platoon and M Company's weapons pla- toon. As soon as the 3d platoon was pinned down, we brought up the support platoon to protect the flank. We built the 3d pla- toon up along some pillboxes. Two German companies were now trying to come in on us. We built up flank protection from north to south. The left flank, on the road, remained open.

"Two machine guns north of the second minefield were firing at us at this point. We suffered several casualties between the two minefields from mortars and artillery. (On the twenty-first we took sixty casualties.)

"In two and a half hours we had secured and organized our position. Company B of the Rangers built up a line to our right. Next morning we had a counterattack in which the Rangers lost several men.

"By the end of the 21st we were the most forward element in the division. Rations had to be hand carried, and that during the night. We had to carry most of the wounded out over the same difficult trail. Some of the men lay for four and a half hours with- out medical attention; didn't have enough litter squads. This helped to increase casualties, since at least three died who other- wise could have been saved. We lost all of our medics during the morning—two by artillery and one in the minefields (all wounded).

"During the next five days we stayed in our holes, suffering six counterattacks. We got our rations and water before dawn or not at all. A number of cases of trench foot developed. We had been lucky in that we had advanced through the only section where an attack could have succeeded.

"On the sixth day, through the magnificent reconnaissance of Lieutenant Hudson Hatcher, who would not send his men but personally went on a one-man patrol, we got information on the area and discovered that the Rangers had progressed on a 45-degree azimuth. We were ordered to attack Hill 54, which was several hundred yards due south of the western edge of Huertgen. On the twenty-seventh we jumped off without preparation. We were in column. The leading elements came face to face with the Germans, but did not fire. The Germans surrendered to elements of the 3d Platoon. We went out to the nose of Hill 54; the shadows were on our side of the hill. We saw Germans to the north. We occupied their foxholes, set up our mortars, and laid fire in on the Germans 50 yards away. We stayed on the hill that night.

"On the twenty-eighth, the 1st Battalion of the 121st attacked north of us, almost due north toward Huertgen. We were ordered to move almost due east to Hill 58, which was due south of the east end of Huertgen. We had to cross a deep draw, nearly sixty feet deep. Near Hill 58 we saw a German officer and some eight men. We told them to surrender, but they were in a good position and they started a firefight. We finally got the officer and twenty-three men altogether as prisoners. We built up our position west of Hill 58. We had Company L behind us. On the twenty-ninth, the battalion commander tried to send Company L around to our left, but it didn't work.

"We were ordered to try an attack on the thirtieth. Company L was to go in on our left after the fight started. To our surprise, the Germans had withdrawn during the night to heavily prepared pillboxes to the east. We occupied the hill about 0730 on the thirtieth. That night about twenty Jerries broke through. They had machine pistols and grenades; they got through our machine gun positions and captured about seven men. My men were in a bad condition. We had just gotten six replacements; five were captured. The terrain permitted a sneak attack, but it is possible that some of the men were asleep (such a thing had not happened before, however). The first of the rushes came from the front, two from the right, and one from the left. The one from the left nearly got us. We threw away all the German souvenirs we had taken so they wouldn't catch us with them. They were trying to destroy our supply lines and they almost succeeded before we threw them back. We sent back word for the 81mm to fire on our positions if they did succeed. We weren't being heroic; we figured we could dig in so that our stuff wouldn't hurt us.

"On the first, second, and third we were in reserve while Companies L and K attacked. They were pushed back the first and second days; they made a frontal assault with tanks and men on the third day.

"The battalion commander ordered us to attack on the fourth of December on an eighty-degree azimuth southeast of Huertgen. I was to take the company to the draw near 360 and occupy the draw. There we were to join elements of Company A, 47th Armored Infantry. It got dark before we could find them, so we pulled back (actually they weren't in the draw). We went back to the road where men of Companies K and L were disorganized. Company I was shelled. It began to sleet and we nearly froze. It was my most miserable night in the army.

"We were ordered to attack on the fifth to take the draw, with Company L to the left and Company I to the right. We had eight riflemen in the company; Company L had ten. We were almost soaked through as we tried to advance. Three machine guns caught us in a cross fire, so we decided to withdraw. The valley was covered by directly observed 88 fire. We attacked again in the afternoon at 1430. Some of our stragglers had come up, so we had thirty riflemen and Company L had thirty. We got a platoon of tanks, but Jerry kept up his artillery fire. We got three prisoners near 360. We reached the corps objective without loss by plain guts. This was the afternoon of 5 December. The 1st Battalion came in that night. We had 134 casualties during the eleven days of fighting. We can't replace these men. We are filling officer losses by battlefield commissions, but we are having trouble finding new noncoms. Company I had the heaviest losses because we spearheaded the attack."

Melton's first sergeant, Howard R. Redding, and three other soldiers (Sergeants Rubinsky and Jacobs and Corporal Edwards)

filled us in on the supply problems during the toughest part of
the period. It took from six to eight hours, they noted, to get the
supplies up the eight hundred to thirty-one hundred yards they
had to be carried: "We usually started with about fifteen men carrying the water, rations, and ammunition on our backs. We had
to go through minefields, under artillery fire, with mud sometimes up to our knees. Some nights it was so dark we had to form
chain lines. There were two pretty steep hills and we had to go
through, sliding and slipping. We had to cross one stream, rough
water, which was almost to our waist. This continued for eight
days. We went at early dawn and late at night; usually had one
BAR man in front and one behind. Sergeant Jacobs noted that
although men were always tired, the first sergeant never lacked
for volunteers. Some of the men who continued to go were: Corporal Charles Brown, company clerk; Private First Class Edwin
Leverette, who once went with bleeding feet, was finally evacuated with severe sinus trouble; Pfc. Lee Sharp, also had bad feet;
and Pfc. C.O. Williams, Pfc. Craig; Pfc. Thurman, who led the
platoons. Staff Sergeant Sherrill Benton worked four days until
knocked out with concussion."

The taking of Hürtgen itself was not difficult, and the story is
of interest mainly because of the publicity given to the town and
because the action was fairly typical of street fighting in the area.
Most of the officers who had taken part in the action had been hit
or were absent on leave at the time of our interviews, so we got
our information mainly from several platoon sergeants who had
taken part in the action. They were Sergeant Clifford L. Adams,
Company E, who had acted as runner for Lieutenant Colonel
Philip Ginder during the action; Staff Sergeant Anthony Rizzo, G
Company; and Sgts. Sylvester M. Damiani and John R. Devore of
C Company, 12th Combat Engineers.

On the morning of 28 November, elements of the 2d Battalion, 121st Regiment, were at the southwest edge of Hürtgen. At
1200, Colonel Ginder, who had recently been attached to the regiment as an extra colonel, ordered Company E to go through Companies F and G into the town. They were told to ride on top of
tanks from Company A, 709th Tank Battalion. Four medium tanks
went in the first wave, with six men on some and eight on others.
The enemy began laying down mortar and artillery fire—"pretty

damn heavy" Sergeant Adams thought—as the tanks came out of a wood into a cleared area. When they neared the town, automatic-weapons fire came from the first buildings on the west side of Hürtgen. Colonel Ginder now ordered Companies F and G to join the advance. Before they reached the town, enemy fire hit the lead tank and all the men on it were injured. Skirmish lines were built up inside the town on both sides of the street. Lieutenant Von Keller (who had come from Russia to the United States after the First World War) and Captain Clyde led elements of their companies through the town. Meanwhile, tank fire kept the Germans inside the buildings down. Then the infantry went to the various houses, fired their rifles and automatic weapons, and threw grenades into the cellars. Usually when this was followed by a demand for surrender, the Germans would come out. More than 95 percent of the enemy were found to be in the reinforced cellars of Hürtgen. A Lieutenant Bosch and his men took some forty-five prisoners from the second house in the town to the left of the main road.

In the course of the advance, the three infantry companies and the engineers who had also been sent in became quite mixed up, but they continued their operations against the enemy. By 1700 the town was cleared of the enemy and some 250 prisoners were reported captured. The chief losses to the Americans were a tank and a tank dozer knocked out near the church and several men wounded.

The problems met by infantry and tanks from mines and weather were graphically outlined by Staff Sergeant Carlton R. Brown, operations sergeant of the 3d Battalion. Brown had been a scriptwriter in private life and he kept a private journal filled with interesting information. At 0900 on 24 November, according to his account, Companies K and L, 121st Infantry, supported by tanks of the 709th Tank Battalion, began an advance along the road leading from Germeter to Hürtgen. Soon thereafter, despite the fact that the road had been cleared the night before, mines disabled the leading tank. The platoon leader left his tank to check on the situation and immediately stepped on an antipersonnel mine; meanwhile, three direct hits destroyed the tank. One man was killed, two wounded, and a fourth was not hurt. The knocked-out tank blocked the road since it was up against a bank on one side and there was a large crater on the other. There were so many mines in this area that the engineers lost twelve men, the tankers lost six, and the infantry thirty in the ditches alone. The tanks were pulled back and engineers were sent forward to clear the roads of antitank mines. At 2100 they reported the road clear, and at 2150 a tank dozer was sent forward to remove the disabled tank. Some two hundred yards from the tank, the dozer hit a mine. The Germans had again infiltrated and mined the road. At 2245 the engineers went out again.

At 0100 the engineers reported that the road was clear. A group was now sent forward with equipment to bridge a crater that had been made in front of the disabled tank. However, when the men came alongside the tank, the Germans fired them on and they jumped into the crater at that point. The Germans had also planted antipersonnel mines in it and two men were killed and two or three others wounded. (The Germans continued to infiltrate because of the difficulty of setting up outposts under artillery fire).

Company L at 0300 was ordered to send up men to the point where the road curved toward Hürtgen and establish a strong point in bunkers the Germans had built there. Within fifty yards of the curve, however, enemy machine guns fired on the forward column. Two men were killed and three or four wounded by mines when they went into ditches at the side of the road. At 0400, another platoon of L Company was sent up, but it was also driven back by mortar and machine-gun fire. Later in the morning the whole company, at about 60 percent strength, was ordered forward but had to fall back after heavy casualties. At 0715 they tried a frontal assault, but were caught by artillery fire and could not advance. When a fifth attack was ordered, one of the lieutenants told the regimental commander that he would try by himself to take the positions, but would not order or ask his men to go with him. He was ordered arrested, but later released and restored to a platoon command.

In later fighting, the men had less trouble with mines, and they were able to take new objectives south of Hürtgen. However, artillery fire hampered their efforts throughout. On 1 December, when men of L Company took some dry log bunkers, it was difficult to get them moving again because of the heavy artillery and mortar fire. Sergeant Brown estimated that sixteen thousand rounds of ammunition hit his battalion during the Hürtgen action. The Germans were not in a happy frame of mind, however, because some sixty-seven men and an officer surrendered to L Company on the 3d. Bad weather—"It began to sleet and got colder than a bastard"—began to cause acute suffering during the day.

The 3d Battalion's attack of 4 December, as we know, found eight riflemen in I Company and ten in Company L. They went forward but didn't have enough strength to consolidate their gains. An officer of the battalion telephoned the regimental commander after the attack: "The men of this battalion are physically exhausted. The spirit and will to fight are there; the physical ability to continue is gone. These men have been fighting without rest or sleep for four days and last night were forced to lie unprotected from the weather in an open field. In some instances men were forced to discard their overcoats because they lacked the strength to wear them. These men are shivering with cold and their hands are so numb that they have to help one another on with their equipment. I firmly believe that every man up there should be evacuated through medical channels." Despite this report, another attack was ordered at 1430. Companies I and L moved out with tanks in support. The companies had been reinforced but still had only fifty or sixty men between them. However, they had their objective at 1630. That evening they were relieved by elements of the 1st Battalion. A number of the men were treated as fatigue cases. At this point, such treatment consisted of being sent to a rest tent near Hürtgen, where the men were given coffee, a shot of whiskey, and some sleeping pills. After a day or two of rest and warm food, they were sent back into the line.

That the sufferings of the regular infantry were also shared by the armored infantry units is made clear in the accounts of Lieutenant Richard S. Lewis, commanding officer, Company B, 47th Armored Infantry Battalion, and two of his platoon leaders, Lieutenant Robert Stutsman and Lieutenant Oliver D. Goldman. Some of their worst trouble came after they had taken Bergstein, a town to the southeast of Hürtgen, with very little difficulty. In the early morning, after they had established positions south of the town, a superior force of Germans hit them and the company's force was cut to about thirty-seven men. They were unable to evacuate fatigue cases, although some of the men were out of their minds. They were told to hold and, after a time, were notified they would get some forty men from the 85th Reconnaissance Squadron, a machine-gun platoon, and some sixty men from the hospital. Of the machine-gun platoon, the first half-track was knocked out as it started to Bergstein and the platoon sergeant was hit. By nightfall only ten to twelve men were effective out of the platoon. The reconnaissance platoon dismounted in the village of Brandenberg and forty men started marching to Bergstein. They were hit by artillery and only fifteen got up. They were counterattacked about dusk and only eight of the original forty remained effective. Then the armored infantry unit was promised twenty-five more men. Some twenty came up between 0100 and 0200. They were straight from the hospital and were in bad shape. They had to pick up any weapons they could find. They had no blankets and it was raining. But, said the lieutenants, "with what we had our spirits were exceedingly high; at each command post they were making coffee; we fed everybody; treated the wounded; gave everybody something to do and kept their minds off the bleak situation.

"We built up our defenses again after two hours of looking at each other bleakly. Positions were consolidated. We might have stopped another infantry attack, but we couldn't have stopped one supported by assault guns and tanks.

"I [Lieutenant Lewis] gave the twenty new men to Lieutenant Goldman and he put them out. We sat down for the counterattack, which we expected would come in the morning. We had a faint promise from Corps of the 2d Rangers but we weren't too hopeful. About midnight a guy came down the road, then two others, each one five yards behind the other. They were three Ranger lieutenants. They asked for enemy positions and the road to take; said they were ready to go. We talked the situation over with the officers. They stepped out and said, 'Let's go men.' We heard the tommy guns click and, without saying a word, the Rangers moved out. Our morale went up in a hurry.

"Next morning about 0400 the Battalion Exec brought withdrawal orders (this was 7 December). B Company strength was about thirty to thirty-five. A Company had one tank; C Company two; and C Company had three plus one which maintenance brought up. We left just before daylight and got fire to our rear all the way up the road toward Brandenberg and beyond."

The story of understrength units was general throughout the regiment. Forty-six officers out of an initial 153, and 1,288 men out of the initial 3,080 were casualties. The 1st Battalion had suffered heavily, particularly in noncommissioned officers, with two first sergeants hit, and a third going blind from an old grenade wound. The battalion had four different commanders in two weeks. Company A lost two officers by relief and three by wounds, Company B lost all six officers, and Company C lost two. The replacement situation was unsatisfactory because most of the officers were staff men, with no prior combat experience (for this reason an attempt was made to commission officers from among the platoon sergeants, which may have accounted for the promotion to lieutenant of one sergeant who had twice "washed out" of OCS), and many of the enlisted men were former airplane mechanics, radio operators, and cooks with high ratings but little battle knowledge. Most of the troops reported missing in action were replacements who had been sent into action almost as soon as they reported for duty. The men of one group were trapped before they could report to the sergeant to whom they were assigned. Many of the men scattered as soon as they received artillery fire and then were easily picked off.

Morale was hard hit by bad weather and continual artillery fire. During the Hürtgen action, the regiment arrested eleven men for refusal to go back into the line—the first cases, according to the regimental sergeant major, Willard Bryan, that the 121st, which had fought since July, had recorded. There would have been more, but the officers watched their men closely and tried to send back older men for lighter duties before they broke under the strain. The great hardships of the fighting still showed in the faces of the men we interviewed a week or ten days after the taking of Hürtgen. However, rest and an occasional warm meal and bath began to work wonders. During the time we were there, Christmas packages began to arrive and some of the battalion headquarters put up Christmas trees. Some of the officers and men had gotten passes to Paris, and the prospect that there would be a larger quota of leaves in the future helped morale.

However, there were constant reminders that the war was not

far away. On the thirteenth, while talking to Lieutenant Colonel Kunzig, commanding officer of the 2d Battalion, we discovered that he was only some six hundred yards from the Germans. As we talked, reports came in that enemy troops were unusually active on his front. He ordered extra watchfulness and alerted the artillery. Later there was the noise of small-arms fire, and a company commander called to say that a patrol was trying to come up the draw toward the battalion CP. The colonel remarked calmly that we might have a little firefight and went on with the interview. I mentally made preparations for the destruction of my notes in case we were attacked. A few minutes later, mortar fire was dropped on the Germans and they withdrew.

Wednesday, 13 December (D+190)

Muddy. Rain and sleet.

Interviewed Major Hogan of 3rd Battalion. Excellent commander. Some good story. Spent all morning there. His place was made pleasant by toy Christmas tree.

Back to I Co. in afternoon. Saw first lieutenant who was from Harlem, Ky; had graduated from UK in 1943.

At night interviewed Major Wiltsie, a Purdue graduate.

To see Lieutenant Colonel Kunzig of 2nd Battalion. Were 600 yards from German lines. Considerable small arms fire. Rumors of possible breakthrough.

Was interesting to watch Regimental CP at night. S-3 kept demanding that draw be mined. "We'll do it if we have to turn out whole regiment." Tended to be superbly ——— here, here which was not present at the front line.

That evening at regimental headquarters I was told that the Germans were getting very restless along the line and it was feared they might try a small counterattack. It was two days before the Ardennes counterattack.

During our stay at Hürtgen, Topete and I stayed at regimental headquarters. The S-2 and S-3 were kind to us and on the first evening permitted us to spread our bedrolls on the cellar floor of their office where several officers and men were sleeping. But we were dispossessed next morning by a colonel who came in, saw the place in considerable disorder, and, remarking that the place looked like "a French whorehouse," ordered everyone there to find sleeping quarters elsewhere. Thereafter we slept upstairs in a room, part of which had been wrecked by shelling so that one wall and part of the roof was smashed. However, Corporal George Loewenberg, guard and translator for the regimental commander, who was at the moment on leave, helped us put up blackout curtains to keep the light in and some of the cold out. He also discovered some pictures in other parts of the house and put them up in a part of the room that he named the Gallery. There was a stove in one corner of the room and fuel for it, but while it was better than the one I had stoked vainly a few days before, it fought a losing battle against the breeze. I had trouble in particular with cold and wet feet since I had no overshoes. Mine, which I had been issued in 1942 and had held on to through basic training and eighteen months of headquarters duty, had been taken from me in Paris a short time before I returned to the front.

Thursday, 14 December (D+191)

Cool. My feet nearly freeze every day. Have no overshoes. Muddy from top to bottom. We have stove, but there is too much wind coming through building.

Interviewed Sergeant Steinberg at PW enclosure. Had left Germany in 1938. Told of telling Nazi Colonel he was German Jew who was glad to be helping U.S.

Friday, 15 December (D+192)

Huertgen. Cold. Ground frozen.

Interviewed Sergeant Major Bryan of S-1 Section in morning.

This is a very interesting spot. . . . Chow kitchen in gallons of mud. Tumbled down place; two dead horses which do not smell 100 feet away.

Mortars constantly firing few hundred yards away.

Church next door knocked down. Stars and Stripes man drawing picture of it and PK next door. We found pictures in this house of tumbled down church of last war which looks like this one.

Replacements came up—look lost. We see young troop who look 40. Have changed in 2 weeks. . . .

Saw a number of men going to Paris. A number going back to showers. Look very happy.

Heavy beards, muddy clothes. Yet clean clothing is coming back from laundry.

Guards look frozen. Stand like scarecrows outside.

High praise for ——— ——— censure for aid station back a way who refuse to receive men from other companies.

Usually griping. Have heard sex mentioned very little.

Some Christmas packages coming in. Some items not usable.

Some men bitter; most of them not very excited.

Have met several German Jews who came to U.S. in 1938. All seem to be glad to be doing job.

Topete interviewing sergeant from U.S. Heavily bearded lad of 23. In the Army for 2 ½ years. Acted frequently as platoon leader. Tells of new lieutenants coming up and asking that he go ahead and take over, since they don't know score. A young lieutenant, just out of Columbia in April [?] came up and talked last night about how to keep after men. Wants educational propaganda.

You can see the human cost of war here. I was back at Corps when Huertgen was being taken. A captain jokingly said "We are taking 3 trees a day," "yet they cost about 100 men apiece." They kept pushing but their men kept going until some got so tired they threw their overcoats and rifles away as being too heavy to carry.

On our last evening at Hürtgen we played host to Staff Sergeant Anthony Rizzo from New Jersey—one of the first people to enter Hürtgen. The acting regimental commander had suggested that we get his story. We found at the moment that he was in charge of a forward company position and that he could be brought out only under a smoke screen. We asked that he be brought to regiment and it was arranged. We had expected a young man, but we saw instead a heavily bearded figure who looked too old to be doing frontline duty. His eyes and face showed great fatigue. He thawed by the fire and soon talked with animation. He asked if he could stay long enough to have a warm meal and a shave. We, quite happy to use our influence with the colonel, told the regimental executive that we needed to talk to the sergeant rather late, so it was arranged that he stay the night with us.

Dinner was served at the regimental kitchen set up across from the headquarters. We had to wade through a sea of mud to get to the shed where the food was served. Two dead horses lay nearby, but the cold had preserved them and they were not offensive. Mortars were firing a few hundred yards away, so we were careful not to gang up. But the food was hot and good, and the sergeant seemed as content as if he were back at the "rear."

After we had eaten, Rizzo asked for hot water and a razor. In a few minutes his beard was gone and he was part of the way back toward his real age of twenty-three—only two and one-half years out of junior college. But he was still tired and the lines on his face belonged to an older person.

Later in the evening, Loewenberg, in an inspired moment, proposed that we have a party in the sergeant's honor. His chief helper, who did most of the work, was a Georgian named Holder, the regimental commander's orderly. We made inventory of our special stocks. Topete had a canned plum pudding, I had tea bags, someone had some canned corned beef, and George found a white tablecloth, napkins, and china in a sideboard in the dining room of the house. Then he said, "We have forgotten the candles." These were not available, so he tore up a sheet and made wicks. Next, two empty cognac bottles were produced and filled with oil. The wicks were lighted, and the table illuminated by the soft but rather smokey light from the "flambeaux." Holder was so much seized by the spirit of the occasion that he borrowed a bottle of gin from the colonel's stock and poured us all something for a toast.

Under these ministrations, the sergeant at last came to life. Warmed by the drinks as well as by the experience, he lost his cares and his years. The war that was only a few hundred yards away seemed remote. For a time we even forgot the booming of the guns.

Loewenberg told us that evening that he had been born some twenty-five miles from Hürtgen. His father had been a well-to-do doctor, and George had been sent to school in Italy and Switzerland. They left Germany for the United States in 1938. Now, like many other German refugees, he was back as a translator. Only a short time before, Loewenberg had been questioning some prisoners when one said, "I know you." He had lived in George's town. I was reminded of a sergeant I had talked to only a day or two before. He had been questioning a German officer, who complimented him on his excellent German. The sergeant replied that he had learned it in Hitler's Reich, but had been forced to go elsewhere, and that he was pleased to be doing his share to destroy Hitler. The officer was silent.

Saturday, 16 December (D+193)

Cool. Talked to Colonel T.J. Cross, Regimental Commander of 121st. In afternoon talked to 12th Engineers. Back to Limbourg at night. At night we had news of parachute landings near Malmedy. They had been landing near Huertgen all week.

Awakened at 5:30 and told to be on the alert for attack. . . .

Counterattack started at 0530.

Shelling of Eupen this morning.

We spent the sixteenth wandering through parts of the forest between Hürtgen and Roetgen, looking for detachments of the 12th Engineers. They were widely scattered, and it was not until after dark when we returned to Dolhain-Limbourg. There we were told that the enemy had shelled the area near the corps headquarters at Eupen that morning, and that there was some German activity along the front. Later in the evening, there were vague rumors about some parachute landings near Malmédy. But there was no great excitement, and we recalled that there had been minor German counterattacks before. To me, the big entry in my diary for the day was that at 6 P.M. Major O'Sullivan from First Army headquarters at Spa called to say that I had been promoted to master sergeant.

Chapter 18

The North Flank of the Bulge

Sunday, 17 December (D+194)– Sunday, 31 December (D+208)

Sunday, 17 December (D+194)

> *Rainy. . . . Definitely announced that I was made master sergeant by army order yesterday.*
>
> *News of German breakthrough along the 99th front. Attacked on the boundary between Vth and VIIth Corps. Parachute troops near Malmedy. No one unduly perturbed. . . .*
>
> *The army moved near Liege at night.*

The Ardennes counterattack didn't seem very serious to us until 5:30 the morning of the seventeenth. At that hour, we were suddenly awakened by Captain Born and told to dress and be on the alert for an attack. The drop of parachutists by the Germans near Malmédy had been confirmed; there were rumors that some of them were in our area, and there was danger of a German armored breakthrough near Monschau, some eight miles to our front. There was no announcement of a general counterattack to the south of us, but what we heard was enough for a pre-breakfast start. We dressed and put on helmets and gun belts, but, after a suitable interval without further alarms, took advantage of the situation to lie down again until breakfast.

That evening we were called to First Army headquarters at Spa for a conference with the other historians. I went up with Topete and a sergeant from corps headquarters. The latter, who had married in May just before leaving for the marshaling area, was going back to First Army on his way to the United Kingdom for several days of what the GIs then called "passionate" leave. At Spa we found there was some concern about Fox, Howe, and Jackson, all of whom had been conducting interviews with regiments of the 28th Division, in the Ardennes area. The fear, even this late on the seventeenth, was not that their units had been overrun, but that German elements might have pushed through north of them. We now knew that there had been a German armored attack in force on the boundary of the V and VII Corps. However, no one was greatly perturbed.

Later in the evening Fox and the others arrived with word that great confusion existed to the south of us, and that they had been able to reach Spa only by making considerable detours. It apparently was generally felt that no real crisis existed, because we managed to hold one of our usual parties with toasts being drunk to the safe arrival of the captains, to my promotion, and everything else we could think of. Jackson, who was from Louisville, and I spent some time talking over Kentucky politics. Jack Shea organized a songfest, and he and Howe put on a make-believe broadcast for the group. As the party grew louder, I could not forbear quoting the lines about the eve of Waterloo: "there were sounds of revelry by night."

Monday, 18 December (D+195)

Cool. Back to Eupen. Breakthrough continues along broad front. 99th being reorganized. Talked to some of the men who had been in the lines through which Germans broke. Said their defenses were light, didn't have bazooka ammunition. Armor by-passed; infantry came straight through.

No one yet is greatly perturbed, although alternate CPs have been chosen. Belgians agitated. Talk of parachutist near here. We go about our business; ——— that when this breakthrough is stopped we can really stop Germans. There is fear that Germans may use up enough reserves that it will take much longer to finish up. Undoubtedly is an all-out attack. Question is to be sure exactly where they want to break through;

which is a feint and which is not. V Corps still being heavily ham-
mered.

Secret news of a certain change in command. Not connected with
battle.

By the morning of the eighteenth, the situation was beginning to look serious, and First Army discussed a withdrawal of
the headquarters. The sections had been given their order of march,
and they began preparations to move during the morning. We
remained at Spa until after lunch and then, paradoxically, because
of the nature of the German drive, went back toward Germany
where, at the moment, we were safer from attack.

Back at corps, we were able to get firsthand part of the story
of the breakthrough. Elements of the 99th Division, which had
been hit south of us on the sixteenth, were coming through
Dolhain-Limbourg to a nearby point where they were to be reorganized. Some of them had been fighting or marching for most of
two days, with practically no food or rest. Many were fed in our
messes as they stopped briefly. Again and again they told the story
which the 106th Division, in particular, and some of the other units
to the south were to relate. The enemy had broken through light
defenses. Neither the 99th nor the 106th had been in the line long,
and they had not dug in or made as much provision against attack as some of the more experienced units. The type of all-night
mine laying at the 121st that we had witnessed was the sort of
action which permitted the 2d Division, on the 99th's flank, to
hold relatively firm in the face of the attack. And it was on the 2d,
one of the first divisions to enter Normandy, that V Corps built its
initial defense of the north flank of the Bulge. Then the 1st Division, which had been heavily mangled in the Hürtgen Forest fighting and was still being refitted, was put into the line. Meanwhile,
VII Corps units were brought southward. The attack postponed a
change in the V Corps command. General Gerow had been named
a short time before to head the new Fifteenth Army, and Major
General Clarence R. Huebner of the 1st Division was selected to
take his place. But for the moment, the two generals were to stay
where they were.

It was clear by then that the Germans had launched an all-out
attack, and that V and VIII Corps had been hardest hit. Alternate

CPs were chosen for us on the eighteenth, but there was no hint of panic in this action. The general feeling was that we could stop the advance, and that the Germans had made a mistake in risking their reserves in such an attack. Our chief fear was that they might advance far enough to destroy many supply depots where ammunition, fuel, and rations were being stockpiled for the spring attack.

Tuesday, 19 December (D+196)

> *Cool.*
> *Transcribed notes all day. Breakthrough grows.*

The nineteenth brought rumors that the Germans were west of Malmédy. We received instructions that evening on what we would do in case of a withdrawal. Thermite bombs were issued with which we could destroy our papers in case of attack. Our field tents and other equipment not in general use was sent rearward to a depot.

Wednesday, 20 December (D+197)

> *Remarkable how little we know of situation; how much the high ranking officers deal in rumor-mongering. . . . Germans have the good ground for armor now as we did from Paris. Much complaint about our failure to go to the Rhine in September.*
>
> *It seems remarkable that few expected counterattack. It was only way Germany could relieve pressure, restore waning hope of her people, forestall unrest, disrupt our plans, postpone the war of attrition. When the attack is beaten back, if we have enough stuff to follow them through we may gain the Rhine and beyond quicker than we would have done otherwise.*
>
> *Later in day learned that several regiments cut off. Germans have thirty tanks as far east as Bastogne. We hold towns behind them in many cases; are in sufficient force to hold. However, they are carrying larger gas reserves. We can't get many planes up. Have been able to evacuate most of our supplies forward. Army has left Spa.*

Our most jittery day of the entire attack was the twentieth.

The day was foggy, which meant that First Army still could not get up the air support we needed.

I wrote that day in my diary:

"We are having very bad air weather. If the Germans are reckless enough their armor may run up and down behind our lines living off supplies and playing the devil generally with our communications. It may be that the best course is not to worry too much about this, but to drive through their points of penetration and try to destroy their lines of communications.

"We [First Army] are bringing up paratroops, new infantry divisions. Some armor plus air force of the 3d and 5th Armies given to First Army. 1st and 30th [Divisions] in the line.

"Everyone still fairly calm.

"6 Infantry and 4 armored divisions of Germans supposed to have swung through VIII Corps and then north in V Corps lines.

"Many people beginning to criticize the command—shows what we might do if we were badly handled. They hate to have Christmas mail held up; one group fussed because they might have to put their newly pressed pinks back into suitcases. Problem of handling liquor supplies arises. I imagine that the Germans felt like that when they had to leave Paris. Some say that the reason for such a spirit is that the Americans are not interested in the war.

"Topete is keeping our stuff packed to move. Has the jeeps filled with gas. . . .

"Men of the 99th, 82d Airborne and other units filter in to V Corps Rear Headquarters trying to find their units. . . .

"Corps is publicizing killing of 200 prisoners taken first day by Germans. Are said to have stood them in field. Killed them with tanks [fire from tanks] as they came by.

"Order at night to prepare all non-essential goods for movement tomorrow."

Near midnight we had an alert. Belgians, who had been worried since the sixteenth about parachutists, reported that there were German airborne personnel in the area. The headquarters soon was involved in a comic opera affair with rear-echelon officers of AG, JA, Finance, and other sections organizing searching parties. We had visions of armed men suddenly rushing the courtyard of the school, when the chief weapon we had for our defense was a bazooka. Several hours later, the posse returned with two German prisoners who had escaped from near Liége. One of our most military colonels would not take this story as true, and kept pacing up and down in front of them, brandishing his pistol, and threatening to shoot "the sons of bitches." They were finally picked up by forward-echelon MPs and peace was restored.

The killing of the two hundred prisoners by the Germans was to be known in the history of the Ardennes battle as the Malmédy Massacre. Photographs were taken of the dead men and circulated to the lower commands with instructions that all units be made aware of the nature of the enemy they were now facing. Orders also went out for all prisoners to be carefully interrogated in order to find who was responsible for the massacre. I knew one of the V Corps officers who engaged in this work and talked to him several times about his activities, which included the establishment of guilt in regard to the killing of a number of Belgian civilians by the enemy. The officer was a midwesterner of Anglo-Saxon descent. He seemed to approach his task like a good lawyer or detective, carefully asking questions that would indicate where responsibility lay. After the war I was amazed to find the investigators under attack for mistreating Germans in regard to the massacre. The photographs were definitely not fakes; the American soldiers were dead.

It is doubtful if news of these killings stirred any more anger than did other photographs discovered on captured German prisoners that showed them standing near groups of American dead and wounded or pictured them wearing pieces of American equipment and gloating as they opened up American supplies.

The whole matter of killing prisoners had been on my mind since the Hürtgen Forest fight. I recalled ugly stories about some unit's record in regard to the killing of prisoners. During the period of the Ardennes I visited a headquarters on the Malmédy road and was told that a sniper had just shot one of their men on an outpost. The men were looking for the German and said that if they captured him they would shoot him. An armored infantry lieutenant, noting my surprise, said that his outfit had captured enemy soldiers on a recent occasion and, after saving two for questioning, disposed of the rest. His excuse was that, being tankers, they couldn't handle the others. Others spoke of opening fire on enemy soldiers who seemed to be on the point of surrendering, so that there would be no need to shoot them later. It was easy to do this sort of thing so long as one thought of the prisoners in terms of the rations they would eat and the men to guard them. Placed against this sort of testimony and this sort of reasoning, a massacre like the one at Malmédy is brutal only because it is larger or calculated to provoke terror.

Thursday, 21 December (D+198)

Hazy.

There was still no air up on the twenty-first. Despite that bad news, there seemed to be some signs that the front was stabilizing and that some of our units, like the 2d Division, were in much better shape than they had been. There was the same fear, however, that other attacks might come at Monschau, to our front, and near Aachen, to the north of us.

Friday, 22 December (D+199)

Raining in morning. Better in afternoon. Some air up.

The twenty-second brought news that Montgomery had taken command of British and American units north of the Ardennes. This was accompanied by reports that Saint-Vith had fallen to the Germans and that enemy units had surrounded Bastogne. Scattered comments in my diary on the Montgomery assumption of command show how I—and my diary tended to reflect comment I heard during the day—misunderstood the situation. I wrote: "British XXX Corps ready to move. One corps to hit at Bonn. Seems we are ready to exploit any counterattack on our front with tactics Montgomery used in Africa.... Remains to be seen if we are weakening lines in north by pulling British down behind Meuse. Seems they have us pretty scared. The bad feature about this is that it makes us more dependent on the British. On the other hand it may cause many of us to hesitate before berating the British for their small part in the war. It may have a very salutary effect at home."

Later I was to read and hear violent American statements about the shift in command, which indicated that all Americans were furious over the shift. So they were at 12th Army Group and Third Army, and I suppose at First Army. But I can recall no great out-cry at V Corps over the change at the time. The general feeling was, I believe, that Monty was hard to take at times, but if he and the British could help, then more power to them.

The big change on the twenty-second was not in command, but in the weather. For the first time since the fighting started, it was possible to get aircraft up.

Sunday 23 December (D+200)

Cold clear.

Germans supposedly through to Givet in the center. We are holding our flanks.

Rumor says we have 4,000 planes up.

Sunday 24 Dec. (D+201)

Cold. Clear day.

Hundreds of planes are leaving vapor trails. Several dog fights; we can follow every maneuver. One shot down and falls leaving great trail of smoke.

The east wall of our office was virtually all glass, and we did little work on the twenty-fourth but sat instead and watched the air show. We speculated at times on what would happen if the planes were coming the other way, but for the most part we watched the steady movement of planes to the east. Now and then one of our planes, after attacking, would fall behind as it started back and two or three German planes would come after it. Just before they got it, ours would turn back in pursuit. Occa-sionally there would be a dogfight, and the cold air would record the movements of the battle in the frozen vapor trails.

The cold, clear air carried the sound of battle for miles, and we were startled at lunch time, as we sat at our tables, to hear machine guns chattering, it seemed almost over our heads. We had visions of a German plane strafing the building and most of us landed beneath the tables, hitting our heads, upsetting food, and creating quite an outcry. In a moment or two some of the calmer or hungrier diners, said, "It's just a dogfight several miles away," and we sheepishly went back to eating.

Christmas Eve was not too cheery because the party we had planned for several weeks had been canceled. The town itself, which had been put off limits when the attack started, was completely quiet. For several days our guard had been tripled and all of the enlisted men from master sergeant down had to pull this detail, something that I was to do for the first time in the army on the day after Christmas. Generally speaking, the mood was not one of happy Noel, although we managed to sing some carols after dinner. We had been put into a proper frame of mind for midnight mass by an alert around 10 P.M. that a gas attack was possible. Most of our masks had long since been lost, so we could only hope it was a false alarm. An hour later, First Army called to say that German airplanes were headed in our direction. We wondered if the cellar would hold all of us. The attack had not materialized by midnight, so some seventy or eighty of us went to the mass. However, we carried our helmets with us, and from time to time someone would slip outside to check with the guards.

Monday, 25 December (D+ 202)

Cool.

Little air activity here. News of 7,000 sorties yesterday which were very successful. Heard tonight that air was out in force on the other fronts. 3rd Army (7th Corps) coming up from south toward Bastogne. Some Germans near Meuse River.

Tuesday, 26 December (D+203)

Cool. Weather pretty good. Worked on routine material.

Wednesday, 27 December (D+204)

Weather worse. Little air. Went to CCR, 5th Armored Division, in Eupen. Roads slick since a little rain fell. Talked to Major McKee and Colonel Anderson.

Some big guns moving on road.

By the twenty-seventh, the situation on our front was calm enough for Topete and me to start interviews again. This was the first time we had been away from headquarters in ten days, and the changes on the road were astounding. The quaint little bridge in the center of Limbourg was heavily guarded by an antiaircraft gun, which in turn was protected by a machine-gun squad. All the roads leading into town were also guarded. We were stopped frequently along the way and made to identify ourselves. The best sight of the day was of several 8-inch guns going forward. We immediately felt better not because we thought the guns would stop an attack, but because we did not believe that First Army would allow those particular weapons to go up front unless they were pretty sure of holding.

Until the end of the breakthrough and the beginning of the American counterattack in early February, everyone on the road had difficulty with the sentries. The trouble arose from the fact that the Germans had organized under Otto Skorzeny some 120 English-speaking men wearing American uniforms and driving jeeps who were to go through American lines and give confusing directions. Interrogations of prisoners indicated that for some weeks German soldiers who spoke English with an American accent had been ordered back to a special training area where they were taught to imitate GIs. This included such things as the manner in which Americans opened packages of cigarettes, salient facts about important cities in the United States, the names of outstanding political figures, and the like. Reports that groups of these men had ordered our troops away from important bridges and had sent them in the wrong directions led First Army to issue its sentries special directives. In turn, officers and men were reminded of the need of complying strictly with regulations, and an announcement of the shooting of a major by a guard when the officer had failed to respond properly to a challenge was carefully circulated as a warning.

First Army instructions listed as sample questions for the sentries to ask the following: passwords, serial number (in this case, one was to throw his dog tags to the guard when challenged and then call out his number while the sentry checked it), state capital of one's home state, who won the last World Series, who had the best football team last year, what is Dewey's first name, what is the name of the Windy City, pronounce "wreath," "with nothing," "rather." Nearly everyone who has written about this period has told of his problems. We were arrested several times because the password had changed since we left headquarters. Each morning we were given a password for the day with alternates in case the original was compromised. It sometimes happened that all of them would be compromised in the course of the day, and that by evening they would have something else in use. Sometimes, a cautious sentry would take us into custody and we would cool our heels until a call could be made to corps. We were particularly suspect because our bumper markings were those of 12th Army Group, we wore First Army shoulder patches, and we claimed to be with V Corps. Worse still, we claimed to be historians and went about asking questions about casualties, troop dispositions, and the like. I still wonder why they did not shoot us.

Topete did not make matters any easier because of his tendency to yell out the password as soon as he was challenged. Since there was a touch of Spanish in his voice, and since the average jumpy sentry supposed that all accents were German, we would sometimes hear a rifle bolt pulled back before I could convince them that we were indeed Americans. On one occasion, at least, the problem was all the other way. One dark night, in an area totally unfamiliar to us, we were suddenly challenged. The password was "Hearth Hollow," especially chosen to try German tongues. The challenge was given in a rather strong accent, and when we gave the countersign, the sentries said, "*Ja, ja.*" We were prepared to sell our lives dearly, when we discovered that the guards were Belgians who spoke with a Flemish accent. The matter of accents often proved troublesome for officers and men of foreign birth. In the Hürtgen area, a former White Russian who served brilliantly as a lieutenant in the winter fighting finally refused to venture outside at night without someone who could speak English after he had been nearly shot a time or two.

My own troubles arose over the capital of my state, Kentucky. First Army had suggested this geographical name to the sentries without giving the answers. The sentries would ask: "What is your state?" and, on being told, they would query: "What is the capital?" The first time or two I said "Frankfort" I noticed a speculative gleam in the eye of the guard and a tendency to raise his rifle into better shooting position. Finally, I got in the habit of answering, "The capital is Frankfort, but you may think it is Louisville."

The questioning always seemed to be more intense the farther one went back to the rear. At Ninth Army headquarters I had to go through the whole list of trick questions, including some information on horse races that I was a little afraid I would have wrong, and finally had to give the name of someone I knew in the headquarters before I was permitted to enter the building. At corps, the routine was less severe, but still rather strict—which became embarrassing at times for some of the officers who couldn't remember the password. The commandant of the rear area was particularly bad in this regard, a fact that led the MPs one night to speak to him rather threateningly. Finally, as they pressed the matter of the password, he turned his flashlight on his face and called out his name, while the guard yelled, "Put out the damned light or the commandant will get you." At battalion and company areas, the routine was varied, often because of the newness of the man. Sometimes it was possible, if one was not sure of the password, to demand it in a commanding voice from the sentry, who would give it without thinking. On one occasion I gave the one for the day before, and the sentry said, "Sergeant, you ought to keep up to date. The new password is so-and-so." My prize example is that of a detachment of the 82d Airborne Division that was set up in a farmhouse. We entered through the kitchen, where two GIs were sitting around a stove. They glanced at us as we went through a door into the next room. The room was empty of officers or men, but the wall had a map showing the division's dispositions and at one side were all the passwords and alternate challenges for a week. We made note of the locations, noted some of the challenges, and went back out, got into the jeep, and drove away without ever being asked who we were or what we wanted.

Thursday, 28th December (D+205)

Weather closed in.

We seem to be containing German push. News of successful holding at Bastogne.

News of Churchill and [Anthony] Eden [British foreign secretary] going to Greece. Fine gesture since failure would increase censure on Churchill. Wonderful maze of politics, ——— inflation, international diplomacy involved. Churchill seems a little more inclined to liberalism than some of his predecessors. It's the old fight for power, topped with class struggle. . . .

Saturday, 30 December (D+207)

Snow.

Back to see Lieutenant Lewis plus Lieutenant Goldman and Lieutenant Stutsman—all of 47th Armored Infantry Battalion. All were college men; very acute observers. Were quartered in ———. Men and officers slept in same building; ate in same mess; enjoyed same jollies; got the same lift out of a chance at a bath.

They were upset about failure of Army to use their forces properly. Had used them as ordinary infantry and had lost personnel which could not be replaced.

I like to visit these units near the front. Maybe a little coarser, but they have thrown out caste and class and artificial distinctions. They obey the men in charge because someone has to direct, but otherwise there is give and take. They will share anything they have and they are grateful that somebody remembers them enough to come and ask questions.

At night back to ———. Captain Shappell came.

Story is that Germans had 20 divisions in the breakthrough—9 Panzer divisions, 2 Panzer Grenadier divisions, 7 Infantry, and 2 airborne divisions. They now have a build-up near Aachen and may make a drive towards Liege or Antwerp from there. PW reports are that next week there will be several days of good flying weather and that an attack will begin then. We have VII Corps ready to move. There is a new Corps in. New Army about ready to furnish 3 divisions (new) in France. At same time they have chewed up 28th and 106th almost completely. 99th banged up considerably and several others lost much equipment. They didn't get much gasoline. V Corps saved its 7 million gallons. Had a big ammo dump (German paratroops within 1 mile of it at one time). We now have artillery firing from the dump. Sent word for everyone to come and get it.

Bastogne garrison, which has held out with supplies brought by gliders, has been relieved by III Corps. 9th Army gathering some new troops in anticipation of attack there.

Sunday, 31 December (D+208)

Cold.

Weather clearing. Perhaps planes will be out today. Heavy bombers have been out lately despite heavy overcast. Have put heavy fire on build-up points.

Party for 325 Belgian children this afternoon. Had 6 piece orchestra. Party in gym. Cook had prepared 800 individual cakes and pies with chocolate. Later gave them a movie and a package of candy, etc., which we had given from our rations the past few weeks. Children beat time to tunes. . . . St. Nicholas was well dressed; very happy.

Bed before 12 although I heard the new year in.

Washed clothes.

Chapter 19

Regaining Lost Ground

Monday, 1 January, 1945 (D+209)–
Monday, 22 January (D+230)

By the end of December, the German attack was well under control. New units were coming in from the States, and elements of divisions in the United Kingdom were flown in to the 99th and other badly hit divisions. Bastogne was relieved, and troops from north and south were pressing in on the flanks of the Bulge, while the eastward push had been blunted. Our chief worry at the end of the month was that an enemy attack might be made near Aachen.

Monday, 1 January (D+209)

Cold.

German plane over. Everybody turned out to see the fireworks. It went leisurely by.

Several bombs have been dropped in Eupen this past week. One fell within 20 feet of the EM mess. One yesterday blew windows out of the Colonels' mess. Buzzbombs over often.

Tuesday, 2 January (D+210)

Cold. Rain and warmer at night.

Attack by VII Corps towards Bastogne set for tomorrow. Germans said to be attacking in Jarr Basin [?].

On guard from 5–8 in morning. . . . Worked on report on Huertgen action.

Wednesday, 3 January (D+211)

Cool.
        Have a cold. In bed most of day.
        *This morning's G-2 report speaks of 28 Divisions in breakthrough.
Says Germans used 3/4 of their armor in the west; 1/3 of infantry* ———
holding action. VII Corps made little progress.
        Snowing.
        *Completed Huertgen Action report as it concerned CCR of 5th
Armored Division.*

Thursday, 4 January (D+212)

Cool.
        . . . Finished Irving Stones Lust for Life. *Got pay (Sept-Dec.). Sent
$200 home. Snow. Read Stewart Holbrook's* Ethan Allen. *Our attack on
German position held up by weather. They have 10 divisions in pocket.*

5–6 January (D+213–214)

Cold.
        Got packages which were sent 21 July.
        *Letter from Ernest Bailey in the Infantry. He is with my old outfit
that was in Memphis (2nd Army; now the 8th Army). . . .*

Sunday, 7 January (D+215)

Trying to snow.
        Read Somerset Maugham's Of Human Bondage.

Monday, 8 January (D+216)

Heavy snow. . . .
        *On guard at night. Hullabaloo over kitchen force giving our food to
prostitutes or to people of the town for cognac.*

Tuesday 9 January (D+219)

Snowing a little. Cold.

Captain Brown tells me that during the breakthrough Germans sent heavy force through (almost 500); got 180 RAF planes on the ground. This was revealed at SHAEF Conference. If it had been a little further South would have wiped out the 9th Air Force.

Have been reading 99th Division report for December. It covers up a great deal of the loss it sustained in the breakthrough. Several rings were ————. A SHAEF G-2 report of 5 Dec., while indicating the possibility of new German infantry divisions, was rather complacent about the situation on our front.

At about this same time, we captured copies of the German order to bus English-speaking Germans (with American dialect) and with American equipment for use in infiltration. I found no evidence of alarm as a result of this. G-2 "Enemy Capabilities" was not changed throughout the month until the breakthrough began. . . . However, there is some defense of our G-2 people in the fact that they were accustomed, in France, to depending on the natives for information.

The Germans managed to know nearly everything possible about our new units—exact positions, time of arrival, etc., which it seems to give the lie to their statements that American PWs are close-mouthed. However, instructions to use the friendly approach probably is responsible. They say that American PWs are more security conscious than others.

Captured orders of the day of the attack show how Germans whipped up great enthusiasm on the part of their soldiers. They believed the project was going through. Their gamble came nearer to succeeding than they could have expected. A few miscalculations, failure to get enough gasoline, the grim stand by certain units—such as 29th Infantry Regiment, 101st and 82nd Airborne, 10th Armored Division and the like, help to explain the story. Four or five good days for the Air Corps helped to explain it too.

We got pretty jumpy; some of our units let too much of our material fall into enemy hands. Special directions have been issued on that point. Warnings as to our carelessness in defense points up the fact that our successes tended to make us less alert. We were staying too close to buildings, becoming good targets for artillery and air attack. Many of our replacements (called reinforcements now) were frightened and didn't want to move up. Replacements have tended to be sent forward in such great quantities that they can't be assimilated in time for attack. We are sending up specialists from the Air Corps, radio operators, ASTP personnel (many of them men sent to school with little training); now being sent into the lines with little preparation.

*Captain Fox and I talked last night about personnel. We were
talking of the low grade personnel in charge of messes and Supply who
treat property as their hoard and sell and give it away. Too often these
men were the early comers to the army who did not have jobs outside.
They naturally went to the top and held on. I spoke of our mess sergeant
at 2d Army, who was arrested for selling our Christmas turkeys. He had
a jail record before coming into the Army. Company officers, who
frequently were of the same stripe as the mess officers put him in his job;
accepted birthday cakes and special deliveries for their families. Some of
the officers had bought the turkeys involved. Finally the charge was
dropped after the men asked for their former company commander as
counsel. At the same time the officer in charge of the officers mess was
transferred after it was found that he was selling surpluses. The mess
sergeant was released, came back and virtually killed the cook who had
given evidence against him. About the same time a technical sergeant
was broken for using an uncomplimentary about an MP. Another was
broken and given 6 months at hard labor for letting a pistol, which had
been inspected by a company officer, fire accidentally. However, a staff
sergeant, who had broken a warning by the company commander not to
break a restriction, was merely fined 2/3 of one month's pay. In this case
he was saved by the intervention of a lieutenant colonel who had had the
sergeant to "cover up" for him once while on maneuvers.*

*Captain Fox said he couldn't understand how anyone could sell
cigarettes, food and supplies while men at front did without. I pointed
out two facts—1. For years nearly everyone in charge of government food
or supplies has tended to look on them as fair game and have used them
as personal property in every way except from the standpoint of thrift; 2.
tendency to say "Everyone else is stealing, why shouldn't I?"*

*We agreed that the only way to have better messes and to stop
stealing of food is to have company officers eat with their men. In that
way they can see that the food allotment is falling, whereas in headquarters where the officers eat apart there is a tendency for them to assume
that the men are merely "beefing" when they complain. . . .*

*It is interesting to note, however, how it has been possible for some
soldiers to get action by writing to high officials. (A recent SHAEF
announcement indicates that many complaints are coming directly to
theater IG and that they should sent through channels. However, this is
not to be construed as discouraging complaints.*

. . . A captured German order saying that EM's could shoot officers

who ordered them to surrender or withdraw. A precaution was added—
"This privilege should not be abused."

I have seen several letters written by negro mothers to Mrs.
Roosevelt indicating discrimination and in each case they were followed
by prompt action.

One letter written by a private to Pres Roosevelt as a fellow Mason,
with the statement "If my officers ever found this out, God help me," was
sent through channels with a recommendation by the War Department
that his request for a transfer to a post near his home be done if circumstances warranted. In all these cases it was indicated that no action was
to be taken against the men for not going through channels.

In the "Yoo, Hoo" incident a soldier wrote to General Lear pointing
out that the soldiers meant no wrong and indicated their feelings about
the matter.[18] It was not through channels. General Lear indicated that it
was better to write such letters through channels and then in a fatherly
way discussed the points brought up by the soldier. . . .

Had interesting discussion the other night with Bob Langham of
Miss. about the Negro question. He was worried about race riots, which
he attributed to Army's efforts to play up to Negroes—praise to Negro
FA units, Negro drivers on Red Ball line, Negro troops (he says Buffalo
Division ———— in Italy), etc. He said the Army didn't want Negroes
(which was true). I have seen General Lear's letter, in peacetime, to that
effect—indicating problems with whites, difficulty of getting sufficient
officers, problems of training in South (incidentally, southern states
which got most insulted by having Negroes originally had demanded
Training Camps). I pointed out that if Negroes were as bad as they said
they were they still had 60% of their 750,000 overseas. 80% of their force
is in supply . . . Langham finally agreed that it would never have done to
have kept Negroes at home while whites left. I pointed out that at the
Kasserine Pass the unit which was commended for holding firm was a
Negro Air Base security unit. This was widely circulated by the Army
Negroes to build up their pride and confidence in their fighting units.

The Army has made considerable efforts to deal sanely with the
Negro question—in some cases having certain days in which towns were
on limits to whites and certain days when only blacks could come to
town; forbidding officers from using terms like "nigger," etc; insuring
that proper equality be shown.

Langham and I took up problem in South. . . . I pointed out, we have
a rapid change in affairs which shows that little by little the Deep South

states are becoming islands in regard to Negro votes—Texas' experience nearly follows what has happened in Kentucky, North Carolina, and Tennessee, where Negroes have gained voting rights when it was found they would vote with the party in power. . . .

The Negro is right in assuming that the right to vote is important. When he has the ballot people give him things. Peculiarly enough the demands of negroes in the north in pivotal states help bludgeon Democrats and Republicans into coercing the South where the Negro vote is negligible—into giving them power. Basically the only reason that the South doesn't revolt permanently against the Democrats is that they think that they at least will have a little show of control if they keep a Democrat in power, whereas a Republican will have no reason to conciliate them.

Wednesday, 10 January (D+218)

Cool.

We are beginning to push Germans back. Talked to Lieutenant Colonel Phan (of Memphis) in civil affairs section of V Corps. He said I could probably get a place in the section if I wanted to. Went up to Kornelimuenster—stopped to see Captain Ferris at XIXth Corps there. Then over to Zweifall to see the 8th Division people. Everything looks about the same up there. Talked to Corporal Adler of civil affairs. I saw him last in Paris.

The V Corps report for December, which was distributed in January, showed the great hopes Hitler had pinned on their attack. His commanders had tried in every possible way to whip up the enthusiasm of the men. Over the signature of Manteuffel[19] there had been issued this order:

"We will march day and night, if necessary, fight all the time. All armored vehicles and even the tanks themselves will roll at night. The founder of our arm, General [Heinz] Guderian, says to each tank commander, 'Night is the tanker's friend!'

"Anyone, whether with the infantry, armored infantry, reconnaissance or engineers, who has trouble with his vehicle will march on foot toward his goal. What we are going to lose on sweat during the following weeks, we will save in blood during the next few months!

"Our ground mission must be continuous. Otherwise we will not achieve our goal.

"No tank officer, no tank man dare disappoint us, they must all be clear in their minds as to their mission.

"On towards the enemy and go through him.

"Regulate your supplies; don't leave *anything* to chance. . . .

"Forward, march, march! In remembrance of our dead comrades, and therefore on their orders, and in remembrance of the traditions of our proud Wehrmacht."

To these words of General Manteuffel, Field Marshal Walter Model, Commander in Chief West, had added:

"We will not disappoint the Fuehrer and the Fatherland, who created the sword of retribution.

"Forward in the spirit of Leuthen. Our motto is especially now: No soldier in the world *must* be better than we soldiers of the Eifel and of Aachen."

Fine words and great spirit, but their great attack, which some prisoners thought would take them through to Brussels or Paris by Christmas, had bogged down in two weeks. They had gained considerable surprise; they had attacked green troops; they had caught us at a time when air superiority was of no help to us. Why had they failed? Laying aside the basic reason—Germany no longer had the means to sustain a great offensive against the western powers—there were other reasons why this particular gamble did not result in permanent gains. From the limited viewpoint of one corps, a great part of the credit belonged to the men on the north flank of the Bulge. In January, Topete and I talked to members of two battalions of the 99th Division's 394th and 395th Infantry Regiments, the 38th Cavalry Reconnaissance Squadron, and of the 26th Infantry Regiment, 1st Division. Material taken from their stories will give some idea of the way in which U.S. forces on the north flank of the Bulge reacted in the last two weeks of December 1944.

The story of the 3d Battalion, 394th Infantry, which we got from Lieutenant Colonel Norman A. Moore, the battalion commander, and eleven of his battalion and company officers at his underground command post two miles west of Elsenborn, has many of the elements common to the accounts of other units attacked on the morning of 16 December. It is a narrative of surprise attack early on the first day, of slow withdrawals to cover positions of other units, and then of less organized withdrawals to assembly positions in the rear. In some cases communications were disrupted, vehicles abandoned, and units scattered.

The 394th saw its first sight of the battlefront when it went into the line on 14 November near positions it was occupying a month later. On the morning of the counterattack it was holding a defensive position around the railroad station near Buchholz, some twelve miles southeast of Malmedy. One of its companies, Company I, plus a detachment of Company L, had been attached to the 395th Infantry on 13 December and to the 393d on the fourteenth. The battalion was about eighty-five men understrength, so that it consisted at the beginning of the attack of approximately 740 men.

German forces along the front of the 394th Regiment consisted of elements of two regiments of the 277th Volksgrenadier Division. Since the battalion was in a defensive sector, it did not send out patrols between 13 and 16 December and therefore had no inkling from prisoners of any enemy buildup to the east or south. No information came from higher headquarters regarding enemy preparations and, as a matter of fact, the reports on the night of 15 December had indicated that enemy artillery along the battalion front consisted only of two horse-drawn artillery pieces. In giving this bit of information, Major George A. Clayton, the battalion executive officer, remarked dryly that after an hour and five minute artillery preparation the following morning, the battalion concluded that the Germans "sure worked those horses to death." (Lieutenant Colonel Charles J. Hendricks, commanding officer of the 1st Battalion, 395th Infantry, told us in this same period that he had received no warning of a buildup. He added that twenty-five years later, monographs published at the Command and General Staff School would probably show the breakthrough as a masterstroke of planning on our part: we made the line thin so the Germans would strike at us just in time to coincide with the Russian attack.)

Headquarters Company of the 3d Battalion was established at Buchholz on the morning of 16 December. L Company was directly to the east with its platoons on both sides of the railroad track at Losheimergraben. The 1st Platoon was west of the railroad, the 2d on its left, and the 3d in support. The weapons platoon and one squad of mortars were attached to the 3d Platoon. L Company headquarters was in the railroad station. M Company, less one platoon, was northeast of L, and Company K north of Company M. A tank destroyer platoon, apparently from the 801st Tank Battalion, and one platoon from B Company, 324th Engineers, were attached to the battalion. The 371st Field Artillery Battalion was in position to give direct support. No one was on the battalion's right except Task Force X, which was supposed to patrol five thousand yards laterally and make reports every hour. On the left was the 1st Battalion of the 394th.

Between 0530 and 0700, 16 December, the enemy opened up with an hour and five minute artillery preparation. Between 0745 and 0800, just as the men of L Company were getting up, a platoon of about forty to fifty men, probably from Lanzerath, came straight up the railroad toward the station in which L Company was located. Private Bond, who thought it was a platoon from L Company coming to breakfast, ordered the men to halt. At this point the leader of the group gave a command in German and the group began to deploy west of the railroad. First Sergeant Elmer Klug opened fire with his carbine and alerted the company. The 1st Platoon, in the building west of the railroad, now opened fire, while Lieutenant Neil Brown and the Headquarters Company men began firing from inside the station. Part of the Germans took cover in a railroad car about three hundred yards south of the station. Others began to run toward this car and toward the woods to the south. A BAR caught one when he was about a hundred yards away. Corporal George F. Bodner, aided by Private Claypool, got four direct hits with a bazooka on the railroad car, but was unable to get to it to check on the damage. The 1st Platoon then went down the track and fired into the woods.

At this point the Germans began to shell the CP. One man, Private Rude, was hit. Five men were in the supply room at the left end of the railroad station when it received a direct hit. A shell fragment bounced off Bodner's bandolier and killed a medical corpsman, who was struck in the head. Private Joe Genovine said, "The hell with this," and they all piled out into a concrete shelter outside the building, where they stayed about a half-hour until the shelling was over. They were joined later by the company commander and supply sergeant, but about 1200 they were directed to move to a house nearby. Artillery and mortar shells were still falling. Altogether about forty rounds were placed on the CP.

To avoid continued fire, one platoon was placed west of the track, a second was placed near a cut to the front of the station, and a third astride the railroad. Two mortars were set up to fire into positions behind the railroad car, and a 37mm gun and tank destroyer were directed to fire directly on the car.

When the firing was reported that morning to battalion, an alert order was sent to Lieutenant Robert E. Martin, the antitank platoon leader, who was stationed in an old beer tavern to the west of the railroad. He took three men and went forward to previously prepared positions near the edge of the woods in which the Germans had taken cover. He advanced from these positions 250 yards into the woods, where he ran upon a reinforced platoon of Germans "standing around." Unable to withdraw, Martin and his men opened fire with M-1s and got nine or ten of the enemy. The firing was heard by Technical Sergeant Savino Travalini, who took a runner and joined the party, helping to cover the withdrawal. Martin soon brought up his squads. Lieutenant John Higgins, one of the platoon leaders, was killed trying to reach Martin. Thinking he was still alive but unconscious, a medical corpsman and three other soldiers evacuated the body under fire to the aid station two hundred yards southwest of the railroad station.

A running firefight continued during the morning. A machine gun in a water tower "beat the hell out of us," according to Second Lieutenant Leonard Clements of L Company. Another machine gun about four hundred yards south of the station pinned down men of Sergeant Travalini's antitank platoon. He proceeded to crawl up the side of the road and knock out the gun with a hand grenade. Later in the action, the sergeant discovered Germans near the roundhouse about three hundred yards southeast of the company CP, and Pfc. Dalton ran across exposed ground to bring a bazooka and ammunition to the sergeant, who fired several times into the roundhouse. This flushed out some of the enemy. As they emerged, Travalini fired into them with his M-1. For his work in this action, he was promoted to second lieutenant. Technician Fifth Grade Janecka, who was wounded after running back and forth for some time bringing ammunition to members of his platoon, was awarded the Bronze Star. During the morning, M Company's mortars fired three hundred rounds in support of L Company. In the course of the fighting, Headquarters Company had an officer killed and seven or eight men wounded. L Company lost from twenty-five to thirty men. Nine German prisoners were taken.

About noon, the fight having died down, the company tried to feed the men, but "instead of chow we got a hell of a barrage." The shelling consisted largely of mortar fire. The headquarters CP was now moved to the vicinity of Company K. The men went into dugout positions where they received intermittent fire during the afternoon and night. A medical corpsman and a man from the antitank platoon were hit.

A radio operator from K Company remained in the house near the railroad station on the evening of 16 December. Barricaded in the cellar and provided with radio and telephone communications, he kept the headquarters informed of enemy activity during the night. At one time he reported that the Germans were ransacking the room overhead. Later he reported the presence of enemy tanks. This information was passed to division, which said the tanks were friendly. The operator insisted, however, that the crewmen spoke German and the tanks had swastikas on them. They went northeast in the direction of Honsfeld; this movement continued during the night.

At 0500 on the seventeenth, enemy tanks and infantry began to move by the station along the road toward Honsfeld. Estimates were made of twenty-five to thirty tanks, twenty-eight truckloads of soldiers, and two battalions of men on foot. As they passed the K Company positions, they fired on the GIs, inflicting some sixty casualties.

During the afternoon of 17 December, 1st Battalion troops on both sides of K Company were pulled back. Platoons of L Company were also withdrawn, so that only one rifle platoon of eighteen men and a weapons platoon were left to hold an eight-hundred-yard front. In the early afternoon a reinforced company of Germans, armed with bayonets and light weapons, attacked. K Company finally beat off the attack by firing most of its mortar ammunition. It then withdrew about a hundred yards and shortened its line. Between 1400 and 1500 it was hit by artillery or mortar fire. Later another withdrawal was made and the company tied in to 2d Battalion on the left. Unsuccessful attempts were made to contact battalion headquarters. K Company's kitchens had moved toward Murringen, so the company started in that direction. Stragglers from other companies then reported that a general withdrawal was in progress. Most of the evening of the seventeenth was spent by the group on a cross-country march in almost open territory. The men were hand-carrying their weapons in heavy snow under artillery fire.

Reports of a withdrawal toward Murringen were correct. Orders had been received during the morning of the seventeenth sending the 1st Battalion in a northeasterly direction to link up with the 2d Battalion, while the 3d was to take up a position behind the 2d's CP. A defensive position was set up by L Company which withdrew about 1500 or 1600 to the high ground east of Murringen. By that time German air activity was getting fairly heavy along the main supply route, and it was evident that enemy troops were piling up along the line. Trails leading directly to Murringen were in bad condition, so it was decided to withdraw along the main supply route. As the troops withdrew, they were fired upon by a party of Germans that had infiltrated and set up a roadblock. A jeep driver was killed, so the decision was made to bypass the roadblock through the short pines to the east of the road. Here again the column drew fire. Captain Carmine J. Perrotta, S-1 of the battalion, halted his men and sent several of them forward under Sergeants Carl Smith, Emil Smelko, and Lloyd Rogers, who later got Bronze Stars for their work. They gathered up hand grenades and threw them at the Germans, who ran. Sergeant Rogers shot one as he was escaping. Enemy fire then stopped and this column of forty-eight headquarters men continued its march. By 1800 the group reached a point east of Murringen. They were supposed to tie in with 1st Battalion but no one was there. No one slept that night as enemy attacks were constantly expected.

Company M, which had withdrawn a thousand yards on the morning of the seventeenth, displaced its mortars again in the afternoon and helped to cover the withdrawal of Company L. Its mortars were then mounted on vehicles and started toward Murringen. Before they could move far, German shells began to fall, killing one man and forcing the company to abandon three vehicles. The others moved out cross-country and reached a point south of the rifle companies that evening. They did not fire during the night.

At 0100 on 18 December division headquarters issued the order to withdraw. The line of withdrawal was to be Murringen–Krinkelt–Wirtzfeld–Elsenborn. Foot troops under Lieutenant Brown of L Company were to follow those of the 1st Battalion, while the motor column, under Major Norman Moore, was to follow the 2d Battalion.

About 0300 the motor column reached the outskirts of Krinkelt. It was stopped there and received reports that enemy tanks were blocking the roads into the town. Rumors were also spread of a tank battle in the town. There was, indeed, "a lot of confusion as to where to go and what to do." German troops had been seen in Bullingen to the southwest on the preceding day and it was known that there was little or no defense. So the order was given to abandon the vehicles and proceed cross-country to Wirtzfeld. These troops were overtaken by the foot soldiers before they arrived at Wirtzfeld at 0700 on the morning of 19 December.

Captain Joseph Shank, the M Company commander, came to Krinkelt after the vehicles had been left. He found a tank blocking the road into the town, but on inquiry found that it was an American tank and that the fire that had stopped the motor column was American in origin. German patrols and snipers were in parts of the town, but it was held by the 2d Division. Captain Shank contacted the tank commander and the column was permitted to come through. Anyone who could drive was put into the abandoned vehicles and they were taken through Krinkelt to Wirtzfeld. German artillery fire hit the road during the withdrawal but caused no casualties. Fire was received near Krinkelt from some American guns that no longer had communications with many of the units and were apparently firing "in the general direction of Germany."

Company K, which was cut off completely from the rest of the battalion during the withdrawal, spent the night of the seventeenth near Murringen. About 0430 the following morning, a soldier from A Company of the 394th escaped from his German captors and reported that there were tanks in the vicinity. About 0530, Captain Wesley J. Simmons, the company commander, took some fifty to sixty men and went out to check on the report. They were caught in a terrific artillery barrage and decided to turn north toward Krinkelt. At two other points they were fired on and forced to turn westward. They finally proceeded along a draw until they reached Wirtzfeld in the afternoon on the eighteenth. Few troops were lost in this withdrawal, but the company had sustained some seventy casualties since the morning of the sixteenth.

The elements of the 3d Battalion under Major Moore and Lieutenant Brown reached Wirtzfeld in isolated groups. They had been divided into small units and lost contact after moving fifteen hundred yards. Captain Perrotta had about fifty men with him. When they were assembled, it was found that they had about 108 foot troops plus elements from tank destroyer platoons, cannon companies, and regimental headquarters. As the groups marched along they had been out of contact with everyone. They knew that Bullingen was in German hands, and on all sides towns could be seen in flames. At one point they thought of hiding in the woods since it was near daylight. At Wirtzfeld, however, they found the 23d Infantry's command post. A major from that regiment ordered one of the captains to turn his troops over to him, but the captain said that he had been instructed to come to Elsenborn. About thirty minutes later he had to take his troops off 2d Division trucks onto which they had been loaded. Assembly points were set up and men were instructed to proceed toward Elsenborn. Points just outside that position were reached that evening.

On the twentieth, the 3d Battalion took up positions that it was still holding at the end of January 1945—some two miles east of Elsenborn. It then had about 350 to 400 men to put into positions. The men had lost their blankets, overcoats, and all of their individual equipment except small arms. All the antitank equipment plus the 60mm mortars had been lost, but the 81mm mortars were still intact.

On the afternoon of the twenty-first the enemy poured in heavy concentrations of tanks and infantry and overran the positions of one regiment. Artillery fire from the 1st, 2d, 9th, and 99th Divisions was then massed on this front and the enemy was hard hit in a concentration that cost the Germans six guns and heavy infantry casualties. This concentration was credited with stopping a counterattack that was supposed to take Elsenborn.

For the next ten days there were varying indications of German activity along the front, but American artillery succeeded in each case in breaking up all efforts at massing infantry. In the period between 16 and 21 December the battalion lost some 220 men, of whom eleven were officers.

Saturday, 13 January (D+221)

> *Very cold when wind came over wasteland blowing glass-like snow particles into our faces. Tanks and troops moving up all along the way. Engineers doing splendid jobs getting sand on all the hills.*
>
> *Ate dinner at Elsenborn (1st Division CP). Talked to a chap named Halloway from Pennsylvania who is interested in going into dramatics [?]. He remembered seeing me at Blandford before D-day. Talked to men from 99th Infantry Division and 7th Armored Division.*
>
> *Talked to Captain Kelley, adjutant of 26th Infantry, at Butgenbach. Back to ——— to see Sergeant Zappella, who writes Regimental after action reports.*
>
> *Back for chicken dinner. Got big mail from home.*

A somewhat different action was fought on the front of the 38th Cavalry Reconnaissance Squadron, which was on the extreme northern flank of the German attack on 16 December. This unit, under Lieutenant Colonel Robert E. O'Brien Jr., held the area near Monschau. Company F (referred to as a company and not a troop since it was the light-tank unit of the squadron) garrisoned Monschau; men of Troop C were in a six-hundred-yard trench on the high ground; Troop B was dug in on the forward slope of Muetzenich Hill with a line running from the hill along the railroad to near Konzen Station. Monschau was situated in a canyon with hills and high ground on three sides. To hold the town and prevent a breakthrough toward Eupen, some eight or nine miles westward, it was necessary to hold the high ground to the east. We were interested in this battle at corps because a breakthrough would have brought the Germans down on the rear and forward command posts of V Corps. Company F had eight light tanks to garrison the town, and these were put in the southeast part. Five more were placed at the blown bridge on the "snake road" which wound its way to Ingenbroich. The 3d Platoon was placed at a railroad cut. The squadron was tied in with the 395th Infantry on its right flank, just at Monschau.

During the second week of December, the squadron, "more on a hunch than anything else," put out mines and booby traps. The 112th Engineers, which did the work, finished it just before the attack. Particular use was made of wire and flares. Some eighty truckloads of barbed wire were used. The wire was placed around platoon positions and flares were put on top. Trip wires set off flares when the barbed wire was touched. Then the squadron fired everything it had in that direction. This was found to be much more effective than using booby traps. In the case of the latter, a patrol usually withdrew, leaving only the man who had been caught by the trap. But with the use of flares, the squadron had inflicted casualties on twelve men out of a fourteen-man patrol.

All positions were dug in; no group occupied a building as a strong point. However, when men were forced out of positions at some points, as in Muetzenich, house-to-house fighting did occur.

On the sixteenth the Germans tried to send infantry into Monschau to clear the way for later armored advances that were to link up with a parachute drop in that vicinity. This was unsuccessful. The chief fight took place on the following day when an attempt was made to break through at Monschau and at points north of Muetzenich. The greatest enemy penetration was made north of Muetzenich, where the squadron was too thinly spread to stop them, and the enemy walked through. About a hundred Germans came through at this point. The line was restored by using Company A of the 146th Engineers as a reserve force and by counterattacking to seal off the gap. During the fighting, some of the Germans were driven back to the east, but more than fifty were left behind the lines. On the afternoon of the seventeenth, Company A of the 47th Armored Infantry was sent down as reinforcements. It was spread out with three platoons abreast and used to sweep the woods; it captured Germans for a week. By evening the line was restored.

Perhaps the cleverest action during the fight, according to Colonel O'Brien, was that of a staff sergeant who was in charge of five tanks around Monschau. He let the Germans come in and then wiped them out. Some fifty to seventy-five enemy dead were found in the fields after the first attack; perhaps two hundred were killed altogether. (Colonel O'Brien, a stickler for accuracy, had his men after the battle list the enemy dead, giving precise coordinate markings at which each body was found.) The squadron itself lost only fifteen men during the attack. Major Charles E. Rousek, the executive officer, described the action around Monschau as follows: "On the 16th the Germans tried to drive directly into Monschau. On the17th they tried to cut our line in half. On the 18th they tried the other side of the line. On the 19th they gave up." Colonel O'Brien declared: "The whole action was an example—not of any heroic action—but of what an efficient active defense can do. There was no great lot of leadership; the men didn't need it."

Just prior to the breakthrough, the 26th Infantry was at Aubel, Belgium, reorganizing and training after the Hürtgen Forest action in which it had been hard hit. Two companies had been entirely knocked out (E and F Companies were completely new). The companies had been brought up to about a hundred men each or about 60 percent strength. G Company was the exception, starting from Aubel with only fifty men. Two heavy machine gun platoons were completely new except for eight men. Officer ranks were depleted: in the whole battalion there were only seven officers who had come in on D-Day. There were only four BARs to a company, but there was no shortage of heavy guns.

Shortly after midnight on 16 December, the 26th Infantry, which had been alerted that morning, moved out for Camp Elsenborn, where it was attached to the 99th Division. On the seventeenth, the regiment was ordered to seize points to the east of Butgenbach. These movements took place without German opposition. They had apparently not expected such prompt reinforcement and had not moved forward rapidly from Bullingen. Seizure of the area would have given them the road net they wanted through Butgenbach toward Elsenborn and would have made up for lack of the road through Monschau. (Captured German documents later showed that the Sixth SS Army intended to send three volksgrenadier divisions through two routes in the Monschau area to pave the way for panzer attacks in the north. The 12th SS Division was supposed to advance along the Losheim–Bullingen–Butgenbach–Weissmes–Malmédy–Spa axis to hit Liége from the north. It was this important route that the 26th Infantry was supposed to hold. We have seen that on the morning of the seventeenth, the enemy was stopped at Monschau. Bullingen was occupied that day, but the Germans failed to occupy Butgenbach before the 26th Infantry arrived.

On the eighteenth, the 26th Infantry was detached from its assignment to the 99th Division and reattached to the 1st Division. By that evening there was evidence of continuous enemy attacks to reach the road net in the Butgenbach area from the east. A 26th Infantry patrol reported about a thousand German infantry in Bullingen. Throughout the day, the division and corps moved up artillery to support the regiment.

At 0225 on the morning of the nineteenth, Company E of the 26th Infantry was suddenly confronted by twenty truckloads of German infantry and approximately twelve tanks. Seven tanks advanced almost to the company positions, where they were brought under fire by bazookas, 57mm antitank guns, and antitank grenades. Artillery fire was directed on the tanks, but three got through this screen and ran up and down the road leading into Butgenbach. Five or six Americans were hit by tank fire before artillery drove the tanks back. Two of the tanks were later reported disabled; patrols later indicated that a hundred enemy dead were found near the German line of departure.

A second attack was made at 1010 when two tanks and a company of infantry advanced from the south, ran through the battalion positions, and blasted them. One tank was halted by direct antitank fire before the antitank gun was destroyed. The other tanks withdrew under artillery fire. It was believed that most of the infantry in the attack were killed.

The 26th Infantry again bore the brunt of attack on 20 December. Two or three hours after midnight, tanks and infantry attacked from Bullingen on the east-west road. The tanks hit a belt of mines, which had been laid on the night of the eighteenth, and turned southward, advancing cross-country to the north-south road running into Butgenbach. The enemy fired into F Company, knocking out three bazooka teams and a machine-gun section belonging to Company H. The attack was stopped by early afternoon by heavy artillery concentrations. A captured German document from the 12th SS Tank Regiment testified to the effectiveness of American artillery fire. The heaviest German attack against the 1st Division was made against the 26th Infantry on the twenty-first. If the 1st SS Panzer Division was to get through to the west, it was imperative that Butgenbach be taken. Prisoners later said that the 25th Panzer Grenadier Regiment was assigned the task of taking the village. At 0130 they attacked the 2d Battalion's positions southeast of the town with machine-gun and tank fire. Artillery and small-arms fire drove them back. At 0300 the Germans countered with artillery, mortar, and Nebelwerfer fire, which knocked out the 2d Battalion's telephonic communications. Fortunately, they were able to radio for artillery fire, which stopped another attack at 0500.

The most dangerous attack of the twenty-first came at 0715 when the Germans threw twelve tanks and a reinforced infantry battalion against the 2d Battalion. The outposts saw them advancing and called for artillery and antitank fire. Despite heavy fire, five tanks broke through the screen near a hedgerow. Two tanks drove up and down south of the hedgerow, firing particularly at American automatic weapons positions. They knocked out a section of light machine guns, a section of heavy machine guns, two or more BARs, and two antitank guns. The 2d Battalion now directed artillery and bazooka fire against the tanks. In the latter case, the bazooka man's assistant was wounded, so he loaded and fired by himself. During the fight another tank came through a gap in the five-hundred-yard-long hedgerow. The tank commander stopped, got out of his tank, stepped up to a foxhole and took an American prisoner. He was joined later by another tank and they repeated the process. Pistol shots were heard from time to time, and it was assumed that the Germans were shooting American wounded. No infantry got through the hedgerow.

At about 0900 five tanks hit eight of Company E's men and about twenty-four from Company G. Three tanks drove through toward the E Company CP in a house in Butgenbach. A bazooka team from G Company tried unsuccessfully to get in firing position in a nearby barn. Fortunately, an American tank north of Butgenbach destroyed one of the tanks in front of the CP. Another, which was firing directly at the CP, was destroyed later. The remaining tank took cover behind the two disabled tanks and blew two holes in the house, hitting nine men. Fortunately, no infantry got through to help the tanks, and shortly after 1600 a 90mm gun near the CP fired three shots at the tank and drove it away.

With the subsiding of the attack, the 2d Battalion reorganized its forces. Company E had sustained thirty casualties (three killed) including the weapons platoon leader, four squad leaders, and three assistant squad leaders. Company G, which started the attack with sixty-eight riflemen and a machine-gun section of nine, lost thirty-five (thirteen killed), including one platoon leader and four squad leaders. The 26th had also lost two tanks and three tank destroyers.

In the fight to stop the tanks, nearly everything that could shoot had been used. Four 90mm guns had been attached for the action. Mortars were used to a great extent, one section firing 750 rounds before it was knocked out by tank fire. In addition to the four battalions of division artillery, four battalions of the 2d Division's artillery were directed to give their support shortly after the attack began. At 1000 ten medium guns of the 99th Division artillery were placed at the disposal of the 1st Division. Approximately ten thousand rounds were used to stop the enemy attack.

On the twenty-second, the Germans turned their attention to the 1st and 3d Battalions of the 26th Infantry. The most serious penetration was between Companies A and K, and a battalion of the 18th Infantry was sent in to restore the positions. Artillery fire was again massed against the enemy, and heavy casualties were again inflicted on the Germans (some estimates ran as high as forty-four tanks and twelve hundred infantry along the entire regimental front for the two days).

Minor enemy activity was reported on the twenty-fourth, but after that date the Germans subsided until the twenty-eighth. Once more they tried an advance and were stopped by the artillery. This effectively ended the German threat; the 26th Infantry was still in its Butgenbach positions in mid-January. The 1st Division in the period from 16 to 24 December sustained losses of 25 officers and 948 enlisted men. Of this number, 13 officers and 487 enlisted men were from the 26th Infantry Regiment.

Several commanders, including General Eisenhower, have given high praise to the units on the north flank of the Bulge for their role in blunting the first drives of the great offensive in the north, but their contribution has been dimmed by the memory of the great defense put up at Bastogne and the brilliant Third Army march northward. But had units to the east and north of Bastogne not slowed the enemy, the Germans would have been west of that objective and perhaps at the Meuse before the airborne divisions could have arrived from Reims.

Montgomery said that the Ardennes battle was won by the fighting qualities of the American soldier. We can safely leave the matter there.

Sunday, 14 January (D+222)

Beautiful day. Cold.

   To 2d Battalion, 26th Infantry, 1st Division at Butgenbach. Went along road which had been under small arms fire yesterday. Got good interview with Lieutenant Colonel David, plus the S-3 and company commanders involved in the action. Movie "Gershwin." Excellent.

Monday, 15 January (D+223)

Cold. Hazy.

   General Huebner takes over V corps. General Gerow takes over the 15th Army. We knew of this several weeks ago; breakthrough held up the change.

   Letter from mother written 25 Dec. in which she says that she got letters from Rip and Jim about changes (probably ——— they were in Ph. Invasion) together with breakthrough news.

Tuesday, 16 January (D+ 224)

Luxembourg back on limits. Was put off limits on 17th Dec. We have come full cycle. During that time we had several alerts. Thermite bombs were issued for the destruction of papers, all non-essential material was evacuated to a point beyond Liege. Extra guards were posted. Alerts were the order of the day. We had a fake gas alert and two air alerts. Twice paratroopers were reported in the vicinity.

Wednesday, 17 January (D+225)

Routine work.

Thursday, 18 January (D+226)

Warmer. Snow melting.

To Eupen to see Major O'Sullivan at the 2d Evacuation Hospital. Saw Captain Fraizer who had stopped by there; met Lieutenant Goldman.

Next to Veriers to see Hal Houston, who is surgeon at 128th Evacuation Hospital. He says that Bill Slayden is at headquarters VIII Corps.

We got a new man day before yesterday, Carl Kuntson from Iowa.

The major talked at length of his interviews with the 82nd Airborne Division. He says that they were amazing soldiers. Many of them have developed a taste for killing to the extent that they can not be sent on patrols when they want to take prisoners because they refuse to take them. One young, blue-eyed, baby-faced lieutenant had killed more than fifty and preferred to cut their throats. Always sharpening his knife.

Educational level of airborne troop probably lowest in the army; very high native intelligence. Act instinctively. If their officers don't take proper action they take over. One officer withdrew from roadblock; they put corporal in charge, went back and held it. No new officer accepted until he has proved himself. Officers eat and sleep with them.

Have discipline in their lines. Once out of the line very high number of AWOL's. No desertions. Always turn up when news of battle reaches them. Are on hand for training, but can't stand boredom of garrison.

Hate helmets; tend to wear knit caps only in fights. . . . Do not think of withdrawing from a position.

They are serious about fighting. Give careful interviews.

Friday, 19 January (D+227)

Snow. . . . Routine work.

Saturday, 20 January (D+228)

Snow. Rainy day.

To Rötgen, Rolt, Zureifall, Kleinhau, and Brandenberg. Met Lieutenant Vasta, 9th Army. I and lieutenant were at 8th Division. He took us to 8th Division forward. We went to the outskirts of Brandenburg. Left jeep there and walked to other edge of town. Was a little scary. We knew we were under observation from three sides although we knew it was unlikely that artillery would waste shells on the two of us. The devastated town seemed deserted but now and then some guard looked out of a building at us. We finally found the 1st Battalion, 13th Infantry Regiment in a cellar. Talked to Captain Wade Brown and Captain Kehal about the Huertgen battle.

Captain Brown—who came into the army from North Carolina State College four years ago (he was studying forestry) was very disgruntled about the war. . . . He was displeased with replacements which were made up of people who had no infantry training. Some men were being sent up who were high ranking sergeants in coastal artillery or the like. They were reduced in a short time because they didn't know what to do. He echoed a frequently expressed desire that they might have time to train their men. His view was that the War Department had made its great error in assuming that it wouldn't need so much infantry [this is something that we found to be true in writing the 2nd Army history] and thus wasn't prepared for what happened when great demands were made on us for more infantry men. This was a favorite statement of General Lear as well as General McNair.

The roads were very slick and I was frightened more than once as we slid around the narrow roads down the hillsides. I find that fear of artillery doesn't worry me while fear of turning over does.

Sunday, 21 January (D+229)

Snowed last night. Clear and bright today.

Stars and Stripes list losses of the 106th Division at 8,003 in breakthrough. Of those, 7,000 are missing. 28th lost two regiments. Others were hard hit. War Department says there were 18,000 prisoners and 32,000 other casualties.

The roads yesterday seemed all to be heavily fortified vs. counterattack. Trees at narrow points of the road were notched and charges attached ready to be fired. Troops and tanks were in most of the towns.

Monday, 22 January (D+230)

Cool.

Have been going through V Corps G-2 reports for December. Although there is some evidence of a build-up in our area no warning is

*given and capabilities of enemy is not changed [of course a standard
capability is counterattack, but this would have been stressed if they
really had expected trouble on the scale which came].*

*Attack came between 0600–0700 on V Corps front after heavy
artillery barrage on the morning of 16 December. Made 3 mile penetration on VIII Corps front.*

*On 17 December full scale attack on V Corps front before 0600. 3
Panzer divisions, at least 3 infantry divisions. Overall gain of 12–20
kilometers. Parachute landings were made under Lieutenant Colonel
[Friedrich] Von der Heydte on morning of 17 December. Estimates of 500
(420 is another figure) were to secure Eupen-Malmedy roads around
813175. Took off from Poderborn, Wesphalia about 0200. Used 25–40 Ju-
52 planes. Failure. Von der Heydte captured when he went to Monschau,
which he thought to be in German hands. Armored attack around
Monschau on 18 December.*

*Captured orders show this was called Greif operation. Was to
include forces carefully equipped with American vehicles, insignia, etc.
Were to identify selves to one another by day by reversing helmets; at
night by red-blue signals of flash lights. . . . Apparently Hitler spoke to
Wehrmacht on 11 and 12 December 44. . . .*

*On 19 December enemy took two towns. Homont and Ronat and hit
at Stavelot. Repeated strikes from armor around Krinklet. Paratroops . . .
failed because only half of the original strength of 800 arrived . . . no
relief.*

*On 21 December, the enemy reported . . . active around Bullingen
and Butgenbach.*

*On 23 December . . . Von der Heydte . . . was summoned by SS
General Sepp Dietrich . . . of 6th SS Panzer Army to get mission of
cutting Eupen-Malmedy road. He would be relieved by 1730 of first day
by SS Panzer Division. Light regiment of 6 companies transported in 2
groups of JU-52's (53 planes in group). Barely 30 percent of regiment
arrived at original assembly spot. Two hours after landing they knew it
was a failure. Reasons for failure:*

1. Too little time for planning.
*2. Too little co-ordination ——— of personnel. ——— to him 5
   days before operation.*
3. The wind—blew at 70 km per hour—scattered men.
4. JU-52 pilots scattered more than wind.
5. Lack of weapons on ground.

Von der Heydte wanted gliders [?] Deitrich opposed.

On 17 December moved a few kilometers out; waited two days for relief. At noon of 20 December, Colonel ordered 200 remaining to infiltrate through our lines and reassemble at Monschau—supposed to be in German hands. Communication disrupted entry. Equipment good.

Full report on 150 or more Germans operating behind our lines in American jeeps and uniforms. Drivers usually speaks little English. One who speaks best English usually high ranking noncom or high ranking officer (Brigadier General in one case). Used SHAEF passes in many cases. Asked questions about their homes. Our sentries told to stop all staff cars; don't worry about brass. (I was stopped often during this time.) . . .

Solar, 15th Panzer Brigade.

Solar is code name of commander. No PWs so far ever saw him. Size estimated 2,000–2,500. Organization was set up at Grafenwoehr in early November. About 900 Germans and American vehicles. American uniforms for all personnel. In November, Brigade split up into 3 CT [combat teams], each with about 800 men. The 3d CT went into assembly area near Stavelot 18 December. 2d CT near Hoenfeld.

Were to block roads, reconnoiter bridges. To secure south bank of river and certain bridgeheads.

To try to kill or capture high ranking officers. Talk of group of 80 men to go to Paris to try to get Eisenhower. . . .

On the 25th we began to capture vehicles out of gas.

Commander of the 15th Panzer Brigade on 26 December was said to be Lieutenant Colonel [Otto] Skorzeny.

Mission upset by:

1. Excessive mining of roads.

2. Air bombardment of Stavelot.

3. Artillery bombardment near Malmedy on 22 December.

4. Alertness of American troops.

. . . Captured German documents that show complete knowledge of forces against them. Point out that 99th and 78th relatively new. Veteran units have many fresh and untried replacements.

Every American will not quickly recover from unexpected attack.

Expected to get gasoline and food on the way.

Replacement question is a big one. A chap from a replacement depot says 5,000 flown over from U.S., after breakthrough. Those just landing in Scotland flown over. Says IRTC now gives only 6 weeks infantry and they are sent over. Can be taught basic infantry in that time, but can't be conditioned. Bad because it is newest man who goes to the front.

News came that COMZ personnel will be sent to front. All right if they are trained (many get 6 weeks now); otherwises bad because they frequently had no infantry training in States.

Chapter 20

Battle for the Dam

Tuesday, 23 January (D+231)–
Friday, 23 February (D+262)

Tuesday, 23 January (D + 231)

Cold. Clear most of the day.

Out early together with Topete to Mützenich to see Lieutenant Colonel Robert O'Brien and Major Charles Rousek of 38th Cavalry Reconnaissance Squadron. . . . We had dinner with them at their desk, while they discussed their part in the breakthrough.

Had to put the windshield down; was very cold. Were 1,000 yds. from our furthest positions.

Got stopped for speeding just outside Eupen. Played cards at night.

Wednesday, 24 January (D+232)

Cold. Snowed last night.

Russians are near Breslau. We made little progress yesterday. Our planes are catching some Germans as they pull out.

Thursday, 25 January (D+233)

Very cold, but fairly clear. . . .

[It] is entirely correct when [it is said] that basic principles of infantry not always thoroughly applied. That was complaint over and over by most experienced people in Normandy. They kept saying that the

infantry failed to take cover, failed to take advantage of artillery prepara-
tion, failed to advance boldly, failed to dig in properly. They still hammer
on the bayonet where I find practically no cases where it is used. In the
breakthrough I found that it was digging in which saved them, yet in
basic we dug only one foxhole.

Artillery is used very extensively. I have been in many CPs when
someone would say they saw two or three Germans several hundred
yards away. 5–30 rounds were frequently dropped on them. However, the
artillery stopped the breakthrough on the Monschau front.

The complaint that armor not well used before St. Lo is a point
backed up by comment of tank people to whom I talked to in the early
days. Tank people admit that they have difficulty in stopping the Panther
Tank. . . .

Supply has been amazing. One million men ashore in 20 days after
D day. Nearly 3 million in 4 months. I saw this taking place and found it
hard to believe. The first 10 days saw divisions pouring ashore on roads
barely wide enough for trucks to get through. Great nets of roads were
soon built.

An interesting statement—"In August and early September the
American armies probably moved farther and faster in a comparable
period than any forces of similar size in this war." I think he is right in
saying that Eisenhower had bigger job than Foch and has handled it well.
I don't know whether he is a good field general. He obviously is an
excellent Supreme Commander. Bradley seems to have inspired confi-
dence. For drive, Patton (although he is disliked by many) is greatly
admired. I think, however, it may be possible for people to argue in years
to come that a desire to keep him in his place may have led to a failure to
allot sufficient material to him for the drives he might have been able to
make. I have heard reports of people in Corps who chuckled at staff
meetings because he couldn't move faster. Tank people prefer 3d Army to
1st Army.

He hits [?] a sore point on the "Army game," "Yes-Yes tendency."
Everybody seems to be trying to please someone above him. The trouble is
that so much depends in the army on saying the right thing. A blocked
promotion over a period of six months . . . may mean the difference
between a Captaincy and a Lieutenant Colonelcy in a year's time. It may
also mean the difference between a company commander and a staff job.
The same thing happens in civilian life, but it is not so apparent.

The cigarette trials in Paris show a failure of officers to have responsi-

*bility down. A more careful interest on the part of officers in men would stop
a lot of the petty graft which takes place in kitchens, supply and the like.*

Red tape is horrible. . . .

*In virtually every section (ours included) 2/3 of the time is wasted.
It is particularly horrible to see the wastage when you see people of talent
assigned as clerks, and then not doing anything. Every headquarters
company has a large staff which waits on the headquarters people. In
[every] Army, Corps, Division, Regiment I have seen carpenters who do
nothing but make knick knacks for the officers; here we have a sign
painter who spends nearly all his time making cute signs like "Close the
door softly"; "No loitering"; "Pick up your laundry," etc.—all done with
special lettering and pictures. Nearly every after action report we got has
much extra art work on the covers. We work about 2 days out of 7 in our
section. While the waiting around . . . throughout the army can be
excused in fact, because of the lag between campaigns and because of the
fact that when action starts a larger staff may be crucial it doesn't
account for all of it. We have about a dozen people who take up their time
serving beer, standing in front of the shower and keeping people from
going in with their shoes on. One fellow does that 4 hours a day—going
through himself about every 20 minutes with muddy shoes on to see that
no one is breaking the rules. Down in regiment where they cry for men I
saw two men spend all their time taking care of the Colonel—(while it may
be true that they help to save valuable time which he would spend in taking
care of his stuff, there is much time that he doesn't do anything either)*

*The COMZ set-up is shocking. 150 hotels in Paris; working on a
schedule of 8:30–5:30. (more nearly 4:30); off one afternoon a week;
frequently other afternoons off. They have no conception of front line life.
It is nearly as bad here at Corps and in many cases clear up to Regiment.
Only in battalions and companies do the headquarters people show most
of the discomforts of the men in the line.*

*In the history set-up we have a function which overlaps with
psychological warfare. . . . Frequently 5–6 sets of people go to units in a
week to ask for the same material. In Paris I doubt if 9/10 of the history
section actually worked more than 2 hours a day (that was the same in
many of our sections at 2d Army). In section after section the day was a
matter of shuffling papers, passing the buck. It's a discourse to be found
in nearly every phase of civilian life, of course. The poem "Echelons on
High" is all too true.*

. . . The men have no great interest in the war. You can't work them

up unless the Germans hit some of their friends—it is the spirit of the men who fought at King's Mountain [during the Revolutionary War] they ran the British out of the section of the country and went home. Many of the people who fought in the Civil War were much the same. . . . It may be well to have the fanaticism of the Germans or the Russians, but I doubt if we have ever had a great deal of it, even in the Civil War. I agree, however, that it wouldn't hurt if discussions were encouraged.

Today's S and S says General Lear is the new deputy ETO Commander. It indicates that the War Department wants some tough action. I think he will get more rear echelon people in the front than nearly anyone else. However, unless the war takes another bad turn no one will succeed any length of time in forcing the headquarters staff to disgorge their "excess fat." Again and again they are told to get down to T/O. They assign the men elsewhere and carry them as DS. When no one is looking the excess gets back. General Lear, himself, engaged in that type of business continually at 2d Army. We would cut down surpluses (usually meant that only those they wanted to get rid of were thrown out). Those he wanted to keep were kept on TD for maneuvers. Once this period was over they were worked in some way until the next house-cleaning began. Unless a tough hombre like General Lear orders the thing done, demands a report in 10 days which shows that the order has been carried through and checks again in two weeks to see that it has been done, it won't be.

Major O'Sullivan out of hospital. Coporas and Captain Shappell came by today.

4th of February is deadline for the outline of breakthrough story.

Saturday, 27 January (D+235)

Cold. Snow.

To the 99th Division headquarters and then to 393d Infantry Regiment in Elsenborn. Met T/4 Robert Armstrong of Miami University there. He was a friend of Tim Hadsel's; did his M.A. in anthropology at Chicago. Had a course under Major Cole.

At night back to 99th Division headquarters. Quarters in a large barn there. Very cold. Snow about 8 inches deep.

Sunday, 28 January (D+236)

Cold. Snow.

Must be about zero. To 1st Battalion of 395th out in the woods east of Elsenborn. Talked to Lieutenant Colonel Hendricks, Major Pearce and company officers.

Back to 99th at night. Stayed at AT office. Met Sergeants Fleming and Blain (Springfield, Mass.) and Captain McCollum.

Monday, 29th January (D+237)

Cold. Snow. Colder.

Stayed out nearly all day and nearly froze. Got stuck in drifts when going well up forward. Main line of supply kept clear however. To 3d Battalion, 394th, well forward in deep holes in the earth; covered by snow. Talked to Major Clayton and company officers. Excellent interview.

Attack didn't start. Heavy guns had fired a great deal the night before; shook us up a good deal.

Very good picture of breakthrough. 99th held pretty well at first. When they were permitted to withdraw, abandoning vehicles as they went, the retreat became confused. In some cases Germans went on through without making any effort to destroy them. No evidence of a wild retreat; definite evidence of disorganization. Seem to have morale back. They got part of 3,000 reinforcements taken from 69th Division which had just reached England shortly before the breakthrough. . . .

Back to Limbourg at night; very cold and tired. Got a big piece of chicken, Topete had chipables and anchovies. We ate very well.

Tuesday, 30 January (D+238)

Warmer.

Topete and I were hard at work all day on the material covering the 99th Division.

Wednesday, 31 January (D+239)

Warmer. Snow melting.

Worked away on story of 1st Division.

Thursday, 1 February (D+240)

Snow nearly gone.

*Captain Healey and Major O'Sullivan down for a visit.
Worked on 1st Division story.*

Friday, 2 February (D+241)

Snow all gone. Completed 1st Division summary at night.

Saturday, 3 February (D+242)

Warm.

Sunday, 4 February (D+243)

Warm. Did very little but read and write letters.

Monday, 5 February (D+244)

*Sprinkled.
Still sitting around.*

Tuesday, 6 February (D+245)

*Cool.
To Spa with Topete and Knutson. Saw Hadsel. Then to Stavelot; part of
the town is quite used up. On way back picked up 82nd Airborne lieutenant.
He had been in army since 1942. Says he has been wounded 5 times and is
about to crack up. Says they took a terrible beating in the breakthrough.
Radio says General Dittman has admitted that Germany can't win;
says she can't accept unconditional surrender, which would ruin her;
says she is bound to lose if she continues the war.
Manila nearly completely taken; Russia still on the march.
Visited a while in Verviers.*

Wednesday, 7 February (D+246)

*Rainy.
Still doing nothing. We are more or less waiting for the present
attack to be over.
Second Lieutenant A.J. Webber assigned to our section.*

Thursday, 8 February (D+247)

Cool.

With lieutenant—A.J. Webber of Missouri and Topete to Lammersdorf to 78th Division. Roads jammed with convoys; largest number of tanks, guns, etc. that I have yet seen.

At night read; argued with Topete. Saw Major O'Sullivan at hospital at Eupen. He went back two days ago.

Friday, 9 February (D+248)

Rain.

Very bad day. Topete and I went to Aywaille to see 1st Division people. The 16th Regiment had moved up near Aachen to go into line. Then [we] went to 1st Division (rear). . . . I talked to Lieutenant John Spaulding of E Company whose platoon, from the 16th Regiment, was the first to get on the hill over Omaha Beach on D day. Spaulding is from Owensboro [Kentucky]. Good interview. Back at 5:30.

Saturday, 10 February (D+249)

Cool.
Wrote up interview.
Very good day.

Sunday, 11 February (D+250)

Rain, snow, sleet, ice, and hellish weather generally.

In the afternoon Topete and I went to Iveldingen near Montenau by way of Sourbrodt and ———. Came back by Malmedy. Went to see Major Christoe of the 69th Division to give him instructions on the coverage of history. He is Chicago Ph.D. in international relations. Studied under Blakeslee at Fletcher School. Knew Major Cole. Horrible trip; roads torn all to pieces by constant convoys. Everybody still moving up Aachen way.

Malmedy is badly torn up in the center of town. . . . The chateau had a nice chapel with an organ. G-3 was installed in it. An interesting line from Beston's Saint Lawrence*—"Sooner or later, guided by its own intelligence or by bitter necessity, a civilization will again remember that* *visible nature is not the immediate spoil of an age or its generations, but the timeless inheritance of man, the ancient mystery to be forever shared with those who forever are to come."*

Another good section about whales—"Presently some five or six or a company will be found wheeling and plunging by, coming like gods with the tide and like gods playing in the waves as if it were [still] the morning of the world."

Monday, 12 February (D+251)

Rain during day. Talk of moving us forward.

Armistice rumors.

Russians open new drives; German commentators insist that surrender means death to German people.

. . . Was decided that Topete and I would cover recent action of 78th Division.

Announcement of end of Crimean Conference (held near [Y]Alta) last night. They still stick to unconditional surrender—end of German Army, German war equipment, German General Staff. Favor control or abolition of German war industry. Luzon line to be eastern boundary of Poland; Poland to be compensated at expense of Germany. Allied control to be set up in Berlin. French to be invited to take part in occupation of Germany. Lubin government to be broadened to include representatives of other governments. Jugoslav question discussed. Another conference to be held in April in San Francisco. Nazi party to be destroyed; war criminals to be punished; reparation in kind demanded.

Tuesday, 13 February (D+252)

Cloudy, warm, trying to clear off.

Topete and I will go to 78th Division tomorrow.

9th Army is scheduled to make main attack. III Corps is in place of ———*.*

Major Shappell and Captain Hechler came by.

Wednesday, 14 February (D+253)

Bad weather.

To 78th Division. We contacted Major Schente and Sergeant

William Baker (a Kentuckian). Set us up in the PRO office—one of people there was Captain Minor (from Lexington).

    Went back to ———— see Staff Sergeant Morris Carter, who went to Murray. Back to Division headquarters in afternoon to discuss plans for covering story with Baker.

Thursday, 15 February (D+254)

Hazy.

    Topete, Baker and I set out for Maastrecht [?] to see Captain Goldman at 9th Army. Went over horribly beaten up roads . . . to Aachen. After that roads were better. Aachen looks rather beaten up. . . . 9th Army headquarters in school building. Spent two hours talking with Major Frazier. Then went over to Gangelt to see Goldman. Found what he had covered. Came back at night.

Friday, 16 February (D+255)

Weather bad.

    Talked to Colonel C.W. Willington, 311th Regiment Commander, Major James Sears, S-2, and Major Guthrie, S-3, of Regiment. The Colonel was very cooperative. Saw them in a pillbox just west of Schmidt. Tank KO'd just outside pillbox.

    Got our first glance at Schwammen Dam from distance. Morning haze over ———— —looked like clouds from airplane. Schmidt very hot since there is perfect observation from all around. We were in and out of town for five days.

    Next went south of Schmidt to see Lieutenant Colonel I.W. Keyes, Battalion Commander, 2d Battalion, 311th, with Captain Herman Jackson [?], S-3, Lieutenants Richard Falloch, Clyde Trimble, Gene Webster. Colonel Keyes gave a splendid story.

Saturday, 17 February (D+256)

Weather still not so good.

    We slept in factory in Loemenberg. Some sort of electric machinery made here; some say submarine parts. Latrine signs in different languages—Polish, Russian, French, German, Dutch, and probably Czech.

To see Captain William Ariail, S-3, Lieutenant Robert Flinin [?], S-2, and Captain Leo McCarthy, heavy weapons commander of 1st Battalion, 311th near Schmidt. In afternoon went to see Major Peter Newton [?] (chemist), Captain Richard Vanniger, Captain William Feery, and Captain Rolph Gero. Vanniger was an interesting character. Talking in a heavy voice he told of shooting Germans on a hill and watching them roll, squealing down a hill. He also told of a German hanging out of a church. It sure shows how civilized they are when they fight from churches. Sergeant ——— ——— who had just broadcast about being the first man in Schmidt, came in while we were there. I found later that his statement was not very accurate.

Very bitter at Company A, 774th Tank Battalion, for failure to help take Schmidt.

Sunday, 18 February (D+257)

Weather a little warmer. Rain.

Out in the woods to the east of Schmidt through horribly muddy roads to see Lieutenant Colonel Harry Lutz and Major Walter Pierce of 3d Battalion, 310th. Got an incredibly tedious story on how this unit helped take Schmidt.

Saw Colonel Hayes of 309th Regiment.

Monday, 19 February (D+258)

Pretty day. Out near Hoenfeld in range of Germans. Talked to Captain John Herzie and Sergeant Schrock of 1st Battalion, 310th. Sat out in open. After about 10 minutes four rounds of artillery fell in about 100 yards of us. Like a fool I remained seated on the water can. Two more rounds came in and we retired to a shelter. 6 more rounds fell after that.

Earlier in the day talked to Lieutenant Colonel Robert C. Wilson, G-2, and Lieutenant Colonel Charles R. McKinney, G-3, 78th Division. Good interviewes.

At night I interviewed Major Charles A. Jenkins, S-2 of 78th Division Artillery.

Tuesday, 20 February (D+259)

Rained. Got stuck.

Interviewed Lieutenant Colonel Robert Shellman, 1st Battalion, 309th, near Silberscheidt. This group got to dam first. Next saw Lieutenant Colonel Floyd Call, Lieutenant George Gossett and Captain Walter Short of 3d Battalion, 309th.

Left for home. Got stuck near Roetgen. Came back thoroughly muddy and filthy. Had 25 letters.

Captain Frank Phelps arrived yesterday.

Wednesday, 21 February (D+260)

Weather good.

Started to work on interviews. Howe has gone to III Corps. Captain Frank Phelps of Baltimore is in his place.

Major Shappell and Captain Hechler came by.

Thursday, 22 February (D+261)

Beautiful day.

Captain Lester Barnes [?] is leaving. Worked on interview material. Kaufman and Phelps to 2d Division.

Friday, 23 February (D+262)

Captain Boron [?] left. Fine gentleman. I worked on 78th material.

Attack to cross the Roer is planned for today. (attacked about 0330)

Chapter 21

The Close-Up to the Rhine

Saturday, 24 February (D+263)–
Tuesday, 20 March (D+287)

Saturday, 24 February (D+263)

*1st and 9th Armies began attack to cross the Roer yesterday at 0330,
after a 45 minute artillery barrage. Went across in assault boats. Had to
put in bridges. Not too much difficulty to get some crossings.*
    Heavy plane attacks.
    Captain Ferris came by from 78th.

Sunday, 25 February (D+264)

Some rain.
    Baker went back to 78th. 1st Army finishes taking Duren.
    *Good news continues to come in on bombing of Tokyo. Fight on Iwo
Jima costly and savage.*

Monday, 26 February (D+265)

Slightly overcast.
    Major Shappell came by.

Tuesday, 27 February (D+266)

Sky overcast. Cleared later.
    Work on 78th Division story.

Wednesday, 28 February (D+267)

Rained a little.
    Moved to Eupen to an old barracks there. Buildings were ones used by V Corps Forward. Have German Mottoes on the wall.
    Knutson and I got a room. We are all set up with easychairs, table, washstand, stove.

Thursday, 1 March (D+268)

Rained a little.
    Attack still going well toward Cologne. Considerable air over here.
    Saw Harry Whayne, now a sergeant with the 5th Evacuation Hospital—one of my former students.

Friday, 2 March (D+269)

Snowing.
    Routine work on 78th Division story.

Saturday, 3 March (D+270)

Spitting snow. Captain Howe came back from Paris. He is going to 3d Corps despite his wishes.
    Harry Whayne came by.

Sunday, 4 March (D+271)

Rain.
    78th Division material still on hand.

Monday, 5 March (D+272)

Rain. Our troops are near Cologne. . . . Trier taken (3d Army).

Tuesday, 6 March (D+273)

Rain.
    Troops in part of Cologne—3d Armored and 104th Division. Later the 8th Division came in. 3d Army 18 miles south of Bonn.

Wednesday, 7 March (D+274)

V Corps being pinched out. May be used for assault. German propaganda talks get more hysterical daily. For the past three weeks everybody from Hitler down has been insisting that Germans can lose nothing ——— freedom; that if she will not surrender she can not be beaten; that if she will hold out the Allies will give up their attempts since they are worn out. They point to the heroic actions of the British after Dunkerque and the Russians at Stalingrad and ask the Germans to copy their enemies in courage.

Great ado is made of the secret clauses of the Crimean Conference at Yalta. (Incidentally the conference seemed to be a good one. I'm inclined to believe that the Polish agreement may have been a little too much like a Congress of Vienna solution, but it is about all that could be worked out. The Poles have not indicated that they are likely to be great, good neighbors anyway. The Curzon Line doesn't treat the Poles as bad as their 1920–21 settlement treated the Russians. FDR's choice of delegates to the San Francisco Conference seems to be a good one. His choices of Stassen and Vandenberg were particularly good.[20] Dewey won't be happy about the latter. France is acting like a sulky baby).

Back to the Germans—everything indicates they are now relying on their voices more than strength now. They made no determined fight after we crossed the Roer River.

News this morning is that the 9th Armored Division is across the Rhine. The 9th Division is to exploit [?]. Lieutenant Webber is with 9th Division. There are rumors of other elements across the Rhine. The whole thing may crack fast.

Thursday, 8 March (D+275)

Cool.

Armies pull up near Coblenz (3d) and Bonn.

At night to hear show of André Kostelantz, and Lily Pons,[21] her floutist, and Theodore Potch. The men were in army garb; she in flowing dress with bright colors. . . . Her program was popular, but good.

Discussion of system of voting in world conferences. A nation must agree to use of force before it is bound. It is the same rock on which the League [of Nations] was heavily built [?], but I doubt if we can hope for a nation to act effectively unless it is willing to do so.

Stars and Stripes *says 1st unit across Rhine at 1640 Wednesday (on same page it says 1550).*

Corps poop sounds something like this—9th Army was to assault. V Corps was to be pinched out by meeting of III Corps to our left, and VIII to our right. We are probably to make an amphibious landing.

On the afternoon of 7 March CCB of the 9th Armored Division reached a point near Remagen (between Bonn and Cologne). A bridge had not been blown so a patrol of company A got across. In 15 minutes Company A, under Second Lieutenant Carl Timmerman of West Point, Nebraska, was across. The 1st platoon led by Second Lieutenant Emmett J. Burrows, probably first Americans across. Germans caught napping (the CCB had pushed 7 miles that day and captured large ammo dump).

Remagen is at junction of Cologne-Coblenz and Ahr valley rail lines. Town is on left bank of Rhine, about 12 rail miles south of Bonn. The Ludendorf Bridge, a double-track rail span, crosses the river at Remagen. The Rhine is about 1200 feet wide at this point. CCB is commanded by Lieutenant Colonel Leonard Engemann of Minnesota.

Opposite Remagen, less than 10 miles beyond east [?] bank, a super-highway parallels the Rhine and provides a northern route to the Ruhr. Near Duisburg the highway veers north east to Hannover, Magdeburg and Berlin. The southern route leads to Frankfurt. First crossing of Rhine in 125 years.—All this from Stars and Stripes.

When III Corps heard that CCB was across it got busy asking for everything. Elements of the 78th and 9th Divisions were thrown in. 7th Armored Division detached from V Corps and sent up. 2000 on 7 March.

By 2400 on 7 March the 27th Armored Infantry Battalion and 14 Armored Battalion of the 9th Armored were across, while the 52d Armored Battalion was crossing. 310th (78th Division) was prepared to cross; 47th Infantry to cross at 0400. 310th attached to 9th Armored.

28th Division rushed up. V Corps now has 2d, 28th, 69th, and 102d Cavalry Groups. The 69th is in reserve. 106th to be relieved 10 March to pick up other two regiments [?] and train together to be committed later. Will be under 1st or 15th Armies.

Bonn about half-cleared. No opposition to crossing save from snipers and a few 20mm MG's.

Rumors that [Field Marshal Gerd von] Rundstedt has been relieved by General [Field Marshal] Walter von Model.

Saturday, 10 March (D+277)

Hazy.
We are to move to Mechernich tomorrow; probably to Bonn by this time next week.
More details on the Rhine crossing in Stars and Stripes. *Company A, 27th Armored Infantry, 9th Armored Division made crossing. Division commander—Major General John W. Leonard; ——— and Division Commander Brigadier General William Hoge (of beach fire [?]). Platoon of Second Lieutenant Carl Timmerman made crossing. Second Lieutenant Emmett Burrows led crossing. Followed almost immediately by other 3 companies of Major Murray Deney [?], 27th Armored Infantry.*
Bridge stretches across between towns of Erpel and Remagen just north of Coblenz. Three-span, steel truss. Railroad bridge. East side of bridge runs directly into a sharp rising hill and railroad tracks go into a tunnel. Hill makes it hard for German artillery to shell.
As Company A came up, a German tried to blow up bridge from American side. Demolition's went off, but the damages were slight. Bridge under small arms and 20mm fire up to 22 ——— used. Three engineers [?] of B Company, of the 9th Armored Engineers killed fixing the bridge. They cut every wire on bridge.
Germans sent 4 bombers over. One bomb nicked bridge. 4 out of 4 planes downed. The Bridge (Ludendorf)—1300 feet long.
General Gerow announced as head of 15th Army.[22] The change came during breakthrough, but is just now being announced. . . .

Sunday, 11 March (D+278)

Up at 0630. Started packing at 0700. Left Eupen in truck and jeep at 1000. Captain Phelps, Knutson and I came by jeep to Mechernich.
We went to Monschau by way of ———; the road is wrecked. Monschau is very interesting. A fortress sets on a high hill. The town is built up and down a narrow valley. To Hofen. Then we came through some interesting country to Dreihorn [?], which is pretty thoroughly torn up. From here on we saw some dead cows, fields torn up by shelling, woods half destroyed, fields heavily mined. To Gemund in narrow valley; almost completely destroyed. Turned north of Kall to east. Then to Roffendorf. Mechernich seems to be near a mining area. The town is not

too badly torn up. We are with AA in a nice three-story building. The woman of the house, expecting vandalism, left a note—"Please take care a little, it is the only rooms I have. A woman." We have four rooms. We have set up beds in one room, have another for our tea and biscuit room, store our junk in another and use the fourth for our office. The people were ordered out two days ago. They all seem to have been fairly prosperous. Crucifixes abound in the home. In the house here I found a book on "Freie Gedmiken" [?] which included ——— and other views. Topete found a splendid drawing board and excellent draftsman's pencils. We found plenty of coal. Items which the British would consider to be luxury items—like lux (made by German firm)—were found. An excellent motorcycle, minus the tires was in the yard. There was an adequate supply of good coal and plenty electricity.

The desolation in much of the countryside is terrific—of course, nearly all the bridges have been blown and much of the railroad system has been torn up.

It was interesting to see German signs on the buildings. . . .

The children were out in force and they gathered around as we unloaded. Several were put to work, getting paid in food.

Part of the hay and beet crop had not been harvested. They were rotting in the field.

Our public address system was going full blast telling the people that they must observe curfew, regulations and the like.

We have adopted a fairly stern attitude in the service but I don't think that we have scared anyone much.

Victor forward will probably move tomorrow and we will likely move in a few days.

Monday, 12 March (D+279)

Clearing up.

Today's Stars and Stripes says that Sergeant Alexander A. Drabik, a 34 year old soldier from Hollon [?], Ohio, was the first soldier into Germany [German line?]. Don Whitehead says he led 10 riflemen across. Lieutenant Carl Timmerman had ordered the 1st platoon of Company A across, but it was held up by fire from stone towers [?] at eastern edge of the bridge. He ran on past and got into Germany.

Tuesday, 13 March (D +280)

Routine. Major Shappell says Colonel Marshall wants me to come to Paris.

Wednesday, 14 March (D+281)

Still at work on 78th story.

Thursday, 15 March (D+282)

Lieutenant Webber back from across Rhine with some books. Carl had a bottle.

Friday, 16 March (D+283)

Found a cache of propaganda.

Saturday, 17 March (D+284)

Major Shappell came by. Colonel Marshall wants me to screen 1st Army material. [Major] General John Millikin of III Corps relieved yesterday. No reason given.

Sunday, 18 March (D+285)

Beautiful weather.
Finishing up 78th Division story.

Monday, 19 March (D+286)

Completed story.

Tuesday, 20 March (D+287)

Beautiful day.
Corporal Knutson and I left at noon. Went to 1st Army at Euskirchen. Then to outskirts of Cologne; saw cathedral in the distance. Town off limits. Down river road (4–5 shells landed near it) to Bonn.

Saw Hodsel at VII Corps. To Altenahr, Ahrweiler, to Münstereifel; back home. Ahr valley very beautiful.
At Bonn looked over into German held territory. Heard rifle fire.

Chapter 22

Chasing the Armor Across Germany

Wednesday, 21 March (D+288)–
Sunday, 15 April (D+313)

Wednesday, 21 March (D+288)

Beautiful Day.

Topete and I went to see 2nd Rangers at Mayschoss [?]. Talked to Major Williams, Captains Arnold and Slate, and Private First Class Helmuth Strassburger (from Louisville). Stayed from 11–6. Excellent interview. From their story it is clear that the attack was a real "rat race" to the Rhine after the Roer was crossed.

Spent the night at Morienthal—a former school for the Fuhrers of farm groups. A huge winery nearby.

Talked to several lads who were interested in getting back to school. Another one told of shooting prisoners. His wife had divorced him and married a former friend of his. He said he intended to kill them.

Got 30 bottles of excellent red wine. Thousands of gallons in the Fuhrer's school.

Thursday, 22 March (D+289)

Beautiful day.

Our bombers and fighters are passing over in great numbers. They are having a great day. They are smashing the German forces in the

Saarland. The 7th and 3d Armies are crushing them as they come together near ———.

Went to Remagen, crossed on first pontoon bridge north of the bridge. We must have 8 pontoon bridges across. They were screened by ——— on the other side of the river. Went up to Honnef and crossed the bridge there. Then went to Bad Godeberg [?] and Bonn and came back to Ahrweiler.

On way to Mayschoss [?] we turned off at Münstereifel (old walled city) and came down to Scheuren and thence to Altenahr.

Interviewed Lieutenant Colonel Saunders of the 102d Cavalry [?] Squadron at Altenahr.

In our whole trip we passed by acres of tanks and trucks. Roads were jammed with supplies. Large dumps on other side. It looks like Cherbourg before the big push on 25 July. It can't be far off.

Friday, 23 March (D+290)

Almost perfect weather.

Bombers over again. 6000 over day before yesterday, and 8000 yesterday. They are smashing everything. The German cities we have seen are gutted. They are obviously using terror methods now. The Germans have up signs—"Knuffen trots Terror."

We are set for an attack on 26 March (originally [?] set for 24 March). VII Corps is already across river. III Corps has part of its units over. We are in reserve. I think when this attack starts we will go as fast as we did against Paris. If weather holds we can be at Leipzig (the 1st Army objective) in the same time it took to go from St. Lo to Paris or from Paris to the Siegfried Line. Patton is to cross at Mainz to take Frankfurt. 1st Army is to head for Kassel and then take off for Leipzig.

Major Ferris down yesterday. Howe in hospital again.

Saturday, 24 March (D+291)

Weather still holds.

Heavy cannonading this morning. The British and Canadian Armies are across the Rhine. 1st Army still parked on the other side. There are rumors that 3d Army is across. 1st Army is poised to throw everything in on the 26th. Everything is ready to go. If the weather holds *the backbone of resistance should be shattered by the middle of April. The Russians are obviously poised to carry the thing through.*

Sunday, 25 March (D+292)

Weather not so good.

British, Canadians and our 9th Army got across yesterday, together with the 1st Allied Airborne Army. The latter dropped 40,000 men in a terrific crossing. Little opposition. The Germans are throwing heavy stuff in on some of our fronts—5000 rounds on one division front.

We are set to move across the Rhine on Tuesday.

Drove to Zülpich and Düren in the afternoon. I did not see a single building in Duren that was not burned out. It was completely deserted.

Monday, 26 March (D+293)

Weather hazy. A little rain. Finished story.

Tuesday, 27 March (D+294)

Weather fair.

Moved. Went to Munstereifel, Eiffelsburg, Kreuzburg, Brohl to Neuwied. Crossed the Rhine just north of Brohl on Victor Bridge ("largest tactical bridge in the world—1340 feet long). We are staying in apartment houses.

Armies still going well.

Wednesday, 28 March (D+295)

Weather hazy.

Still on the move into Germany. Patton's 4th Armored still going strong.

Heard that Patton's units are in Bavaria and may have units as far as Nurnberg. Nobody doubts anything any more.

Spent day getting set up. Tanks and trucks pass endlessly. Major Shappell here this afternoon. Saw Major ——— of G-2.

In afternoon to PW camp. About 2000 prisoners in ——— enclosure near railroad station. Guard is very light. Men were crammed together. There were a number of young chaps and a number

A prisoner-of-war camp for captured German soldiers.

of old ones. Their uniforms were not so badly beat up. They look rather well fed.

The guards told me they made the SS men stand for some time with their hands in the air. When they tried to drop them they hit them over the head with belts. They chuckled about 2 colonels the day before who had demanded to be fed. They said—"Bring your own stuff to eat." They said they kept them overnight without food since it made them more docile. A number of soldiers, who had donned civilian clothes, were brought in. AMG had given them 24 hours to register if they wanted to be treated as honorable PWs.

*Six truckloads came in while we were there. Two or three uncouth
characters jumped on and began pushing them around to get belts and
other souvenirs. Others pushed the fellows around.*

Went down to Urbanv [?], just above Coblenz at night.

*Saw a number of liberated Frenchmen driving back, flying French
flag and waving to everybody.*

Saw barges on the Rhine flying flags of nations who once owned them.

Thursday, 29 March (D+296)

Cold. Rain.

*Called back to 1st Army at Euskirchen. Went with Sergeant Dix and
Major Ferris to Gemund, Dreiborn, Einruhr, Kesternich, Ruhrberg,
————, Steckerbern [?], Schmidt, Kommer-Scheidt, Hoenfeld, and Dam
no. 5. Showed Dix photos to make.*

*Roads were full of trucks moving east. Continuous stream of traffic.
Gas pipeline built across Rhine now. Stream of French, Belgian, Russian,
Polish, Italians going back. Some in our trucks, others on bicycles, carts,
afoot, waving and smiling.*

*German children begin to ask for cigarettes as we pass. Schmidt was
absolutely deserted save for an old man, woman and child at a pillbox
which served as Regimental CP of 311th. To Euskirchen at night.*

Friday, 30 March (D+297)

Cold.

*Back at noon. In morning Major Ferris showed me some ambiguities
in 78th Division story on Schmidt. Said was one of best stories which has
been done.*

*Master Sergeant Patterson brought me back through Rheinbach–Bad
Neuenahr–Bad Niederbreisig–Neuwied.*

*Topete, Knutson and I went to Ehrenhreishe [?], Coblenz. Went to
barracks and got some German uniforms.*

*Saw 100s of prisoners and hundreds of freed French, Italians, Polish
workers and prisoners going home. Some have old uniforms they evi-
dently wore several years ago. Others have supplemented these with
German clothes.*

*As we went through German uniforms we saw dozens of Germans
getting clothes and books to take home.*

War still goes well. Victor Forward will be 140 miles from us tomorrow.

Saturday, 31 March (D+298)

Cool.
Got paid. Captain Fox went forward.

Sunday, 1 April (D+299)

Beautiful in morning. Cloudy in afternoon. Easter parade very good [?]. Even Red Cross girls lent [?] little variety. Services in chapel. Chaplain didn't mention war.

In afternoon met a Dutch interpreter—Theodore Vandenberg—who told me of conditions in Herlee [?] under the Germans. They took most able-bodied men to work for them, shot some hostages. Took considerable food by requisition.

When invasion started they said we were driven back as at Dieppe. As time went on American and British planes nearly wrecked Dutch cities. Took 11 hours by train to go 80 kilometers because of air attacks by Allied planes.

Thought we were not very religious in America. Shocked at our views on women. . . .

Monday, 2 April (D+300)

Weather threatening.

Have just seen some of our damage to buildings. Nothing is willfully smashed but soldiers had pawed [?] through everything and left it on the floor. Southerners should understand now about Sherman's men. I can understand how Germans may have been called vandals, for doing no worse. Many Germans put up signs saying "Dutch" or "French" live here. Some put up flags of friendly nations. Top hats, tail coats, radios, books, pots and pans still go out of the house. Everything else is pulled down.

People look well fed. In the cupboard here in our kitchen (which has both coal and electric stoves) I found white flour, meal, sugar, etc. Their clothes look all right.

An ironic touch—I just found a copy of the Neuwieder Zeitung *for 1 July, 1930, announcing* "Der Rhein ist Frei."

Tuesday, 3 April (D+301)

Rain.

Started at 9:30. Made good time to Kasselbach. Ate dinner in school building. Belgian soldiers and American tankers were eating there. Children gathered round and offered Easter eggs and apples. Topete gave them Camels. (Children along the way had asked for cigarettes.)

Were held up on road, 1 1/2 hours just beyond Kasselbach. Roads were jammed with supplies, artillery, infantry. Coming back from the east were hundreds of liberated prisoners—Poles, Russians, French, Belgians and perhaps Germans. They waved, saluted, grinned. Poignant scene. Some had rides in empty trucks. Others, unwilling to wait, were walking home. Were in groups of 5–25. None seemed weary, although they must have been. Several times we saw them still staying at the house where they worked. They seemed content there.

As we came along we saw the people working in the fields. Trees, fields, countryside was becoming green again. There was no evidence of war save for an occasional KO'd gun around which children were playing. The villages in this area—save Geissen—which was smashed, were in good shape.

Followed following route—Neuwied, Beudorf, Vallendor, Ebrenbreisher, Montaubor, Limburg, Allendorf, Broufels, Wetzbor, Geissen, Kasselbach, Hamburg, Neustadt, Swester, Bad Wildungen, Naumburg, Wofthgen, and Volkmarsen.. We set up in the latter town at 9:30 at night. Got beautiful beds. Town was tense. Taken only 2 days before. Prisoners had been coming in all day. Fear of counterattack.

Wednesday, 4 April (D+302)

Rain. Cold.

Less tense. Prisoners still coming in. Artillery coming up. Usually "liberation" going on.

Several Russians freed here. They are working with us.

Interesting to see people getting accustomed to occupation. No evidence of Volksturm activity. People seem pretty content. Not happy at being moved out. Afraid we will smash mirrors.

Thursday, 5 April (D+303)

Bad weather.

Chaplain Goldstein tells of reopening synagogue at Ahrweiler. Had become a ———, *but Decalogue still stood. Human excrement in building.*

Friday, 6 April (D+304)

Rain.

War still goes well. Patton pushing towards Erfurt. Last night Russia denounced neutrality pact with Japan.

Chaplain Goldstein tells of giving service for 43 Polish Jews near Worburg [?]. Says were better treated by Germans than by other Polish PWs.

Thornwald, Allen, Peterson, Knutson, Topete and I sat around and drank some cognac which had been taken from the German Army.

Saturday, 7 April (D+305)

Cool and windy.

Went driving. This is a beautiful country.

Washed clothes in electric washer. This house is old; has no bath or toilet facilities, but has lights and electric washer. Furniture is new and modern in design. Barns in the rear could have belonged to the 1800s.

Sunday, 8 April (D+306)

Cool. Day is beautiful.

To church in Lutheran church. No sign of any connection with Nazis. Lieutenant Colonel Hamblen, the chaplain, told me he had found no evidence of Nazi flags in the church. Thinks Niemoller's influence may be responsible.[23]

Talked to freed French prisoners. They asked of home, De Gaulle. One of them said "C'est le siecle de l'Amerique" [It is America's century]. He wanted to know if De Gaulle tended to the left. They were pleased that the young were having a chance in the government. They were pleased at what our planes had done to the Germans. They spoke of their unpreparedness—uniforms were incomplete, airplanes non-

existent, artillery antiquated. They hated Laval, but not Petain (although they thought his ideas were Fascist). They insisted that France must trade more; produce more. These people did not seem bitter, but they were thoughtful. None were the pale, anemic type of Paris. I felt helped by their spirit. It is wonderful to see how they look when they are going home. It is one of the finest things we have done. They won't forget us.

Took shower. Road around countryside. Beautiful hills.

Saw PWs in afternoon. Some were very young. Fathers, mothers, wives had been bringing them in. As the guard said—"Once they leave here they've got it made." He said they were told to treat SS soldiers as rough as they could under the Geneva Convention. He said after they had beaten one SS officer severely, he said "You are too soft; we would kill somebody."

Monday, 9 April (D+307)

Cool.

Moved to Altmunden—barrack near Hann Münden. Went through Cassel, which was terribly destroyed. People were streaming back to France.

Tuesday, 10 April (D+308)

Cool, but beautiful.

Looked around barracks. Germans had left hurriedly; clothing was scattered everywhere.

Wednesday, 11 April (D+309)

Cool, but beautiful.

Ready to move to Heiligenstadt. Went through Gottingen (lovely town) to Heiligenstadt, where we arrived at 1515. Stayed in private home. Advanced without difficulty. Are to move tomorrow.

Thursday, 12 April (D+310)

Beautiful day.

Spent day doing very little. Down to PW cage from 5:30–8:30. About 3000 were there. They were across a small stream from the town, guarded by 3 guards. Many of their relations came down and brought food. There were a number without arms and legs who were still fighting. One man had been crippled since birth. A number were very old and a number very young.

Friday, 13 April (D+311)

Beautiful.

Moved to Weisensee. There heard that Roosevelt died last night at Warm Springs, Ga. of cerebral hemorrhage. The first reaction was one of disbelief, since we have had no news for two days. Later the news was confirmed.

Roosevelt's death brings up many questions:

1. The Dewey I told you so people: I believe that Roosevelt's election still was important in that it forced the Republicans to internationalism and it helped to win approval for his policy.

2. Will Truman work? Many people fear that we will have another case like Johnson.[24] He will likely work all right with the Senate, which ultimately would fight Roosevelt. . . . Truman is committed to Roosevelt policy and will have backing of the Roosevelt liberals.

3. What effect will it have on the war? The war question is settled. Roosevelt's death will make little change.

4. What effect will it have on Roosevelt policy? FDR, himself, had changed many of his views to more conservative idea. His advisers like Harry Hopkins may become obscure. Madame Perkins may go. Undoubtedly conservatism will have its innings. Labor will be as strong as its vote getting power.

5. Effect on the peace? Undoubtedly a Roosevelt in full possession of health would have been our greatest asset at a peace conference. If he had broken down like Wilson he would not have been valuable.

Roosevelt might have straightened out many snarls with Stalin and Churchill which Truman can't do.

Truman may get a peace treaty through the Senate more easily than FDR.

Truman should not try to play Roosevelt role at conference. Will be necessary to find [?] Laurence ——— Steltin ———, though Grew is of same value. Sumner Welles[25] should be picked up.

Six months more of Roosevelt for the peace conference would have helped. However, the Yalta Conference settled a number of points which otherwise would have been troublesome.

6. Effect on the stature of FDR. Like Lincoln he may have gained by dying now. He didn't settle down to a period of fighting with the Senate, of strikes, of economic difficulties, of troubles with business, of anti-climax.

There is no chance of writing the history of FDR's importance here. However, it may be noted that he gave the country confidence in a period of great economic distress, he paved the way for many important economic regulations—SEC, he fostered TVA, he helped to strengthen England's will to buck the Nazis's, he forced our hand on an international foreign policy, he helped to lay the foundation for the most powerful armed force (Army and Navy) in the world, he achieved for us real world leadership.

His financial policy was not too logical. His spending to prosperity may later be proved unusual but the war bonus vindicates the idea of prosperity coming from spending (this only for the short term period). He wrote thoroughly into the laws and the spirit of the people the idea of government's responsibility for jobs and welfare. His appointments were not always of high level. As a political manager he was superb. He weighted things in favor of labor to offset a balance of business which had been top-heavy for several years. He struck a blow at legislation by the judiciary. If we should come to fascism he would bear a share of the blame for increasing the role of government in the life of the citizenry. He was willing to experiment for the good of the individual.

Would Wallace have been better for V-P?[26] I would prefer Wallace, but in view of the —————— shown to him for the Secretaryship of Commerce it is likely that he would have wound up in the position of Johnson.

There is no reason why either our war or peace effort should be crippled by Roosevelt's death. The war effort could almost run itself. It is too late for his death to discourage the Allies or encourage the foes.

We are too powerful to lose the peace if we use our power. While he could have avoided some friction by his contacts he might have made some concessions which others might avoid. It will be in large measure a Roosevelt type of peace, whether he is there or not.

Saturday, 14 April (D +312)

Cool.

Did a little work in the tavern at Weissensee. Rode around town. People, as usual, going about their business.

I got word that I was to go to Paris soon.

Sunday, 15 April (D+313)

Cool.

Moved to Naumburg—30 miles from Leipzig. Our CP was supposed to be at Werisenfals but it is being fought for. Went within 15 kilometers of Weimar. We are in German barracks. Evidences here are that they retired in good order; none of the confusion we noted at Altmunden.

Many children gave the V sign to us as we came along. They had collected cigarettes for it.

Made long visit to large air base at Kölleda which Allied planes had thoroughly bombed.

One of 9th Army bridgeheads across the Elbe was pushed back. 1st Army is 3 miles from Leipzig and 3d Army is near Chemnitz.

Paper says Truman is to keep the policies of Roosevelt and the Roosevelt cabinet. I think he may fool many people by his sane handling of things. He knows the Senate and will work with it. He apparently has the ability to work hard at a job. His health is good. That he can give world leadership in the manner of Roosevelt is unlikely, but he has a pattern to follow. The U.S. has the power and prestige, he can find capable representatives. The parallel of Pitt to Roosevelt is better than that of Lincoln. England did well with second and third rate prime ministers in winning the war against Napoleon after Pitt died.[27]

There is no need of getting stampeded by Truman's conservatism. He knows he owes a debt to PAC and has been committed to much of the New Deal program.

Roosevelt was buried today at Hyde Park. Anthony Eden represented England.

Chapter 23

Another Form of German Culture—Buchenwald

Monday, 16 April (D+314)–
Tuesday, 24 April (D+322)

Monday, 16 April (D+314)

Cool.
    Routine work. Drove around town.

Tuesday, 17 April (D+315)

Beautiful weather.
    Visited wrecked railway yards. Saw PW cages and places for liberated prisoners. Germans fill the hospital across street from us.

Wednesday,18 April (D+316)

Cool.
    To Weissenfels [?]. Attack on Leipzig under way.
    Got a German command car.

Thursday, 19 April (D+317)

Beautiful.
    Leipzig about taken.

Friday, 20 April (D+318)

Cool.
    Routine work.
    Sent packages home.
    Leipzig completely ours. Nuremberg ceased fighting.

Saturday, 21 April (D+319)

Stormy.
    Russians 16 miles from heart of Berlin.

Sunday, 22 April (D+320)

Rainy, cold, sleety, terrible.
    *To Leipzig with Captain Fox, Knutson and Private First Class
William L. Seiter,* Detroit News, *14800 Penrod Ave., Detroit, Michigan. Seiter is First Army photographer. We took pictures of castle at
Weissenfels. AA defenses near Bad Dürsenberg. Then to Leipzig. Much
of the damage was old. To City Hall, recently hit. Then to Volkerschlacht
———.Sharp fight there. Saw American MP's heading [?] up French
and ——— who tried to get wine.*

Monday, 23 April (D+321)

Cold, sleet, rain.
    *In convoy with Hadsel to Buchenwald (concentration camp). Camp
for 60,000 normally. There were 120,000 just before we arrived. A young
Polish Jew showed us around. He said he and about 1000 others escaped
being killed by the SS just before we came because he and they hid for two
days while friends of theirs tore up their cards and substituted cards of
dead non-Jewish Poles. The boy had been there a year; didn't look badly
treated.*
    *We saw about 100 dead—naked, emaciated, gaping horribly, ready
to be cremated. There were said to have been a thousand bodies there.
Some of the men said one died every 3 minutes. 150,000 had died there.
Problem seemed to be not so much bestiality as neglect and overcrowding. 1600 in one barracks, large enough for 500–600. Six in a bunk large
enough for 2; one blanket per man. Soup and black bread for workers.*

A pile of human remains and the broom used to sweep them up at Buchenwald, April 1945.

There was not so much wanton cruelty as disregard, although there was much evidence of torture. The crematorium, while horrible with its skulls and bones, was a logical way of disposing of the dead. The revolting thing lay in putting people there because of race and political beliefs.

We had apparently killed or beaten up all SS guards found there. The Pole said we were too humanitarian—we had killed the SS immediately instead of letting them die slowly.

The Red flag flew over many buildings; others showed French, Belgian, Czech, Polish flags.

The stench in buildings was terrible.

Went through Weimar and Jena. Both smashed up.

In afternoon got a false report that Russians were ready to contact 69th Infantry Division. Fox, Phelps, Topete and I all took off for the Division at Naumberg—beyond Leipzig. Picked up Al Newman of Newsweek *on the way. Found it a false alarm. Back at night.*

Tuesday, 24 April (D+322)

Cold, with a little sunshine.

Topete and I drove down in "the Monster." Made good speed on the autobahn. Got down about noon. Spent the rest of the day going around in circles with reports of Russians on the 2d Division front.

That night Captain Phelps went to 2d Division. Seiter and Captain Fox also left, purportedly for 2d Division, actually for 273d Regiment.

Chapter 24

A Non-Sober History of the
Meeting with the Russians

Wednesday, 25 April (D+323)–
Monday, 30 April (D+328)

Wednesday, 25 April (D+323)

Cool.

*Interviewed Lieutenant Colonel Snead G-2 and Lieutenant Colonel
Conran [?] of 69th Division.*

*At night ———— told us that the Russians had been contacted
during the afternoon. The following statement was issued that night.*

"Telephone conversation between Tracer 5 and Tryhard 6, 252135.

*"Contact was made at 1640 at Torgau with the 173d Company
[Regiment] which belongs to the 58 Cardie (Guards) Division, commanded by Major General Rusokw [?]. He requested a meeting at 10 AM
tomorrow morning. The coordinates are 6441 on the Elbe River. A
Russian officer comparable to a major commanding the 173d Company
[Regiment] returned with the patrol to Tryhard CP. He has radio
communication with his next higher headquarters.*

*"Tryhard 6 also has a message from Captain Morrey's patrol which
also has made contact on the Elbe at Riesa. His message was—'I am
staying here until you arrive. Have two guide parties on the way. No
resistance.' Lieutenant Katzbue commanding another patrol also has
contacted the Russians and also Captain Morrey's patrol.*

"Tryhard 6 received a later message from Captain Morrey. It reads

'Have met the General and toasted the armies. He wants a meeting here at the Elbe. No bridge but hand ferries. Sending guide back. I will remain here."

The sitrep of V Corps G-3 shared the following:

"Patrol from 1st Battalion, 273d Infantry contacted 58th Guard Division, U.S.S.R, at Torgau (6542) at approximately 1600. Three Russian officers reported. (There was also a sergeant.) Returned to Division CP and arrangements were made for the meeting of the Division Commanders at 26 1600 April at Torgau. A patrol from the 273d Regiment, I and R ———— contacted elements of the 15th Guards Division at Riesa (188151) at approximately 1530. Patrol will remain in Riesa and return at first light.

"First Lieutenant William Robertson and 3 men contacted the Soviet forces (the 173d Regiment, 58th Guard Division) at Torgau at 1640. Three Russian officers—Major Lexionou, Captain Neda and Captain Solviancev returned to our lines with this patrol. These officers are from the 58th Guard Division of the 34th Corps. The Corps Commander is Major General Baklanov. A meeting of Division Commanders (69th and 58th Guard Division) has been arranged for 26 1800 April.

"Lieutenant Katzbue led another patrol to Riesa where the 15th Russian Division was contacted at 1530. The patrol remained in Riesa."

Captain Fox and Seiter were with the patrol led by Major Craig (of Friendship, Tennessee) and Captain Morrey.

About 11:30 at night we heard sirens. Topete investigated and found it to be the four Russians. Seiter also returned. I spent until 2:30 trying to get through to Master.

Thursday, 26 April (D+324)

Cool.

The patrols had broken instructions not to go more than 4 kilometers east of the Mulde River. Colonel Adams of the 273d was bawled out, but actually the 273d was praised.

About 0930, Seiter, Topete and I set out for Torgau. We found a party of about 15 jeeps filled with correspondents and photographers ready to go to Torgau. We stopped to ask if it was the right party and they started without us. We were delayed about 15 minutes and then took off, following the cloud of dust they raised or making gestures to civilians who pointed the way.

We reached Eilenburg and noted the town still burning from the shellings of previous days. The town was filled with displaced persons and German prisoners. (The latter sat in an open field guarded by 2 men with a machine gun).

As we went outside Eilenburg, across the Mulde, we met a large column of Germans, with arms slung, walking in to surrender. The correspondents made a quick turn around and we got set to make a turn when the accelerator tore loose and Topete had to use the gas feed on the dash board to drive. We lost the party again and went back to Eilenburg to find the party. They hadn't come through so we waited until we saw them turn back again, from the second road they had come down, and take off for Wurzen. We set off in hot pursuit. This time we got behind an Air Force officer who stood in his jeep and waved wildly at people, trying to get them out of his road . . . while the driver sat on his horn. At Wurzen we joined the convoy and took off at high speed for Torgau. It was very dusty and we were black when we reached the appointed spot. We were going through towns through which only patrols had found and the people turned out to see us. Many waved and the liberated prisoners waved excitedly as we passed.

We reached Torgau about 1130 finding the town deserted save for Russians, Americans and liberated persons looking for loot. We went to a parapet on the west side of the river and looked out at the 2 destroyed bridges. Russian peasants were gathered on the bank of the river waiting to go across. Some Russians soldiers were on the west bank and the photographers set to work.

A Russian captain, a lieutenant and several soldiers posed for numerous photographs, firing weapons in particular. They were very reckless with guns. One soldier came in with lieutenant who had been shot by accident. We were told of a young girl who was killed during a party on the bank of the river. She was buried there. Several civilians were said to have been shot.

The only transportation consisted of four racing shells. I went across with another American, a Russian woman (carrying her baby) and a Russian who rowed the boat. The baby and mother were both crying. The mother held on to my jacket for dear life while I held on to her parcels and tried to help balance the boat as we went across the 300 foot wide river.

On the other side we got into a party of a Russian captain, five women correspondents and some soldiers and walked up to the barrack or

One of the racing shells used to ferry troops across the Mulde River to Torgau to meet with the Russians.

warehouse on the hill. About 15 minute walk. We walked by some Russian field pieces pointed westward in to Torgau. As we came in sight of the men, who were lying on the ground, they sprang to attention and saluted smartly.

We reached a courtyard leading into a building. There correspondents and soldiers gathered to sample some vodka. It was so crowded that Dows and Arnest (I met them in the building) and I went outside and sat in the courtyard. The grass was beautiful. There were some lovely flower beds (one in the form of a star) and the sun was warm. Soon afterwards we were joined by F. L. Stokes of the St. Louis Post-Dispatch who told us of his lead for his story—"Today a belt of power stretching from the Bering Straits to the Elbe met to determine the destiny of Europe for 50 years" (I have written slightly differently in another account of this).

We started to open some K rations when a Russian came up and motioned to us to wait. He went into the building and returned with a cook. They brought black bread, kraut, sardines, fig cookies and vodka. A sergeant brought a huge pot of pure lard. We undertook to drink the vodka at one gulp as they told us to.

Sergeant Pogue with Russian soldiers at Torgau, April 1945.

About 1530 we started to the river. We stopped along the way to talk with some liberated British soldiers. Then the photographers got some soldiers to dance while we clapped our hands. A lad with the Red flag, gave the flag to his comrade and joined in. Soon afterwards a Russian major arrived and ordered the men to the river.

When we reached the river about 1600, Major General Emil F. Reinhardt of the 69th Division had arrived. The Russian major came down and greeted him. Shortly afterwards the Russian Major General and his party came down the hill. He shook hands with General Reinhardt while the photographers ground away and everyone pushed to get in the picture.

Just before the meeting an American MP, holding both the American and Russian flags, handed me the Russian flag to hold. I gave it to a Russian soldier later when we started up the hill.

We went back to the barracks where a meal was prepared for the general and his staff. The little room was crowded full as photographers tried to get pictures.

The lesser fry got fed in the kitchen. They got chopped meat, onions, black bread and wine. This meal was supplemented by four eggs apiece

Major General Reinhardt, commander of the 69th Infantry Division, meets with the Russians in Torgau, April 1945.

for the official guests. Only one bottle of champagne was available for toasts, but this was supplemented by wine, cognac and vodka, as the heads of the various governments were toasted.

The meeting was over about 1800 and we back to the river. There to chuckle as General Reinhardt tried to get into the rowing shell. He tottered uneasily as he got in. We crossed with a tipsy Russian soldier who almost let us be swept down the river before beginning to row.

About 0630 we set out for the 69th CP at Naumburg with the armored cavalry of the 69th Recon Troop.

Friday, 27 April (D+325)

Cool.

Major Shappell sent us to find Captain Fox. I found that he was at Torgau. We drove down and found him as he got off the improvised raft being used to ferry guests. We stayed about 30 minutes and went to ——— Trebitz [?] to interview Major Hick and Major Merman [?] of the 271st Regiment.

(Major Christal was exceedingly helpful throughout.)

Saturday, 28 April (D+326)

Cool.

To the 1st Battalion, 271st, at Eilenburg. Interviewed Captain Baird.

In afternoon to Trebnu [?] to 273d Regimental headquarters. Saw Captain Fox. Long interview with Major James R. Sykes, S-3. They were located in beautiful private house. Chandeliers and everything.

Sunday, 29 April (D+427)

Cool.

Back to continue interview of Major Sykes. Interviewed Lieutenant Colonel George C. Knight who arranged the surrender of the ——— in Leipzig.

In afternoon to Maukrhena [?] to interview Major H.P. Green of the 272d. Back after dark.

Monday, 30 April (D+328)

Cool.

To Jezewitz to interview Lieutenant Colonel Carmack and others of 2d Battalion, 271st. Stayed until 1400.

In moving picked up Harry Wiggleworth, a ——— ——— who had lost his outfit.

Back to Naumburg. Ready to move. Major Ferriss down for a few days. . . .

Chapter 25

Pilzen on VE-Day

Tuesday, 1 May (D+329)–
Sunday, 13 May (D+341)

Tuesday, 1 May (D+329)

*Cold. Left Naumberg at 0950 in convoy. Went to Autobahn near St——,
thence south to Bayreuth and thence to Grafenwohr, about 20 miles from
the Czech border and about 40 miles from Nuremberg.*

Extremely cold. Was bundled up like an Indian.

*Hitler's death announced. Admiral [Karl] Doenitz takes over.
Deaths of [Heinrich] Himmler, [Joseph] Goebbels also reported. Peace
rumors float about. Count [Folke] Bernadotte [of the Swedish Red Cross]
was intermediary. Himmler willing to surrender to British and US, not
to Russia.*

Mussolini shot in Milan. Got pie-eyed.

Wednesday, 2 May (D+330)

Some snow. Very cold.

Berlin gives up.

*All German forces, nearly are beaten, give up in Italy and part of
Austria. Von Rundstedt and others captured.*

Thursday, 3 May (D+331)

Cool.

Hamburg gives up. Prague declared a hospitable [?] city.

German soldiers laying down their rifles to surrender.

Friday, 4 May (D+332)

Cool.
  Kiel declared open city.

Saturday, 5 May (D+333)

Warmer.
  Working ahead on story of 69th Division.

Sunday, 6 May (D+334)

Rain.
  Rumors of peace.

Monday, 7 May (D+335)

Rain.
  Were told that Germans signed unconditional surrender at Reims.
Will take effect at 1201 9 May.

Cease fire starts today.
General [Alfred] Jodl signed for Germans, General [Walter Bedell]
Smith for U.S.

Tuesday, 8 May (D+336)

Beautiful day.
Moved from Grafenwohr to Pilzen. Left at 1000; arrived at 1530.
Were near Pilzen when Churchill at 1500 made official announcement of
V-E day. Was glad I heard it in Czechoslovakia—one of the first of
Germany's victims.

We could tell which country we were in by the welcome. Once we
passed Weidhis we began to get smiles and waves again. The flags were
up. The streets of Pilzen were crowded and it was one long triumphal
procession through the town with flowers being thrown, etc. It was not
as spectacular as Paris, but interesting just the same.

First Army is ready to leave for the States and then for the East. V
Corps is under 3d Army for the time.

S.L.A. Marshall has called for me in Paris again. Orders will come
through shortly.

Am listening to great overseas hook-up in celebration of V-E.
No real excitement on our front. It is too anti-climatic.
No blackouts. To many of the fellows it was the best thing they had
seen.

Wednesday 9 May (D+337)

Warm.
Worked away. Went out about 10 miles on Prague road to see
German columns moving up to surrender. They lined the roads for miles.
Some were from Prague garrison.

Thursday, 10 May (D+338)

Warm. Worked. Finished Leipzig story.
At night Captain Fox called and said I was to go to Paris. He,
Phelps, Shappell, ————, George and Knutson are to go with First
Army.

Friday, 11 May (D+339)

Hot.

> *Too much champagne last night.*
> Stars and Stripes *on surrender of Germans—*
> *Surrender at 2:45 (Monday) 7 May. Hostilities to cease 0001*
> *Wednesday 9 May.*
> *Signed by Colonel General Gustof Jodl, Chief of the Wehrmacht and*
> *C/S to Karl Doenitz.*
> *Lieutenant General Walter Bedell Smith, C/S to Eisenhower;*
> *General Ivan Susloparoff, head of Russian Mission to France; General*
> *Sevez (France).*
> *War Room at SHAEF headquarters at Reims—55 miles east of*
> *Campiegne Forest. German Admiral Hans-Georg Friedeburg, C-I-C of*
> *her Navy had arrived on Saturday to begin negotiations. (He had*
> *surrendered to 21st Army Group on Thursday.)*
> *12 Allied officers present—General Sevez, General Bedell Smith,*
> *General Susloparoff, General Carl A. Spaatz, Commander of the U.S.*
> *Strategic Air Forces; Admiral Sir Harold Burrough, British Commander*
> *of Allied Naval Forces; Air Marshall Sir John Robb, Chief of Allied Air*
> *Staff; Lieutenant General Sir F.E. Morgan, Deputy C/S; Major General*
> *H.R. Bull, Colonel Ivan Zenkovitch, aide to S.; Colonel ———— Pedro,*
> *aide to Sevez; and Lieutenant Ivan Chernoff [?].*

Saturday, 12 May (D+340)

Hot.

> *Knutson and I drove command car from Pilzen to Weimar—via*
> *Eger (ate dinner there). Passed Germans driving in to surrender. Were*
> *headed into field to near Eger for Russians. We drove about 80 miles per*
> *hour on autobahn.*
> *At night arranged for place for the next day. Beautiful ride.*

It is interesting to speculate on what I have done since twenty-one, my last significant birthday. When I left the University of Kentucky in 1932, with my master's degree, I wrote that the next ten years would be important ones for me. I felt at the end of that time I would have my personal philosophy settled and would know where I was going. Actually I am far from that.

The war, while giving me a chance to see more of the world and of all kinds of people, nevertheless confused me. It had many effects, on the physical side. I lived more thoroughly an ordinary life than ever before in my life. For the first time I found how much man lives next to the animal. To what extent this consumed my thoughts, I do not know. That it made me tougher-minded and more tolerant and sympathetic of human frailty, I am sure. It was good to find that I could make friends with people who disliked academic folk on principle and it was pleasant to try something entirely new, taking qualities not found in books and still being able to get along. Life in the army seemed so far from reality, but it is a better Ivory Tower than any Academic Tower of escape. And of course the war and the aftermath left me sufficiently confused, so that I have not yet been able to discover any answers, and I find I am not anxious to look for them.

At twenty-one I hoped to be in the diplomatic service or politics. Both seem less likely than ever.

Epilogue

When World War II ended in Europe in 1945, Forrest Pogue, an army historian attached to V Corps, had accumulated pocket-sized notebooks he had filled with jottings made while accompanying American troops from D-Day in Normandy across Europe, to Patton's Third Army in Pilzen, Czechoslovakia. "We knew the war in Europe was over before the radio broadcasts," Pogue said later, "because the lights came on in Pilzen and in every village near us."

Pogue hoped to expand his diary into a full account of experiences with the American troops driving eastward. Most pages of his little notebooks were packed with his scribbling, but he was certain his memory would flesh-out the details. Then he finally decided to expand the contents of the little notebooks into a publishable form. He was severely jolted to find he could not read a word in them. It was not a failure of memory, but of eyesight. He was told that he had degeneration of the retinal macula in both eyes. There was no cure. He would never run into furniture, but he never again would be able to read or write, or see anything in detail. University history majors were assigned to read to him daily, to keep him abreast of scholarly research. They were eager to try to decipher the notebooks, but none could do so.

Pogue's death in 1996 made it likely that the notebooks would be confined to a filing cabinet to crumble away into bits unless some future scholar could interpret them. Pogue's cousin Jeannine Stallins was especially chagrined at her failure to read the notebooks, because she had always been the most successful transcriber of his family letters. She could recognize a few words here and there in the notebooks, but not enough to make sentences.

She and Frank Anderson were married in 1954 and both began a career in public education, and the notebooks lay forgotten. Frank had been too young to serve in the war, but in 1957 he was drafted and sent to Germany as a soldier in the Army of Occupation for two years. This experience led him to examine the notebooks more carefully and to try to transcribe Forrest's writing. He began to decipher several lines of work that became more recognizable because they pertained to the military. The project was finished in two years. For names of persons who were not especially famous they searched the indexes of published books to ascertain spellings. They wore out geographical dictionaries and maps of Europe. Frank said, "I believe most of what we have transcribed is accurate, because when I read it, it sounds like Forrest talking."

Christine Brown Pogue

Notes

1. Marshal Henri Phillipe Pétain, a World War I hero, had headed the Vichy government that collaborated with the Germans.

2. Charles de Gaulle led the Free French government. Pierre Laval, who served as foreign minister and premier in the 1930s, was premier of the Vichy government. After the war he was tried and executed by the French. Pétain was also tried, but he was sentenced to life imprisonment.

3. Named for its leader, Fritz Todt, this paramilitary construction organization built the West Wall defenses.

4. Famed movie star and singer.

5. Honore Daumier was a nineteenth-century French artist.

6. Koening was commander of the French Forces of the Interior— the Resistance movement.

7. Diplomat and nephew of General MacArthur.

8. Django Reinhardt was a famous jazz guitarist.

9. Pablo Picasso, the renowned artist.

10. Stein was an expatriate American writer and Alice B. Toklas was her companion.

11. Edouard Daladier, Leon Blum, Edouard Herriot, and Paul Reynand had served in the first years of the war. Joseph Darnand was later executed by the French for treason. Georges Mandel, a cabinet minister who opposed the armistice with the Germans, was murdered by French collaborators in early July 1944.

12. William D. Leahy had served as ambassador to Vichy, then throughout the war as Roosevelt's chief of staff.

13. Camille Chautemps had been premier briefly in the 1930s. Georges Bonnet, Daladier's foreign minister, was also an appeaser of the Germans.

14. Georges Clemenceau was the premier who led France to victory in World War I.

15. Georges Robert, who commanded the French fleet at Martinique, refused to go along with Admiral Jean Darlan's cooperation with Allies. Darlan, who was the commander of Vichy military forces, agreed to work

with the Allies after the Americans invaded North Africa in the fall of
1942.

16. Novels, biographies, and other such books published in paper-
back editions for distribution to the armed forces.

17. Carlo Sforza, who became foreign minister after the overthrow
of Mussolini, wanted Italians to cooperate with the Allies.

18. Lieutenant General Ben Lear, Second Army commander in Memphis, brought on a storm of media criticism before the war when he ordered group punishment of a unit after some of the soldiers shouted at
girls playing golf.

19. General Hasso von Manteuffel led the Fifth Panzer Army in the
Ardennes Offensive.

20. Former governor Harold Stassen of Minnesota and Senator Arthur
Vandenberg of Michigan were prominent Republicans.

21. Kostelantz was an orchestra conductor and Pons an opera star.

22. General Gerow commanded V Corps, the 29th Division, and was
former head of the War Department War Plans Division in Washington.
He graduated from the Virginia Military Institute in 1911, and was born
in Petersburg, Virginia. His name was originally Giraud. He came to the
ETO in 1942 as head of the 29th Division.

23. Martin Niemoeller, a German clergyman who opposed the Nazis.

24. Andrew Johnson, Lincoln's vice president who succeeded him
after the assassination, was a weak president.

25. Sumner Welles had worked closely with Roosevelt as under-sec-
retary of state.

26. Henry A. Wallace was vice president during Roosevelt's third
term and was appointed secretary of commerce after Roosevelt selected
Truman to be his running mate in 1944.

27. William Pitt, as British prime minister, led the fight against Napoleon.

Glossary

AAR	After-action report
Abn or A/B	Airborne
Ack-ack	Antiaircraft guns or fire
AD SEC	Advanced Section
AEAF	Allied Expeditionary Air Force
AEF	Allied Expeditionary Force
AG	Adjutant General
APO	Army Post Office
ASTP	Army Special Training Program
ATS	(Women's) Auxiliary Territorial Service
BAR	Browning Automatic Rifle
Br	British
CIC	Counter Intelligence Corps
CinC	Commander in Chief
Cmdr	Commander
COMZ	Communications Zone
Conf	Conference
COSSAC	Chief of Staff to the Supreme Allied Commander
CP	Command post
C/S	Chief of staff
DSC	Distinguished Service Cross
DUKW	Amphibious truck
ETOUSA	European Theater of Operations, U.S. Army
Exec	Executive
FAAA	First Allied Airborne Army
FFI	French Forces of the Interior
FO	Field order
Führungsgruppe	Operations group
FUSA	First U.S. Army
FUSAG	First U.S. Army Group

G-1	Personnel section of divisional or higher staff
G-2	Intelligence section
G-3	Operations section
G-4	Supply section
G-5	Civil Affairs Division of SHAEF
G-6	Public Relations and Psychological Warfare
Gestapo	Short for *Geheime Staatzpolizei* (state secret police).
Gp	Group
GO	General order
Hq	Headquarters
Intel	Intelligence
IRTC	Individual Replacement Training Center
JA	Judge Advocate
Kampfgruppe	German combat group of variable size
KP	Kitchen police
LCT	Landing craft, tank
LCVP	Landing craft, vehicle and personnel
LST	Landing ship, tank
Luftwaffe	German Air Force
MP	Military Police
NAAFI	Navy, Army, Air Force Institutes
Oberkommando	Headquarters of an army
OCS	Officer Candidate School
OPA	Office of Price Administration
OSS	Office of Strategic Services, an American spy organization whose operatives worked behind enemy lines.
PRO	Public Relations Office
PX	Post Exchange
RAF	Royal Air Force
RCT	Regimental Combat Team
SAC	Supreme Allied Commander
SCAEF	Supreme Commander, Allied Expeditionary Force
SEC	Securities Exchange Commission
SGS	Secretary, General Staff

SHAEF	Supreme Headquarters, Allied Expeditionary Force
SO	Special operations
SOP	Standard operating procedure
SOS	Services of Supply
SS	*Schutzstaffel*, the Nazi Party's elite, black-uniformed bodyguard. Led by Heinrich Himmler. Its military arm was known as the Waffen SS.
TVA	Tennessee Valley Authority
UP	United Press
USO	United Services Organization
TAC	Tactical headquarters
TD	Temporary duty
VIP	Very important person
VOCO	Verbal orders of commanding officer
WAAF	Women's Auxiliary Air Force
WAC	Women's Army Corps
WD	War Department
Wehrmacht	German Armed Forces

Code Names:

ANVIL	The planned 1944 Allied invasion of southern France
BIGOT	Special security procedure for Overlord
COBRA	Operation launched by First U.S. Army on 25 July 1944
GREIF	German deception operation in support of the Ardennes Offensive
MARKET-GARDEN	Airborne-ground operation intended to establish a bridgehead across the Rhine in the Netherlands
NEPTUNE	Detailed plan for the invasion of Normandy, spring 1944
OVERLORD	Overall plan for the invasion of northwest Europe, spring 1944

About the Author

Master Sergeant Forrest C. Pogue was awarded the Bronze Star and the French Croix de Guerre for his frontline interviewing during battles of the Second World War, in France, Belgium, and Germany. He also earned a Bronze Arrowhead and four Battle Stars, the former for participating in the invasion of Normandy, the latter for the campaigns.

He was the author of *The Supreme Command*, the official history of General Dwight D. Eisenhower's command in Europe during World War II. He was a contributing author to the books *The Meaning of Yalta, Eisenhower: A Centenary Assessment, Command Decisions* (1959), *Total War and Cold War* (1962), *D-Day: The Normandy Invasion in Retrospect* (1970), *The Continuing Revolution* (1975), and *The War Lords* (1976). He was a contributing editor to the *Guide to American Foreign Relations Since 1700* and the author of the four-volume biography of General George C. Marshall.

Index

Central Machine Records, 221
Cerisy, 167
Chambois, 187
Champs-Elysées, 196, 197, 213, 232,
    247
Charles I (king of England), 11
Château Chevrival, 185
Château Hennemont, 219
Château Ledoux, 179–80
Château le Rilly, 179
Château Rothschild, 202
Chautemps, Camille, 243, 383(n13)
Chemical Corps (US), 234
Chemnitz, 362
Cherbourg, 40, 124, 132, 133–37, 146–
    47, 169, 171–72
Chernoff, Lt. Ivan, 378
Chief of Staff to the Supreme Allied
    Commander (COSSAC), 222
children: Belgian, 305; in Dolhain-
    Limbourg, 261–62; in Germany,
    357; in liberated Paris, 200, 212,
    214–15; in London, 12; in
    Normandy, 101–2, 103, 125
Christal, Maj. (271st Regiment), 373
Christoe, Maj. (69th Division), 338
churches: in Germany, 358; in
    occupied France, 243
Churchill, Winston, 10, 206, 247, 248,
    268, 303–4, 377
cigarettes, 199–200, 209, 230, 232
Clancy, Sgt. Ervin, 162, 163
Clark, Lt. Blair, 3, 5, 133
Clark University, xv, 4
Claypool, Pvt. (394th Infantry
    Regiment), 314
Claypool, Sgt. Charles A., 163
Clayton, Maj. George A., 313, 336
Clemenceau, Georges, 244, 383(n14)
Clements, Lt. Leonard, 315
Clift, Maj. M.G., 104, 105, 106–10
Clifton College, 20, 21
Clyde, Capt. (121st Infantry Regi-
    ment), 282
Coblenz, 215, 345, 355
COBRA, 160
Cole, Maj. Hugh M., 2–3, 18, 181–82
Colleville-sur-Mer, 29, 71, 74
Collins, Maj. Gen. J. Lawton, 152, 177
Cologne, 344, 349

Colombières, 98, 106, 107
Colson, Sgt. Clarence, 69, 70, 72
Colwall, S.Sgt. Curtis, 67
Combat (newspaper), 239
Combat Command R, 273, 274, 275
combat historians: assigned to cover
    D-Day, 51; casualties among, 222,
    262; controversy over journals,
    155; European theater group, 2–5;
    V Corps directive on purposes of,
    81–82; First Army team, 18–19, 21,
    132–33, 138, 155, 156, 187; first
    phase of work in Normandy, 137–
    38; William Ganoe, 8–10; S.L.A.
    Marshall, 185–87; Pogue's career
    as, xvi–xvii; Pogue's suggestions
    for improving accounts by, 234–
    35; preparations for D-Day, 23–24,
    25–26, 27–33, 34–35; Third Army
    team, 18
combat history: combat journals and,
    31; difficulties in establishing
    times, 220; William Ganoe's
    theory of, 8–9; history of, 1–2;
    George C. Marshall and, 2;
    problems of establishing casualty
    figures, 221; problems with
    battlefield reconstructions, 221;
    problems with soldiers' testimo-
    nies, 220–21; War Department/
    ETOUSA controversy, 8–9, 23–24,
    176, 187
Comédie Française, 234
Committee of National Liberation
    (France), 238, 240
Communists: French, 243, 244, 245;
    partisan bands and, 268
Company C, 175th Infantry (US), 46,
    55–56
Company K, 175th Infantry (US), 37–
    38, 39, 92, 161, 162–66
concentration camps: Buchenwald,
    364–65, 365(photo)
Conde, Prince of, 259
Condon, Lt. Paul, 162
Condren, Lt. (Capt.) (Historical
    Section, VII Corps), 222, 252, 262
Conran, Lt. Col. (69th Division), 367
Consultative Assembly (France), 235–
    36

relieved of command, 111–12;
Pogue's methods in, 99; problems
with soldiers' testimonies, 220–21
field jackets, 262
5th Armored Division (US), 160, 167,
215; Ardennes, 300; first forces in
Germany, 262–63; Hürtgen Forest,
272, 273, 274, 275; Wallendorf, 262,
264–67, 268–69
V Corps (US), 182, 249, 377; *Ancon*
command ship, 126–27; Ardennes,
292, 293, 294, 299, 304, 329; Army
Post Office, 168–69; attacks in
Germany, 215, 262–64, 345;
combat historians, 21, 22, 81–82,
130; D-Day invasion plans, 27–31;
at Dolhain-Limbourg, 258–62; in
England, 22–23, 24; at Eupen, 254–
55, 257–58; Falaise trap, 187; L.T.
Gerow and, 24; Gen. Huebner
and, 326; Hürtgen Forest, 270,
272–73; in Normandy, 76–81, 113,
124, 160, 168; in Paris, 188, 192,
199, 200; Pogue's orders,
153(photo); Schmidt action, 256–
57. *See also individual forces and
units*
5th Evacuation Hospital (US), 344
5th Ranger Battalion (US), 54
15th Army (US), 294, 326
15th Guards Division (USSR), 368
15th Infantry Battalion (US), 265
15th Panzer Brigade (Germany), 330
52d Armored Battalion (US), 346
56th Field Artillery Battalion (US),
274
58th Guards Division (USSR), 367,
368
Figaro, Le (newspaper), 216, 239
1st Airborne Division (Great Britain),
255–56
1st Allied Airborne Army, 353
First Army (France), 256
First Army (US), 116, 293, 355, 377;
Aachen, 256; approach to Paris,
188; Ardennes, 293, 294, 296, 299,
300, 301; attacks in Germany, 352,
362; combat historians, 18–19, 21,
132–33, 138, 155, 156, 187; Fourth
of July (1944), 144–45; Hürtgen

Forest, 253, 271; move to Vouilly,
145–46; Normandy breakout, 139,
178; Roer River, 343; in Spa, 251–
52
1st Battalion, 115th Infantry (US), 98–
100, 106
1st Division (US), 32, 116, 338;
Ardennes, 294, 296, 312, 319, 323,
324, 325; D-Day, 51, 53–54, 60, 64–
75; exchange of German nurses at
Cherbourg, 146–47
1st SS Panzer Division (Germany),
324
Fleming, Sgt. (99th Division), 335
Flinin, Lt. Robert, 341
Flying Fortresses. *See* B-17 Flying
Fortresses
Folies Bergeres, Les, 223
Fontainebleau, 244
forced labor, 114
Forêt de Cerisy, 158
Formigny, 84
Fort du Roule, 134
Fort Harrison, 4
Fort McClellan, 5, 113, 234
Fournay, le, 98
Fourth of July (1944), 144–45
4th Infantry Division (US), 18, 51, 83,
155, 215, 264, 273
14th Armored Battalion (US), 346
.40 caliber machine guns, 164
44mm guns, 164
47th Armored Infantry Battalion
(US), 280, 284–86, 304, 321, 346
Fox, Lt. (Capt.) William J., 19, 20, 21,
22, 23, 24, 25–26, 34, 36, 50, 79, 81,
84, 89, 90, 113, 115(photo), 116,
126, 130, 132, 133, 134, 138, 140,
145, 146, 152, 155, 159, 172, 203,
254, 257, 293, 309, 358, 364, 365,
366, 373, 377
foxholes, 79, 158–59, 160, 333
France: 1944 American presidential
election and, 246; Consultative
Assembly, 235–36; Leftist groups
and, 268; liberation, 238–39;
newspapers and political opinions, 239–41; Pogue's descriptions
of towns between Paris and the
front, 249–50, 251; political

Lightning Source UK Ltd.
Milton Keynes UK
UKHW040916070220
358352UK00001B/22